ALCANTARA

Contents in Augmented Reality (AR)
This volume is enhanced by Augmented Reality (AR) contents that enable readers to see the videos related to the different topics.

1. Download the Skira application from your App store
2. Select the Scan tool and point your smartphone on the images that have this icon

Luca Masia

ALCANTARA
The material of art

SKIRA | **ALCANTARA**

Design
Luigi Fiore

Editorial coordination
Vincenza Russo

Editing
Emanuela Chiesa

Layout
Serena Parini

Translations
Susan Ann White
and Gavin Williams
for Scriptum, Rome

First published in Italy in 2022 by
Skira editore S.p.A.
Palazzo Casati Stampa
via Torino 61
20123 Milano
Italy
www.skira.net

© 2022 Alcantara S.p.A.
© 2022 Skira editore
© Alberto Biasi, Constance Guisset,
Chiharu Shiota, Georgina Starr
by SIAE 2022

All rights reserved under international copyright conventions. No part of this book may be reproduced or utilized in any form or by any means, electronic or mechanical, including photocopying, recording, or any information storage and retrieval system, without permission in writing from the publisher.

Printed and bound in Italy.
First edition

ISBN: 978-88-572-4825-7

Distributed in USA, Canada, Central & South America by ARTBOOK | D.A.P. 75 Broad Street Suite 630, New York, NY 10004, USA. Distributed elsewhere in the world by Thames & Hudson, 181A High Holborn, London WC1V 7QX, United Kingdom.

Photo Credits
Archivio Alcantara: all the images
Photo © Hufton+Crow.
Courtesy Fondazione MAXXI: p. 36

CONTENTS

7	Preface: Alcantara and Art *Andrea Boragno*
11	Islands in the Sea
17	Artists' journeys
23	Alcantara Design Museum
37	Can you imagine?
49	The house of dreams
57	The landscape of the future
65	Luxury glam
71	The Prince's Apartment
81	Magic Hotel
89	A coffee at Momus
105	Local icons
113	The sound of Alcantara
123	Waves of energy
127	Studio Visit
135	Beyond the body
141	Mobile structure
151	Fluid space
159	Reality, imagination
171	The material of vision
179	Out of the blue
185	The nearby East

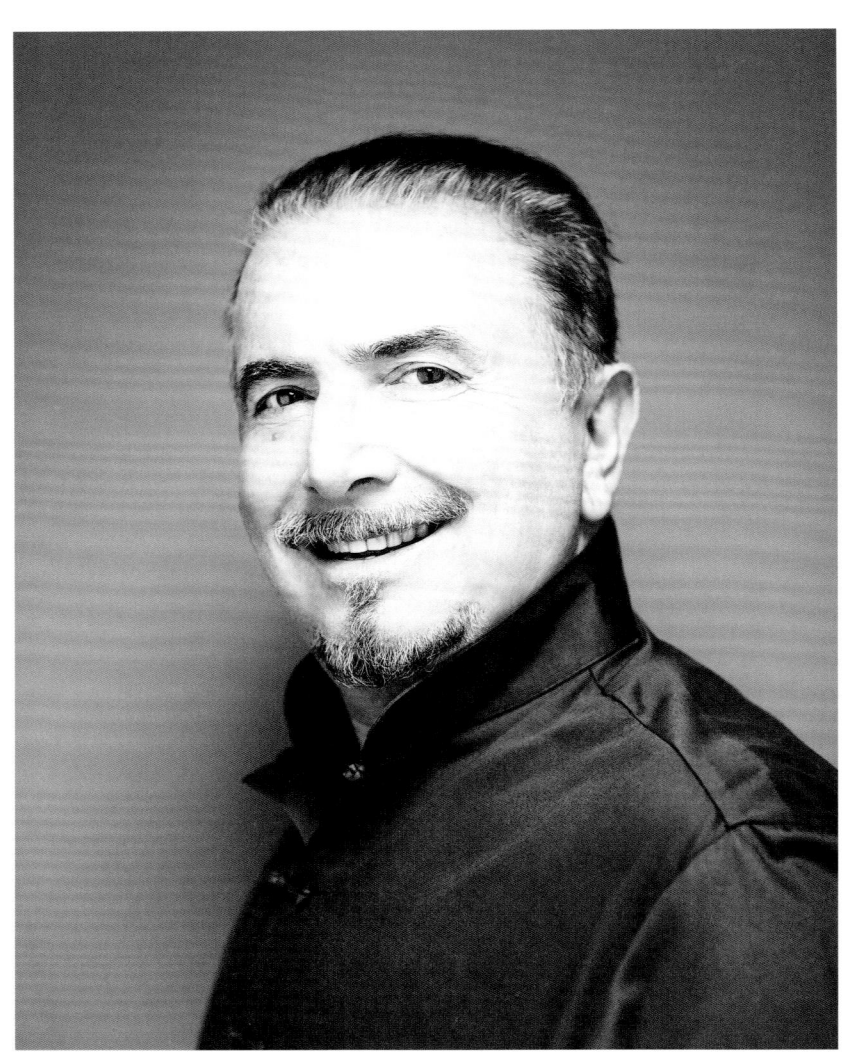

PREFACE: ALCANTARA AND ART

Ever since the beginning of its history, Alcantara has collaborated positively with designers and creatives from all over the world, in the widest ranging design fields. Subsequently, in 2006/2007, the company adopted a highly proactive role in relations with artists, seeing the potential for developing a dialogue to seek new forms of expression and possibilities of applying them.

The earliest collaborations immediately highlighted the valuable nature of a unique and extremely versatile material, which, as well as having unquestionable functional properties, is also an endless source of inspiration. A material that has the ability to "speak an infinite number of languages", continually reinventing itself, and always becoming "whatever you want it to be".

Accordingly, the close dialogue between Alcantara and Art has driven a process of continual experimentation, which, over the years, has enabled us to explore, and go beyond, the boundaries of the material: Alcantara does not restrict itself to dressing vision, but generates it.

In the same period, the Company came to the belief that the international market it looks to would express more and more clearly a growing demand for products capable of combining functionality and technological qualities with aesthetic and sensory values, and that an even greater demand for personalization would emerge in this context.

Thus, there was a growing conviction that successful products cannot simply be represented by a list of technical specifications, but should be capable of connecting emotionally with the consumer.

The relationship with art, through a mutual process of giving and receiving inspiration, has become a strategic aspect that has allowed

Andrea Boragno

Alcantara's potential to explode in its many and varied forms and functions, also to meet the demand of the most sophisticated and exacting sector of the market.

This has led Alcantara to systematically step up its relations with the art world at the international level, developing highly-productive collaborations with prestigious museums and galleries, and countless artists, be they icons or young talents, from the most diverse cultures. The Alcantara material has become an integral part of the creative process: the "medium" via which the artist expresses his/her creativity.

In this context, the now more than a decade-long collaboration with the MAXXI in Rome, the museum with which we have developed a new model of artistic co-production, is emblematic. It is also significant that all the works created with Alcantara are now in the MAXXI's permanent collection.

In line with this vision, Alcantara has gone beyond the traditional forms of sponsorship and patronage, establishing new relations with creatives, curators and institutions, based on the development of joint research projects. These initiatives have become powerful generators of innovation, creative experimentation and constant research on material.

This book documents Alcantara's activities in the world of the arts: a long-running journey where every goal is also a point of departure towards new horizons to be explored, new limits to be overcome.

Andrea Boragno

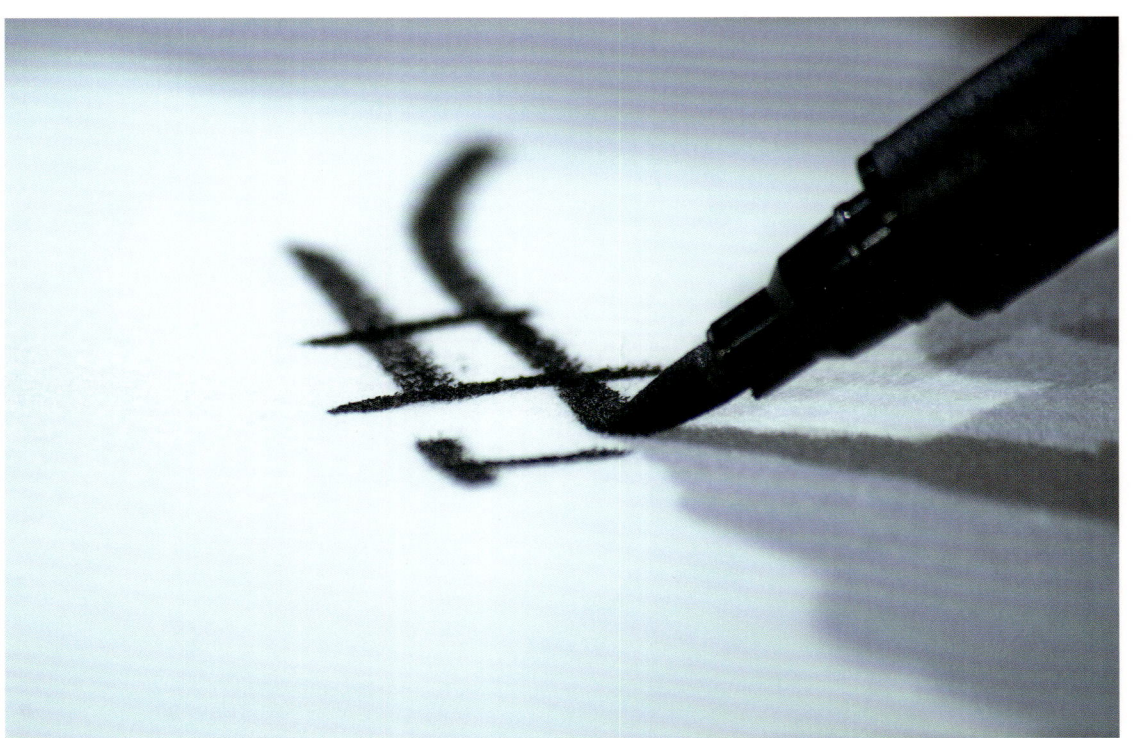

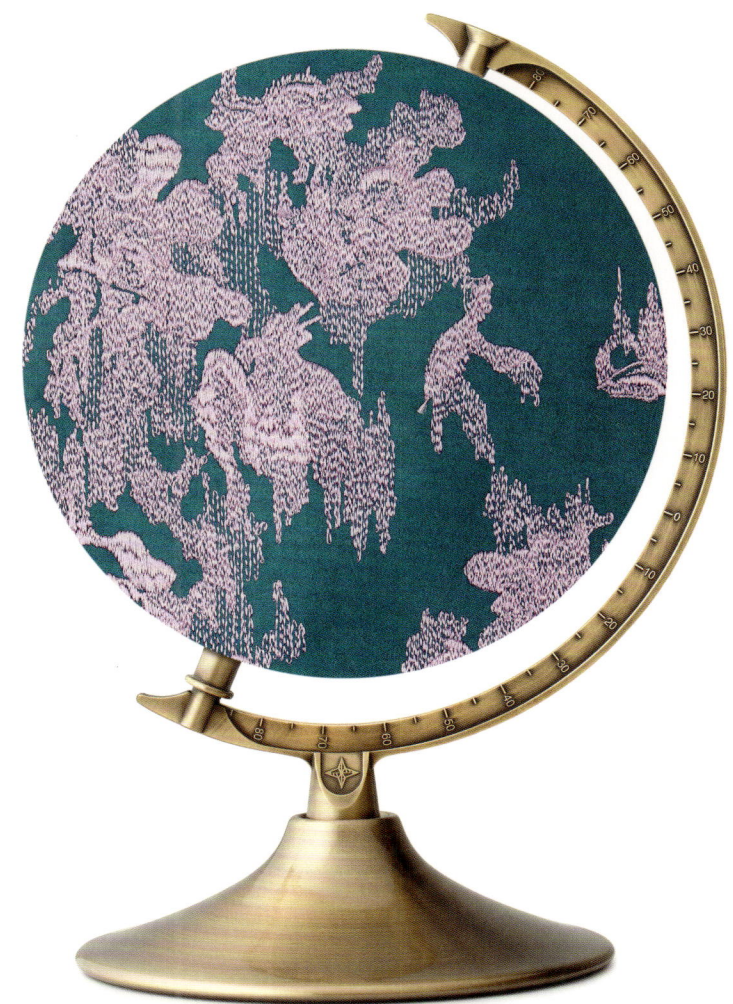

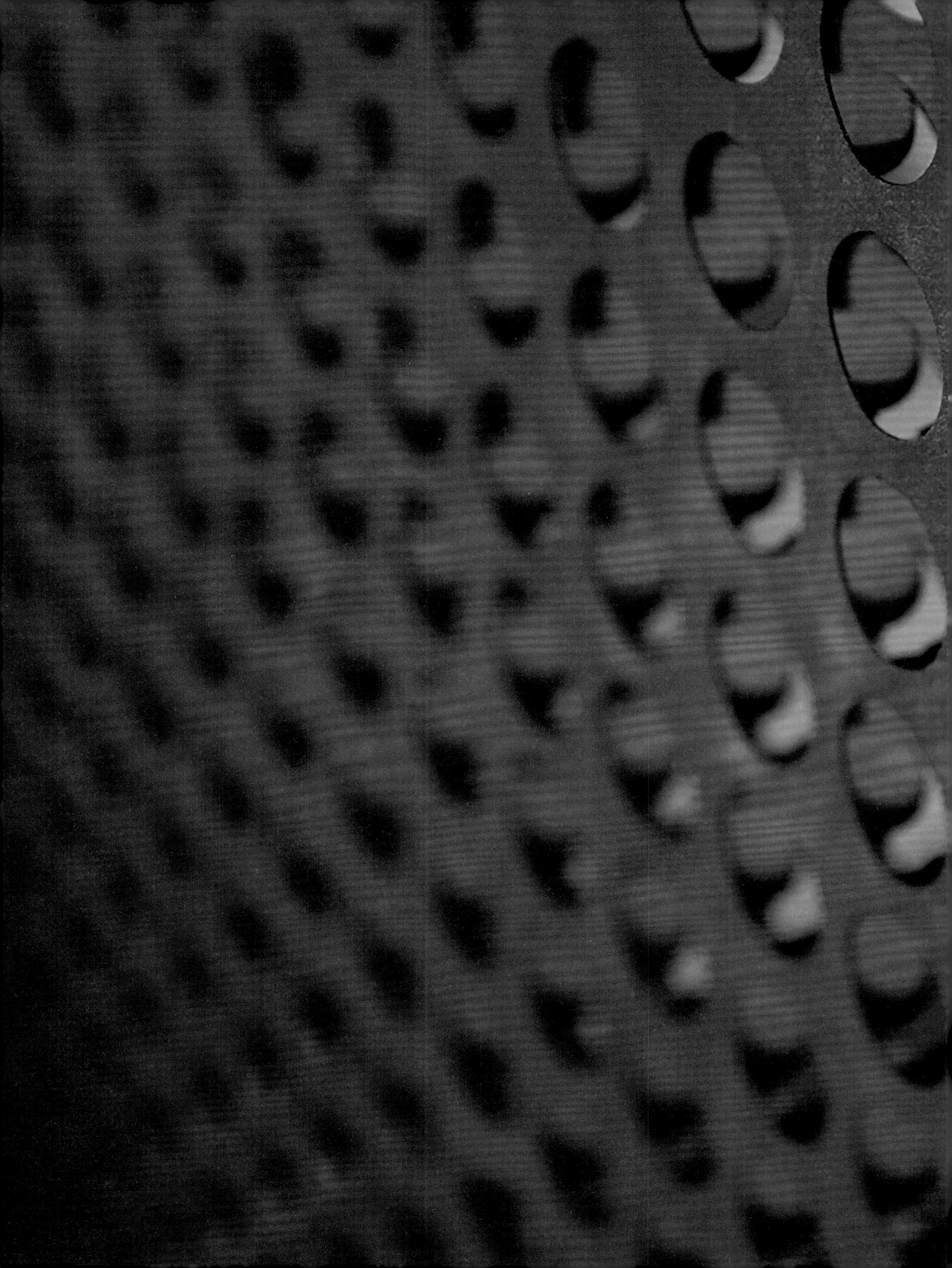

ISLANDS IN THE SEA

The key is not to be intimidated. It takes nerve to lift your gaze to the skies and watch the flight of the first spaceship. Mankind closed ranks and tried to get inside Yuri Gagarin's Vostok 1. The Russian cosmonaut's orange suit seemed way too big for him; he watched from above while we followed him from below, in our mind's eye. We were so very small, but what we were doing was so much bigger. For the first time man had detached his shadow from the ground, and was flying beyond the atmosphere. A historic journey, in the spring of 1961.

Alcantara under an electron microscope

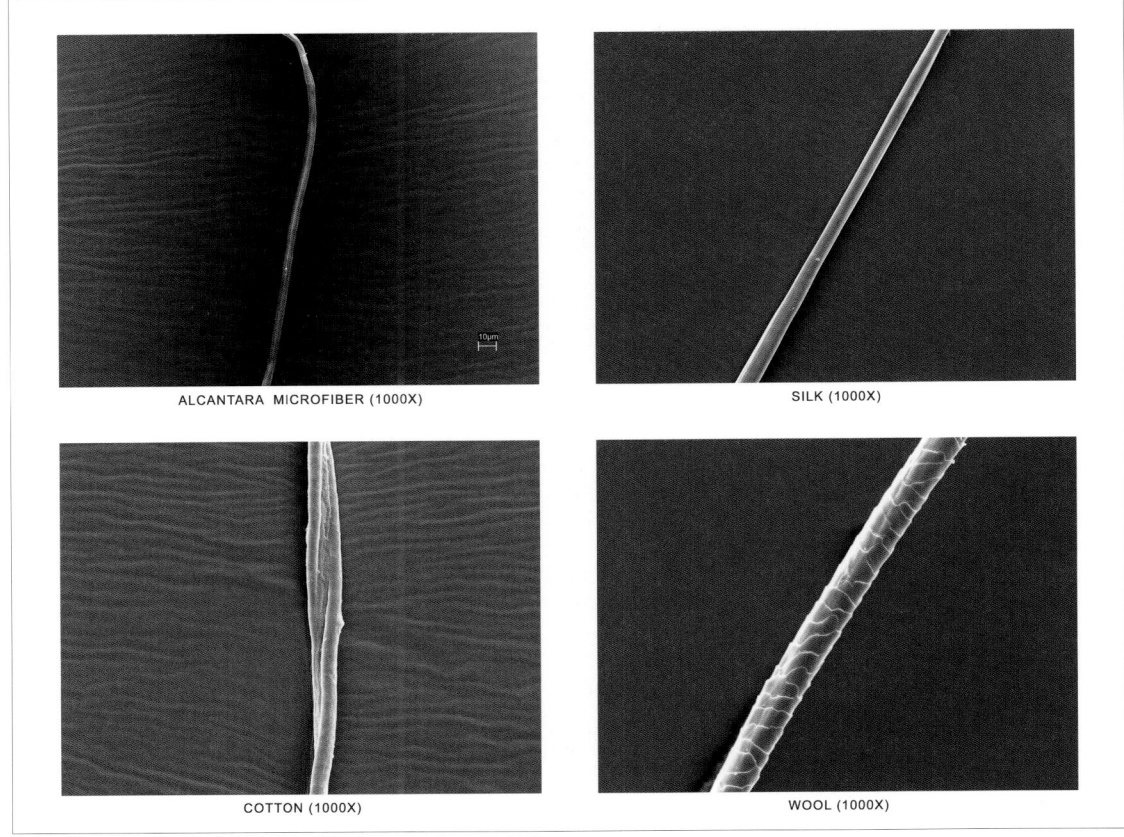

The journey around the earth's orbit lasted as long as a soccer game, with a few minutes of extra time. Just long enough to say things that will remain in the collective memory. For example: "The sky is black along the edge of the Earth; near the horizon there is a beautiful deep blue aureole". Yuri Gagarin saw the planet as blue, and from that moment on we all started to say it was blue, like a great sea with a few islands in between. It must have been mind-blowing to see the Earth without borders. For the first time, after a couple of million years.

Around the same time, in Japan, a young research chemist graduated from the University of Nagoya. His name was Miyoshi Okamoto, and he was a genius. He was immediately hired by Toray, a company that was full of geniuses. For one thing, they had invented Rayon, the fibre derived from cellulose that looks like a transparent natural silk. The laboratory was on the island of Shikoku, in the western part of the country. Okamoto's job was to work on the materials of the future: acrylic and polyester. The young researcher also began a journey into space, but the infinitesimal space of the molecules of new synthetic fibres. It is not difficult to imagine him gazing downwards, eye glued to his microscope, while the rest of humanity was looking upwards, in the direction of the US spaceships that were approaching the Moon.

Okamoto invented new materials, he became a celebrity in his field, and at the end of the 1960s he created a kind of chamois leather that he thought could be used for shoe uppers. A type of calfskin, pleasing to the touch, soft and velvety. Highly resistant, flexible, and waterproof.

Okamoto must have been a poet, too, because when they asked him to describe the new material, he said that it looked like a cluster of "islands in the sea". It was not a woven material, there was no weft or warp, only interwoven synthetic fibres. Under the microscope they really did look like islands in the sea.

The research went on, and when the time came to give the material a name, people thought about how to connect those islands in the sea together. *Al-Quantarah* is the Arabic term meaning "bridge". That would be the name of the new material: Alcantara. The first patents were filed in 1970. Now, after water, air, earth and fire, there was Alcantara. It seemed like a new element, created by man.

To produce the Alcantara material, the Japanese met up with the Italians. An industrial plant as big as a town sprang up at Nera Montoro, near Terni: a small world built around a complex manufacturing process where extremely high-quality artisanal and industrial procedures were carried out: long sequences of secret operations, covered by patents.

It all seemed like magic, but it was industry, in the service of research and creativity. Alcantara is a versatile, malleable material, able to give personality and character to an endless variety of design solutions. To make things simple, we could say that it was just a covering. But this is too generic

Alcantara under an electron microscope

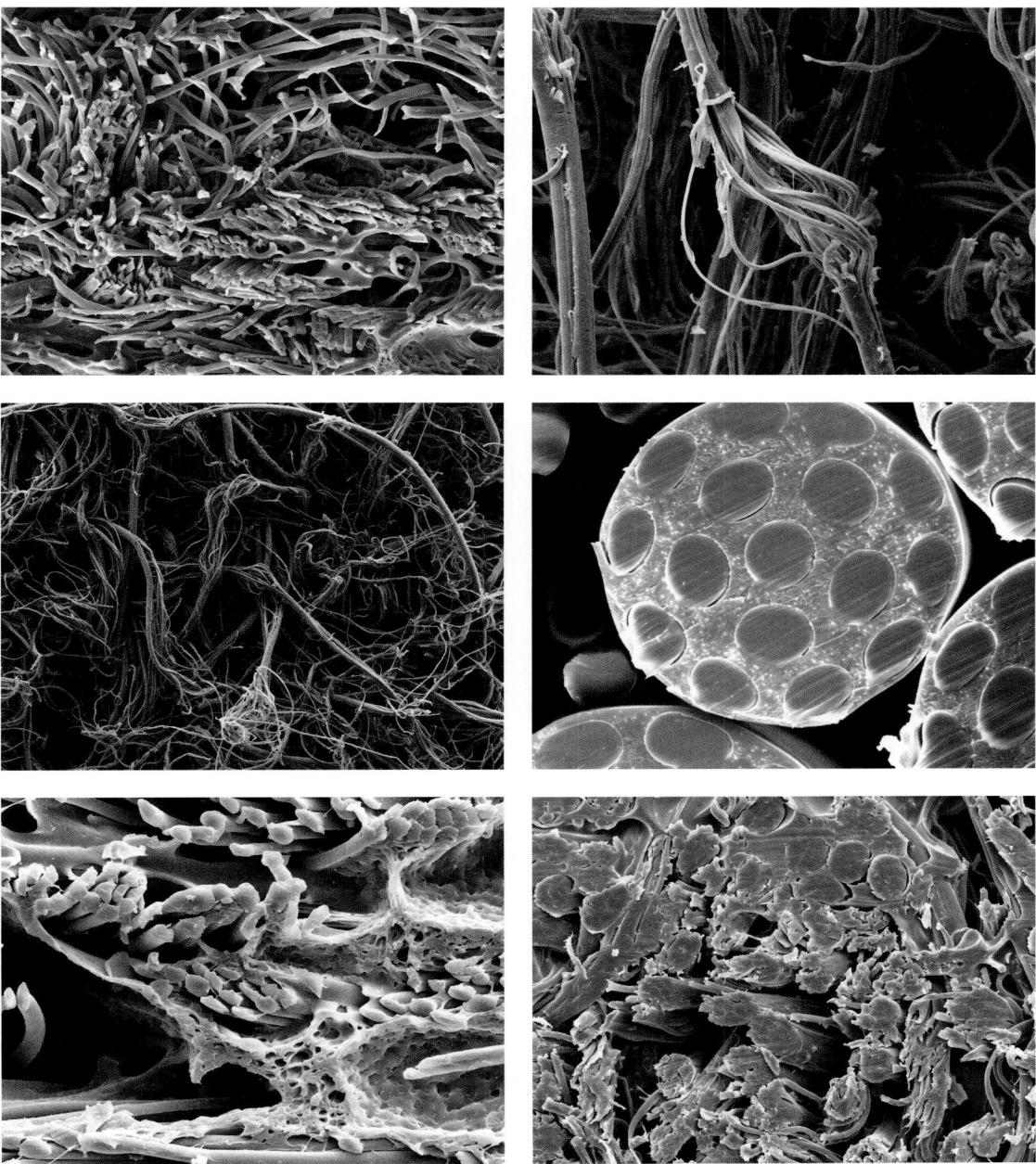

and reductive a term, because Alcantara is a material that becomes whatever you want it to become. The 1970s and 1980s were the golden age for Japan's economy, and also for Italian style. Fashion discovered Alcantara, followed by interior design and the automotive industry. These were years of great successes. Alcantara became synonymous with beautiful, refined, exclusive. Italian.

    In order to understand a material like Alcantara, you must learn how to see the islands in the sea – as Okamoto did in the 1960s. Alcantara is an alphabet: it contains combinations of letters forming sentences, and whole languages, which make it possible to convey emotions. Alcantara is elegant and soft to the touch, cool, waterproof, and resistant to twisting and tearing. It is receptive to light and sound friendly; you can print on it in very high resolution, like photographic paper, and it can be painted on like a canvas. When you look at it, it has two dimensions, but as soon as you touch it you perceive a third. A depth that exists even before the material is used to cover objects. Alcantara speaks and says much about us, through the places it furnishes, the things it clothes.

In the early years of the new millennium, the company experienced a radical shift. A new leap forward, triggered by profound self-reflection and examination of its values. Taking a step back, in order to go a long way forward: like an athlete's run-up. In 2004, as part of a strategy to reposition and strengthen the brand, the new Managing Director, Andrea Boragno, decided to focus on Alcantara's uniqueness and its potential for infinite possibilities of expression and application. Relations with the art world became the generator of a process of constant innovation and experimentation. Alcantara chose to inhabit the landscapes of art, innovation and research. To stimulate creative thoughts and enable their exchange, like a bridge between ideas.

Thus, began a process aimed at forging an identity. More than 10 years of research in the fields of design, the performing arts, and figurative art. With a clear idea in mind: always standing alongside the artists, asking them to think in terms of Alcantara. To think and communicate in Alcantara. To then stage their narratives by collaborating with curators and museums across the world. to become cultural producers, and create something unique, something precious.

Alcantara has become the material of art: a new inner grammar for project designers, leading artists and younger talents. This book tells the story of their journeys with Alcantara. All the way to the Moon, even, to see the islands in the sea.

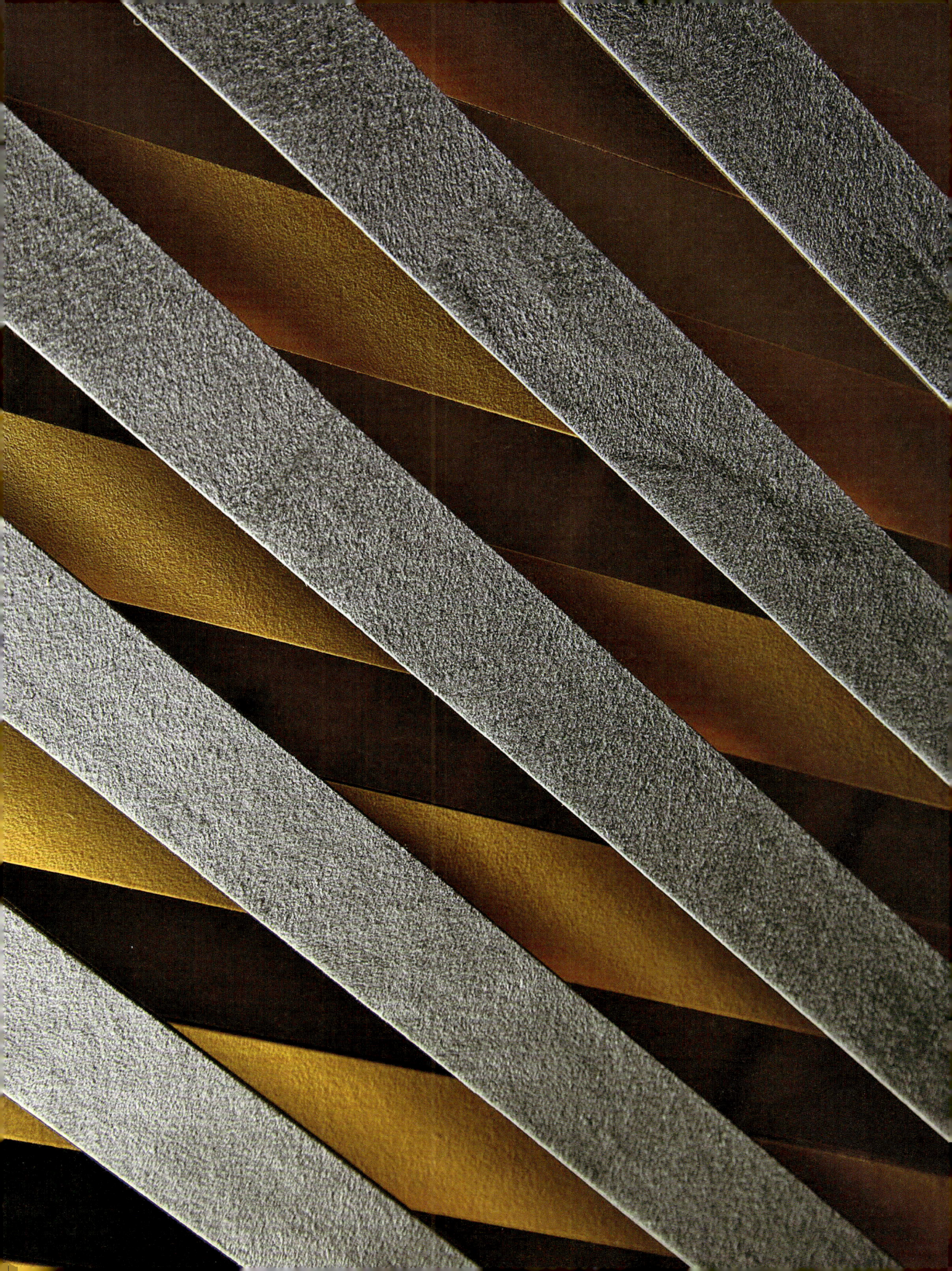

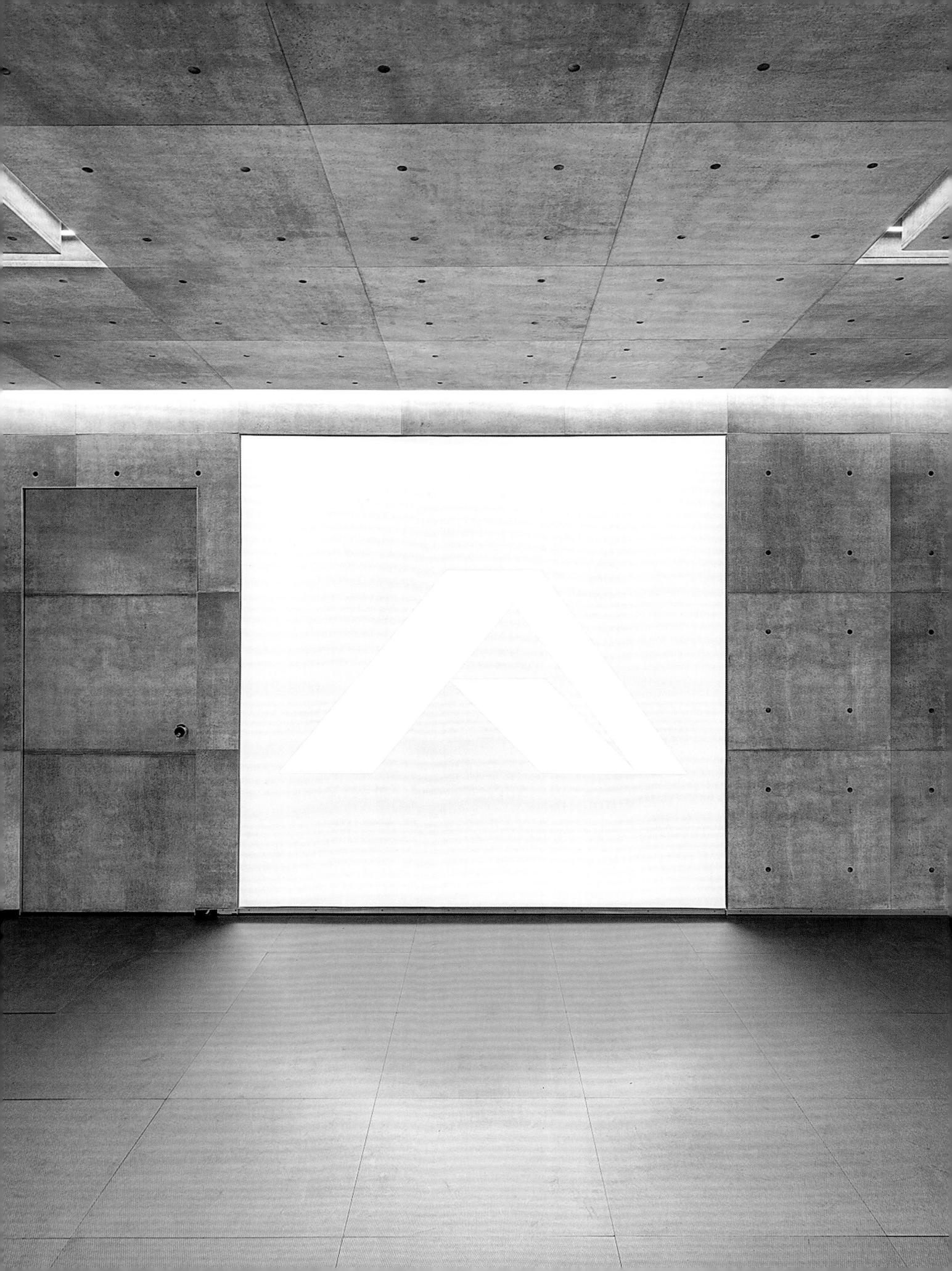

ARTISTS' JOURNEYS

The town stretches along the river, amidst the hills. There are houses, a long thoroughfare and side streets, various places where people's paths may cross. In actual fact, the town is one big factory containing other factories, all of them highly specialized. Each department in the Alcantara plant is responsible for one phase in the manufacturing process. Viewed overall, the production site is impressive: it expresses the strength of a vision, man's dynamism as he creates an impossible material.

Alcantara headquarters, Milan

Alcantara headquarters, Nera Montoro (TR)

Following pages
Aerial view of the headquarters, Nera Montoro

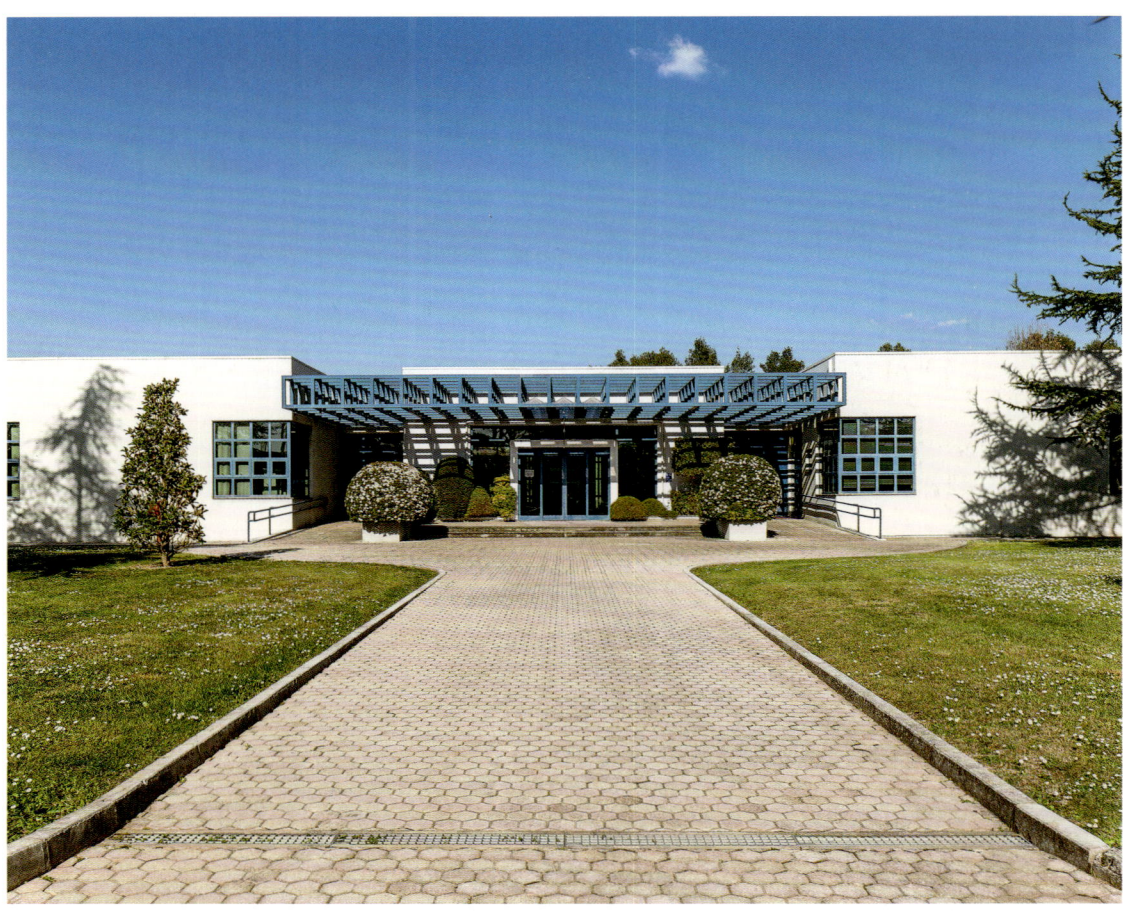

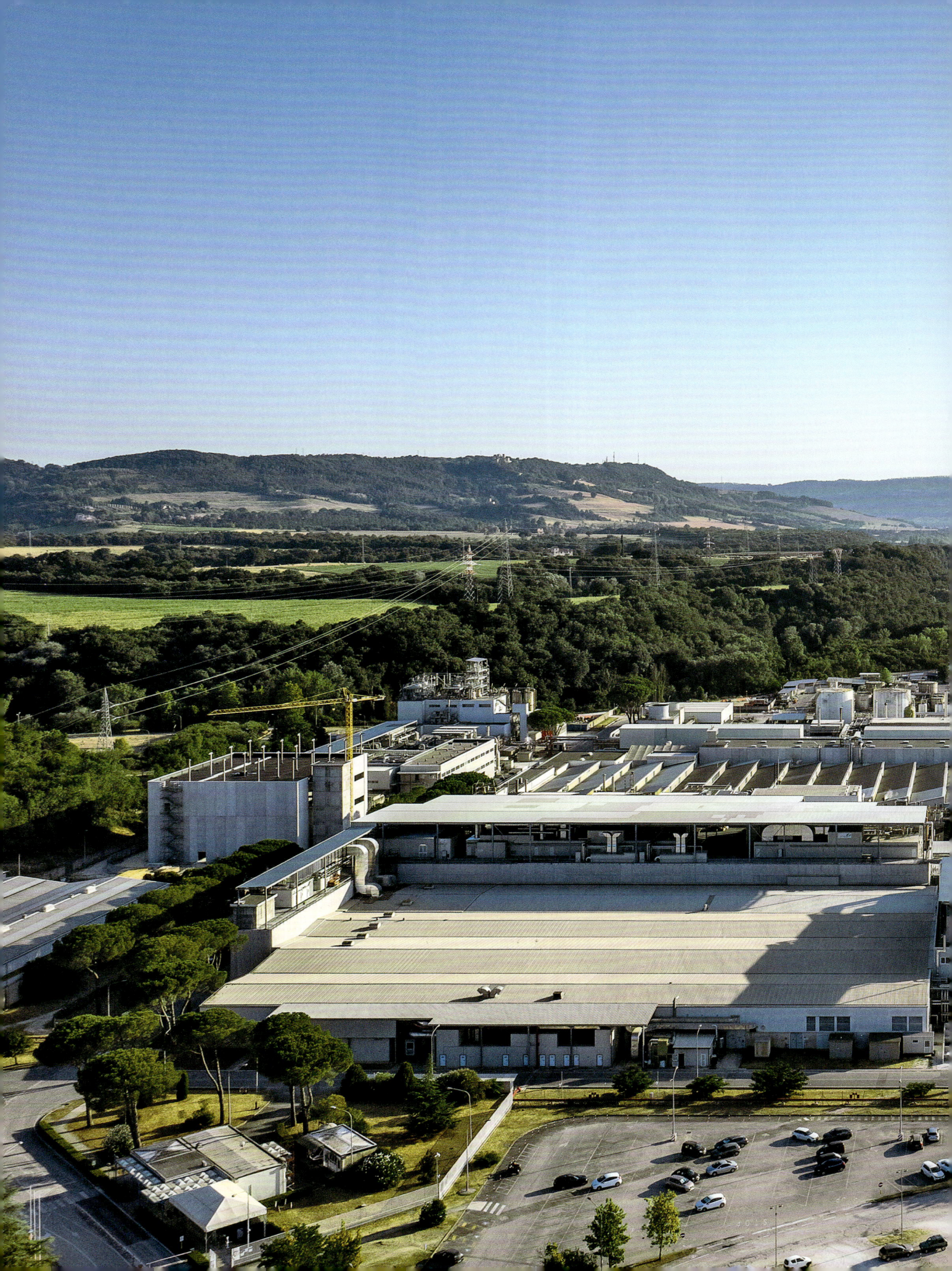

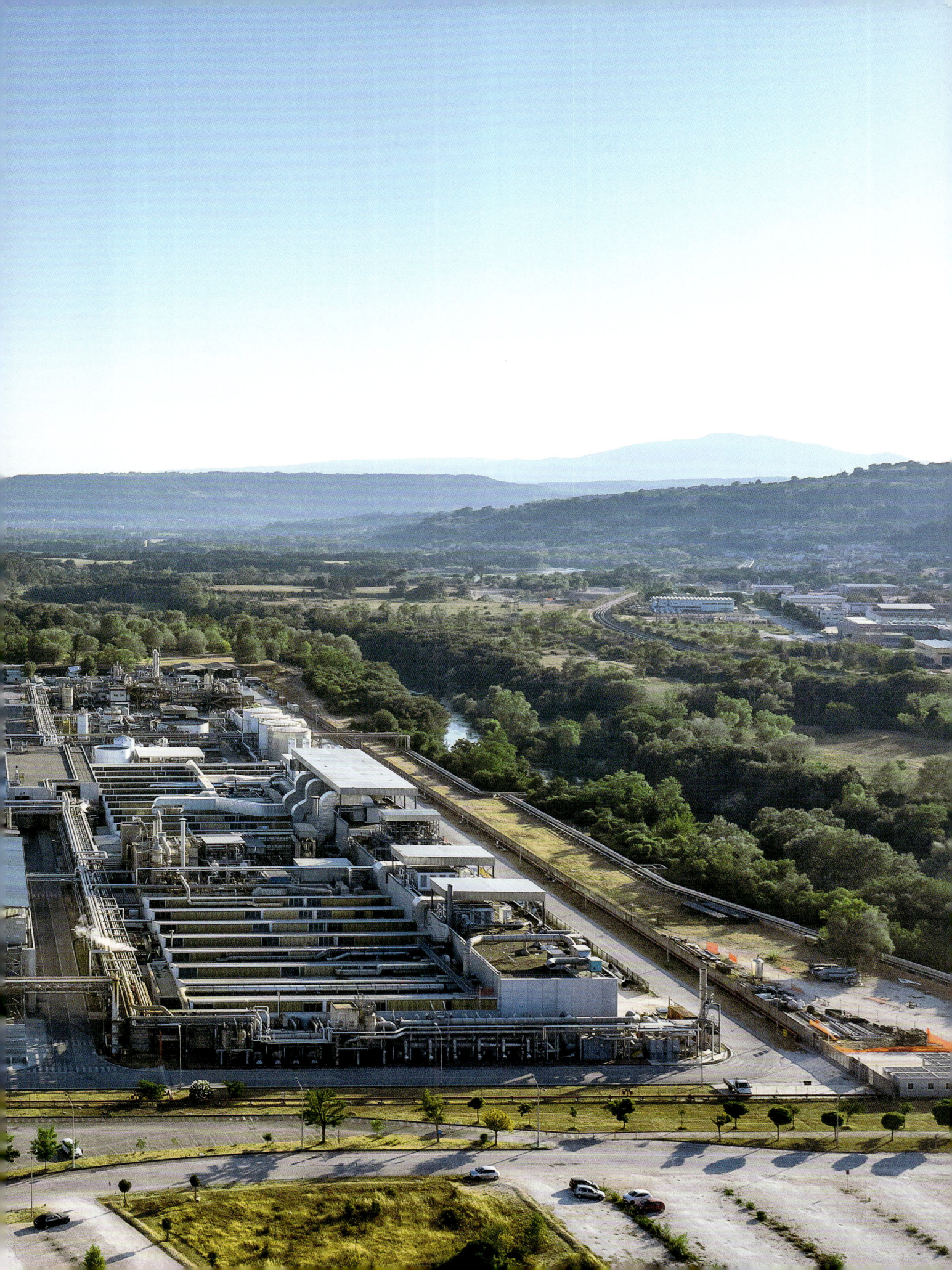

The entrance is low, clean-cut, and symmetrical. White walls, and decor consisting in interlinked blue tubes above. The window frames are also of the same colour, like the waters of the river that flows nearby. It is complemented by the contrasting green of the countryside all around. The light is crystal clear.

The greenery is also symmetrical: one tree on the right, one on the left; one bush on the right, one on the left. In the middle, as if trying to break up the precision of the scene, a small group of people are holding hands and dancing. They kick their legs in rhythm: first all to the right, then all to the left. They are a group of artists, they come from every corner of the globe, and they are familiar with the ages of life. They are talking intensely, exchanging ideas and thoughts.

The scene is the start of a new exhibition. Every creative project by Alcantara begins with a visit to the plant. The aim is to create a hands-on experience with the art material: to start to think in terms of Alcantara.

Beyond the entrance, a new world opens up. The factory seems like some kind of parallel universe. The artists suddenly fall silent, they observe, they listen. They walk, and begin their journey through the world of Alcantara. There is only one word for it: astonishing! This is not a textile factory, a chemicals plant, or mechanical engineering plant. It is like one of Calvino's invisible cities: a unique place that incorporates all three.

Noises become sounds: a constant, composed and orderly downbeat and up-beat: the rhythm of creation. The uniqueness of the production process, and the secrecy that enshrouds every stage of the work, lend mystery and magic to the journey. To become Alcantara, the material continually passes from one state to another. In nature we are not used to a material changing state. It is something of a puzzle, enough to drive you crazy. Something that artists are very good at.

Alcantara is a miracle of softness and lightness. Ultra-thin fibres are stretched, curled, and cut until sequences of flakes are obtained. Ninety kilometres of it weigh no more than a gram! If you look at the fibres, protected by special casings, under the microscope, you see islands in the sea. One of the artists stretches out his hand, lightly touches the Alcantara flakes, and asks if he can take one. He must have had an idea. The first of many.

Then the material is combed and carded, and distributed in very thin superimposed layers, creating a kind of mattress. The time has come for needle-punching: the fibres are interwoven using long needles, forming a compact and resistant felt.

But this is only the beginning, so make yourself comfortable. Now the textile industry steps back, and the chemical side comes to the fore. The sea that held the islands together is dried up. The felt is impregnated and then immersed in a liquid that solidifies and coagulates the raw fibres. One of the creatives points out that, while Okamoto was inventing Alcantara, Giulio Natta won the Nobel Prize for research into the chemistry of polymers.

Today, the production of Alcantara is steeped in the dimension of sustainability. Since 2009 the company has held Carbon Neutral certification, the fruit of a total commitment to reducing carbon emissions to a minimum. At the Nera Montoro plant, production is entirely fuelled by electricity obtained from renewable sources. Residual emissions are tracked and offset by reforestation plans and projects designed to protect the environment.

The raw material is then cut and treated with special abrasive papers that make it soft to the touch. When you run your finger over an Alcantara surface you'll find you can write on it, like children do on windows when they get steamed up. Sheer pleasure.

The last stage is dyeing. The department looks like a painter's studio, with endless small bottles of various colours lined up next to each other, and connected to the machinery. Finally, once tinted, the Alcantara material is dried and heat-treated to fix the colour. What colour? Every single shade that you can imagine. Researchers are always at work: every creative proposal becomes a technical and manufacturing challenge, to be met and overcome.

Visitors also observe the work of the quality control staff, who seek perfection and inspect every square inch of material. Then they go into the offices of the Research and Development Centre. There are cabinets full of Alcantara samples, of which there seem to be no two alike. The adaptable material proves capable of speaking an infinite number of languages. You study them, touch them, hold them up to your nose, finger them, then let them go. They seem to fly. You wonder: "Are they all Alcantara?"

An endless source of inspiration, the expressive potential of Alcantara knows no bounds. The same material can become anything, while remaining itself. The first comments circulate among the visiting creatives. One says: "All materials have limits, Alcantara has potential." Another adds: "Alcantara begins where other materials end."

It makes you want to create, knowing that you can do anything. You just have to imagine it.

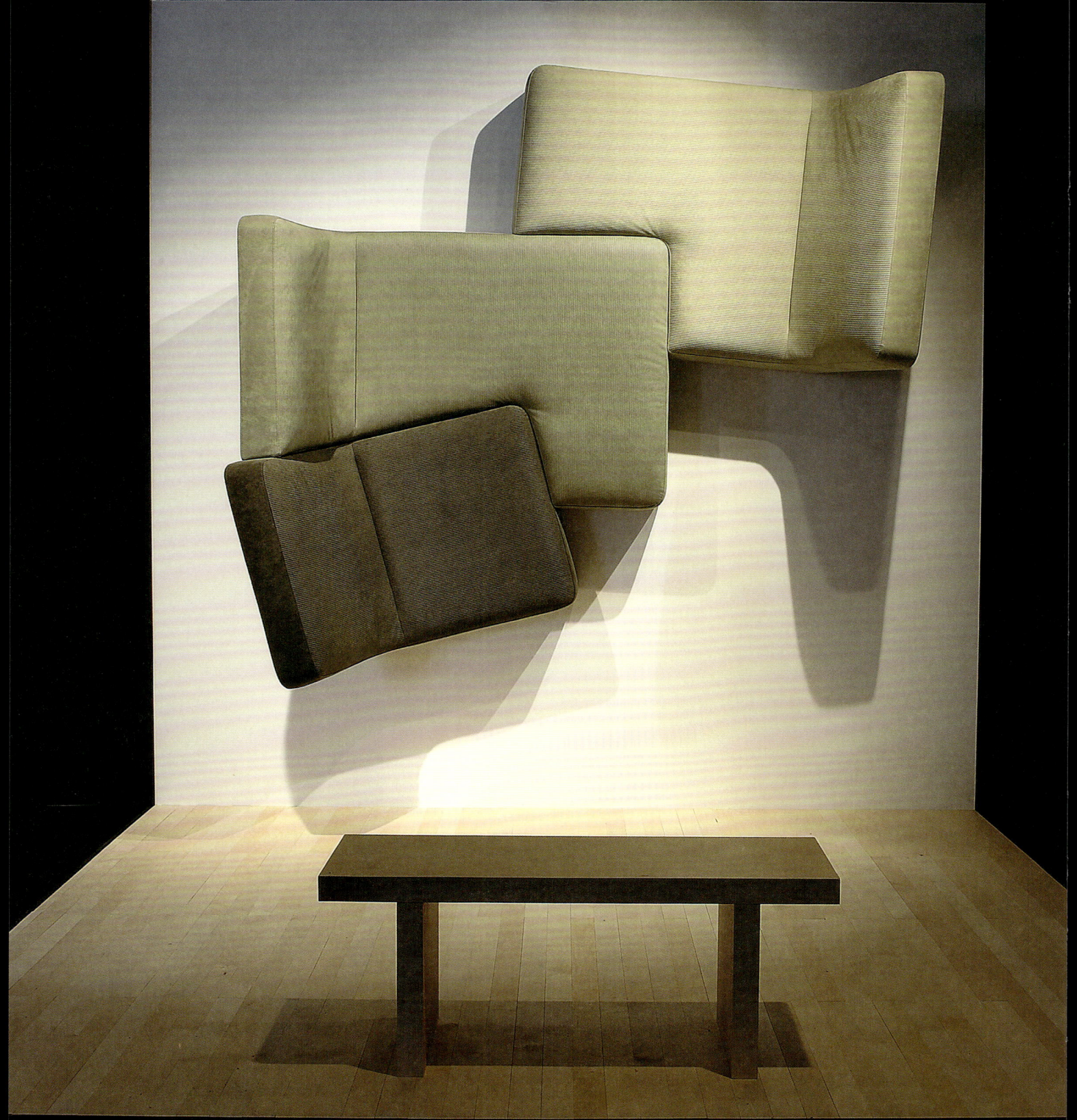

ALCANTARA DESIGN MUSEUM

Springtime in Milan. The taxi crawls along Via Tortona in the traffic. This street used to be in the suburbs, until the last century. Along with the railway, the Naviglio canal, the industrial buildings; now it is the new fashion district. The car pulls over just before Superstudio, the image hub. There's no point in going right up to the entrance, there are too many people. The taxi-driver suggests we stop here. He knows how things work during the Salone del Mobile. The passengers are foreigners, they come from the other side of the world. They get out and allow themselves to be caught up in the crowd. But it is not confusion: the show has already begun.

Confluences sofa in embossed Alcantara by Nigro for Ligne Roset

Net-Work Alcantara sofa by Dordoni for Roda

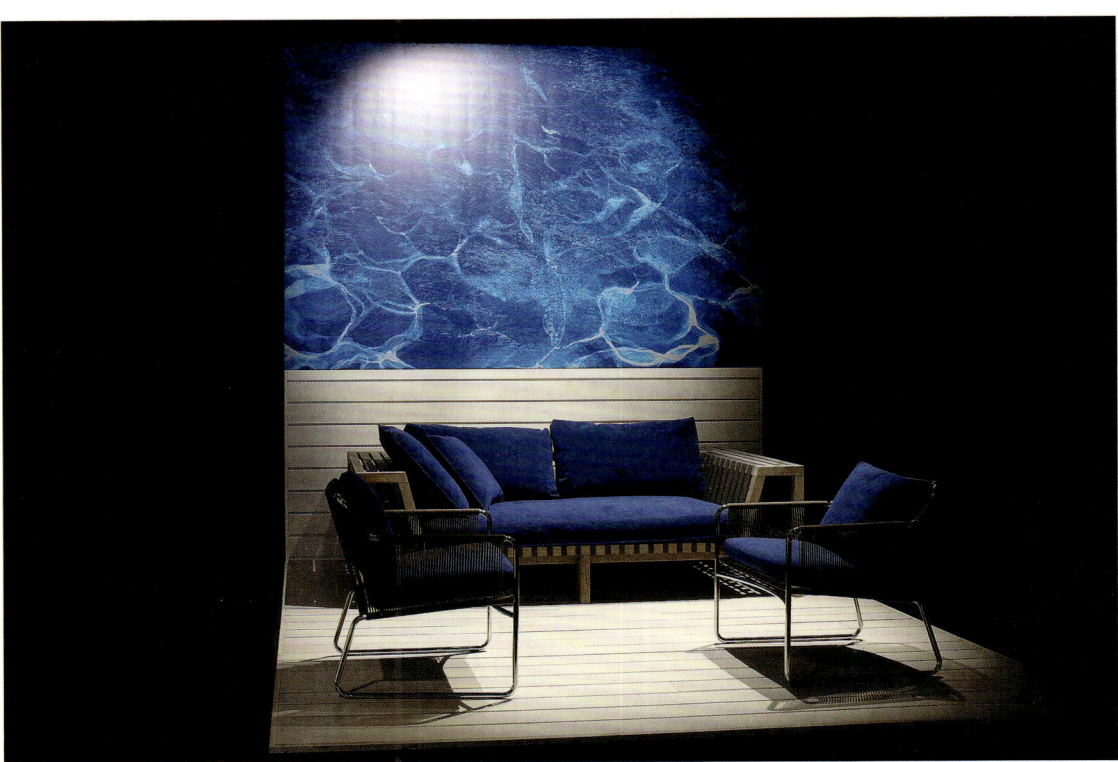

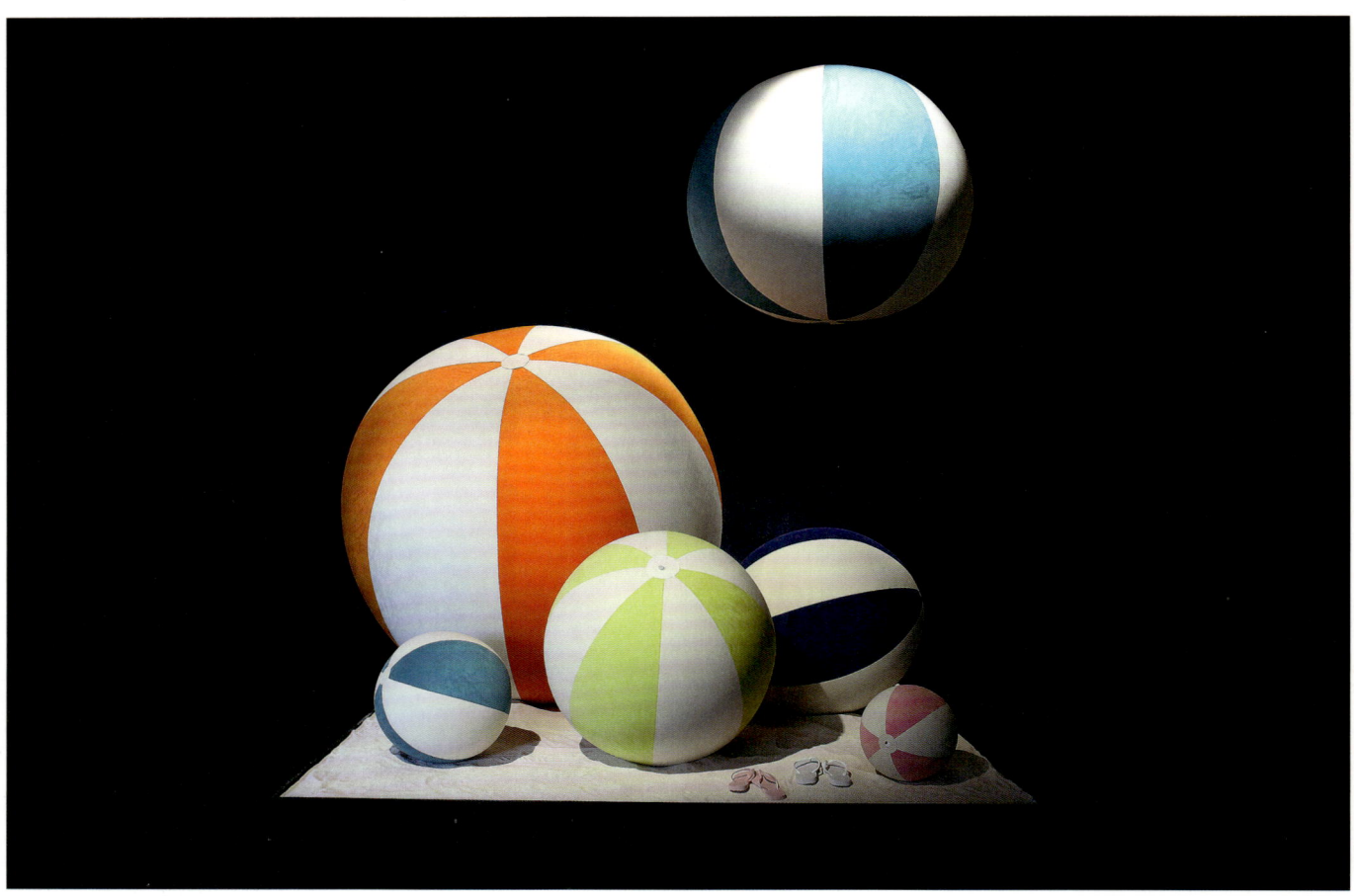

Matteo Thun and Antonio Rodriguez, *Lido*, Alcantara Design Museum, Milan 2009

Every year, Milan Design Week offers a wide range of events revolving around the culture of design, communication and art. Alcantara is a leader on the international scene, and in 2009 it proposed a Design Museum, the first of its kind, that grew out of the close collaboration with the curator and artistic director, Giulio Cappellini. The exhibition presented long-running research work on the material. The idea was to invite world-famous artists and designers to reinterpret objects made by important companies in the sector, using the languages of Alcantara. To think about the expressive possibilities of the material, and discover how a furnishing material can become form, and the stuff of dreams: giving new personality to things, suggesting new end uses.

Cappellini created a neutral theatrical space where designers displayed their works in Alcantara. These creators differed in terms of sign, culture, and tradition. The theatre was designed to spotlight their ideas and approaches. Different, and even opposite, perspectives, which spoke to the public through the eclectic language of a single material: Alcantara.

Matteo Thun took the stage with a glimpse of summer. He created an expanse of pale sand on the floor, then placed two pairs of flip-flops on it. The vertical flat, like a sky resting on the horizon of the sea, was made of deep blue, almost purple, Alcantara. It merged with the black

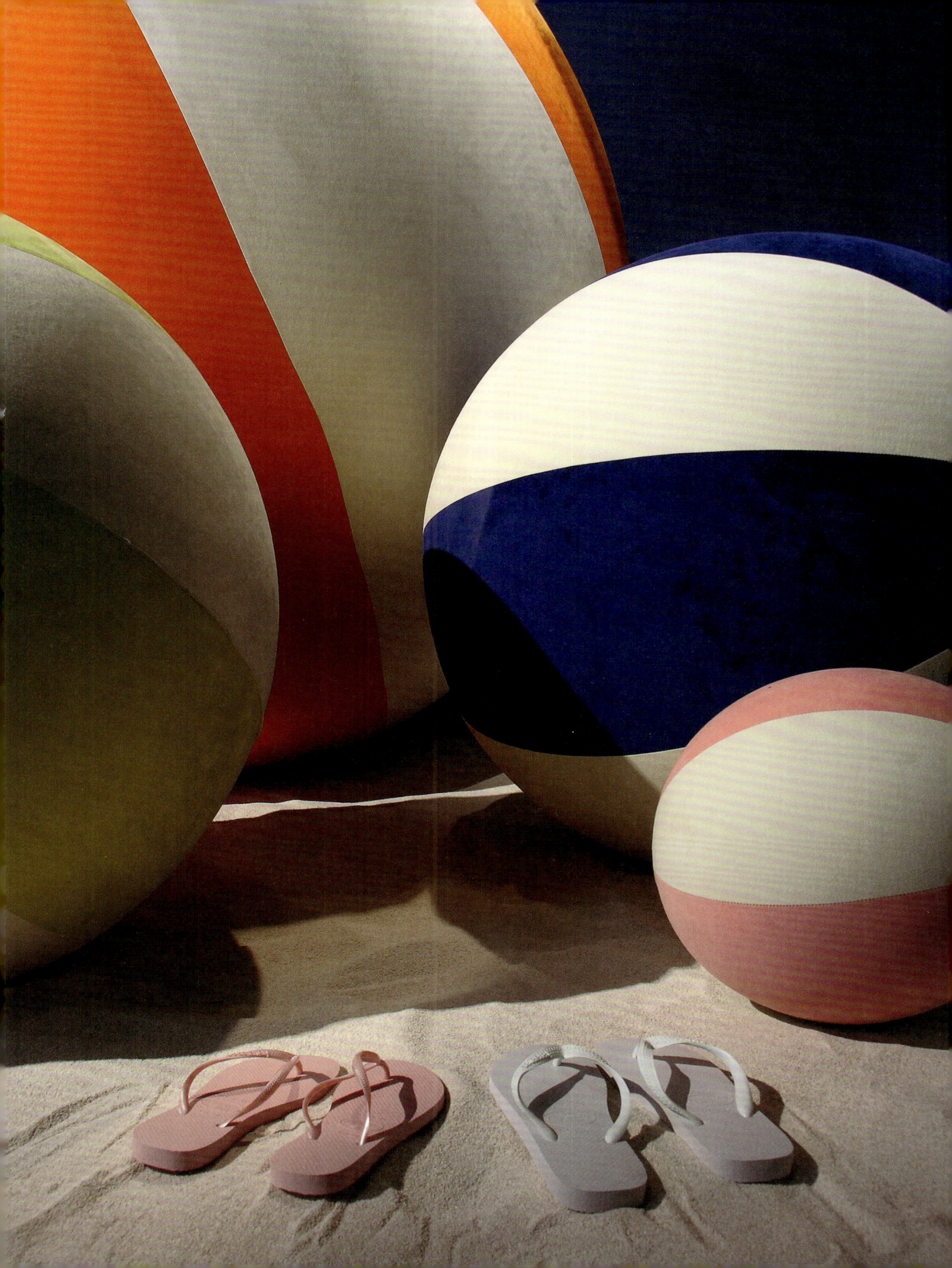

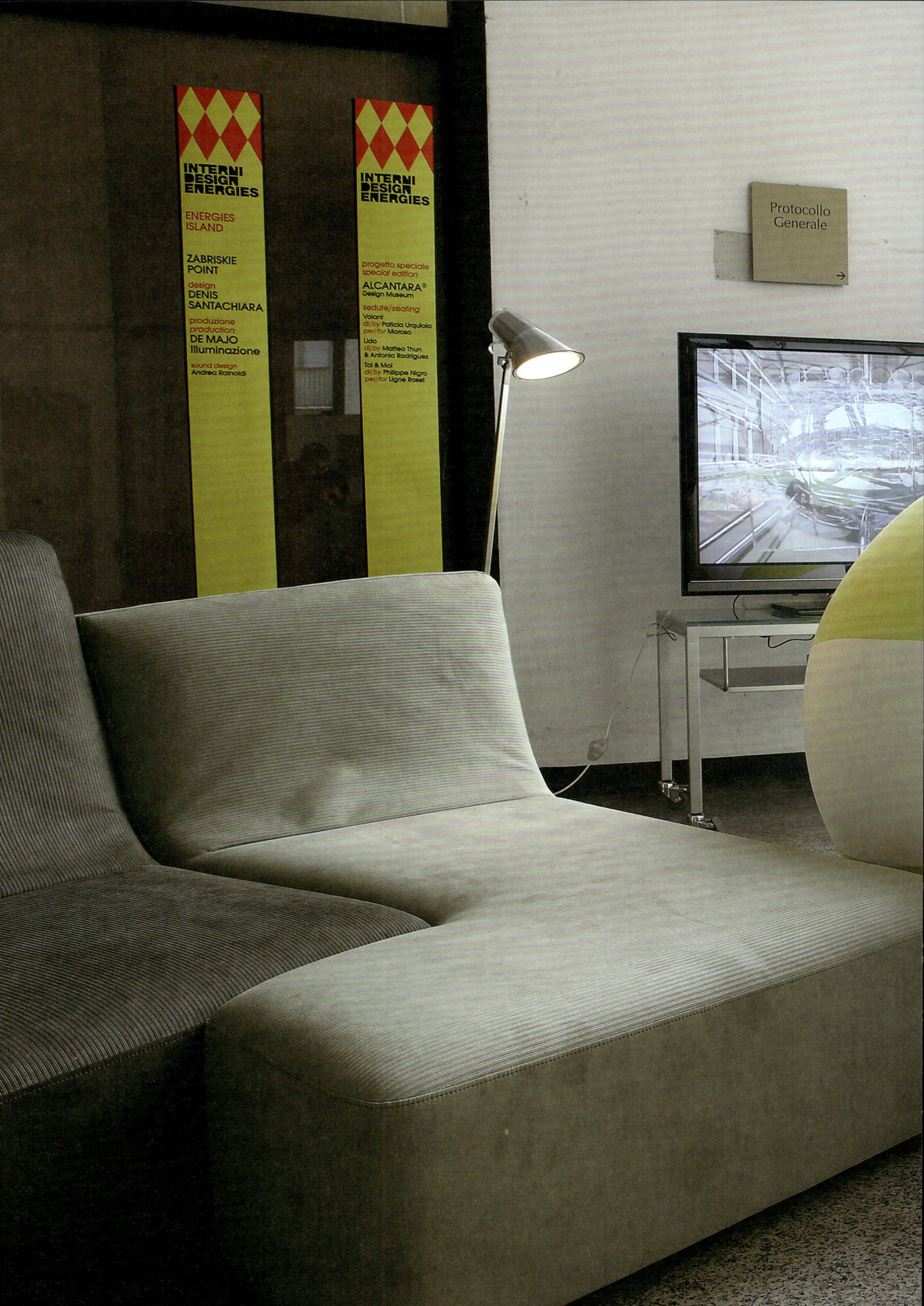

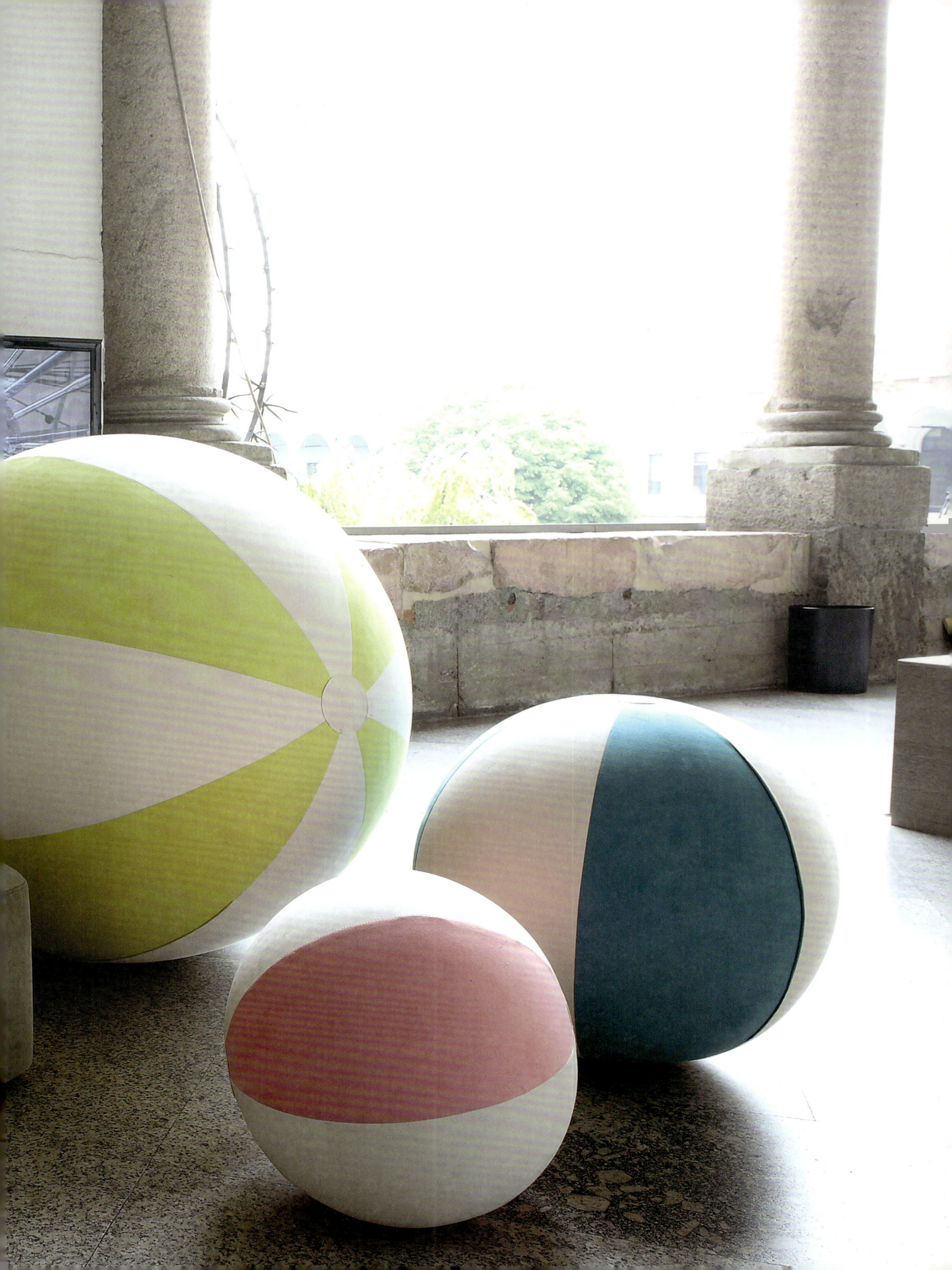

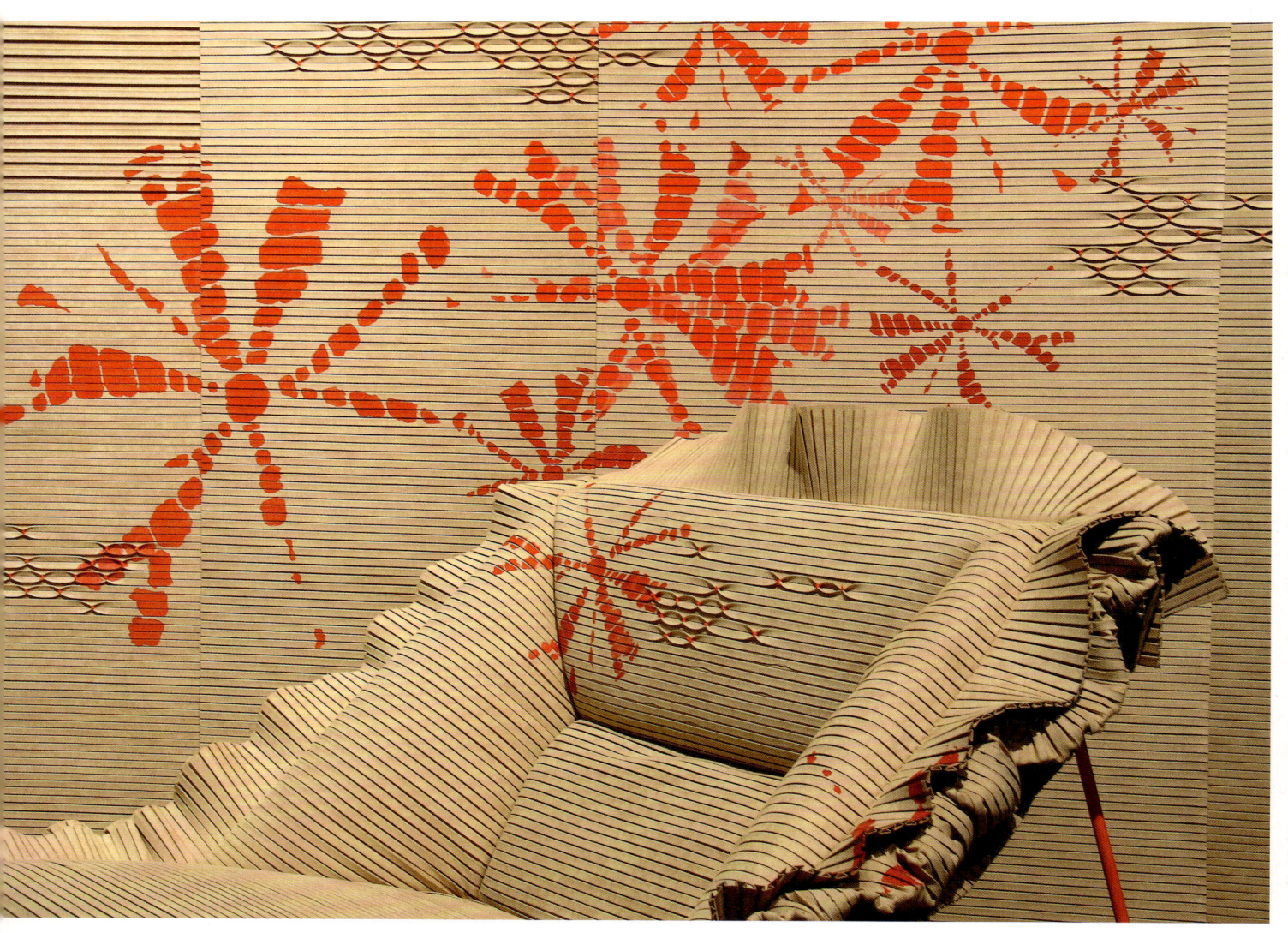

Patricia Urquiola, *Volant*, Alcantara Design Museum, Milan 2009

of the walls. There was also an airy composition of Alcantara balloons, in colourful segments, resting on the sand. As light as a midsummer night's dream. One of them even floated upwards, like a hot-air balloon. You thought of *Baron Munchausen*, *The Magic Flute*, or *The Little Prince*, as you stepped sideways with a smile and immersed yourself in Patricia Urquiola's pleats. She was attracted by the possibility of folding, gathering, curling and twisting Alcantara to create textures of folds punctuated by the rhythm of lines. She chose a warm beige hue to cover a Moroso chair, making it look like something out of *Madame Butterfly*. The Alcantara folds were wrapped around the body of the armchair, the curls clustered all around, like puffs of steam. Sighs of joy. She furbished the space around the object, creating a background with the same material, which resembled a traditional Japanese interior. Red splotches forming flowers, lines and drops, stood out on the Alcantara surface. It was all very lively, but also sedate, subdued. An idea of fragile preciousness, like cherry trees in bloom.

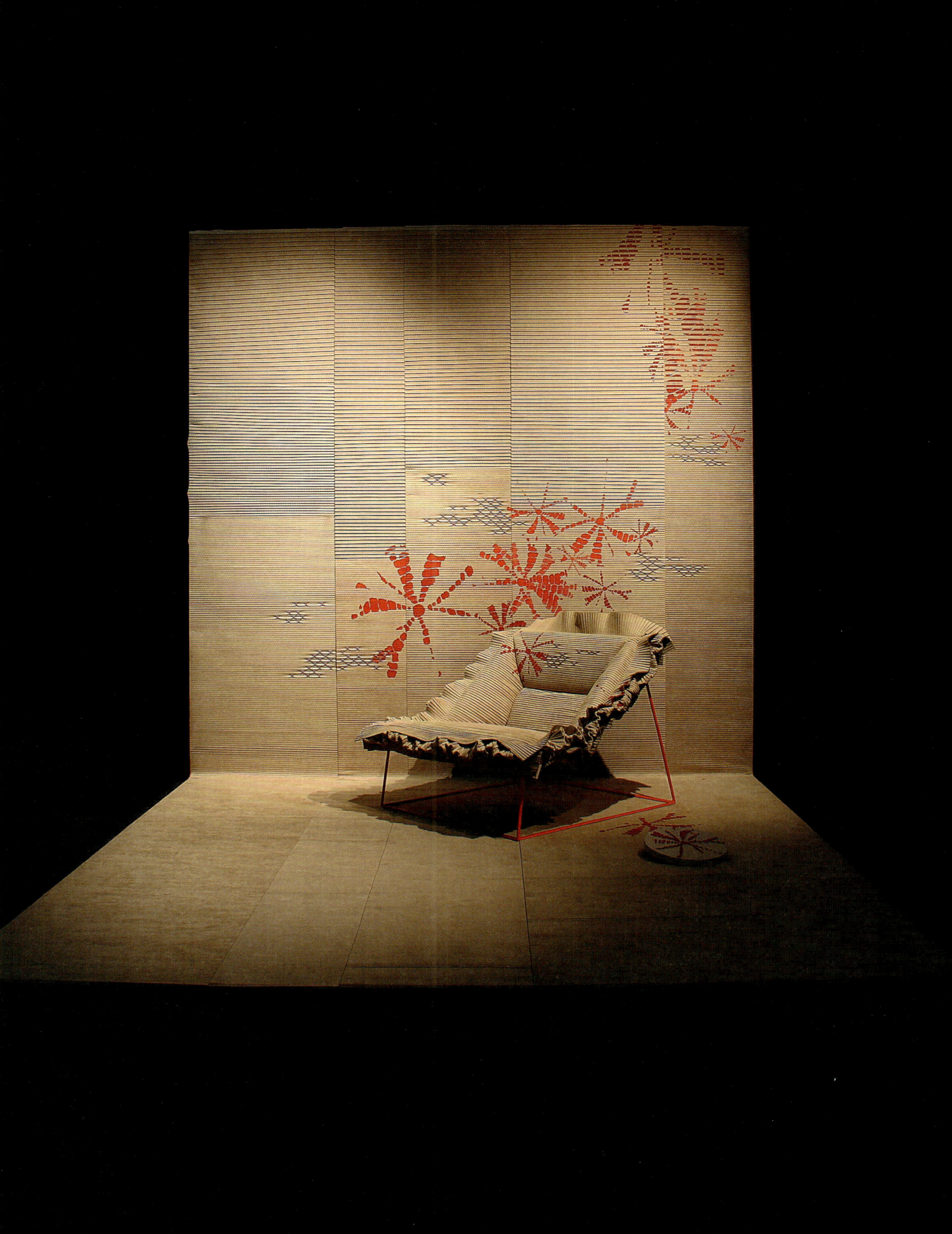

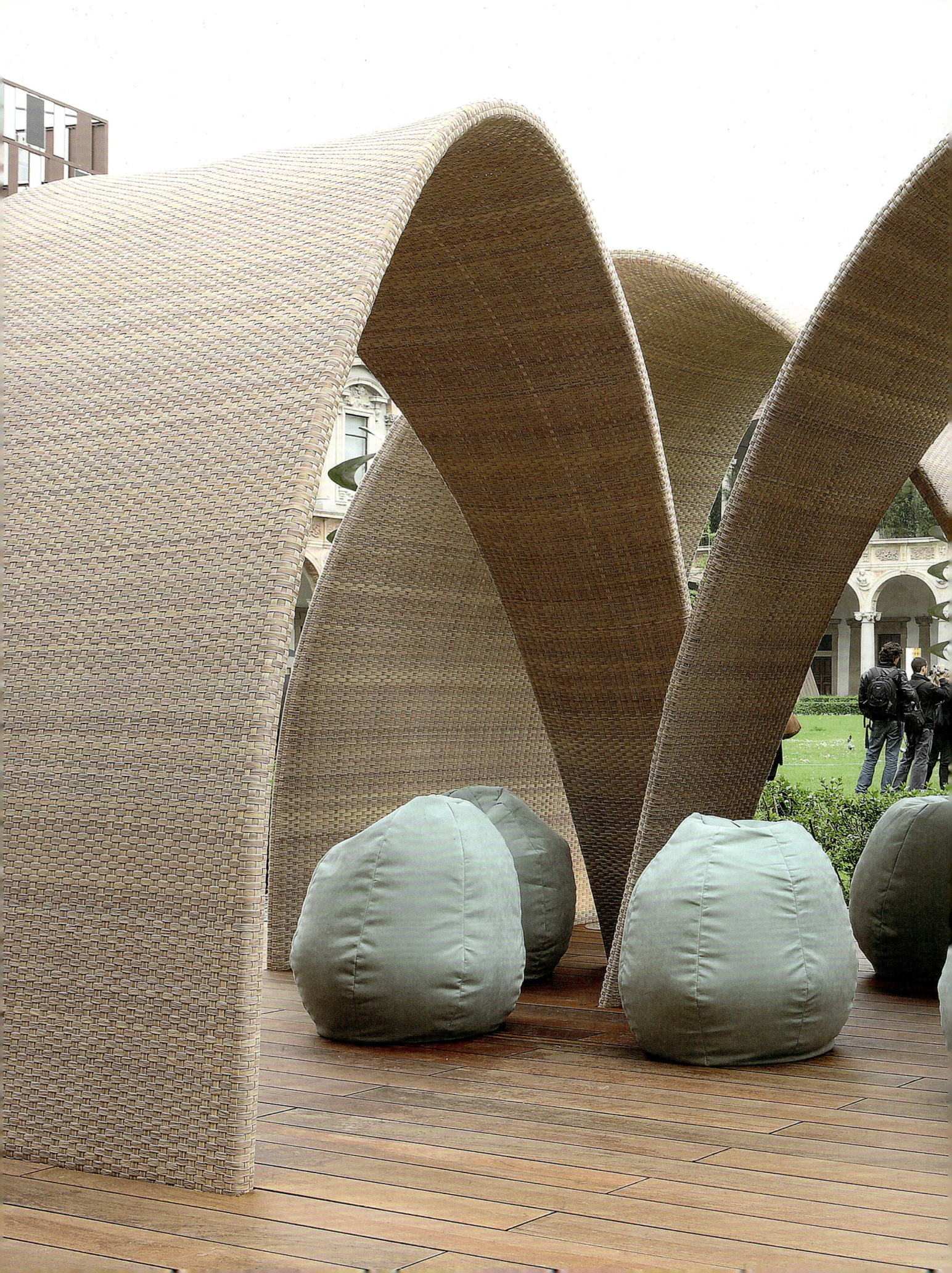

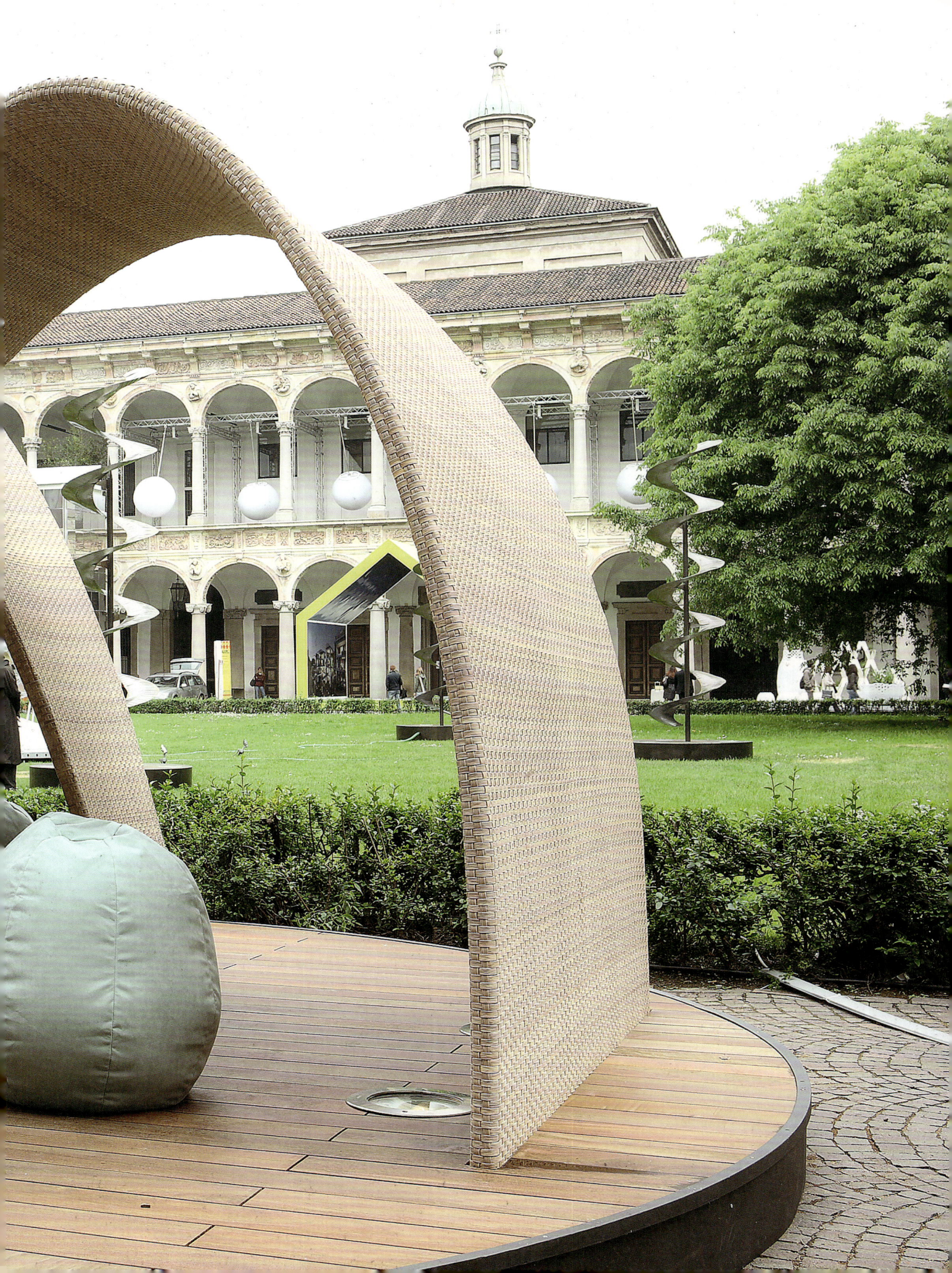

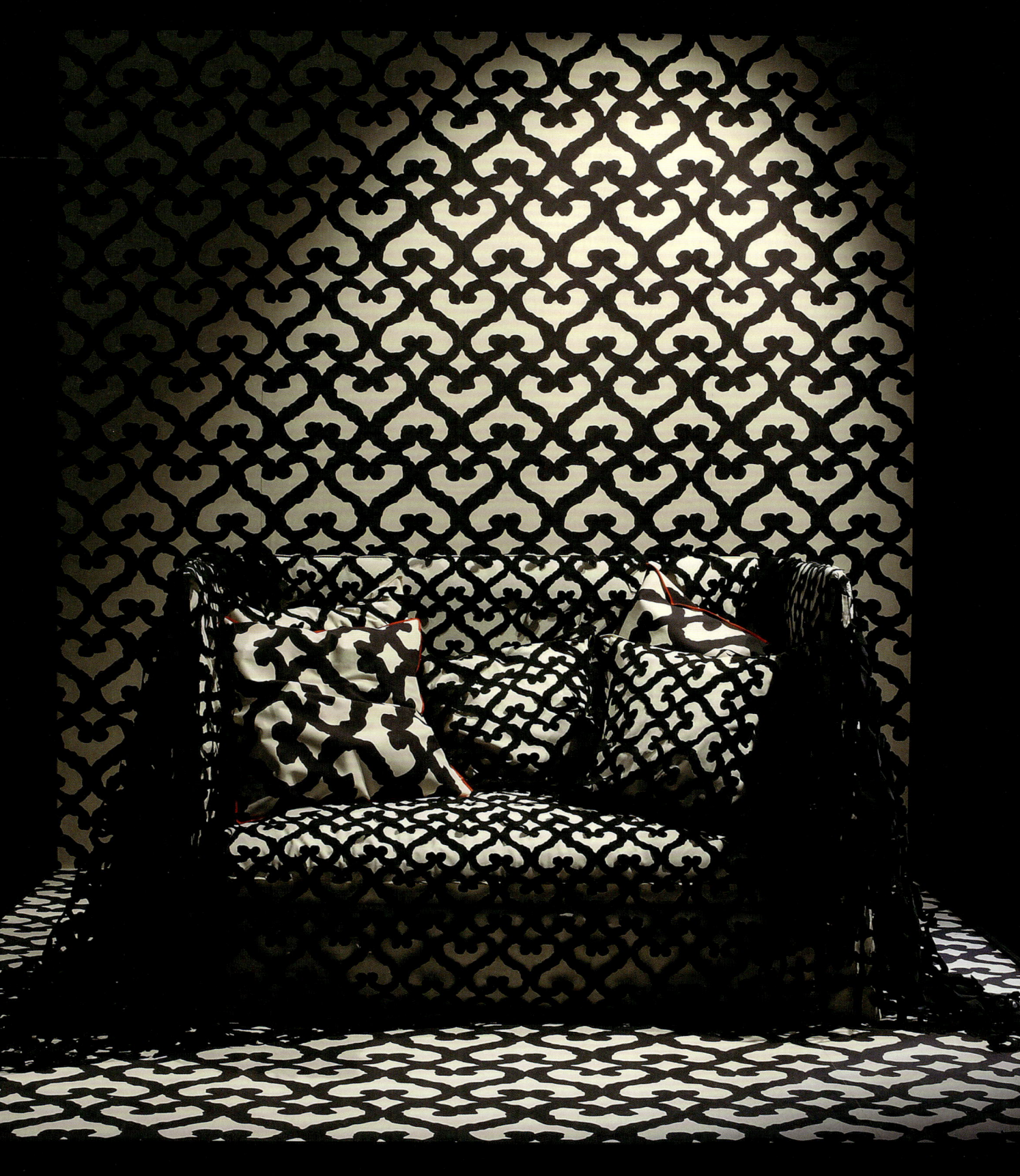

Paola Navone, *Ghost 18*, Alcantara Design Museum, Milan 2009

Another step sideways, and the Alcantara Design Museum featured a sofa that Paola Navone revisited in an Arab vein. She multiplied a pattern resembling inlay on Alcantara. A sort of reverse, duplicated treble clef reminiscent of the grilles of certain antique confessionals, or the shadows cast by awnings and plants in the courtyards of houses in the Medina.
An exercise that is possible with Alcantara, which can become a surface printed on like wallpaper, or a robust piece of openwork. You almost felt the urge to go up onto the stage, step into the spotlight, and sink into the sofa. And with the fingers dig to appropriate the material, make it even more personal, unrepeatable.

The exhibition continued, maintaining a balance between design and art. A deliberate, refined ambiguity: a mix of languages that created variety, and interest. Quality, as a story that narrates differences.

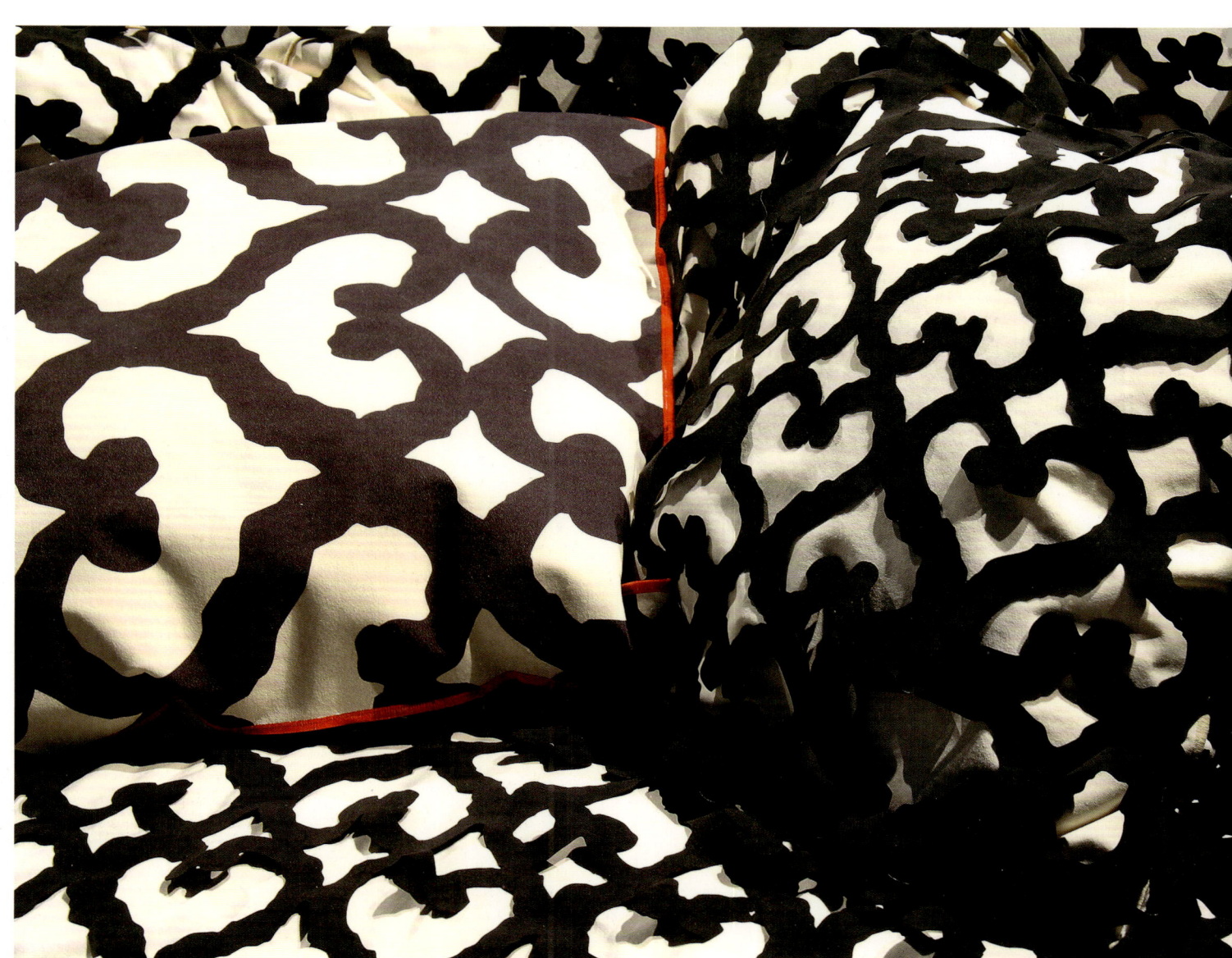

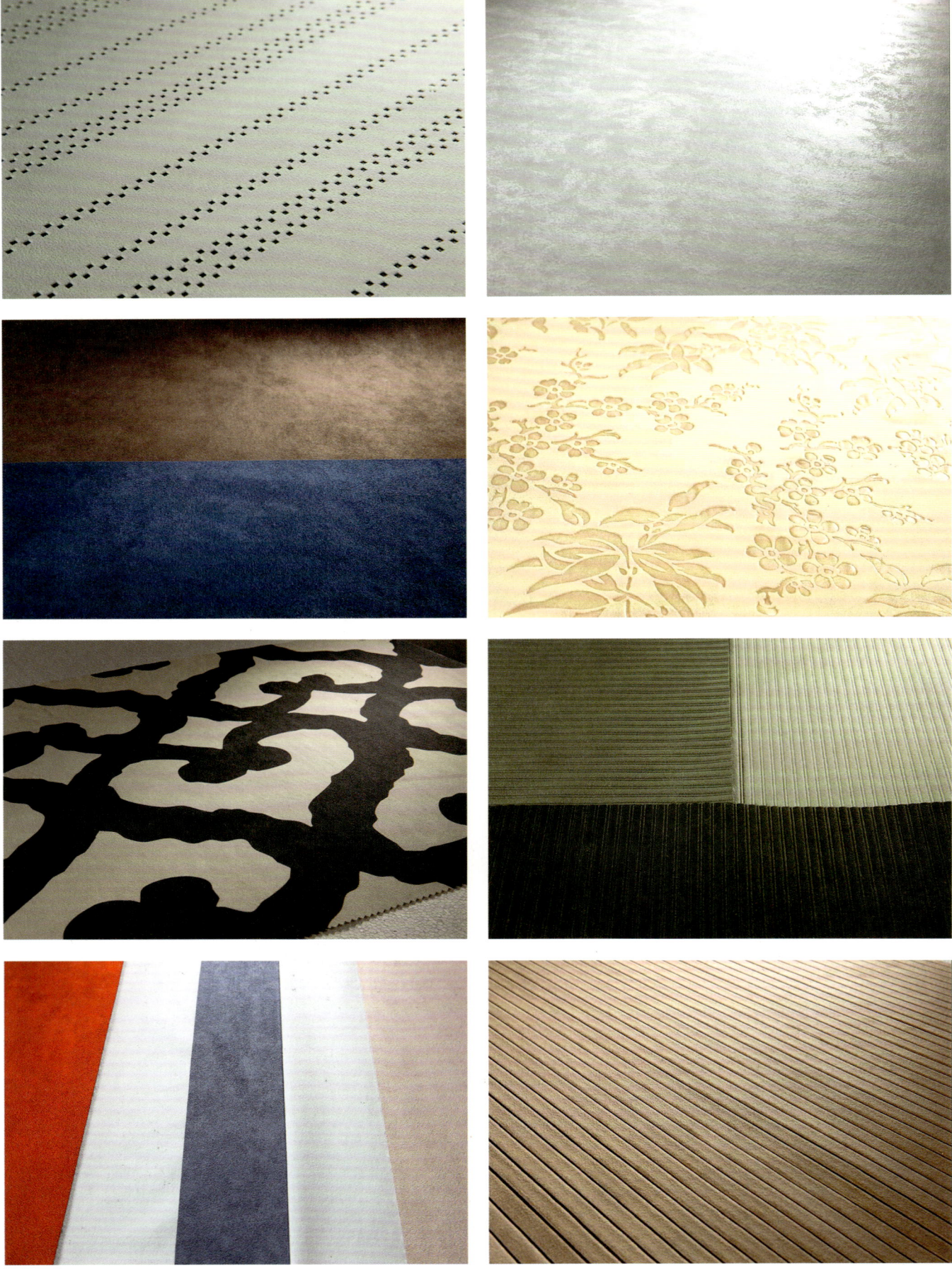

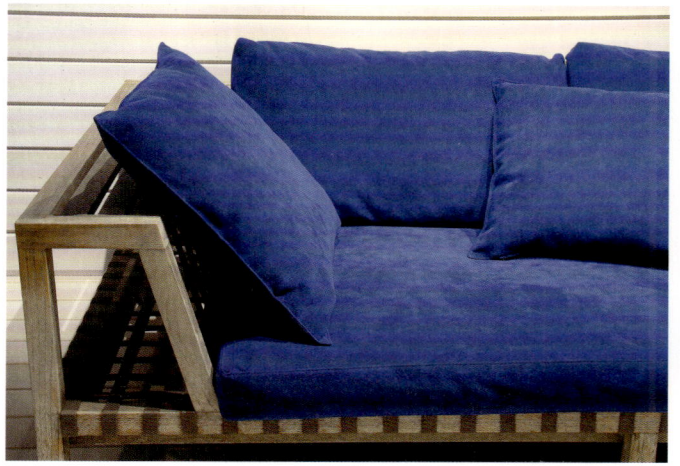 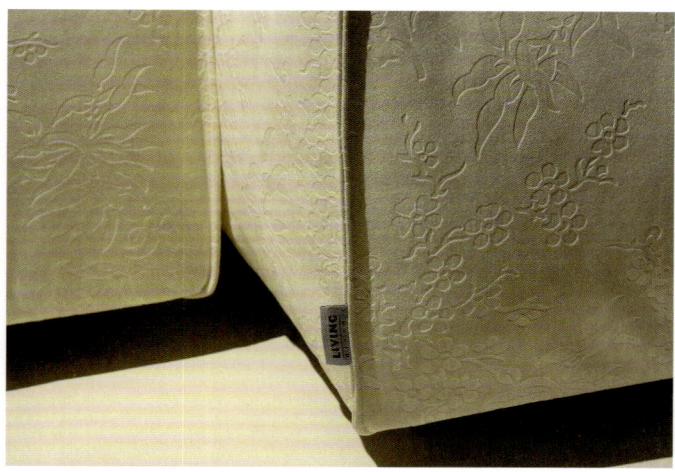
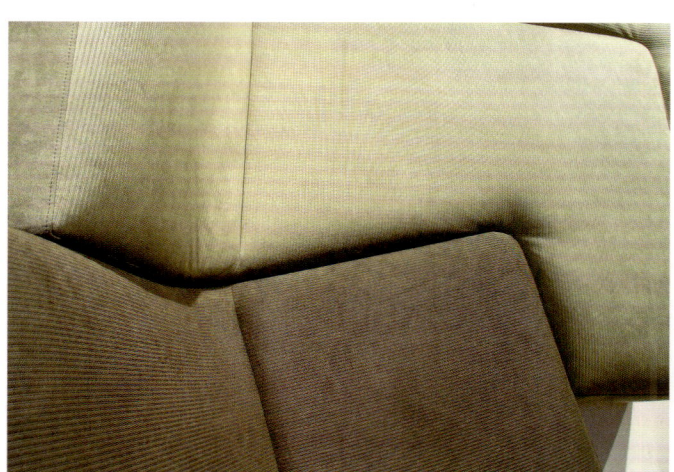 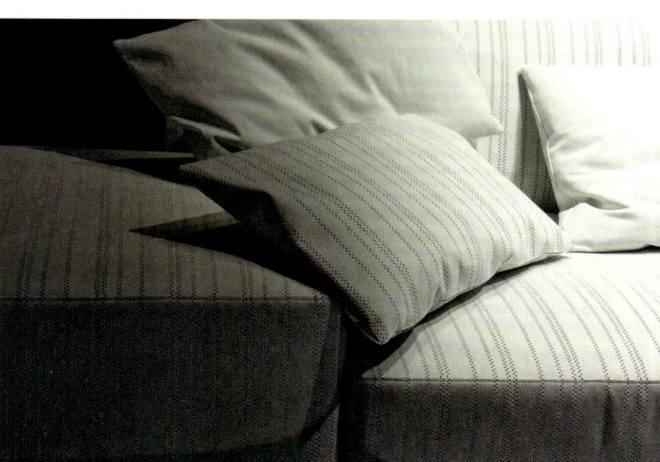

Alcantara produced a collective project, and began to explore the material's possibilities. Adding a touch of wit: the quickness of intelligence. This first exhibition indicated the path to be followed. It seemed like an exhibition, but it was actually a landscape, a collection of ideas.

The following year, 2010, Alcantara presented the second edition of the Design Museum. The show was even more international, reflecting a company that, with one foot in Italy and another in Japan, embraced the whole world. Artists such as Kati Meyer-Brühl, Marcel Wanders and many others developed a wide range of themes such as fashion, autos, and sustainability. New ideas, to recount the contemporary world through the complexity of a unique material, and its infinite languages.

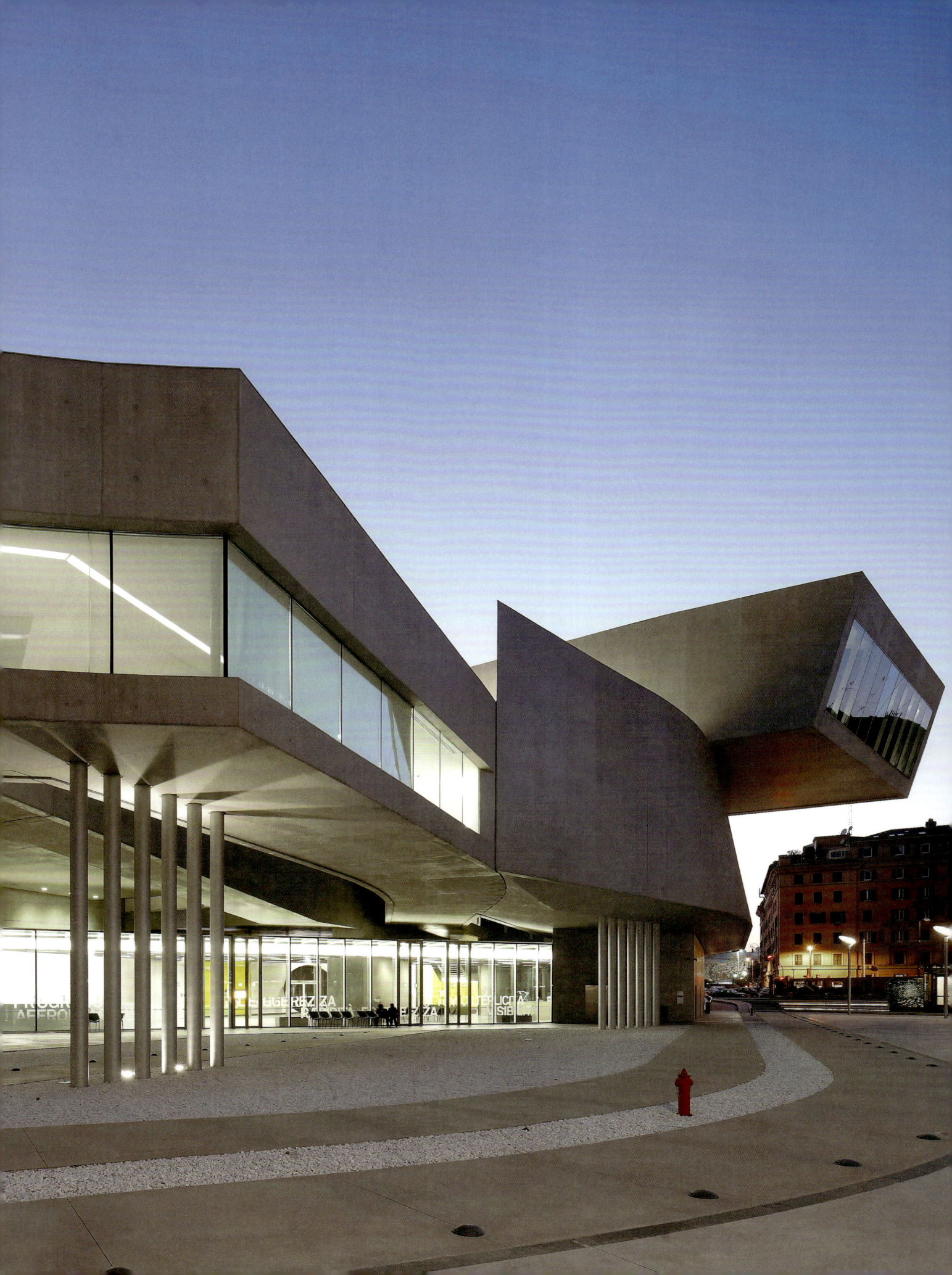

CAN YOU IMAGINE?

MAXXI Museum, Rome

"Can You Imagine?" (overview), MAXXI Museum, Rome 2011

The Flaminio district, in Rome. Where there was once an abandoned military barracks there is now a new contemporary art and architecture museum that goes by the name of MAXXI. It is important to write the name in capitals, so that readers understand that it is the National Museum of XXI Century Arts.

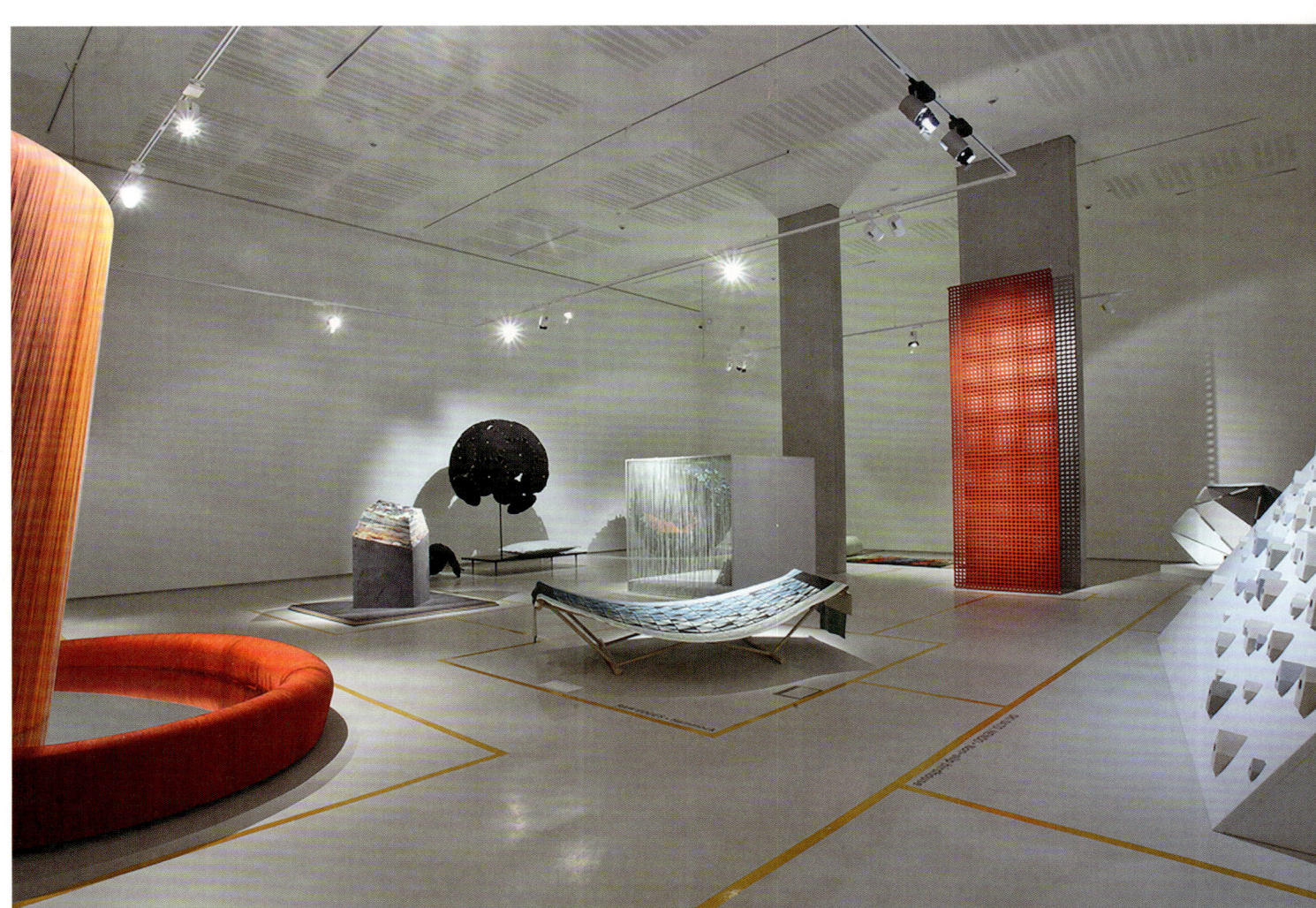

A wide-ranging, fluid vision that the building designed by Zaha Hadid interprets with sequences of curved lines, accelerated perspective, and vanishing points accented by the light that shapes the exhibition spaces. The complexity of the volumes melds with the urban fabric of the district, the levels intersect, creating a sequence of spaces like unexpected landscapes that visitors can walk through: they change as the lighting changes. Losing yourself to find yourself, following the paths of creativity.

The museum's first stone was laid in 2003. Seven years later, when the building was still not complete, MAXXI and Alcantara began a dialogue. The goal was to start a collaboration between the company and the institution, with a view to producing culture. To invent a new kind of relationship, between the public and private sector.

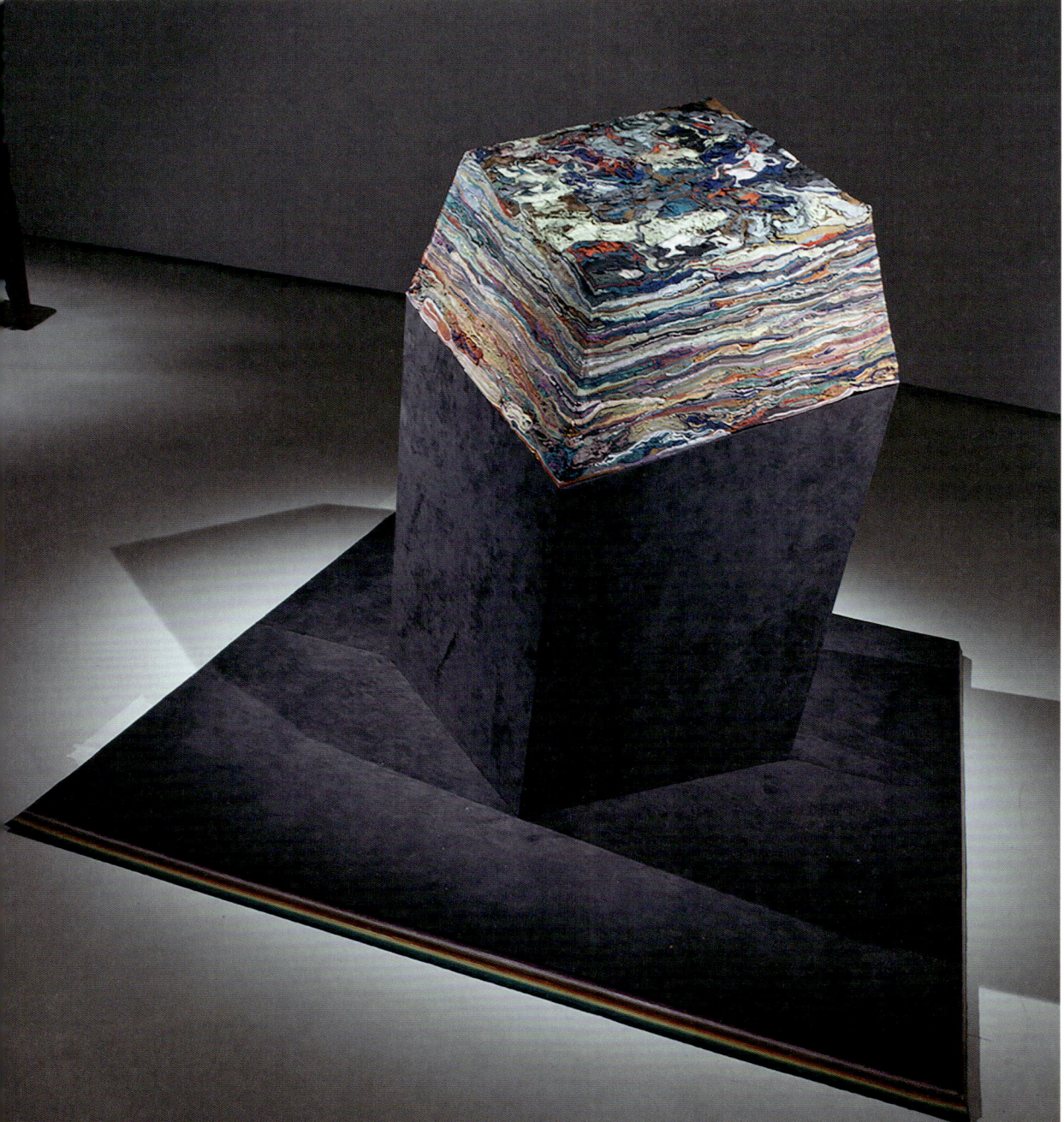

Massimiliano Adami, *Alcantara Remix*, "Can You Imagine?", MAXXI Museum, Rome 2011

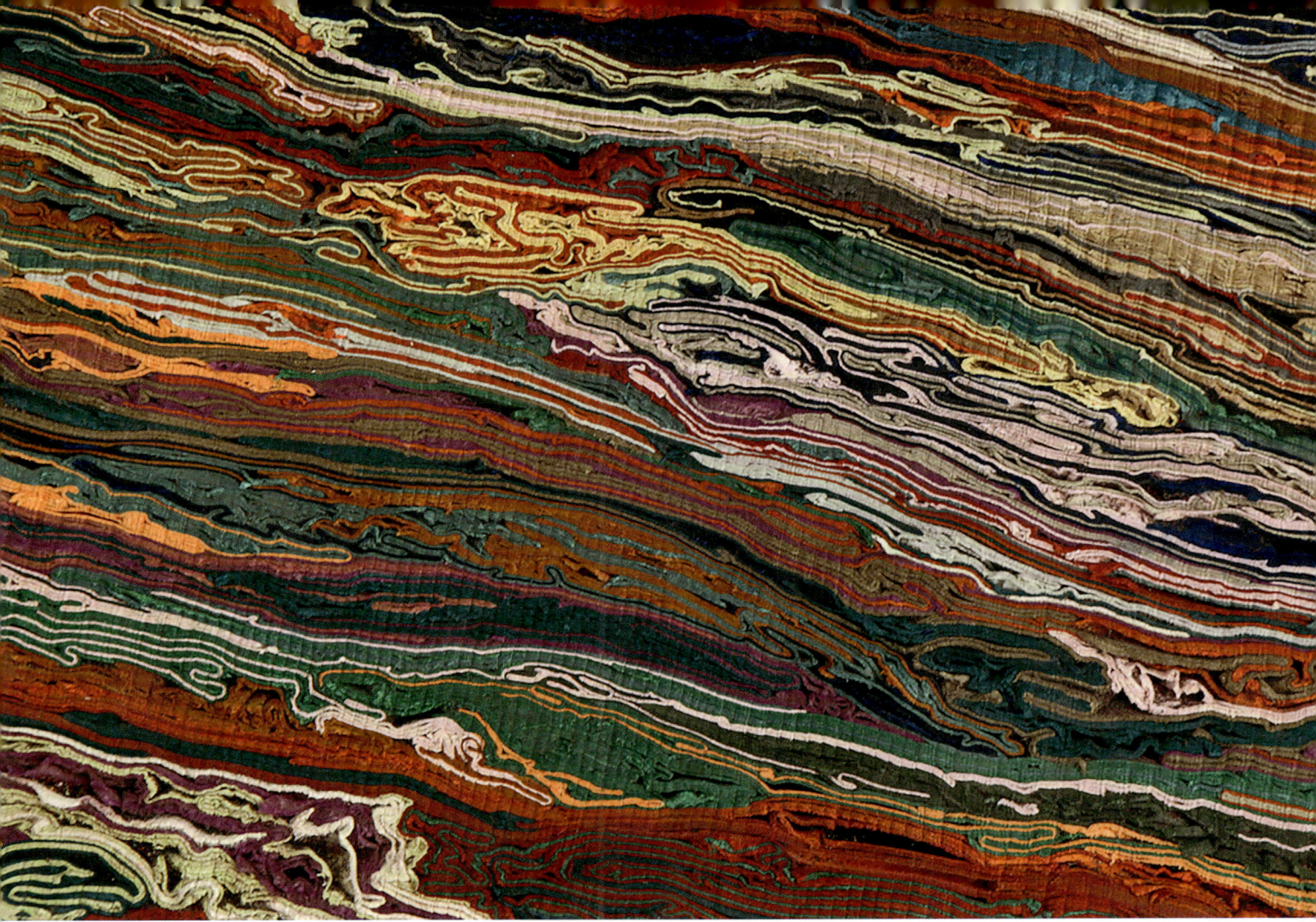

Massimiliano Adami, *Alcantara Remix* (detail), "Can You Imagine?", MAXXI Museum, Rome 2011

The first exhibition was held immediately afterwards, in 2011. It was entitled: "Can you imagine?" Having a question as the title was the result of a sophisticated reflection on the endless expressive possibilities offered by the Alcantara material, in the narrow borderland between art and design. The curators – Domitilla Dardi for MAXXI Architettura, and Giulio Cappellini for Alcantara – met and understood one another, never getting lost. They combined their respective languages, and organized a group exhibition that brought together eleven designers from all over the world. The challenge was to imagine what Alcantara could become, to turn this into a reality that went beyond the known and what had already been tried. The designers were constantly backed by the company's Research and Development Centre, which churned out one technical solution after another to meet the creatives' needs.

But the question "Can you imagine?" was also addressed to the public. Alcantara invited everyone not to limit their imaginations: to satisfy their desire for discovery by exploring the links between reality and dreams, between technology and fantasy. This led to an exhibition devoted to the culture of project design, in the etymological sense of the word "project": literally, to project oneself forward, to go beyond.

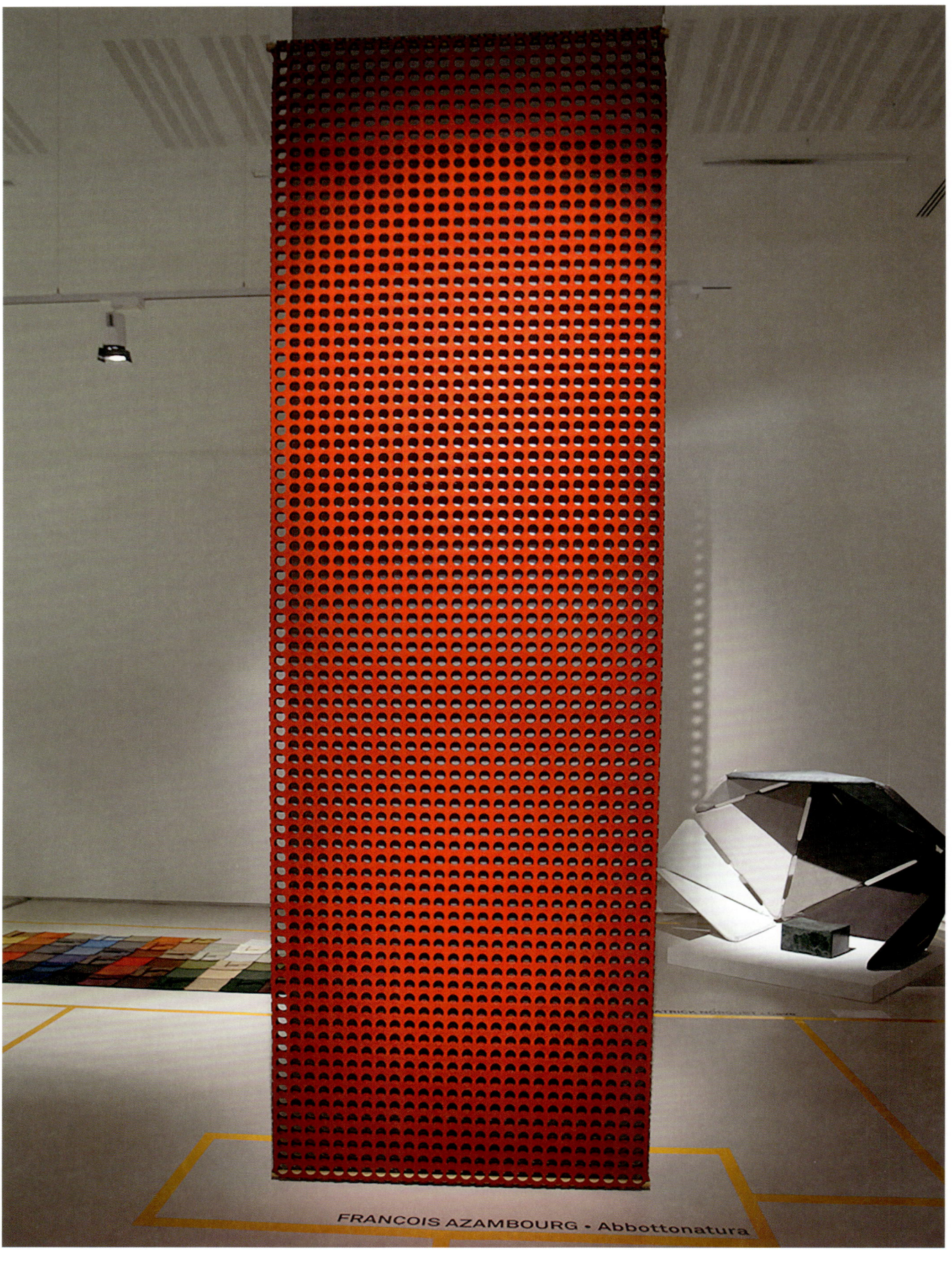

FRANCOIS AZAMBOURG · Abbottonatura

François Azambourg, *Abbottonatura*, "Can You Imagine?", MAXXI Museum, Rome 2011

Marcel Wanders, *Pool Table*, "Can You Imagine?", MAXXI Museum, Rome 2011

Light accompanied the public on their visit, who were invited to interact with the works: to touch them in order to experience them with all their senses. To intuit the ideas behind the forms.

Massimiliano Adami presented an agglomeration of superimposed layers of Alcantara. The object resembles a prehistoric monolith, a soft, multicoloured stalagmite. Material in the pure state, unknown, alien. An unidentifiable object, a silent volume, sculpted by angled cuts that reveal its internal structure. Thin sheets detach themselves from the upper surface of the work and appear to float, illustrating the nature of the material in sequence. It's always Alcantara, from which Alcantara is regenerated and recreated.

By contrast, François Azambourg, from France, was fascinated by Alcantara's hidden depth. He created a panel constituting a conceptual module: a single surface which, by exploiting a simple origami technique, becomes a double wall. A small folded Alcantara element enables the eyelets of the surfaces to be buttoned up, creating a self-supporting structure. The designer presented the work as a close-up vision of the material, seen through the lens of a microscope.

Marcel Wanders played ironically with an Alcantara billiard table: his lanky frame is bent forward, he brandishes the cue – also made of Alcantara – and shoots a ball into a corner pocket. The softness of the material is an open invitation to touch. The player's fingers run over the

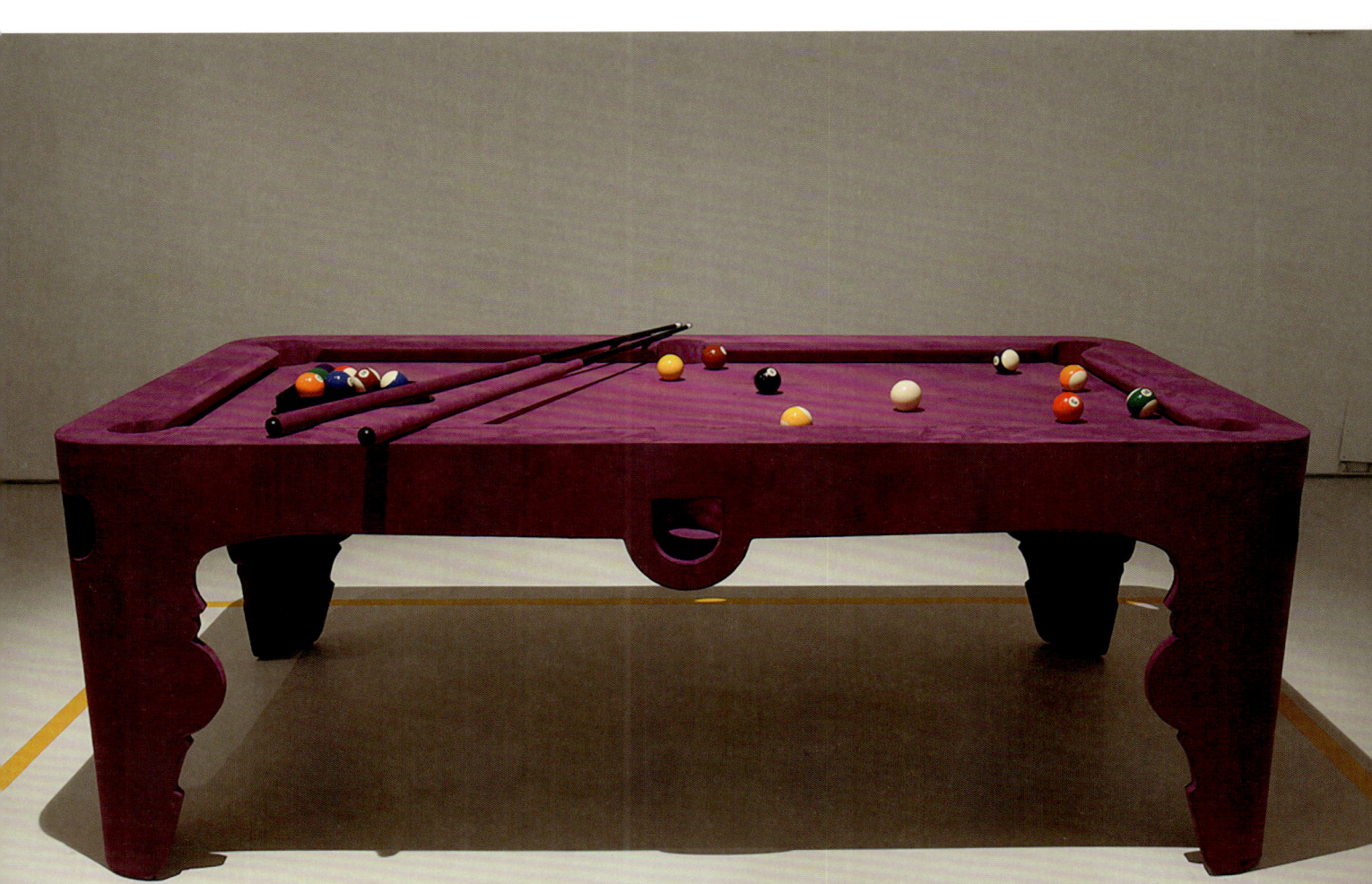

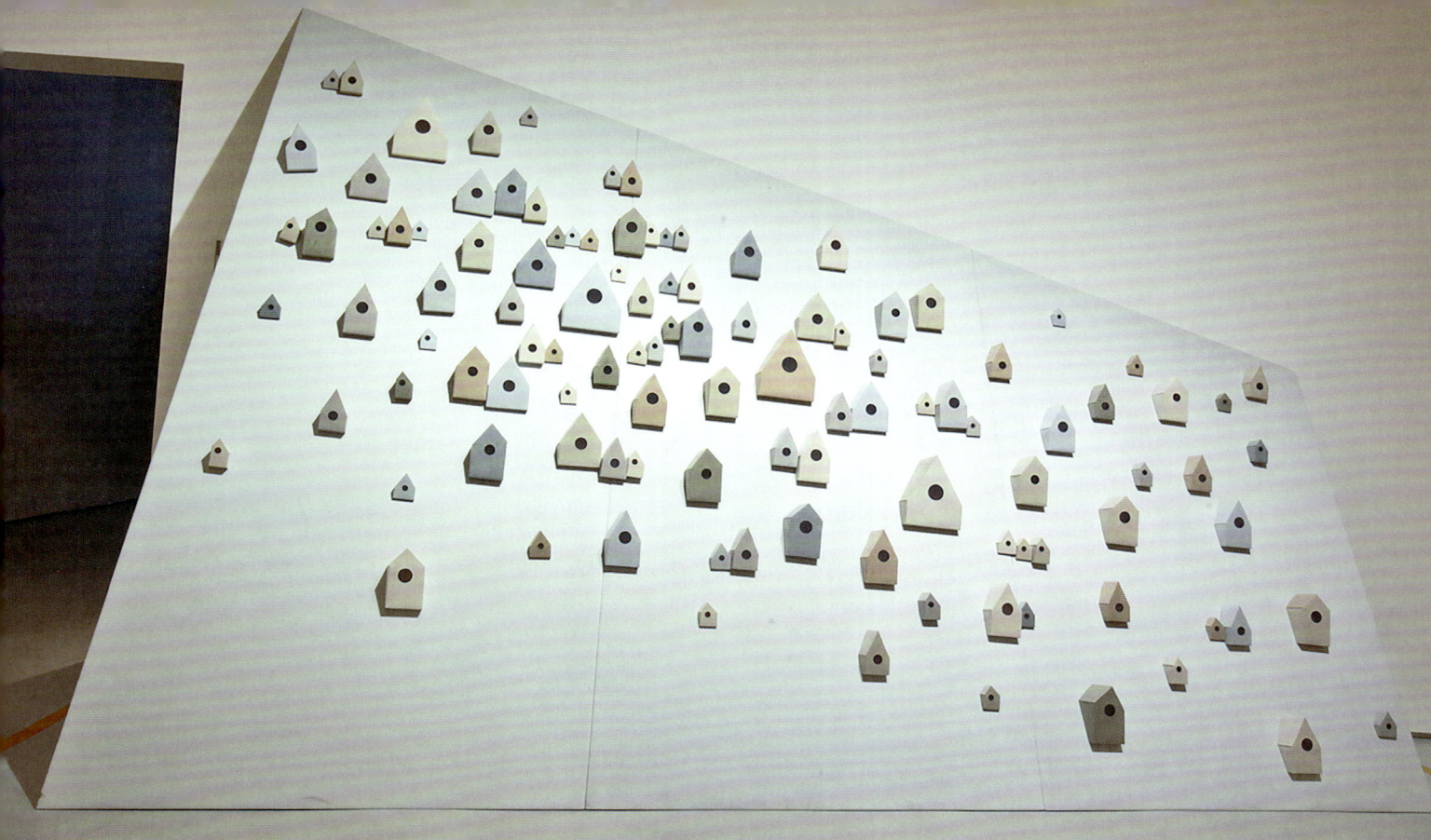

Oki Sato, Nendo, *Non-Slip Birdhouse*, "Can You Imagine?", MAXXI Museum, Rome 2011

cloth, his eyes follow suit, and his senses allow themselves to be caught up in the game.

With his studio, Nendo, a young Oki Sato offered the poetic image of a suspended landscape. An inclined plane, made of Alcantara. On this plane there is a series of birdhouses of various sizes and colours. They are as simple and precise as the words of a *haiku*, as balanced as the lines of the poem. The public is invited to touch them and move them. The birdhouses do not fall over, even though they are not fixed. Alcantara has a good grip, holding them in a strong embrace. Friction is one of Alcantara's characteristics, and in car seats this holds the driver's body securely, ensuring safety.

Light led visitors to discover Paola Navone's *Pet basket*, which joins together thousands of tufts of Alcantara to create a welcoming spherical structure. Inside, the cushions are made of fine threads of the same material knitted together. A refuge against life's storms; a shell that rocks; a nest of leaves; a cradle to isolate and envelop, to protect and cuddle.

Satyendra Pakhalé's work, instead, derived from the ideas that the artist picked up when he visited the Nera Montoro plant. "When you see all those threads of micro-fibres coming out of the machinery," he said, "you think about the endless aspect of the manufacturing process". With just a mirror as the base for cascading Alcantara threads, the artist recreated the illusion of a flow of material that disappears within itself. A fountain? A waterfall? A gate? The object is ever-changing, it emerges like a dream. It is whatever you imagine it to be.

Paola Navone, *Cuccia*, "Can You Imagine?", MAXXI Museum, Rome 2011

Satyendra Pakhalé, *Endless Alcantara*, "Can you imagine?", MAXXI Museum, Rome 2011

Following pages
Nika Zupanc, *Protect me from what I want*, "Can you imagine?", MAXXI Museum, Rome 2011

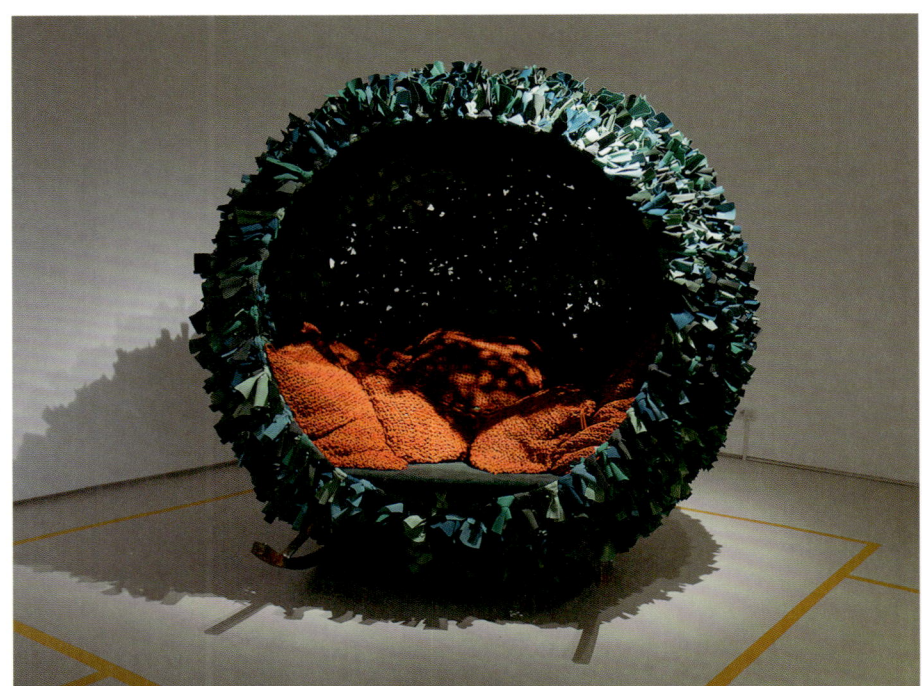

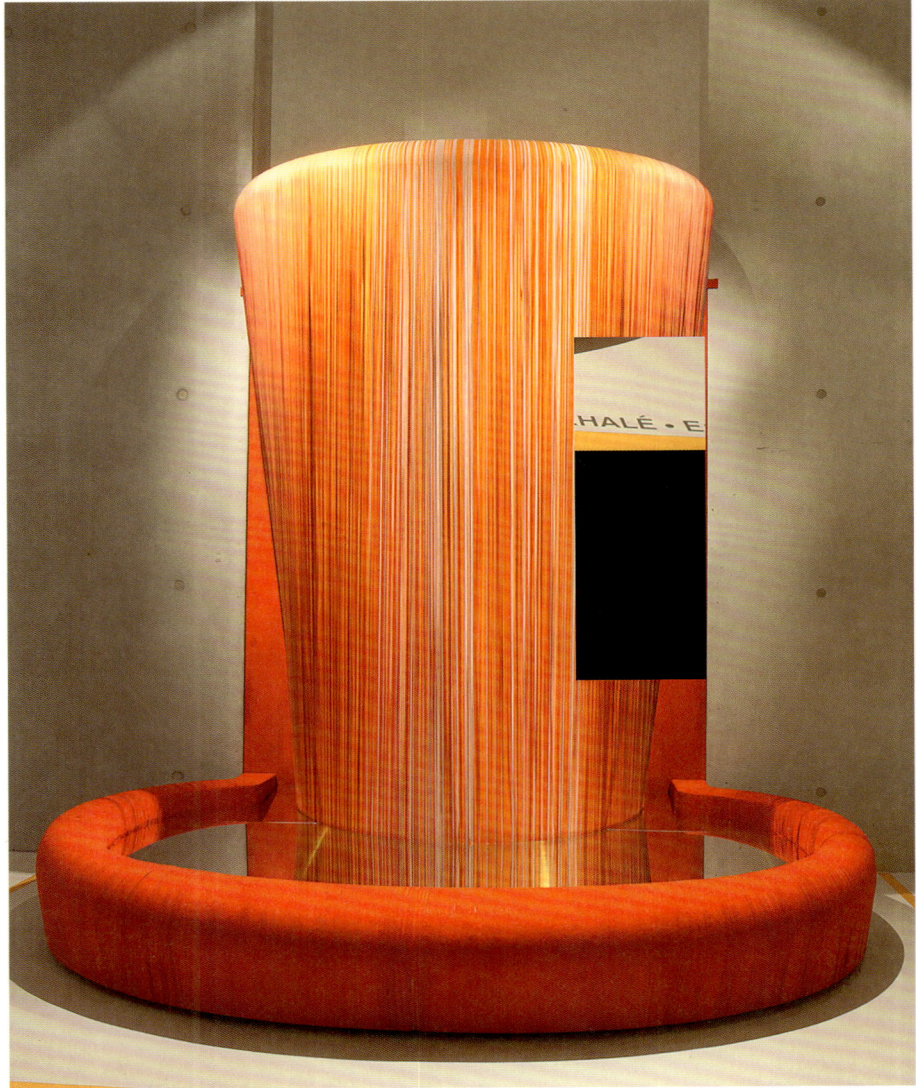

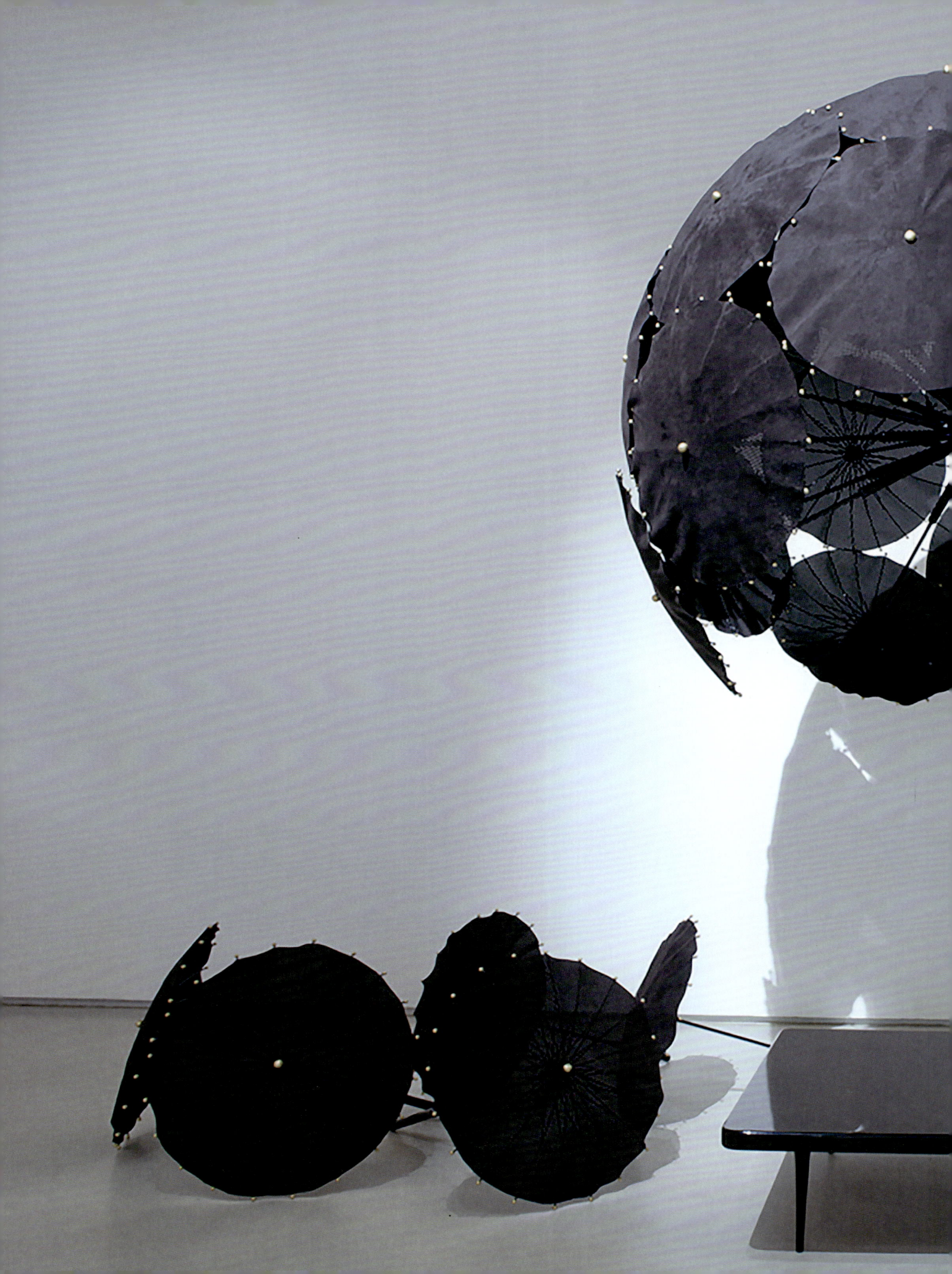

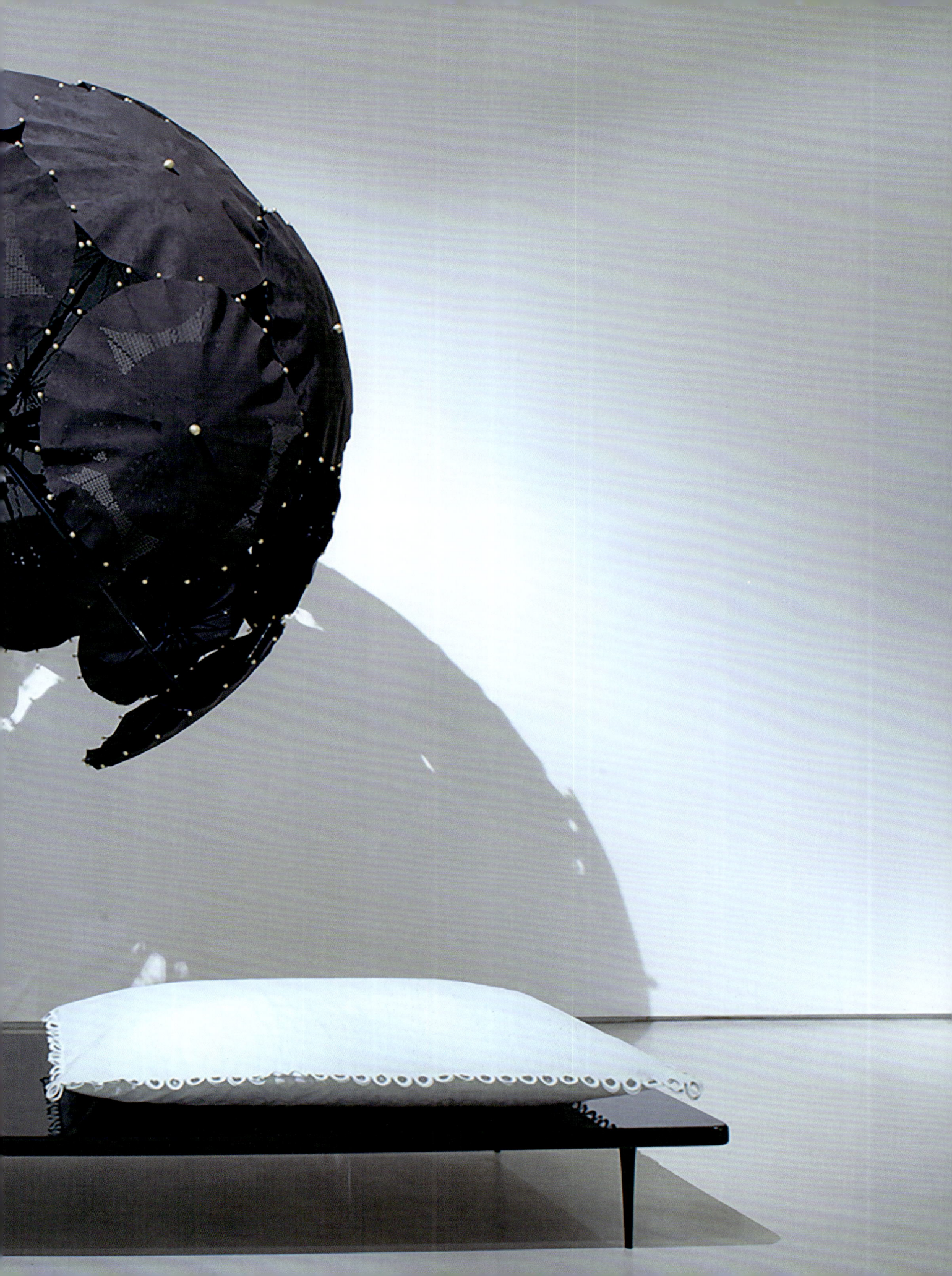

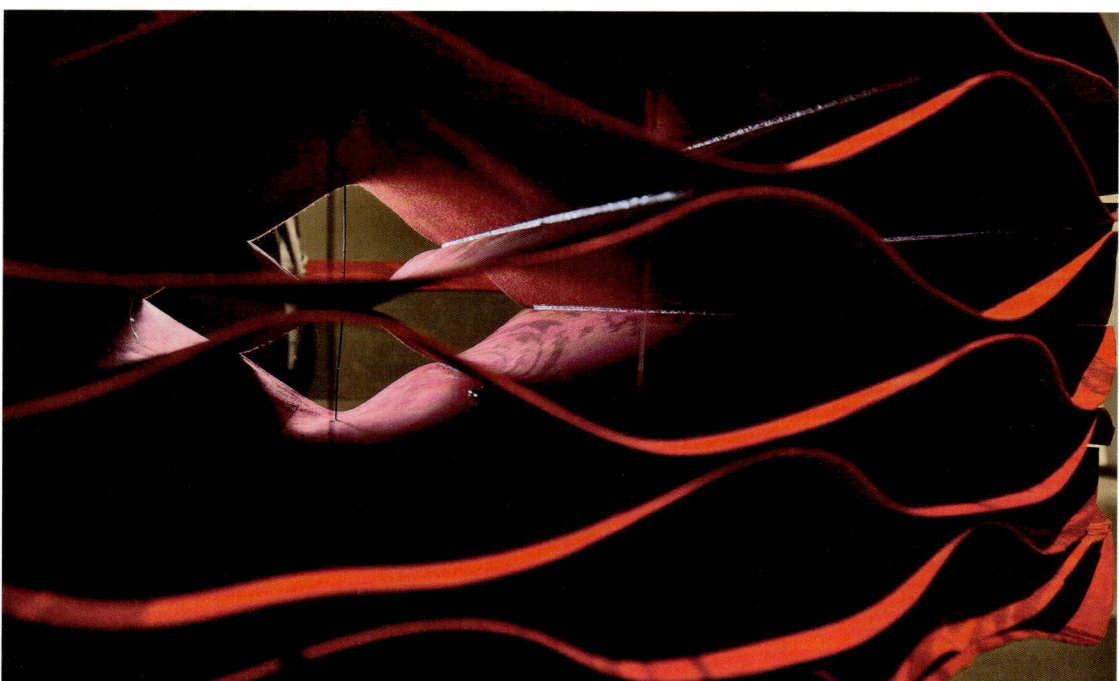
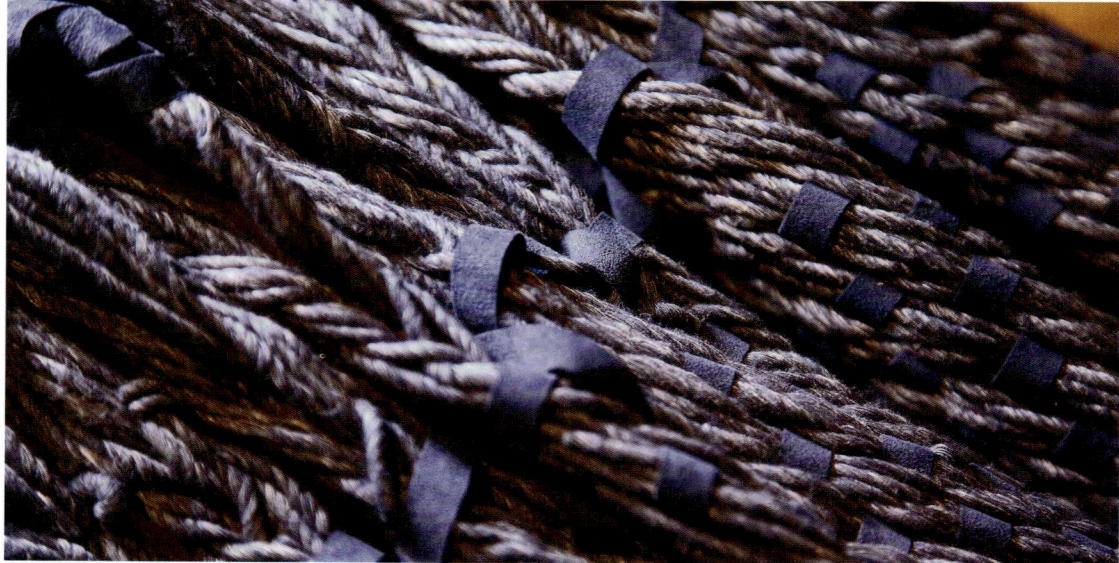

On the right
Lorenzo Damiani, *Roller*, "Can you imagine?", MAXXI Museum, Rome 2011

After "Can you imagine?" Alcantara and MAXXI continued their intense collaboration. Some years later, the Museum's President, Giovanna Melandri, said: "We have inaugurated a strategic partnership based on a new form of understanding between an institution and a company. MAXXI and Alcantara support and promote creative talents; they jointly develop new forms of design that go well beyond the traditional concept of sponsorship."

The company and the museum have embarked on a path geared to the future: from Rome to the world, in an increasingly international dimension. The works in Alcantara have become part of MAXXI's permanent collection. They are the only ones on display with a sign saying: "Please touch".

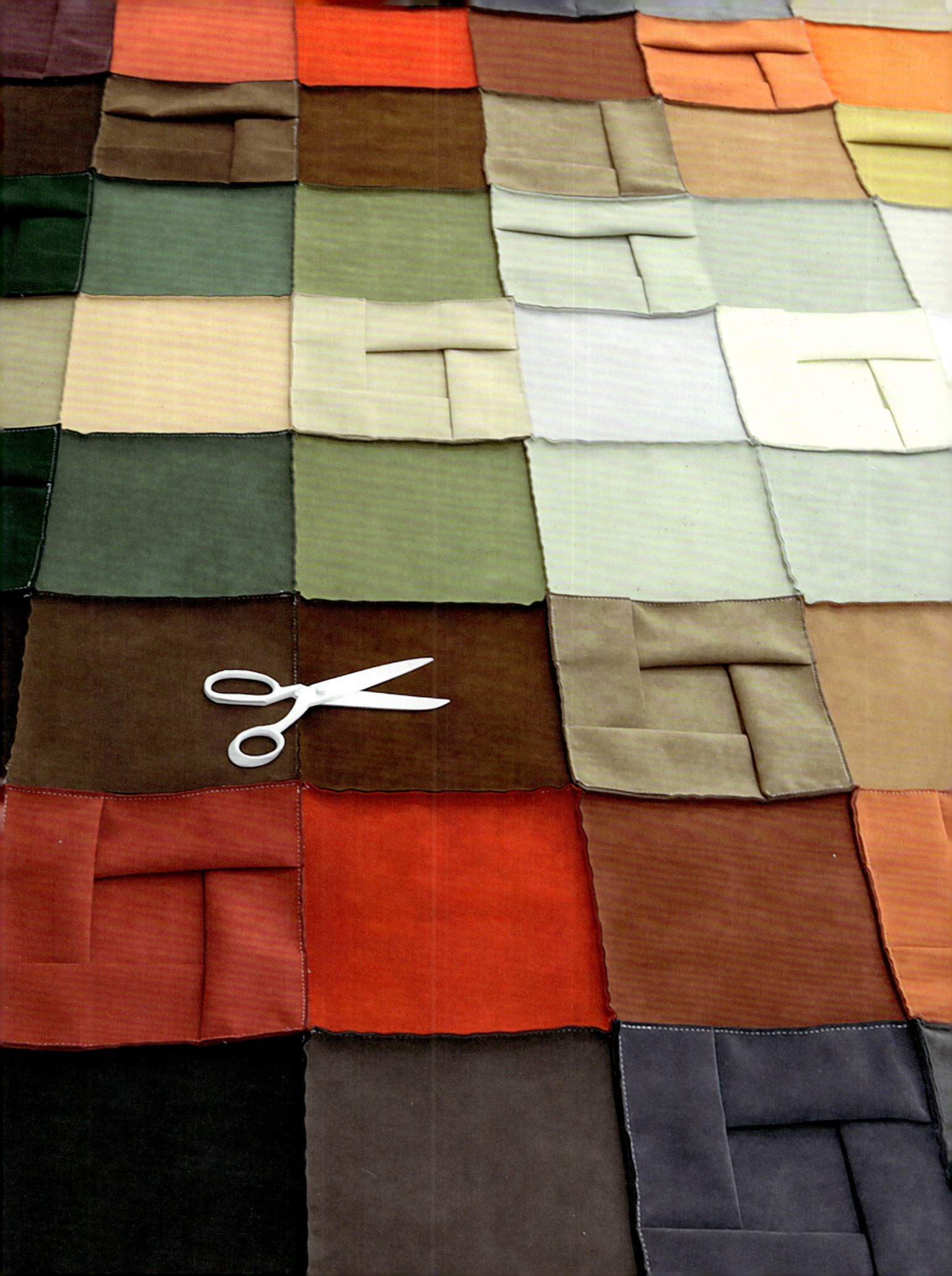

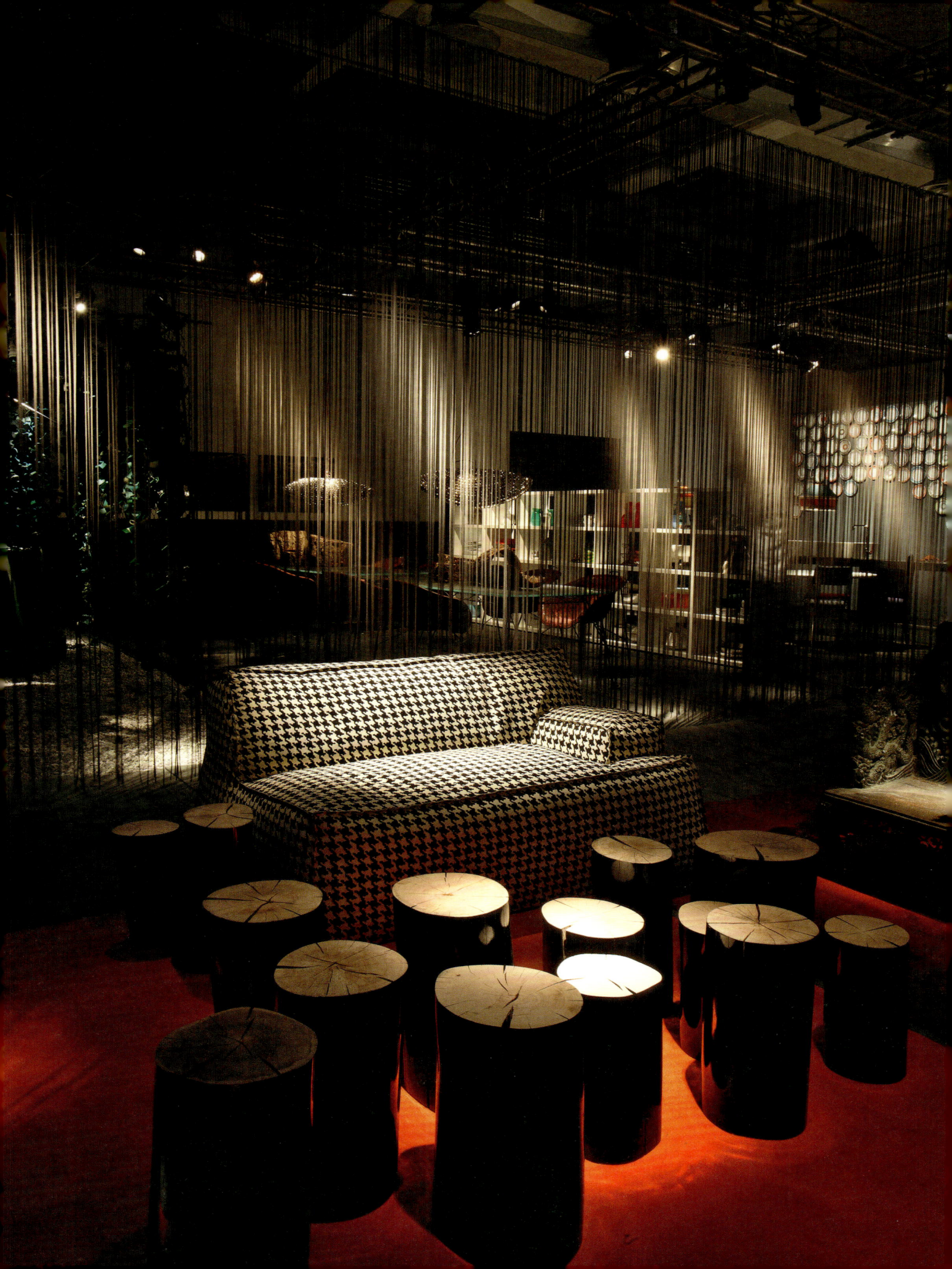

THE HOUSE OF DREAMS

A space designed to excite the senses, the stuff of dreams. The Alcantara Dream House welcomed its international public at the Superstudio Più in Via Tortona, in Milan. The year was 2011; the setting, once again, was the Fuorisalone event.

    There were no bells to ring, or doors to open. All you had to do was to screw up your courage and step beyond the thick barrier of glittering, iron-grey Alcantara threads. They had the appearance of artificial forest creepers: a dense forest which you abandoned yourself to, before entering a new dreamlike dimension. You only had to shut your eyes, allowing your fingers to stroke the material, and the way opened itself up. A sort of initiation, a rite of passage. Like daylight, when it slips into the darkness of night and enters the world of dreams. Sheer emotion.

Giulio Cappellini and Paola Navone, "The Dream House of Alcantara", Milan 2011

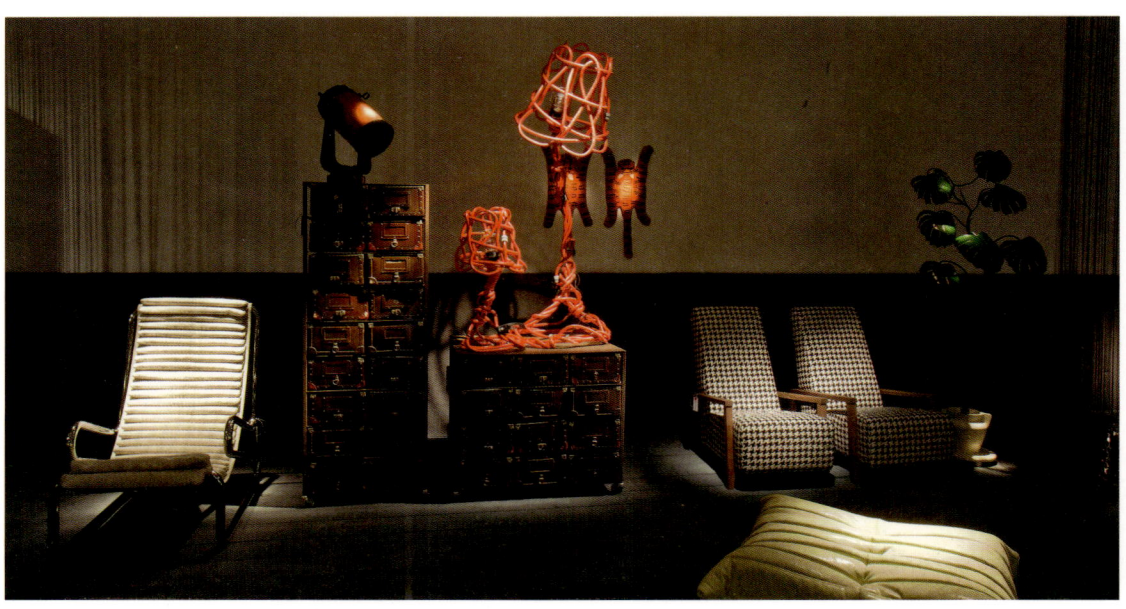

The interiors were there to be experienced, using all your senses.
The subdivision of the spaces set the pace, a slightly Baroque alternating sequence of anticipation, discovery, and surprise. Cappellini and Navone had mixed together their personal and professional experiences, their passions, and their visions of time and space. They created a place that incorporated everything: a collection of opposites that communicated with each other, forming relationships. In the house of dreams there were no smooth, neutral surfaces: everything was Alcantara. Tables, chairs, lamps: every single thing had to be touched, observed with your hands. Usually we are happy just to look; here you had to feel, in order to understand.

    The heart of the house was the living room. Thin Alcantara threads separated it from the other rooms: the kitchen, the night-time area, the study, the garden. The material covered and transformed objects; they were icons of contemporary design and souvenirs of journeys collected along the routes of the world. Alcantara, soft and seductive, invited you to discover, to live and relive experiences. Reality exceeded the imagination. That's how dreams work.

    The visit came in handy when following the chromatic trails left by the objects. The natural colours of the Alcantara material indicated routes ranging naturally from the incisiveness of black and white to gentle blue horizons, not to mention the intensity of greens, reds, and blues. There was a lot of painting in the Alcantara house of dreams. One was put in mind of Tiepolo, when he

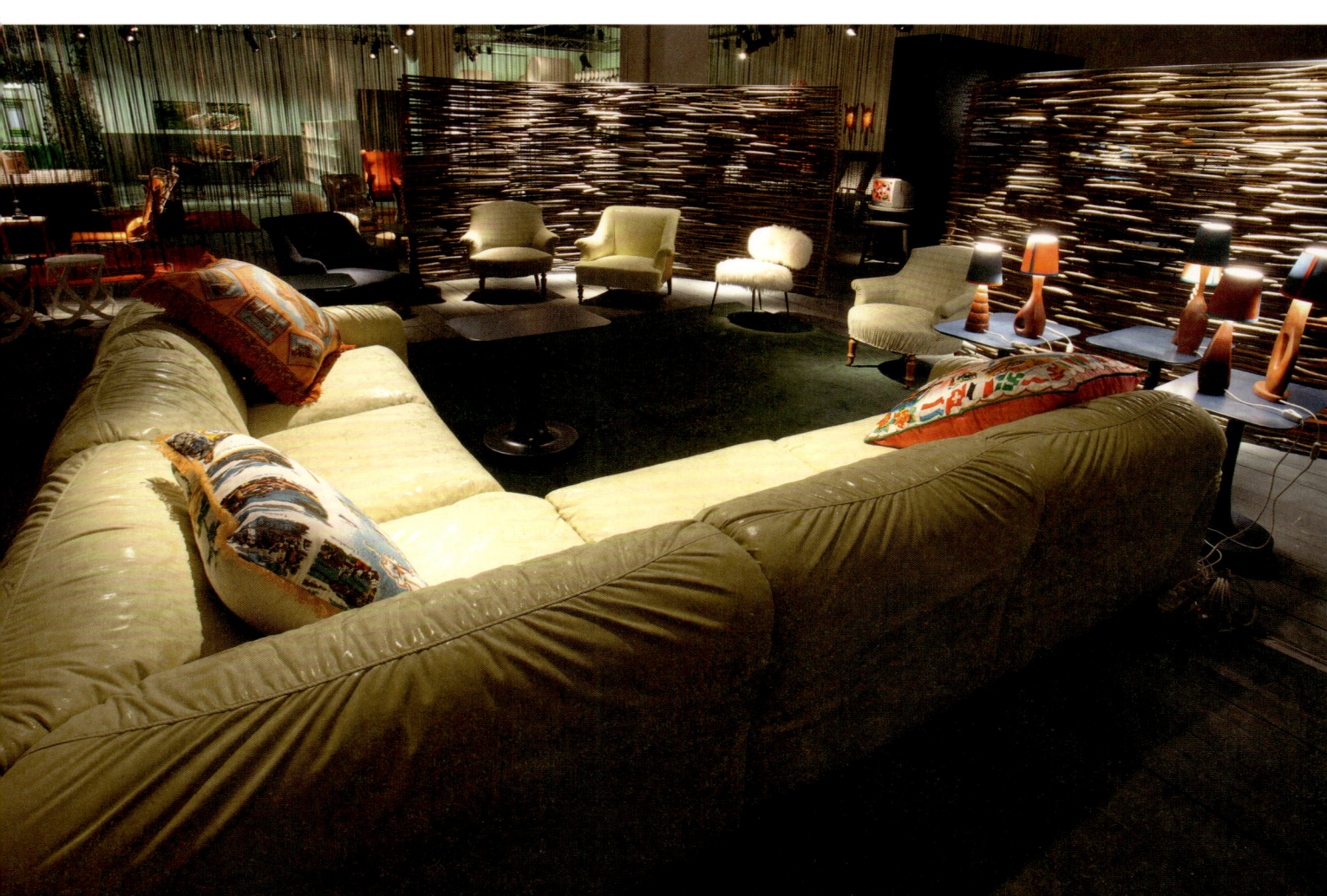

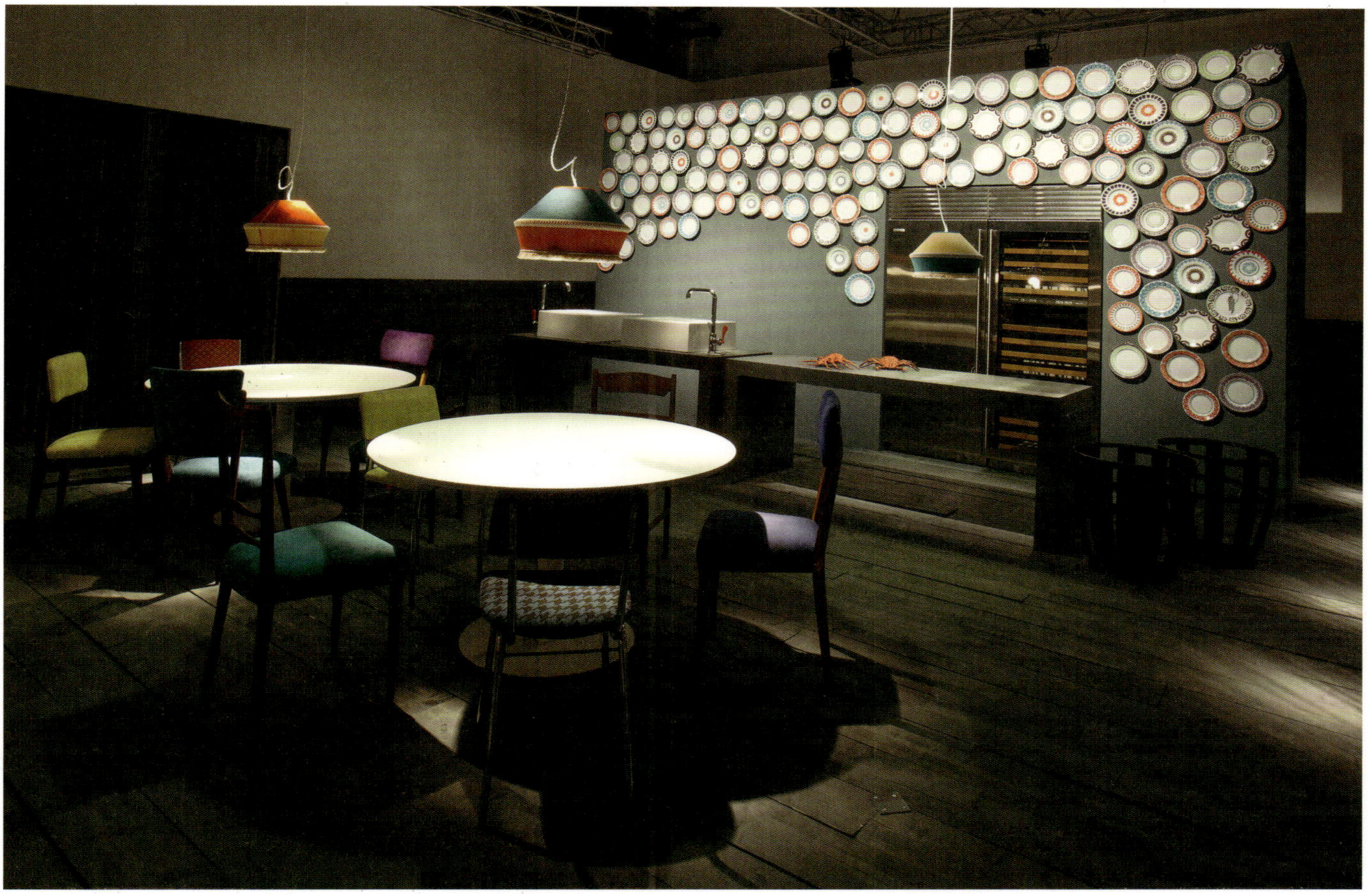

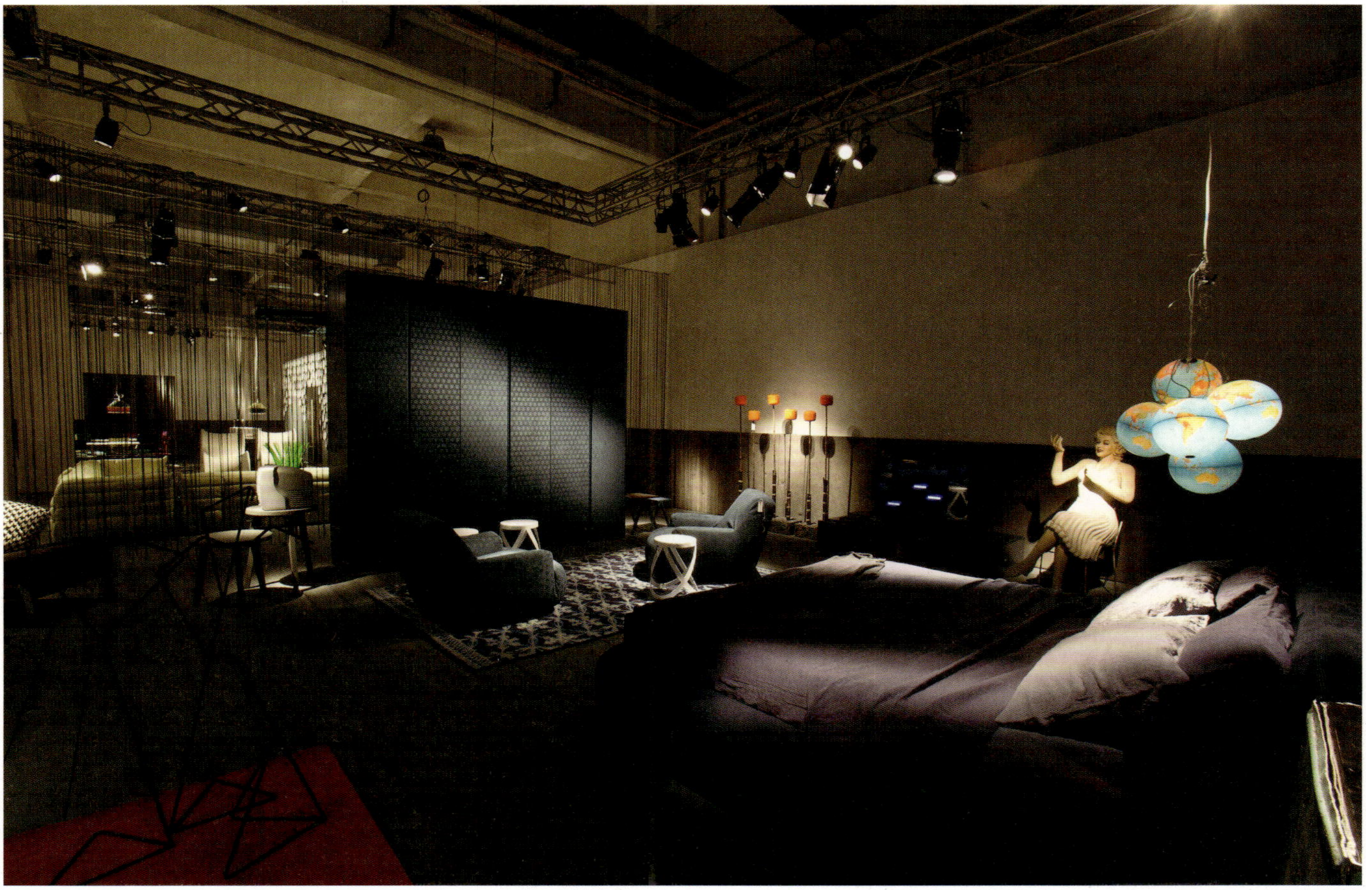

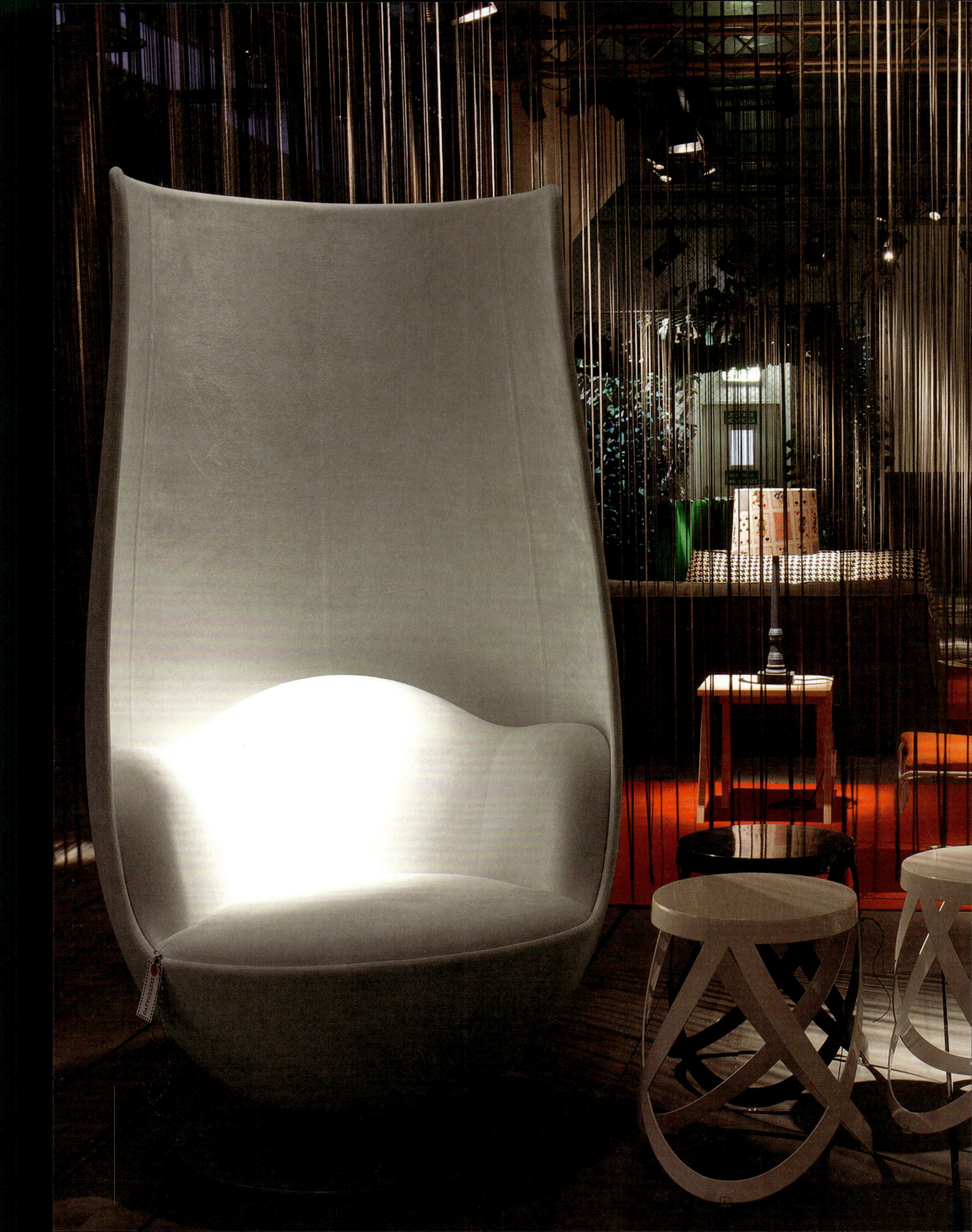

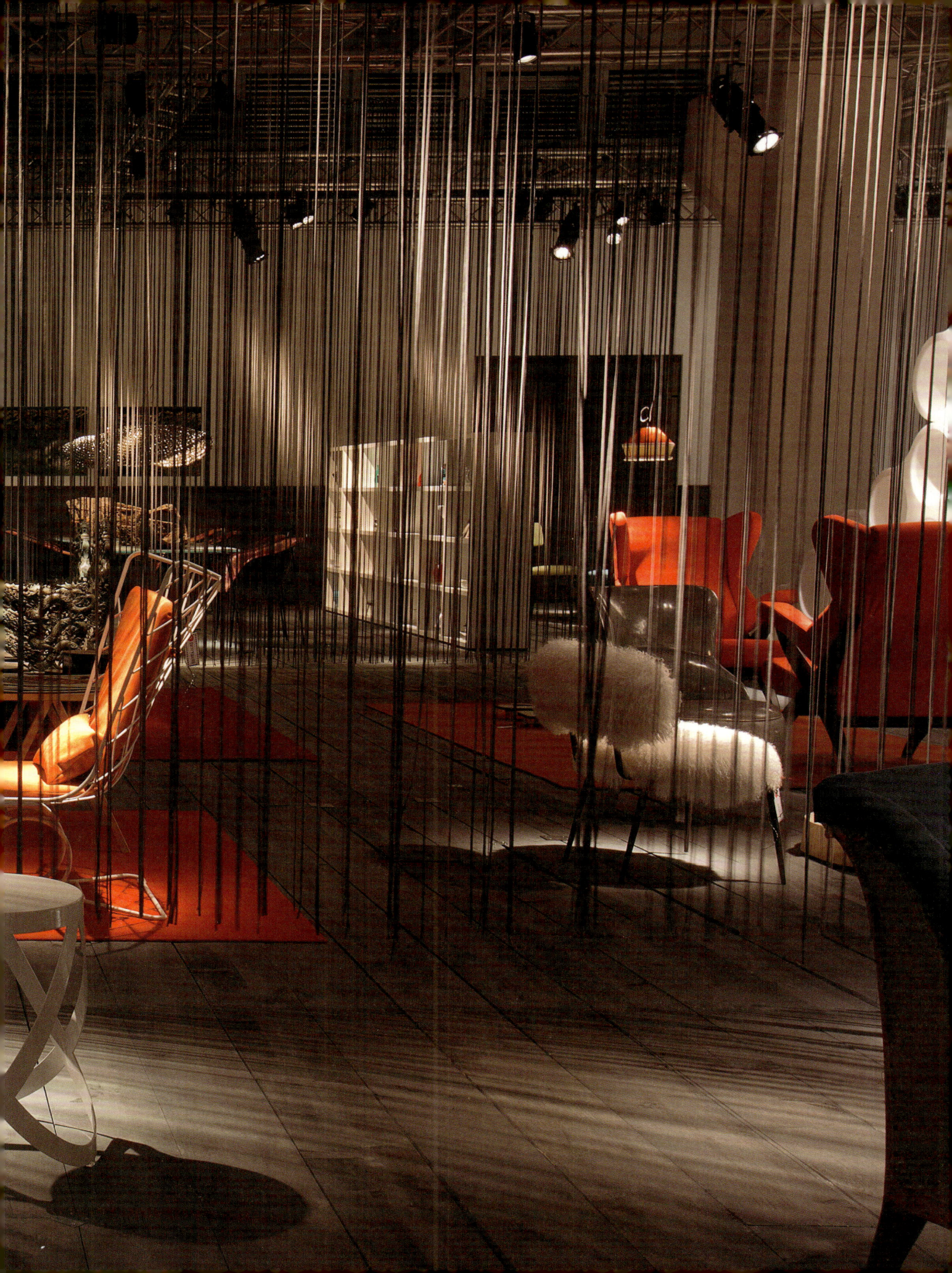

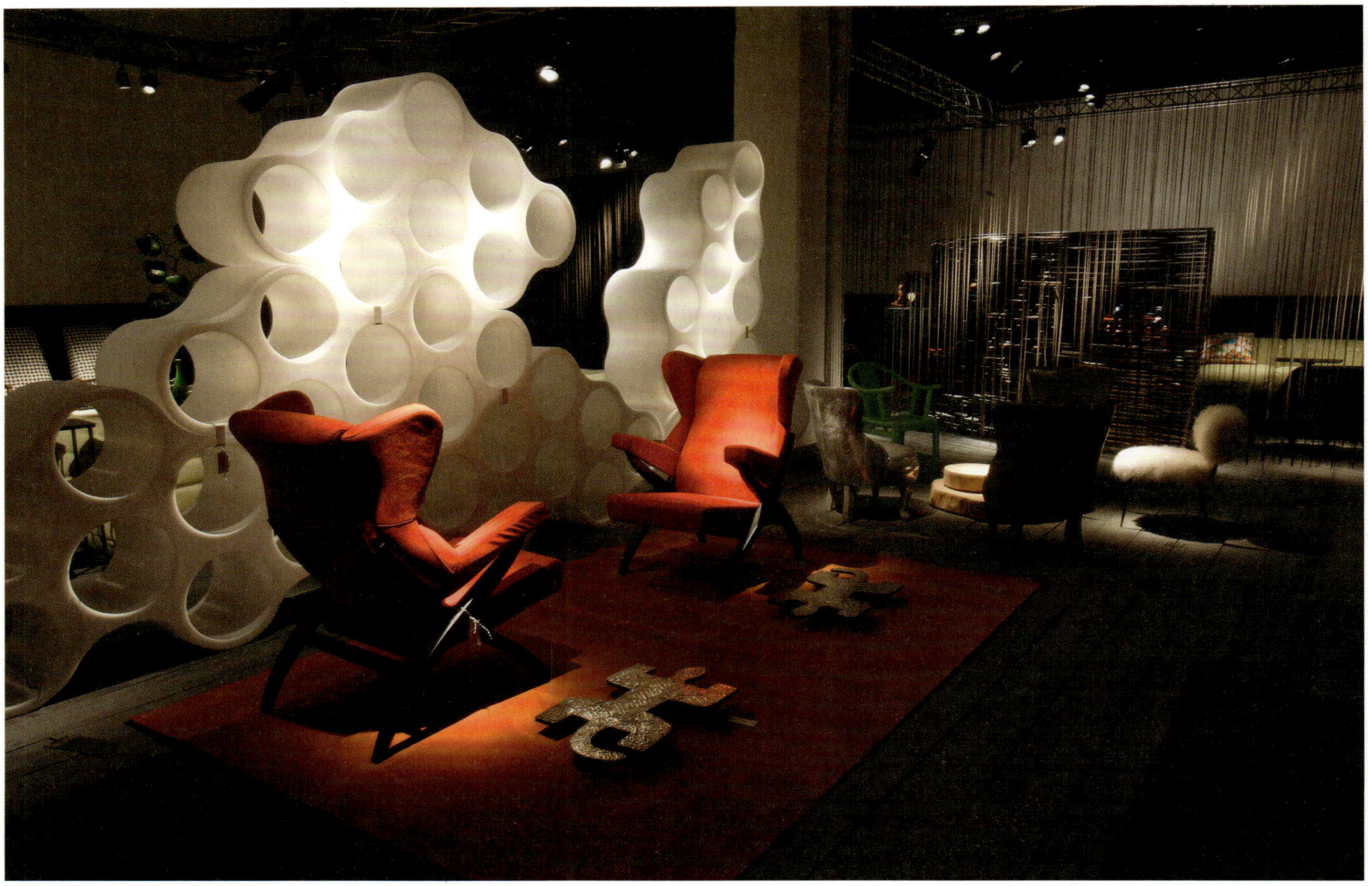

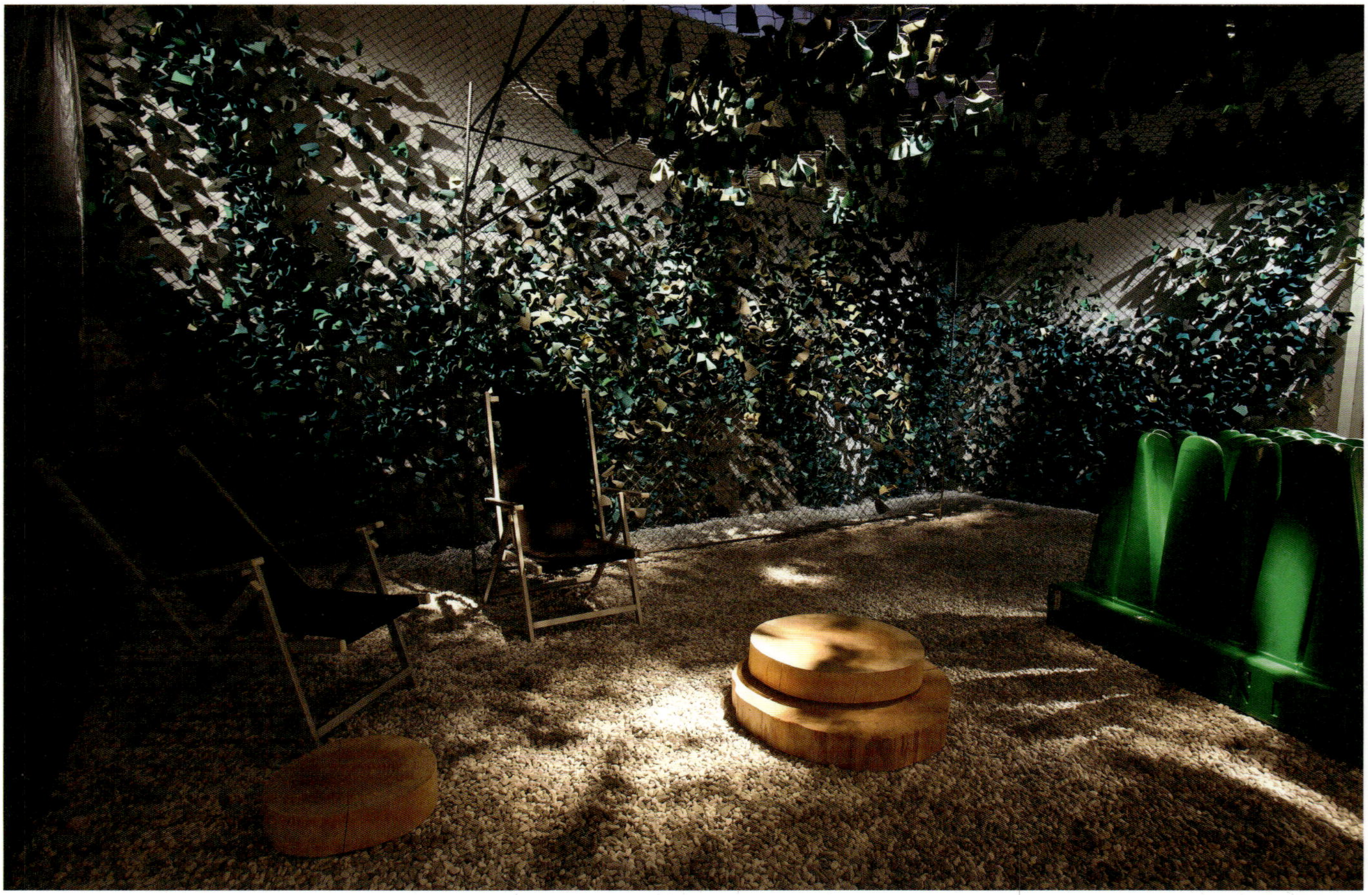

54

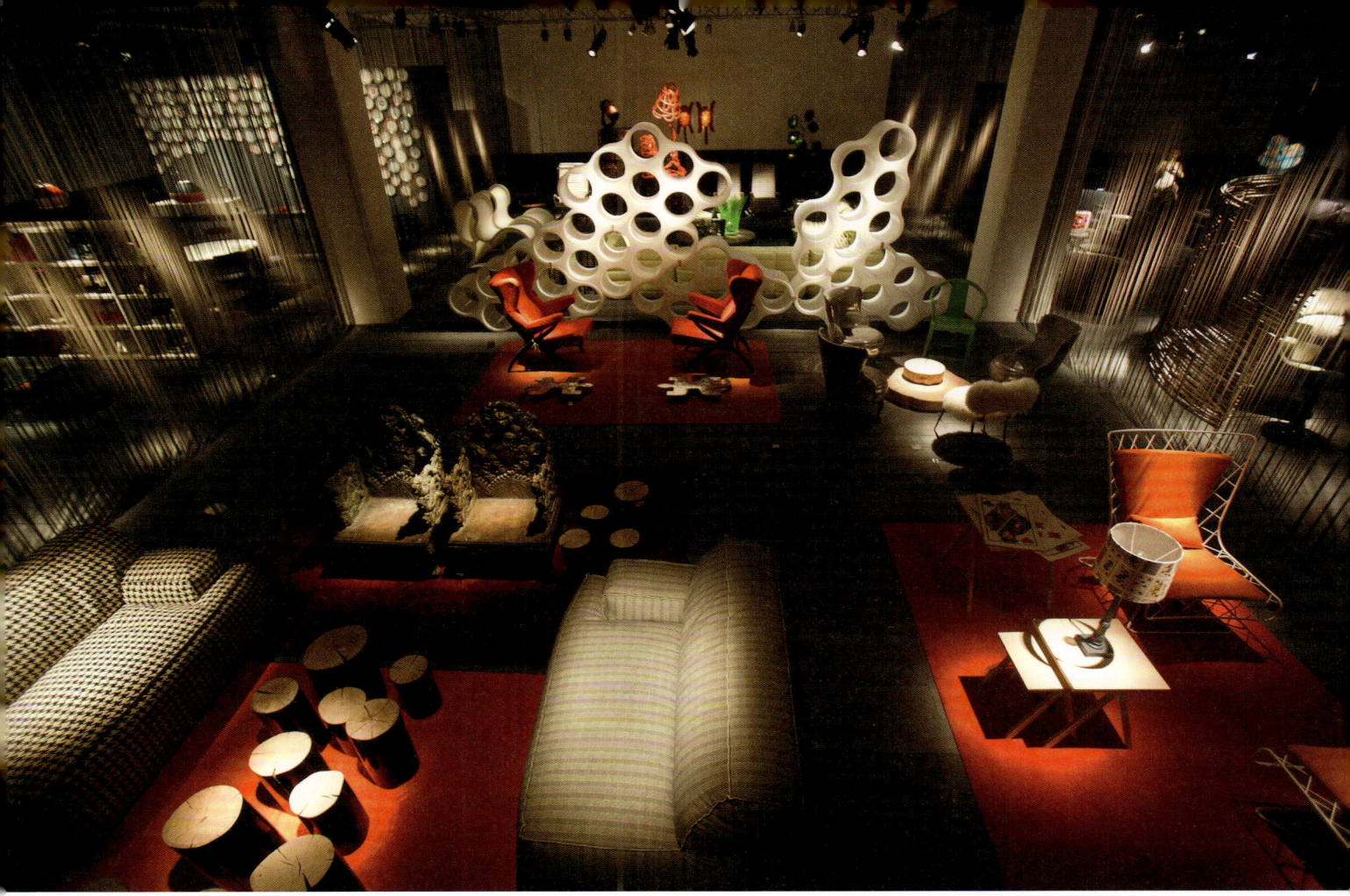

explained that a picture is: "a mezzotint background, one pale colour, one dark colour". Light is material, too. It came to rest on objects, which revealed emotions, and recounted stories. You followed it and you touched it, in search of places of intimacy. Your eyes explored the colour spectrum, and they relaxed in the atmospheres of interiors that were a collection of corners. "May each person find their own!" the designers seemed to be saying. The house of dreams was above all a sanctuary, a place for receiving thoughts, and cultivating the memory of them. A collection of points where you could stop, sit, and lie down. Another thing to be found in the Dream House was smell. Alcantara stimulated its guests' sense of smell, and added seduction to the dream. The unique and unmistakable scent of Alcantara when it is new, or freshly washed. The voices of the public spoke all the world's languages. They were heard one after the other, one on top of the other, and they became muffled within the body of a material that absorbs noises and turns them into sounds. The Alcantara Dream House stood as a powerful kind of stage scenery in which collections of moments, and stratifications of ideas, converge. In the way it was carefully staged, each object narrated a story, and people's hands certainly picked up on this. They listened by touch, and they could read, through their fingers. Your eyes and nose and ears followed, confidently. In the garden of the house there were frayed curls of Alcantara that became climbing plants. They were illustrations of fairy tales, tactile narratives. One's senses continued to play with one's dreams, until one reawoke.

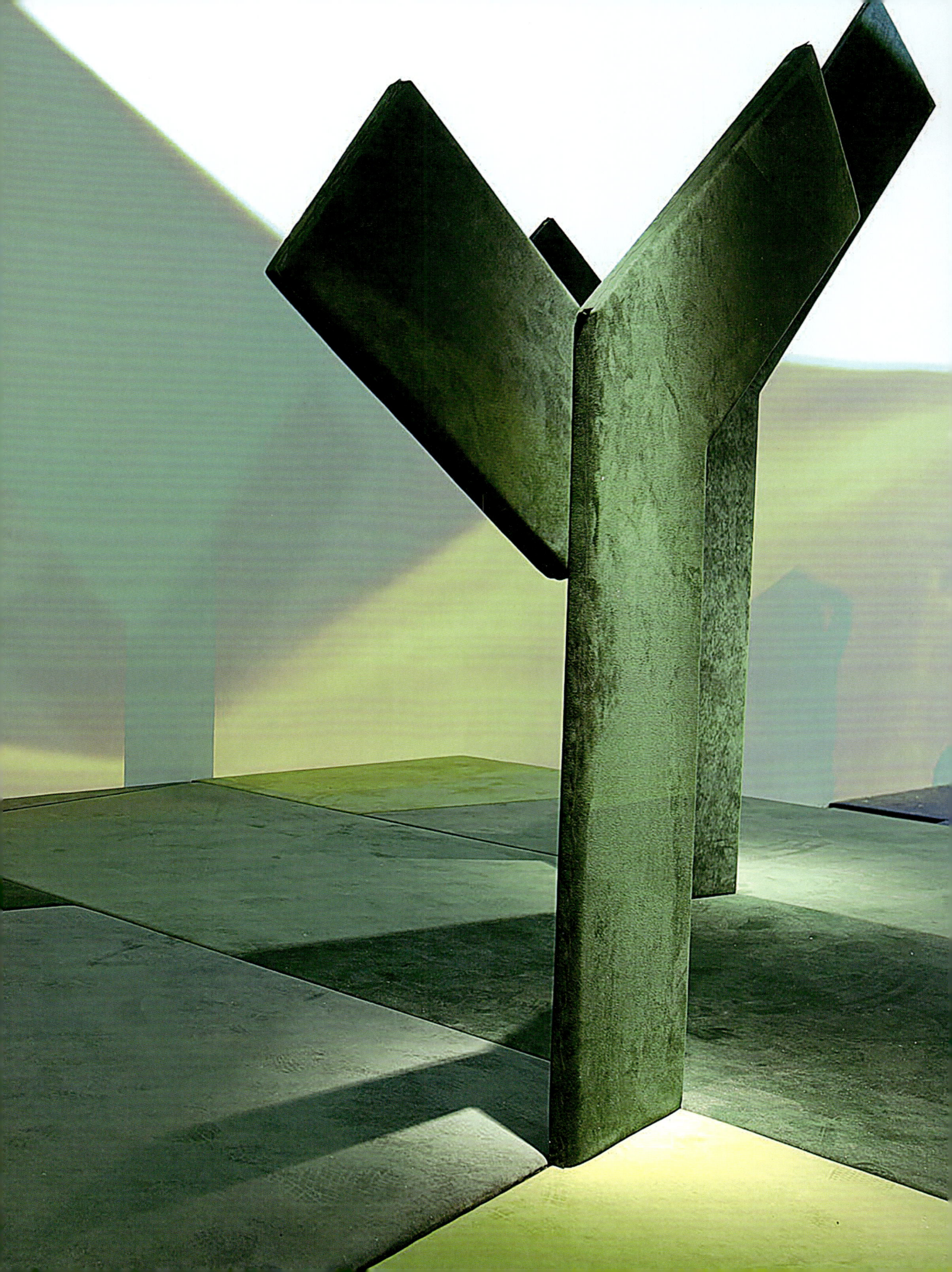

THE LANDSCAPE OF THE FUTURE

Visitors to the dream house went out into the garden, to brush against the climbing tassels of Alcantara: they seemed like evergreen trees that were the product of your imagination. The following year – also at the Superstudio, also at Fuorisalone – the horizon expanded; the tactile material became a landscape, and led the visitor to seek a moment of rest. The Alcantara space became a joyous collective sensory experience. There was a hidden structure mapping out gentle hills and valleys, wholly covered with Alcantara in the most different shades of green. If you allowed your mind to wander freely, you could make out woods and fields and hills. There were stylized trees stemming from the development of a simple linear module: as if it were a seed, that grows and remains recognizable in the plant's development.

Giulio Cappellini and Yuri Ancarani, "The Future Landscape", Milan 2012

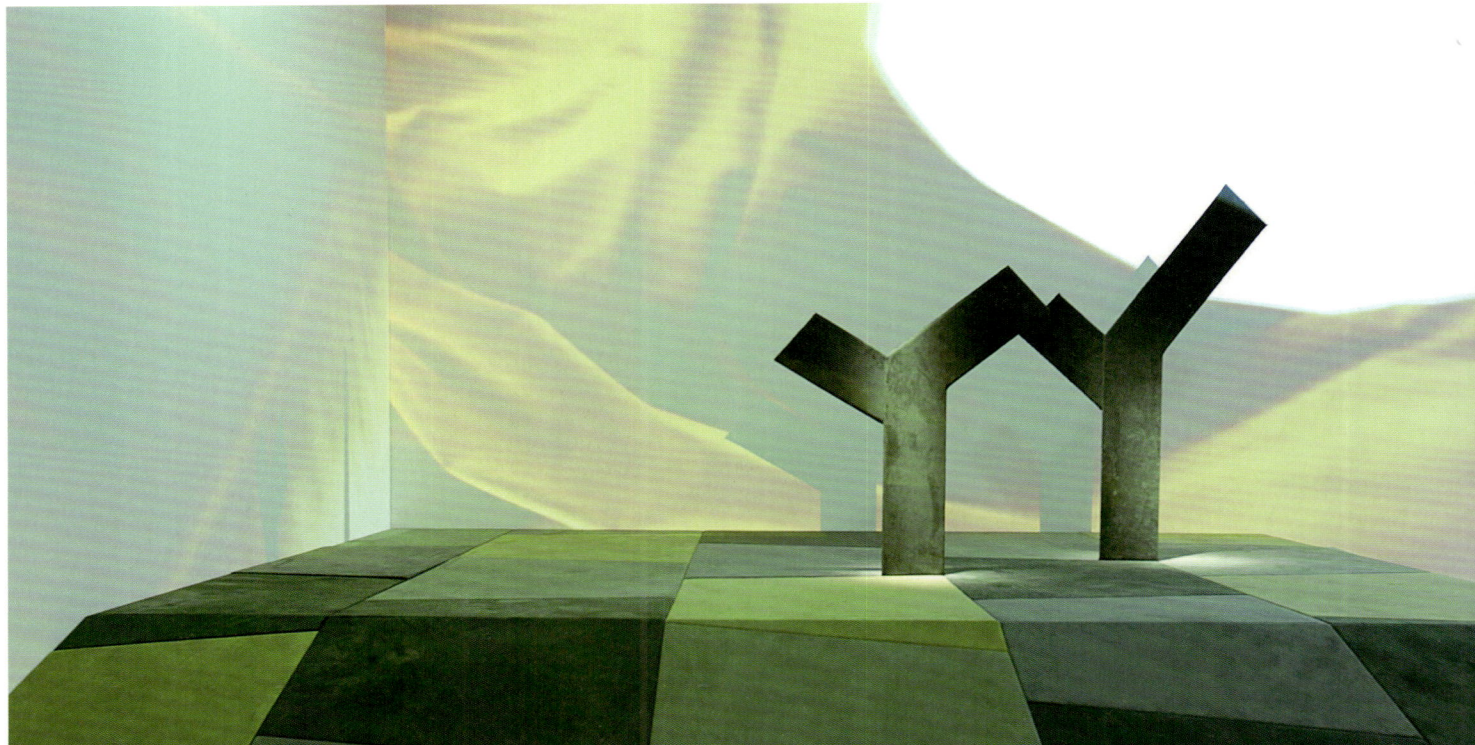

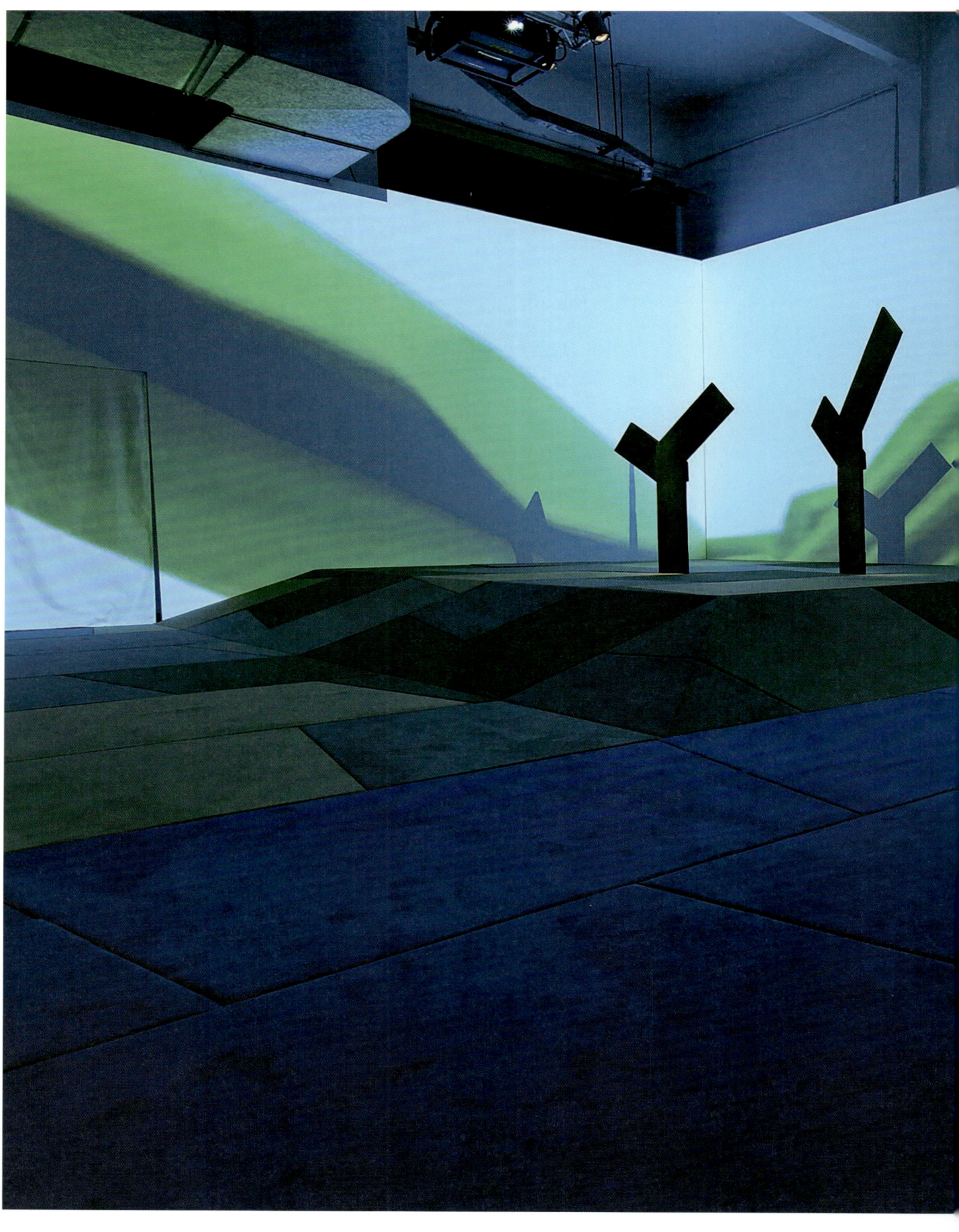

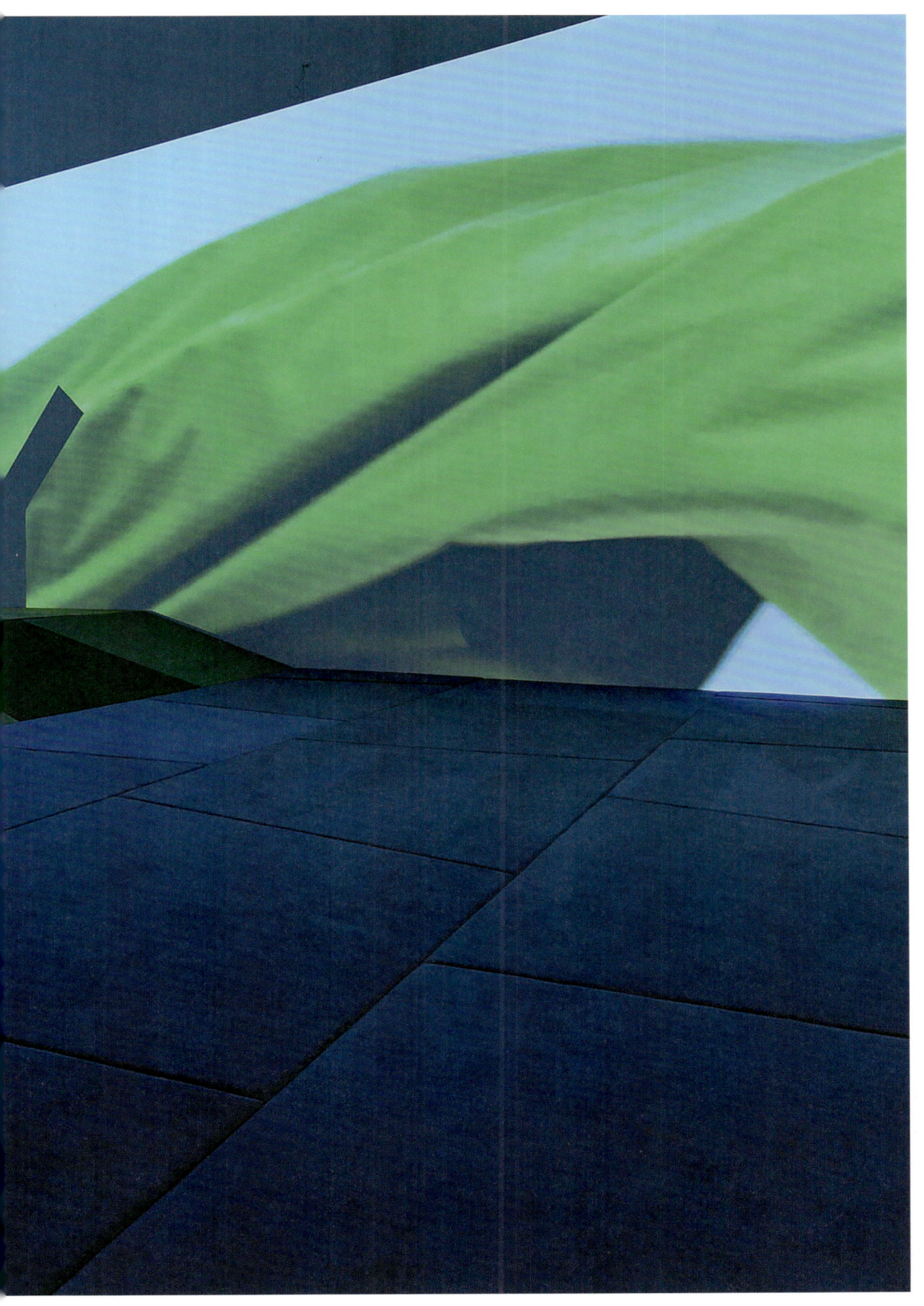

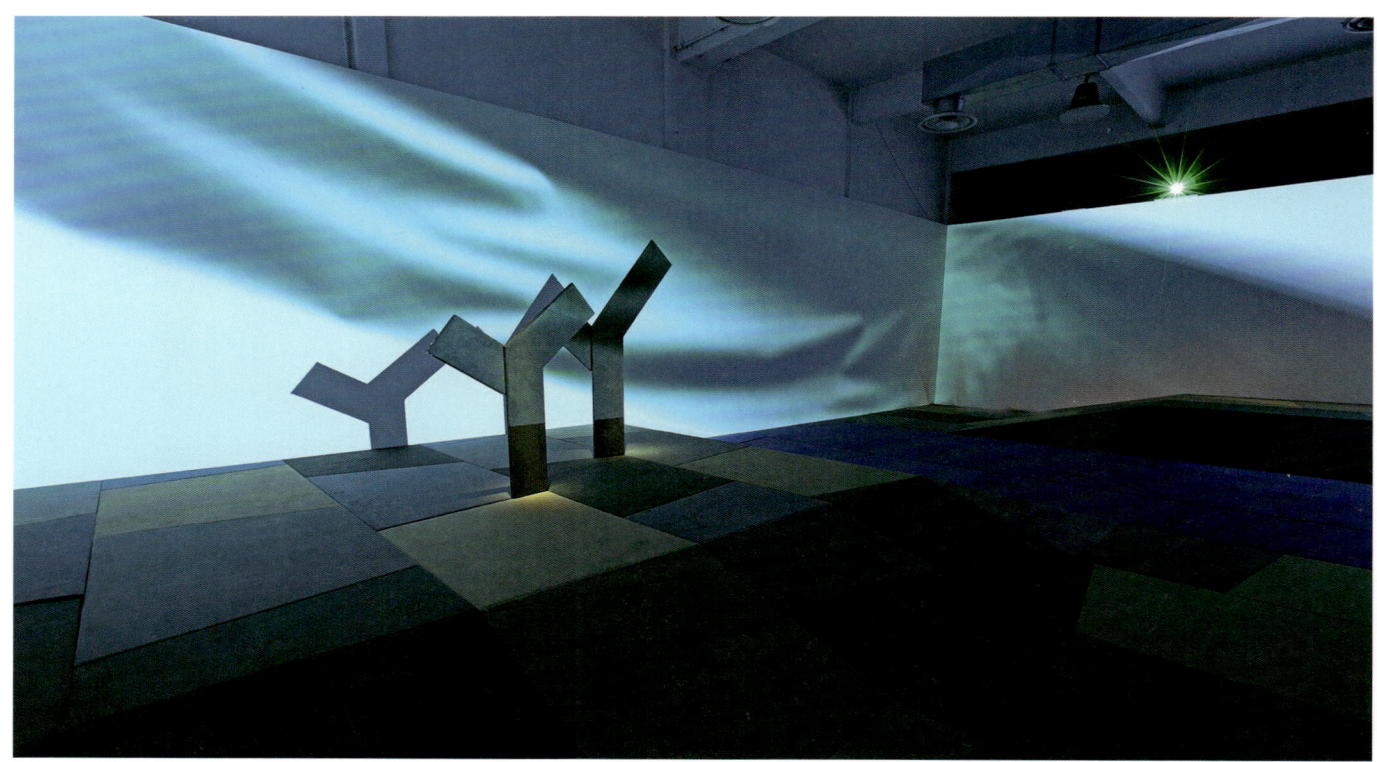

All around was the sky, with clouds of Alcantara driven by the wind.
But since this was a landscape of the future, the skies were fifty linear metres of video projection! A powerful installation from the visual point of view, but very simple from the technical viewpoint. The videos made by Yuri Ancarani showed waves of Alcantara gently rising and falling in the coloured space. He made them by hand, shortly before the opening. The artisans who erected the framework for the hills, and who covered it with Alcantara, had to force themselves not to stop working, distracted as they were by the artist, who would gather up lengths of Alcantara several metres long, and flick them firmly against the floor, his movements timid to start with, and then more and more rapid, terse, resolute and final. The snapping sound made by the material on the ground caused turmoil, and sent clouds of dust flying up into the air, glinting in the light. The Alcantara surface would come to rest again, and then there would be another shockwave, with the artist gripping the edge of the material and snapping his arms in a rapid, coordinated motion. The video camera filmed everything, at three hundred photograms per second. In the end, after the video was edited, Alcantara was seen to float softly in the sky, in slow motion, enveloping the landscape of the future.

    The international public attending Design Week converged on Milan and ventured into this grove of Alcantara trees: a flat expanse for people to talk, eat and think. Nothing was there by chance, and there were no repetitions, in the practice of dogged, daily innovation. After covering objects, now the Alcantara material created a space where people could calmly go and relax. It was reminiscent of a medieval garden, the *hortus conclusus*, in contrast to the dark forest. A landscape of the future that was also a voice: the announcement of a hard and fast commitment entered into by Alcantara for the defence of the environment, sustainability, and workers' health. It was way back in 2009, when discussion of these issues was somewhat feeble and distracted, that Alcantara was awarded Carbon Neutral certification. As such, it was the first company in Italy, and one of the first in the world.

Alcantara's landscape of the future was also a metaphor of Italian style asserting itself internationally; a culture of knowhow bringing together artists, artisans, and businessmen. "Becoming *Carbon Neutral* was not a decision made in order to abide by a law, indeed there is no such law," states Andrea Boragno, the company's President and Managing Director, "instead it was a specific choice on our part. We will never tire of underlining the importance of the relationship between design, art and the environment".

Thus, ethical values become identity-defining characteristics, distinguishing features of a community of work that translate into a competitive edge. The Alcantara "Future Landscape" firmly conveyed this sensibility, that looks to the future. Meanwhile the lights of the installation changed, precisely and regularly, reflecting the different times of day, and times of the year. From the pale blue of dawn, with a faint tinge of red, to dark orange, streaked with the typical yellow and red hues of sunset. Then night-time, and rest, and dreams before a new day. A gentle poetics, accompanying the natural way events unfold, the providential repetitiveness of life-cycles.

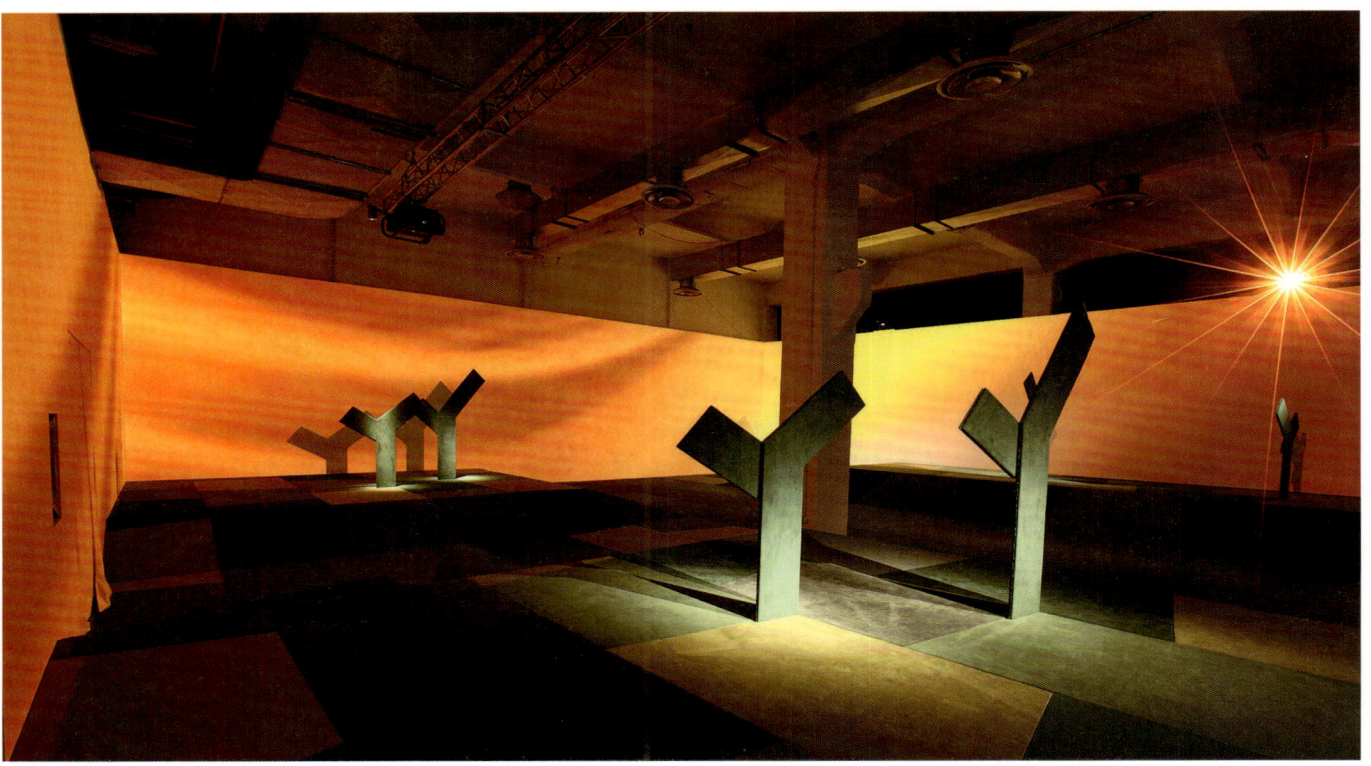

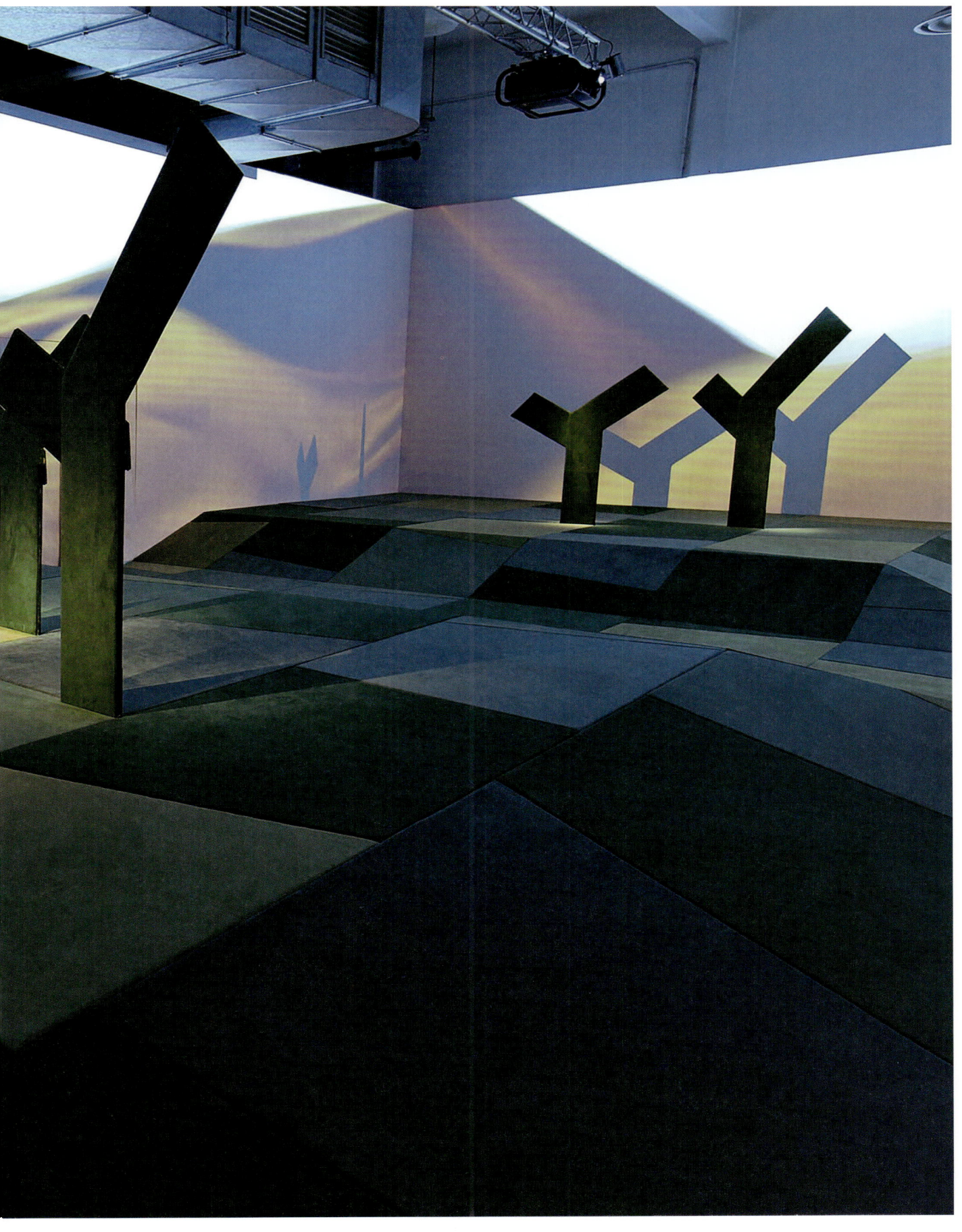

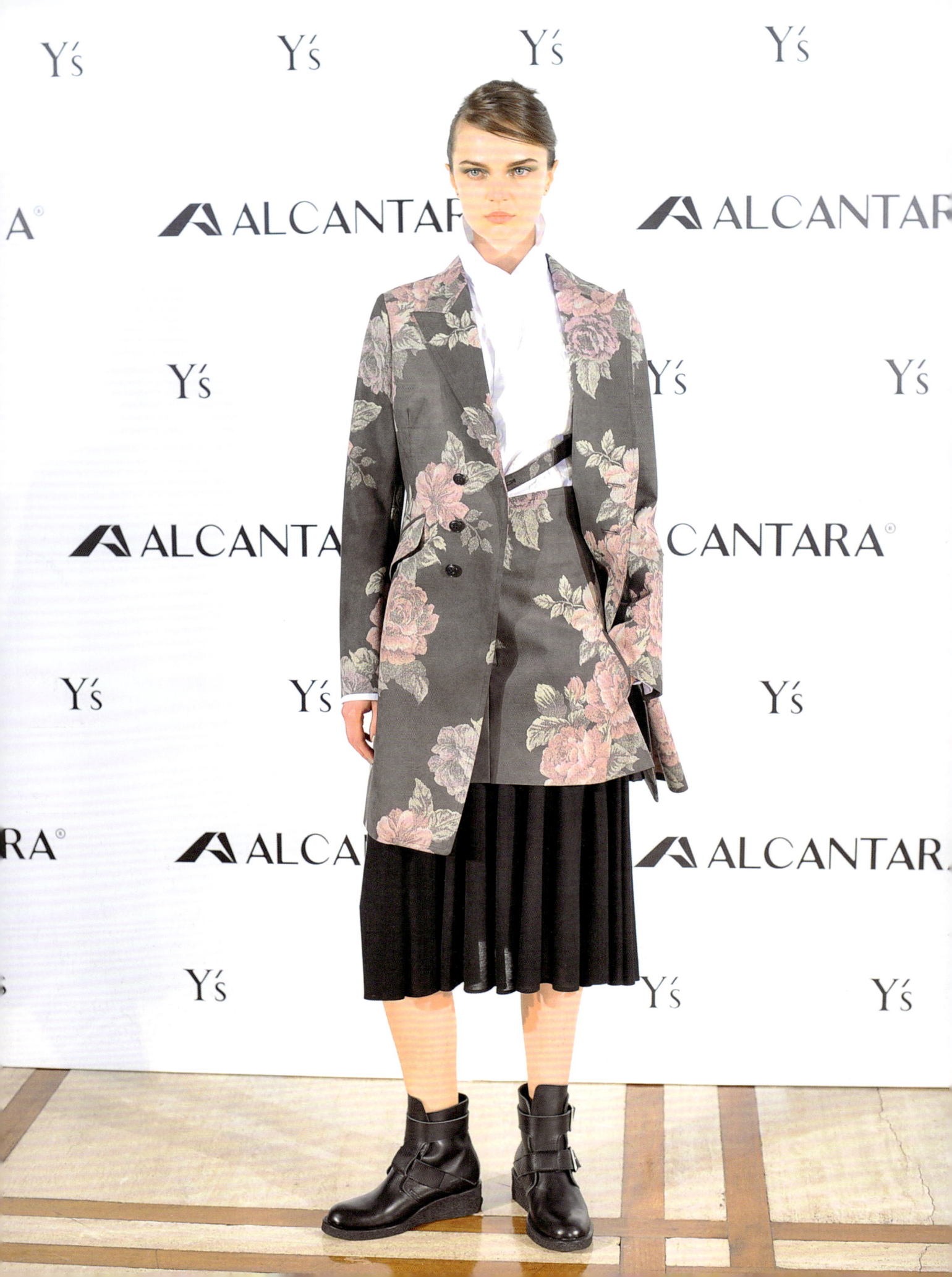

LUXURY GLAM

There is something magical and surprising in Alcantara's journey. It began life in Japan, and came to maturity in Italy. When it went back to Japan it did so as a symbol of Italian style. The year was 2014, the place was the Italian embassy in Tokyo. Alcantara was the protagonist of an event combining Japanese technology and Italian art. Creativity, design and artisanal skills as universal languages of an international culture.

Yohji Yamamoto,
Italian Embassy,
Tokyo 2014

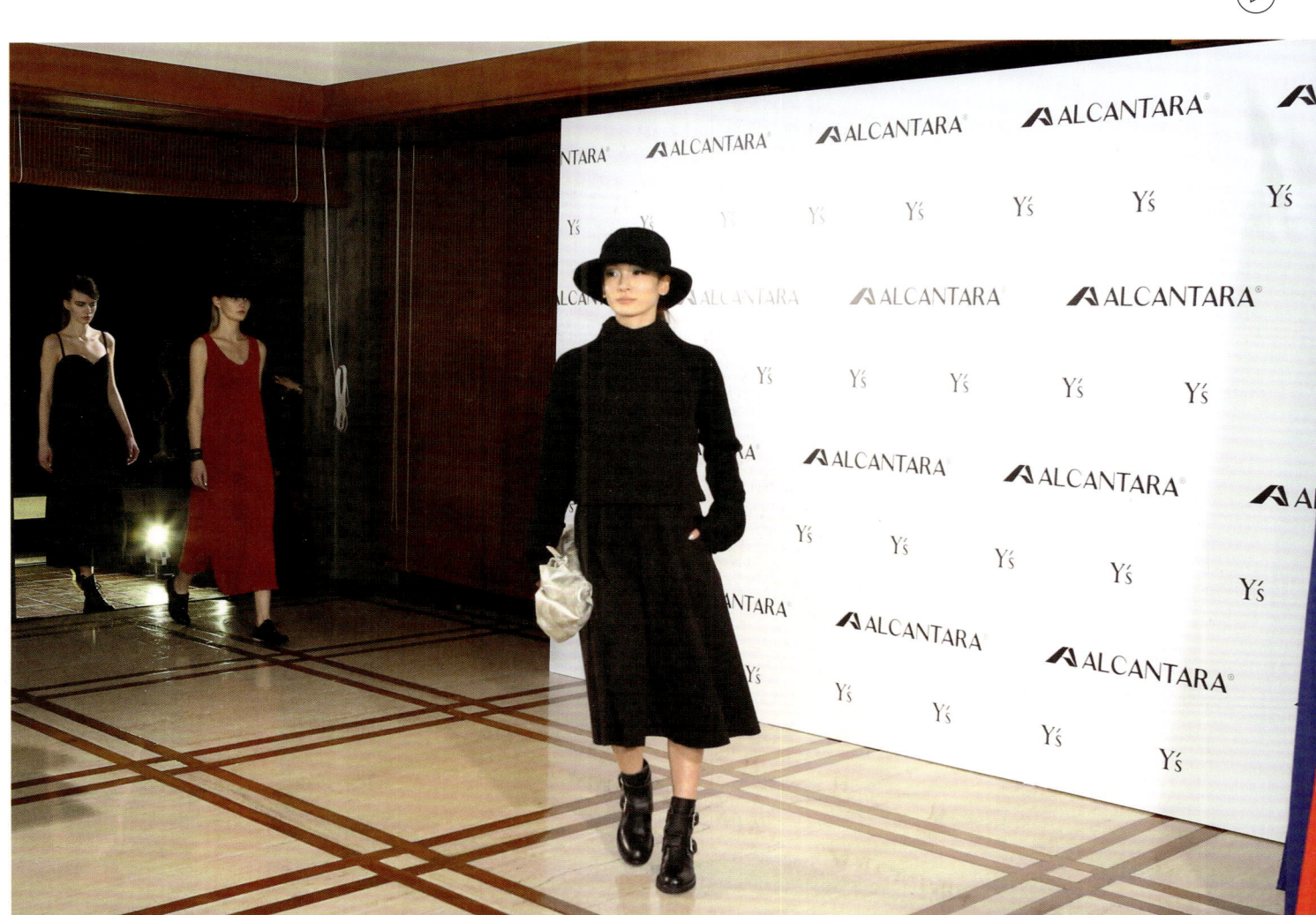

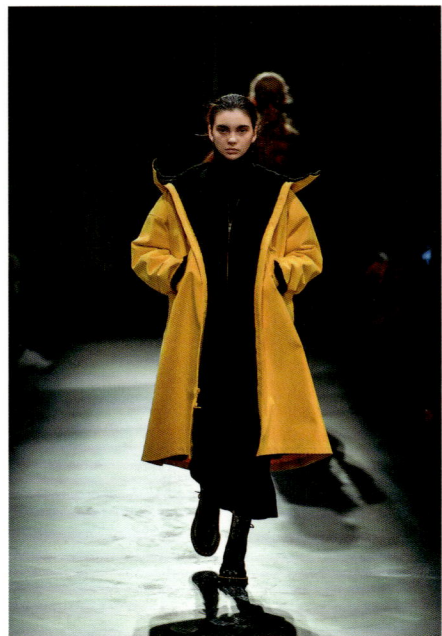 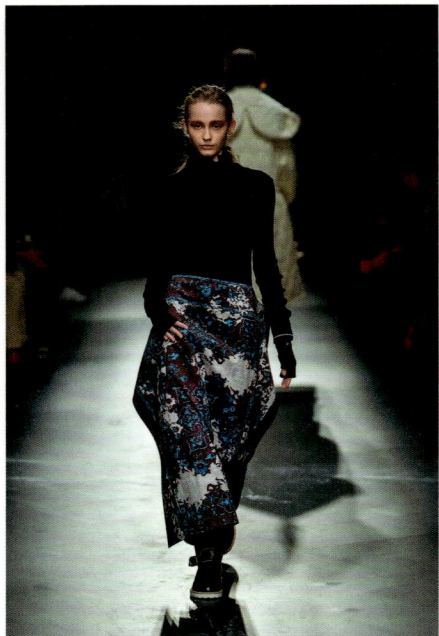 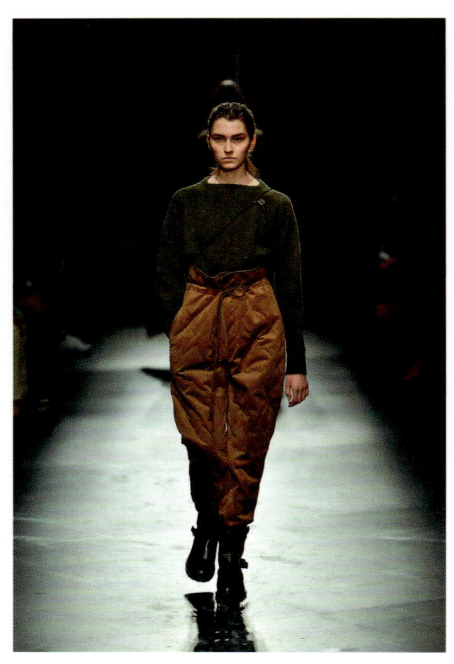

Yohji Yamamoto, "Capsule Collection", Omotesando Hills, Tokyo 2019

The collaboration began between Alcantara and the Japanese designer Yohji Yamamoto, who approached the material with a designer's feel for project design, and an artist's creativity. The idea was once again to explore the endless possibilities for transformation of the Alcantara material, this time to create exclusive outfits.

The site of the fashion show was highly unusual, a long way from the traditional locations of fashion. In its architecture, too, the Italian embassy in Tokyo manifests the potential of the combination between Eastern and Western culture. The building dates from the early 1960s, designed by Italian and Japanese architects. It combines elements of extraordinary simplicity and elegance, such as the overhanging eaves and the two-section roof. The garden is a masterpiece of harmony with nature: one of the oldest and noblest in all of Japan, being over four centuries old. There are ancient trees, a small lake surrounded by hills, grassy clearings and stone lanterns. The cherry blossom in the spring is a sacred event, and the palette of autumn colours is breathtaking.

Yamamoto and Alcantara created an unusual and sophisticated collection, introducing, for the first time in the fashion sector, solutions such as woven Alcantara material, first reduced to fringes and thin threads. Also explored are the qualities of the material as a support for printed designs. References to nature, and the embassy gardens, are happily married to the principle of sustainability of Alcantara, which for years now has been committed to reducing its carbon emissions. Yamamoto worked the Alcantara material, creating luxury surfaces, overflowing with sensory effects. He added ostrich feathers and outsize crystals to the clothing and accessories, alternating with metal details. Retro floral prints and delicate embroidered motifs suggested new themes reminiscent of poetry and Romanticism.

Colours borrowed from the Taoist garden, with soft shades of sky-blue and light grey, were juxtaposed with strong colours such as rust and bright pink.

When the collection left Tokyo, it travelled to Los Angeles. The journey by an international brand such as Alcantara continued, and fashion was one of the most interesting markets, where luxury became associated with art and creativity.

Five years later, in 2019, Alcantara returned to Japan, again with Yamamoto. This time the setting was a modern one, and close to the world of fashion: the Omotesando Hills centre, designed by Tadao Andō. After the experience of 2014, the material's creative development explored new territories, and cut across old boundaries. Yamamoto tried out a great many different expressions of Alcantara's versatility, always supported by the company's Style Office. The clothes in the show offered a variety of shapes that stemmed directly from the myriad possible faces of the same material. There were silvery coats that were the product of lamination processes, puffball garments in which Alcantara returned to its old vocation as a facing material for padded clothing. The material also took centre-stage in its range of bright colours, its monochrome and fluorescent flights of fancy. There was a return to Alcantara's extraordinary versatility when it is cut and reduced to

Yohji Yamamoto, "Capsule Collection", Omotesando Hills, Tokyo 2019

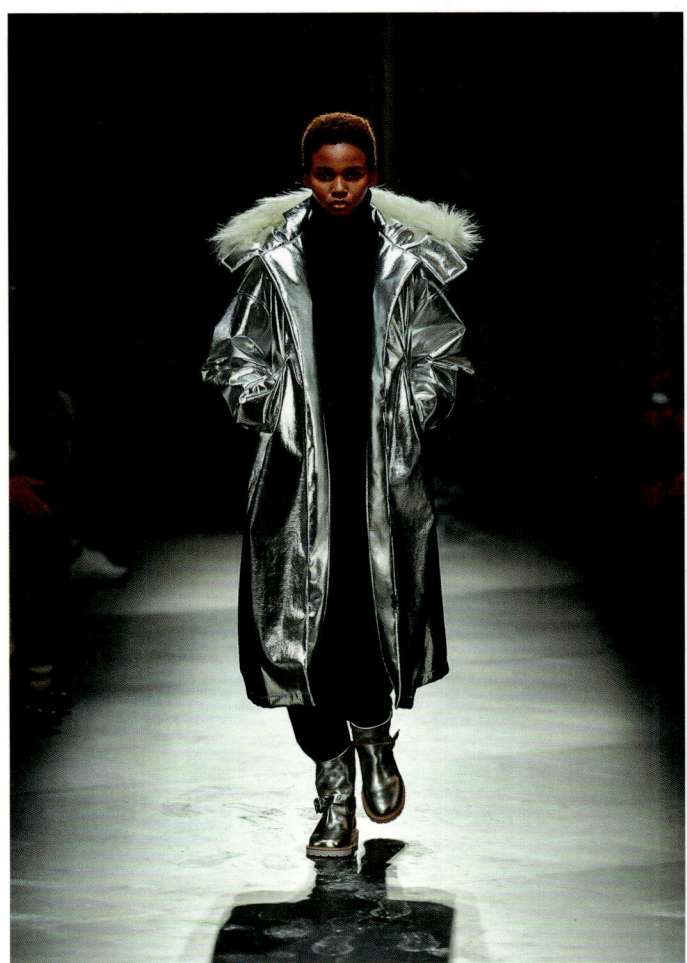
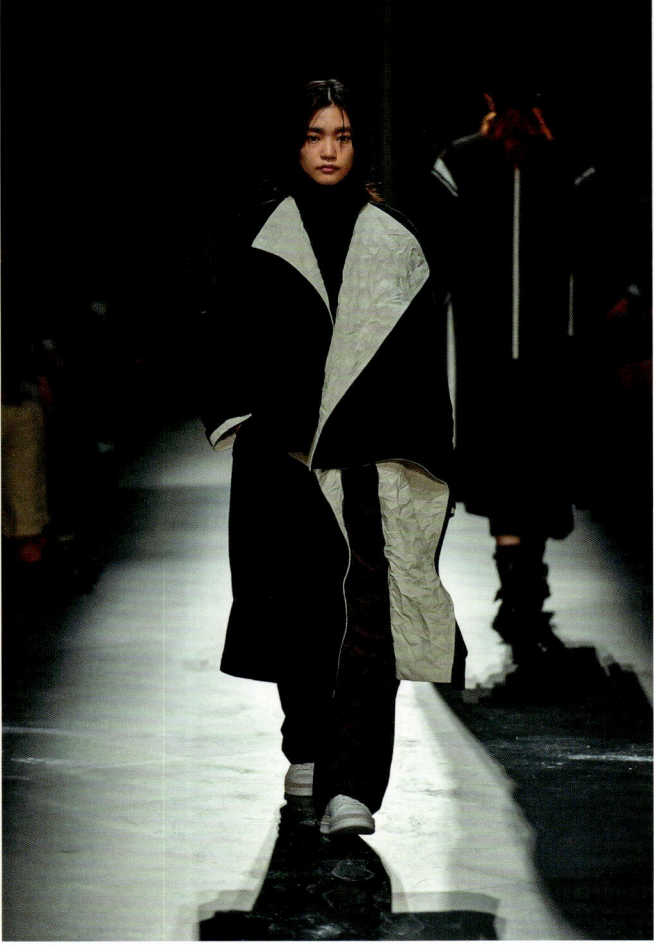

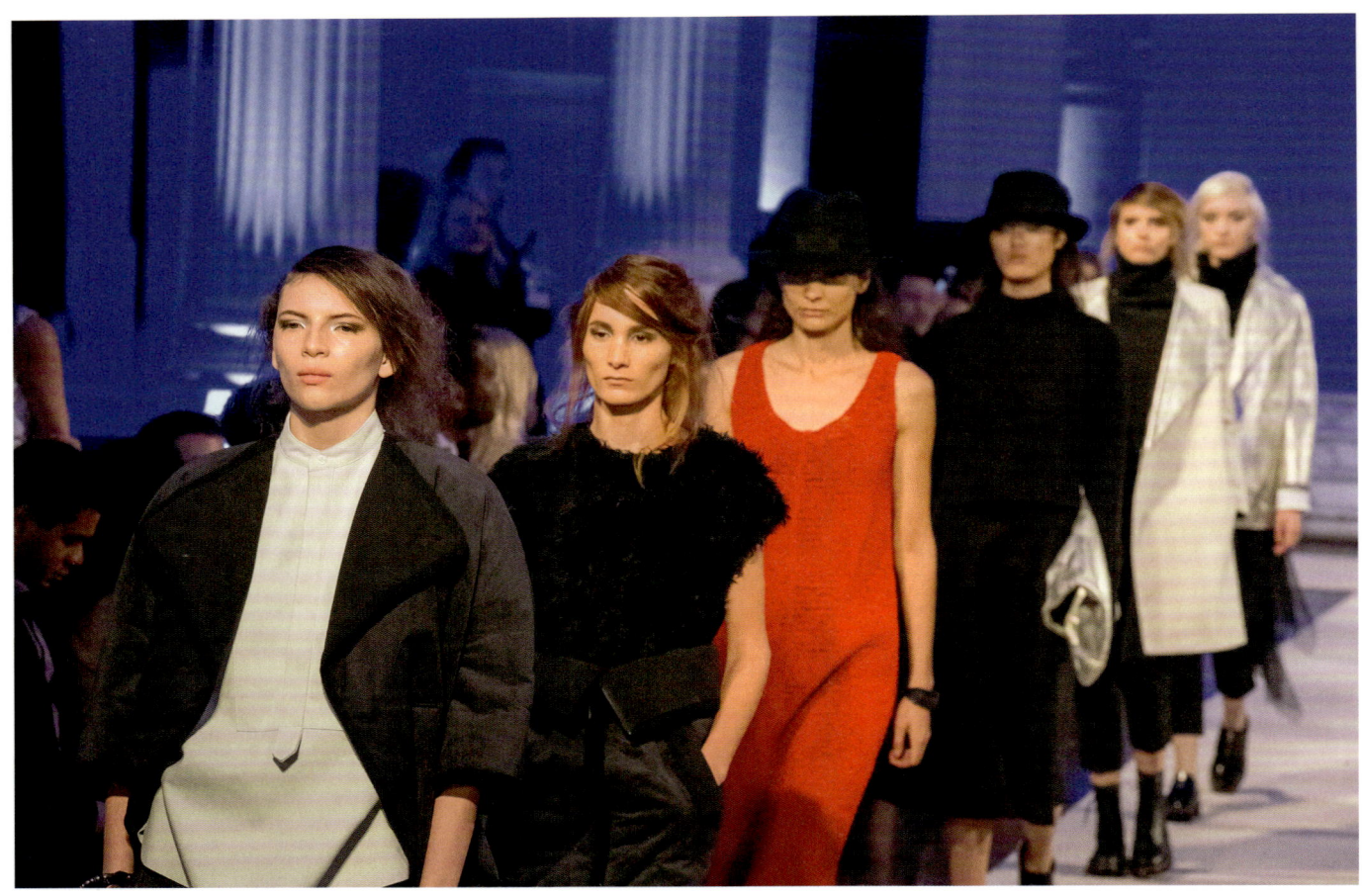

ultra-thin fringes, which are then woven or made into plaits. There were the endless possibilities of combination with other materials; for example, the handmade Alcantara coat with woollen lining, or jackets with the outside treated in leather and the linings crumpled like crêpe paper. Finally, printed garments, with a Persian rug motif adorning a long wrap skirt.

The public gathered around the Omotesando Hills fashion runway applauded. The photographers' flashes were akin to silent fireworks flaring in the half-shadow. There were journalists from international newspapers and Japanese celebrities, such as the actress and singer Ayaka Miyoshi.

The following year, Alcantara held a new fashion show in Japan, this time in collaboration with Lanvin, the prestigious Parisian brand. Once again the location was Tokyo, but the actual site was not advertised. There was no public, only male and female models, with staff reduced to a minimum, video makers, and streaming engineers. The pandemic required social distancing, and Alcantara returned to Japan to take a new leap into the wider world, by means of live video coverage. A new formula that came about as the result of a need, but which offered interesting opportunities. Digital technology is expanding the horizons of communication. New stimuli, to be reprocessed in the future, when the present will have become a past that is gone but not forgotten.

Yohji Yamamoto, "Capsule Collection", Los Angeles 2014

Lanvin, "Special Capsule Collection", Tokyo 2020

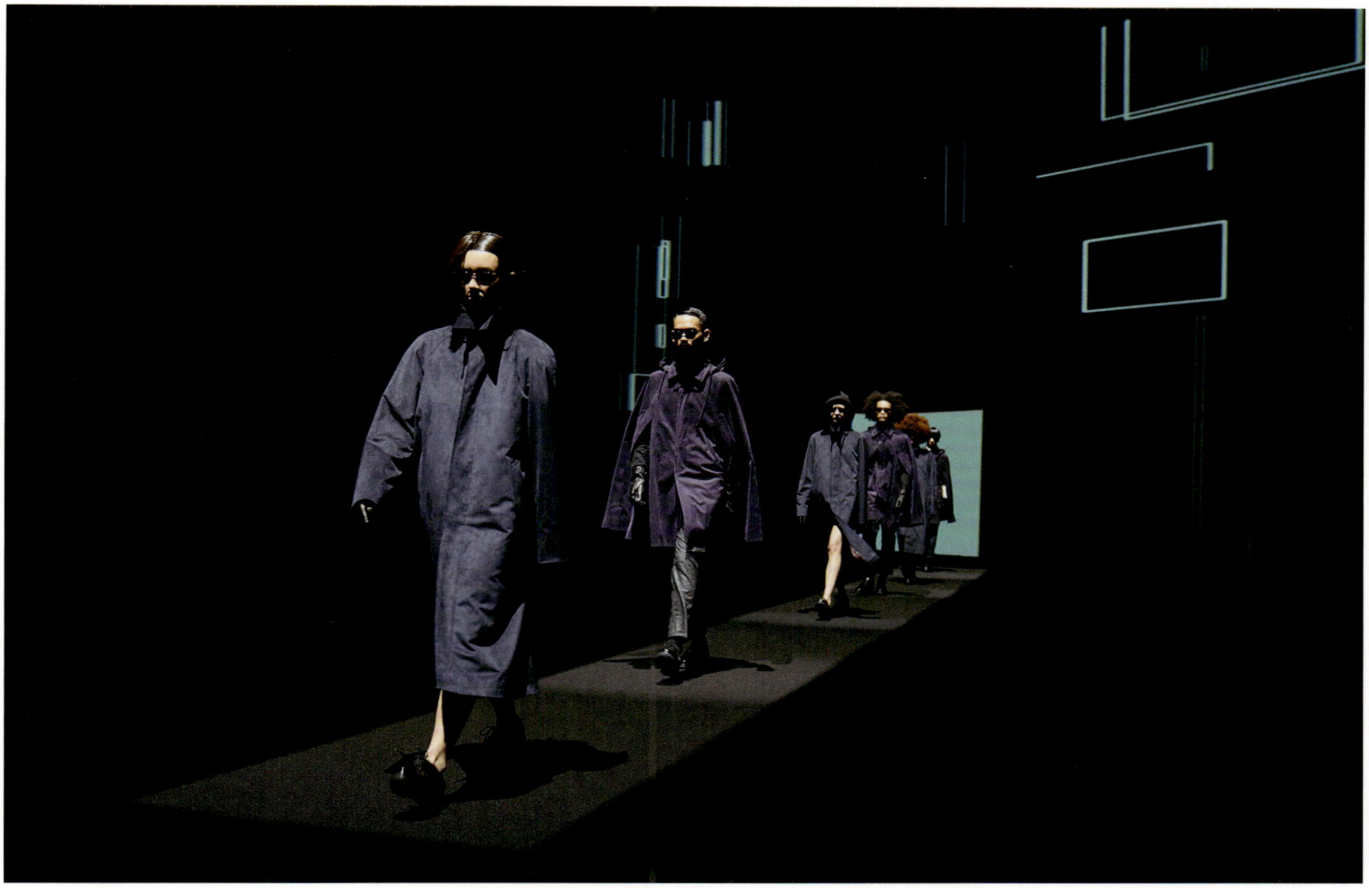

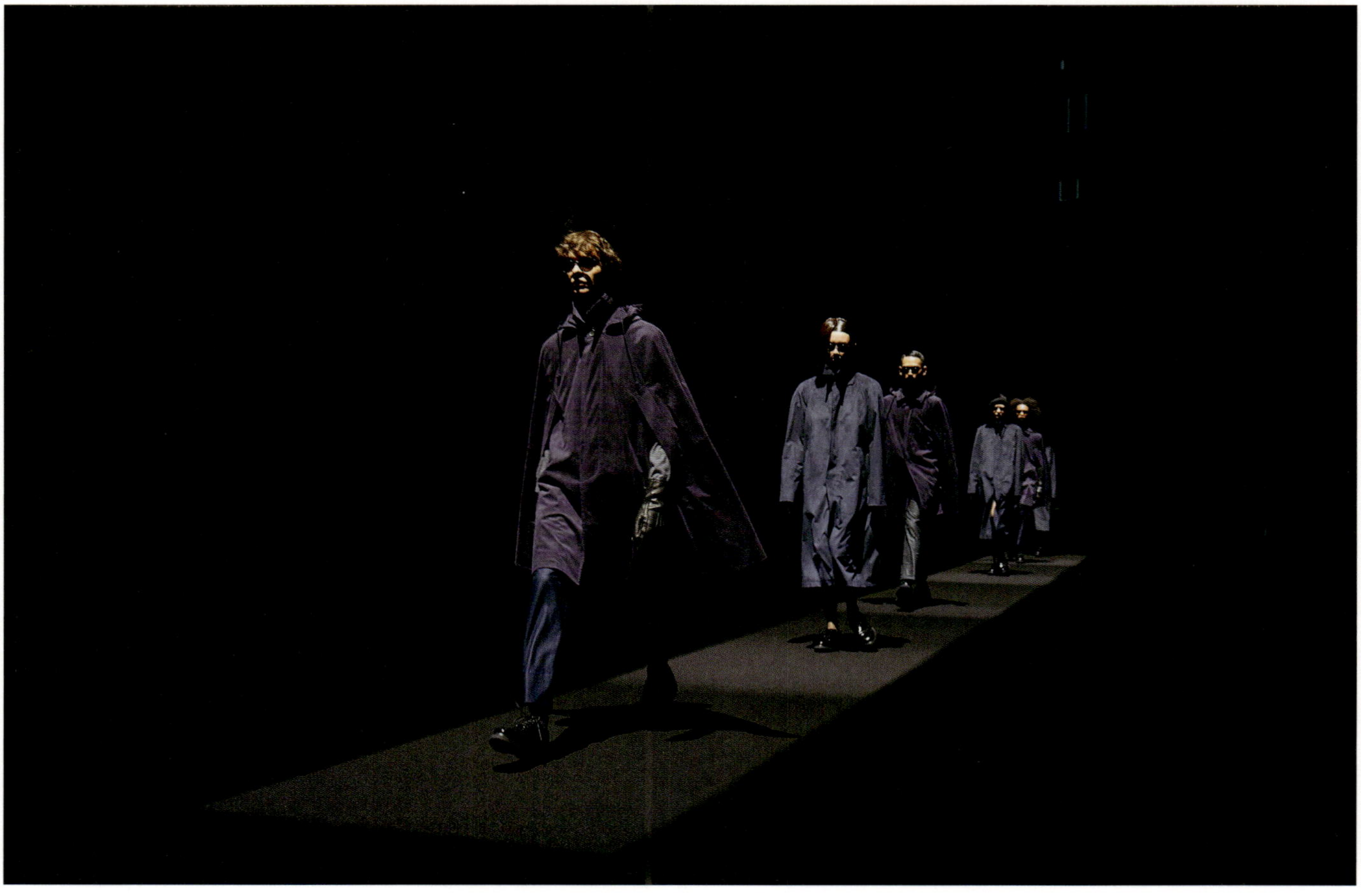

69

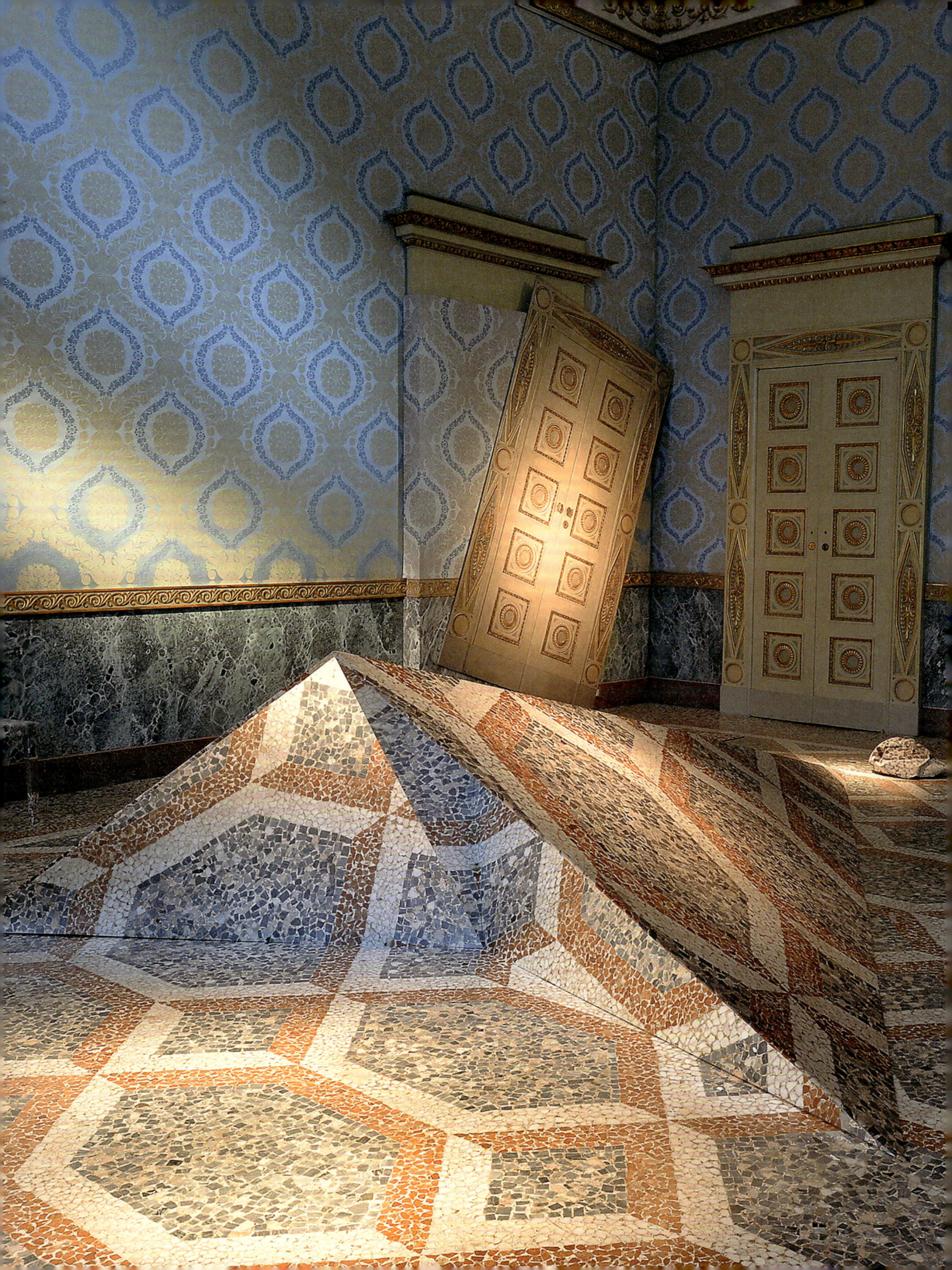

THE PRINCE'S APARTMENT

If you happen to find yourselves in the centre of Milan, try and leave the Cathedral behind you, cross the Palazzo Reale square, and ascend the grand staircase. That's all it takes to travel back in time. Step by step, the stairway becomes a bridge uniting different eras and cultures, different ways of life, and visions of the world. The building becomes stripped of its walls, inside and outside start to fall away, and the whole site becomes a threshold of the imagination.

Gentucca Bini, *Sul-reale*, "Alcantara, Technology of dreams", Palazzo Reale, Milan 2015

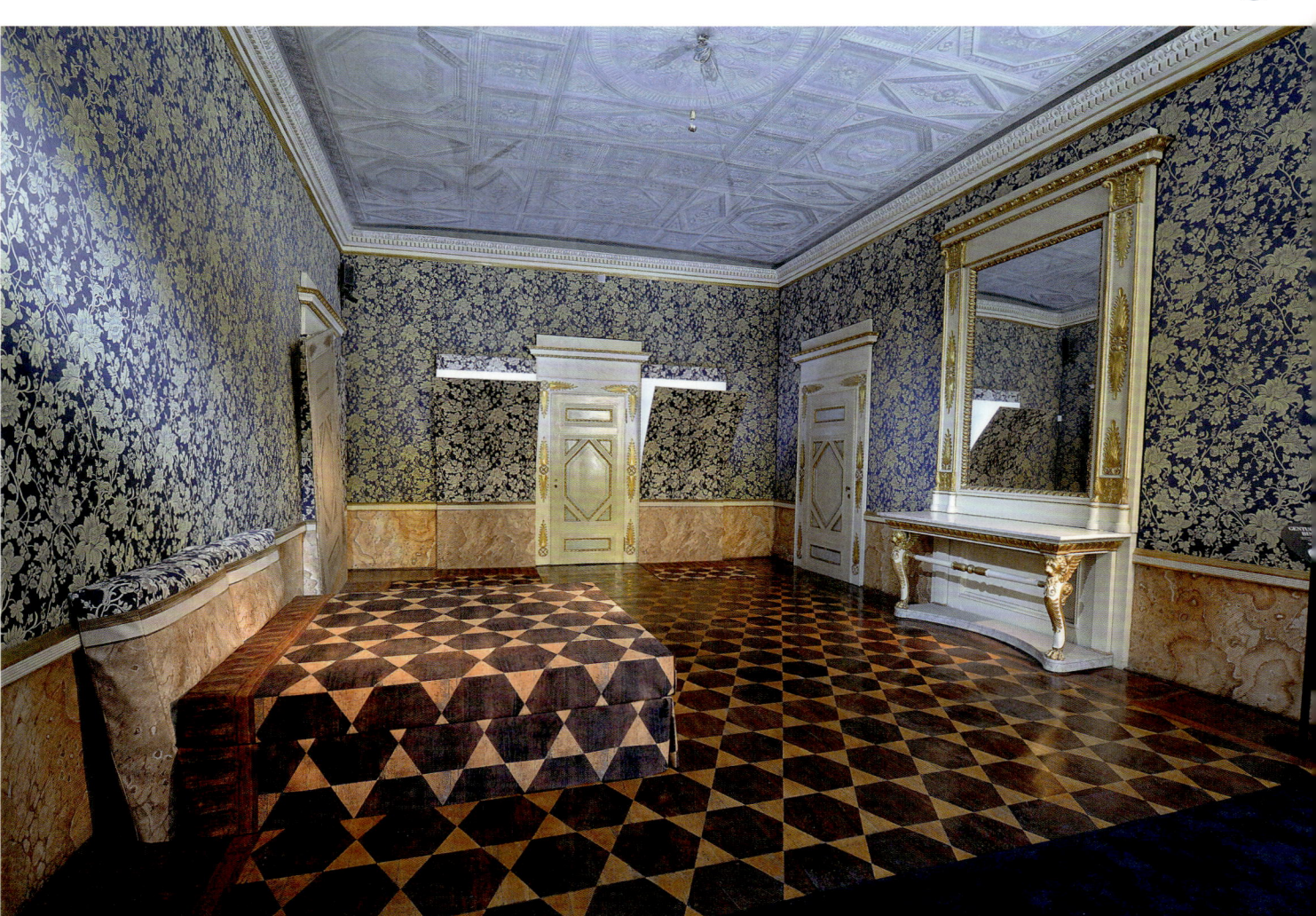

In the beginning the palace's incumbents were the Visconti family, and later the Sforza. They used to live in the Castle, but this was where they engaged in pure theatre, in the sense that in the formal chambers on the first floor, the rooms that the stairway connects to the city, they used to conduct official ceremonies: here they enacted the scenes where power was wielded. Then generations of residents came and went, one after the other: the French, the Spanish, the Austrians, and the Savoy dynasty. Almost a millennium of histories, in turn interwoven in the history of Milan itself.

In recent times the Prince of the palace was Alcantara. For over a month, in spring 2015, the art material became the protagonist in the royal rooms that played host to the interpreters of contemporary style. The palace came alive, and memory resonated in the lavishly decorated rooms: the Tapestry Rooms, the Hall of Caryatids, the Rotonda, the Ministers' Chamber, and the Throne Room. But the quivering of life was felt even more intensely in the small private rooms, simple bedrooms with one door in and one door out, fragments of a corridor within a larger labyrinth. A tangled collection of lives and events, all bound up together, winding its way back through the past. Palazzo Reale played host to Alcantara, and demanded that the works engaged in a dialogue with the building, its architecture, the frescoes, the wall-hangings, the decor, and the colours. It called on it to do so in the present, the right time for attuning the vision of the future with memories of the past.

The curators, Cappellini and Dardi, had already collaborated before to put together the MAXXI exhibitions. They briskly ascended the ceremonial stairway, and came knocking at the prince's doors. As a gift, they came bearing Alcantara. With them were six designers with the spirit of artists, called in to cross the threshold of the historic space in order to project it beyond the contemporary dimension. A technological material such as Alcantara must be worked with the same artisanal skill as the Renaissance masters. Italian knowhow is also a bridge: it is capable of time travel.

Gentucca Bini worked *On (top of) the real*, and created an installation with a surprising visual impact. She seemed to tip whole pots of paint onto the floor and walls of the rooms, using surprise and irony, which she then spread with the brushes of perspective, optical illusion, and disorientation of perception. Real or surreal? The idea was founded on an intrinsic feature of the Alcantara material: its ability to absorb light and to take very high-resolution prints. As in a digitally processed image, the artist copy-pasted whole sections of rooms, and moved them, creating the illusion of doors ripped off their hinges and coming apart from walls, three-dimensional solids emerging from the floors, and even walls coming apart and allowing fragments of light to filter in from outside the building. It was all about wonder, amazement, and fun, as well as the malleable ability of the material to shape space, crossing the boundaries of time. Through photographic printing, the material of the future merged with the stucco-work and marble features of previous centuries.

Studio Nendo, *Il Teatro del Principe*, "Alcantara, Technology of dreams", Palazzo Reale, Milan 2015

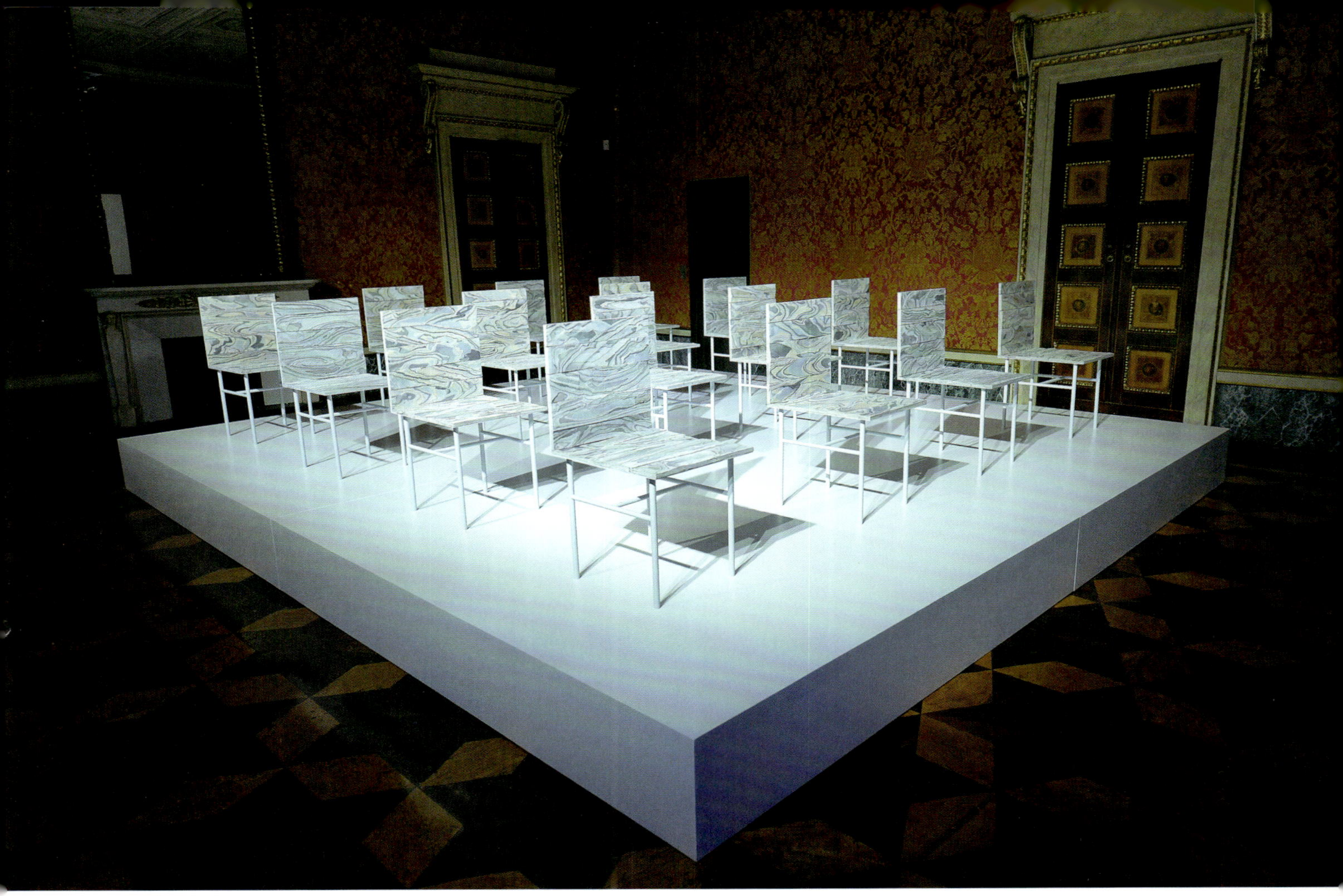

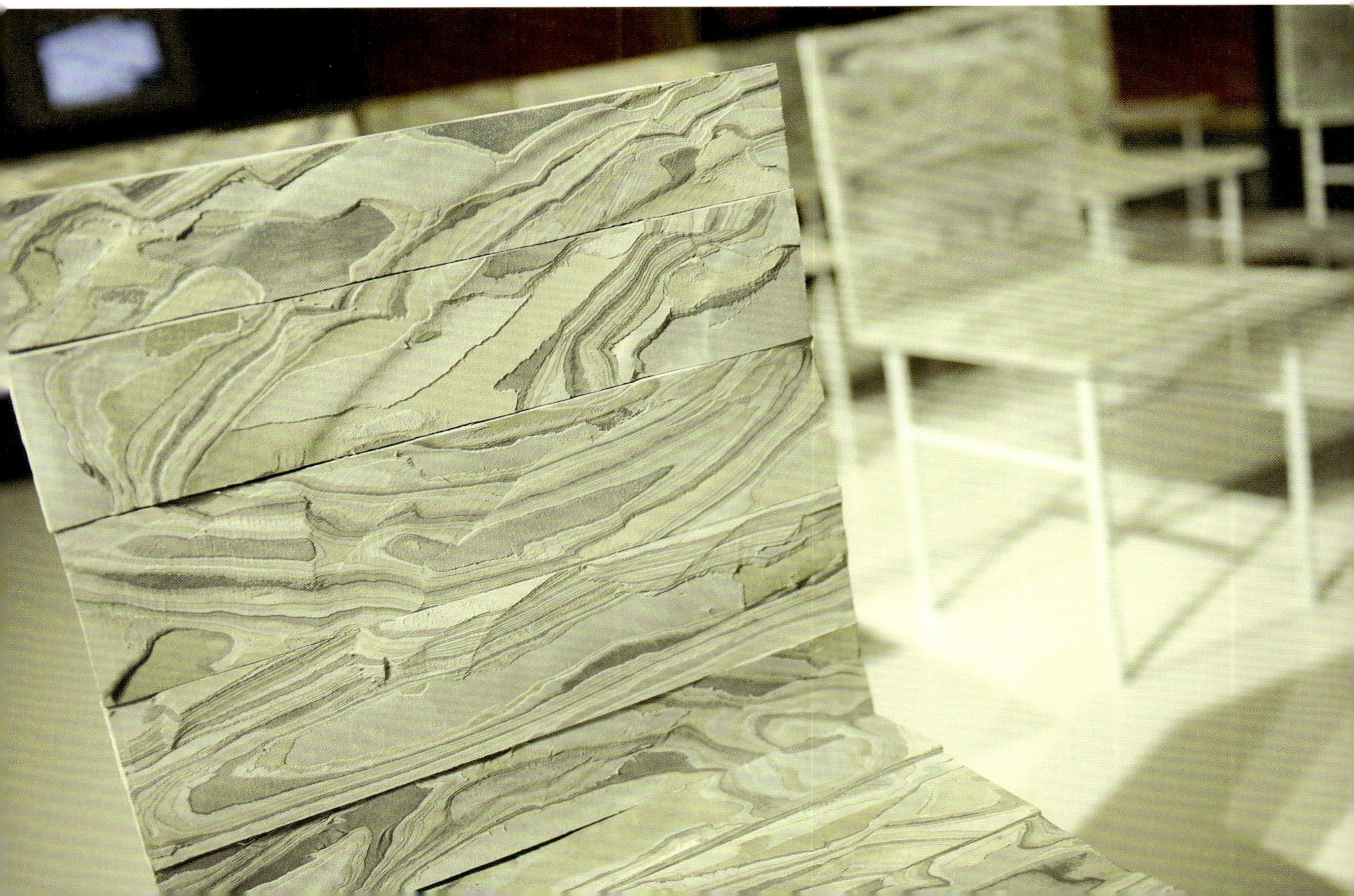

In another room, Nendo, the Japanese studio, reworked layers of Alcantara, creating the illusion of a new material. It used wraparound offcuts of material in differing shades of the same colour and created a cylinder from which it extracted the central portion. What resulted was a superimposition of Alcantara that put one in mind of the internal pattern of a tree, its central core. The designer created a sort of virtual wood referencing the artisanal skills of master carpenters. Finally, with this reinterpretation of Alcantara, it created the chairs of the "Prince's Theatre".

The reference may not be familiar to everyone. Palazzo Reale was once the site of Milan's first-ever theatre, later demolished in the second half of the 18th century, when the Teatro alla Scala was built.

However, the link between the work and the site was not only historical, it was also a material connection. The new Alcantara design made by Nendo set up a dialogue with the decor of the room: the drawings on the walls, the floor inlays, the frames, the doors, the mirrors.

The exhibition continued, more works entered into a relationship with the interiors. Paola Navone's *Fortress of Silence* had the appearance of a curved wall of soft, multicoloured Alcantara cushions. A room within a room: silence enclosing more silence, for intense internal reflection, ensured by Alcantara's capacity for sound absorption. Then there was the *Chromophone*

Paola Navone, *La fortezza del silenzio*, "Alcantara, Technology of dreams", Palazzo Reale, Milan 2015

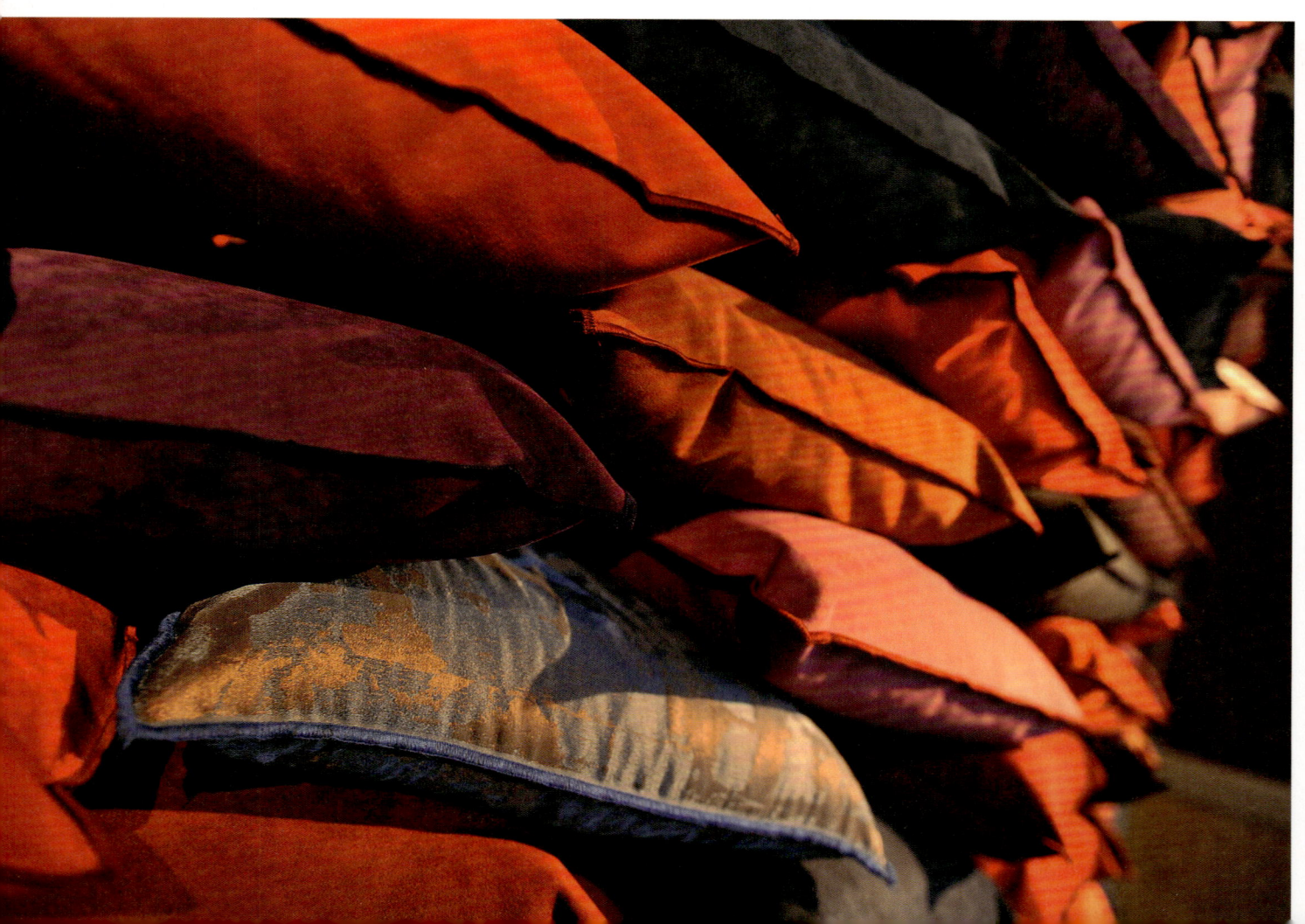

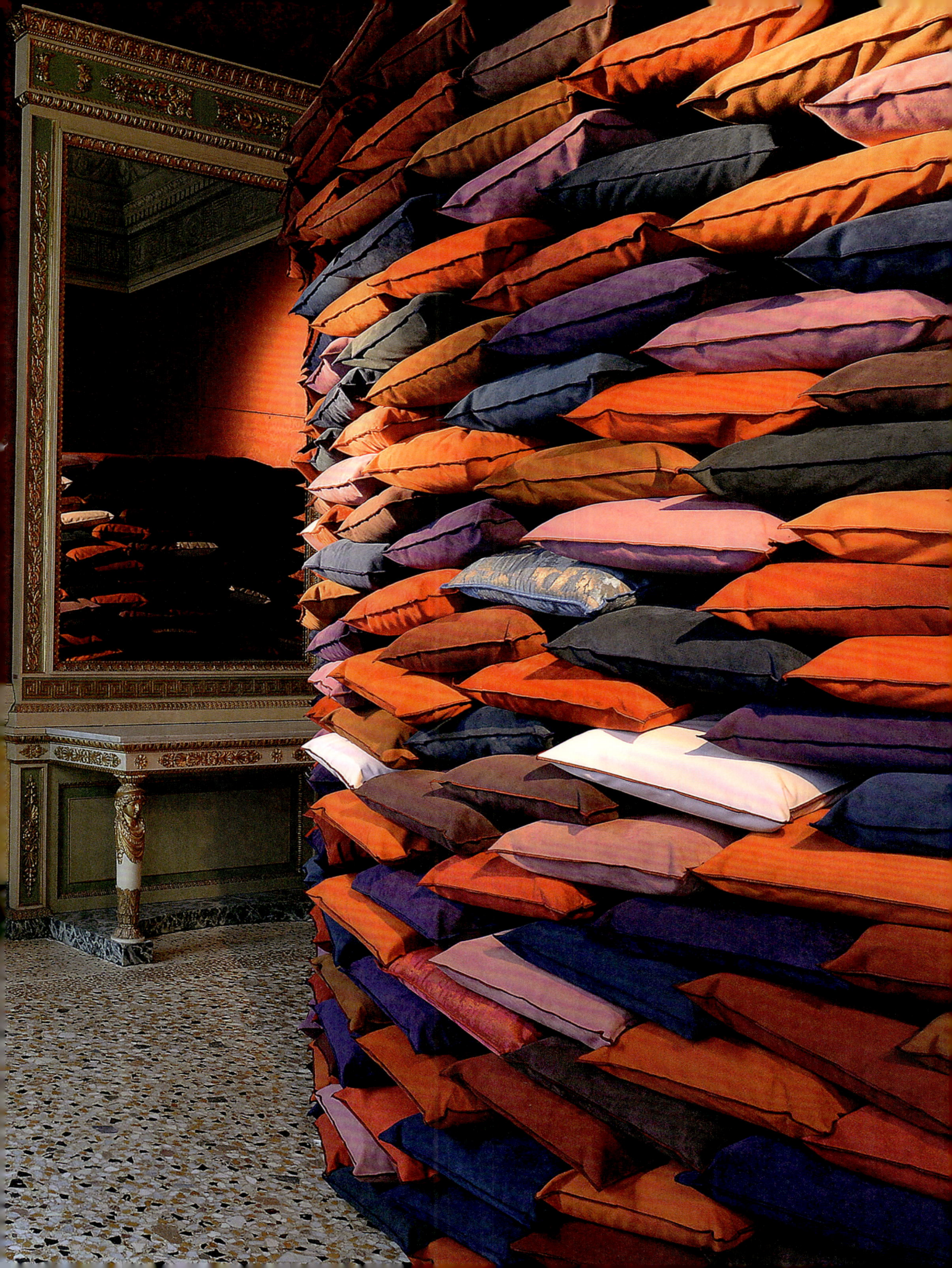

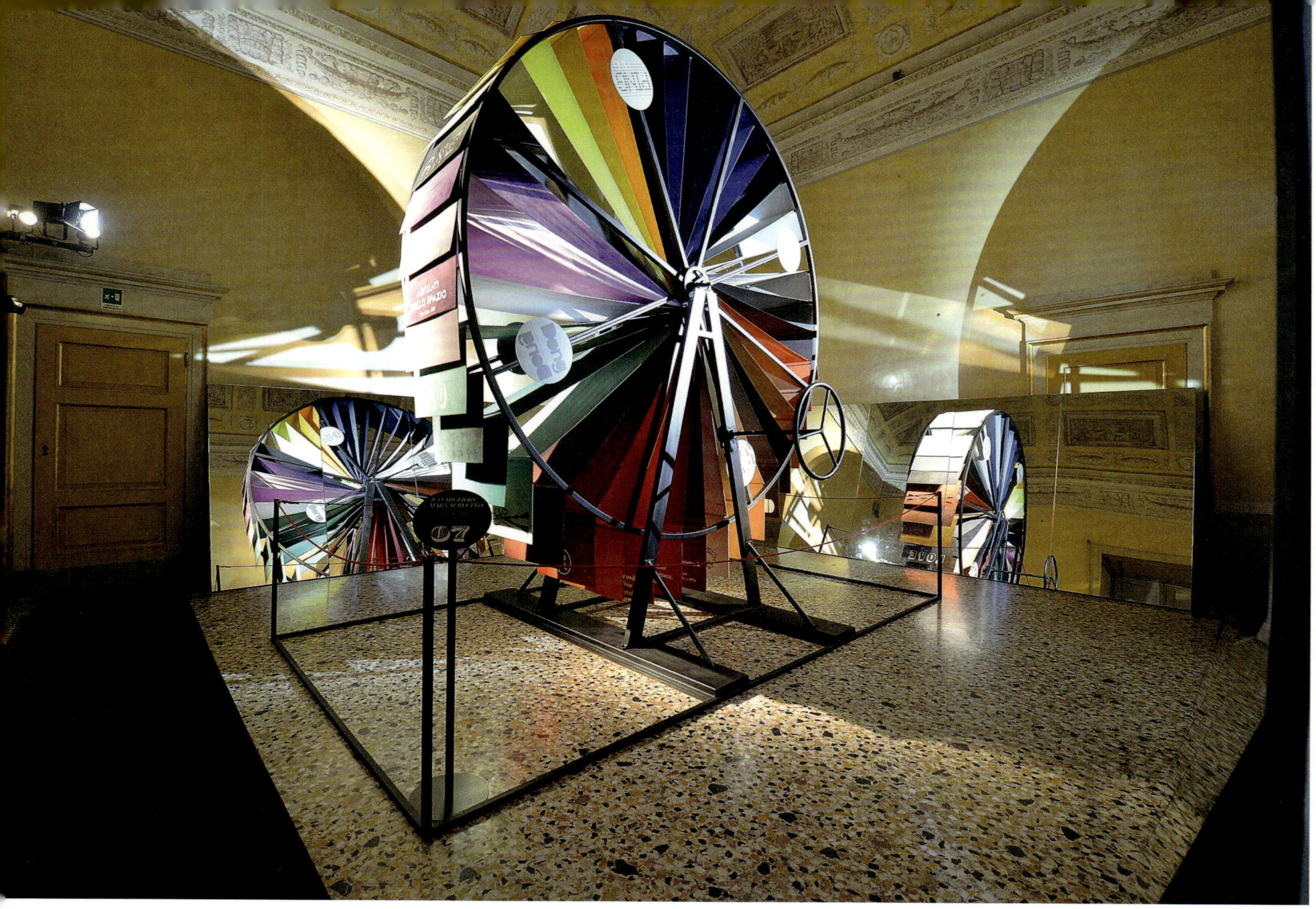

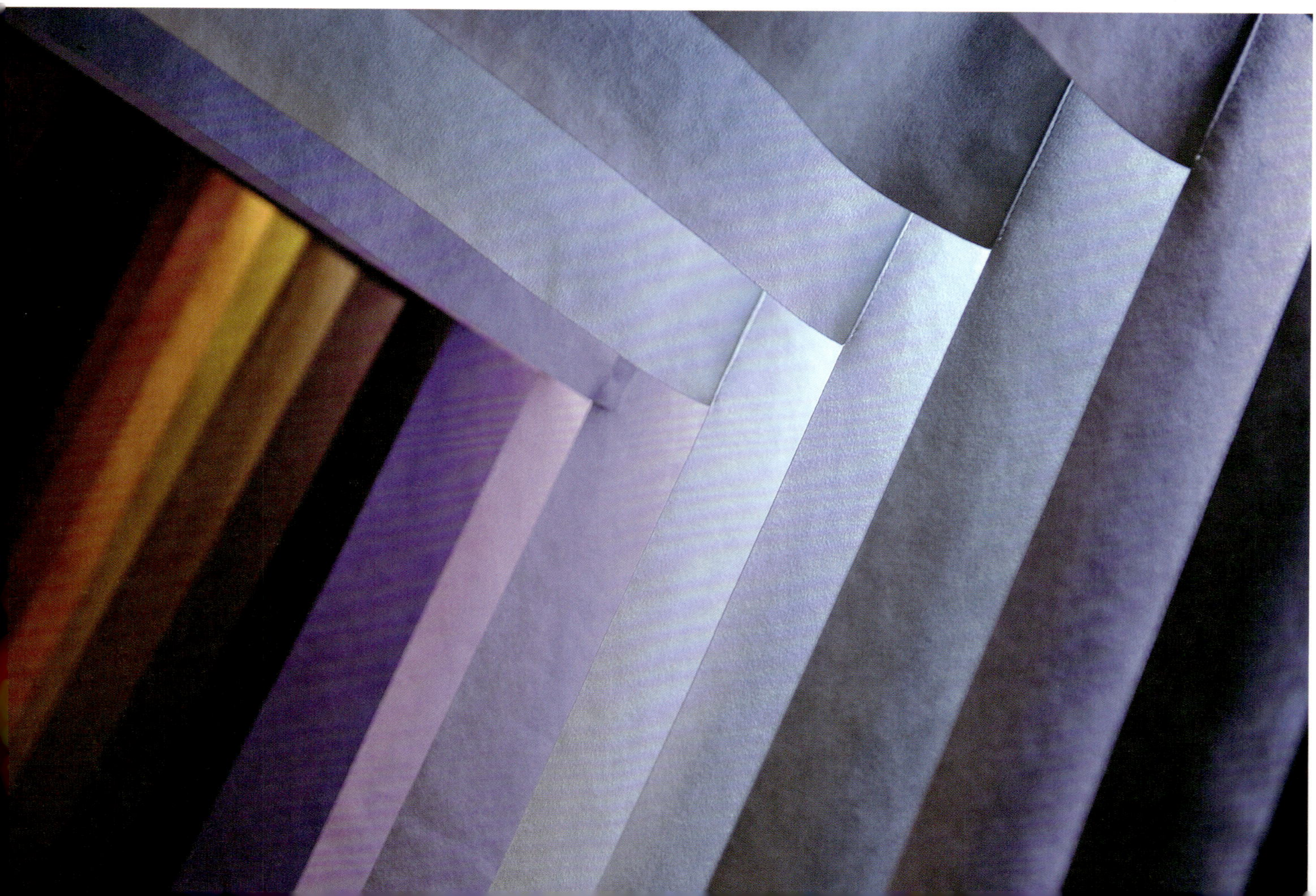

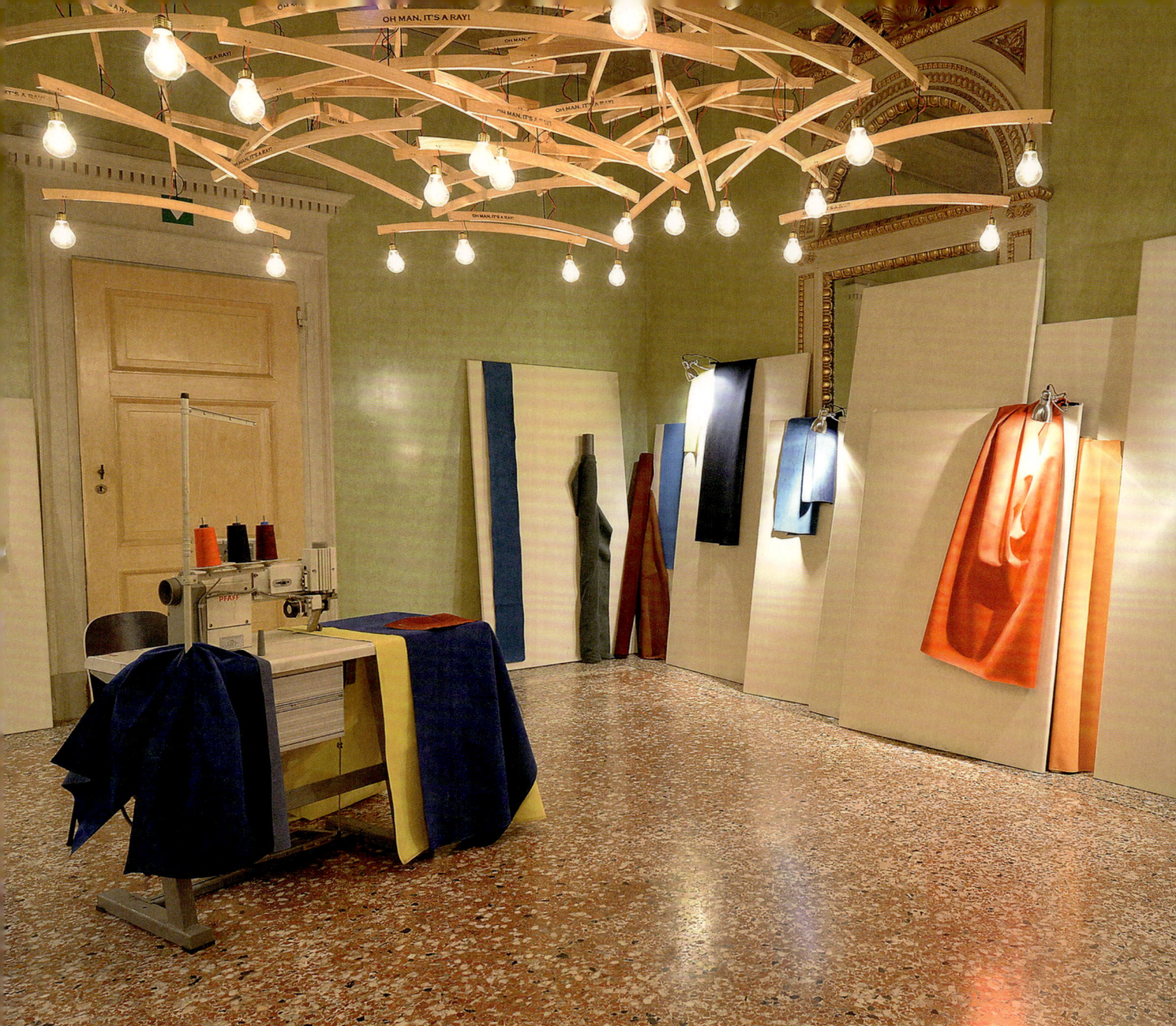

Ico Migliore and Mara Servetto, *Cromofono*, "Alcantara, Technology of dreams", Palazzo Reale, Milan 2015

Ingo Maurer, *Oh Man, It's a Ray*, "Alcantara, Technology of dreams", Palazzo Reale, Milan 2015

Following pages Giulio Cappellini, *La tavola delle meraviglie*, "Alcantara, Technology of dreams", Palazzo Reale, Milan 2015

by Ico Migliore and Mara Servetto, a great wheel formed from multicoloured strips of Alcantara: when it span, it produced a chromatic concerto, the variety of the material's visual and sound-based languages. Cappellini laid out a *Table of Wonders*, as once found at court, with place settings made from Alcantara and decorated with colourful plants made from the same acrobatic material.

Indeed, there is no limit to imagination. The Prince's Apartment was a never-ending source of inspiration which the creatives drew from, and translated into the many and varied languages spoken by Alcantara. Timeless languages that operate in an increasingly international dimension: echoes of the past that resound in the contemporary world, before then launching themselves into the future. What kind of future? Nobody can say, that is something only art can imagine.

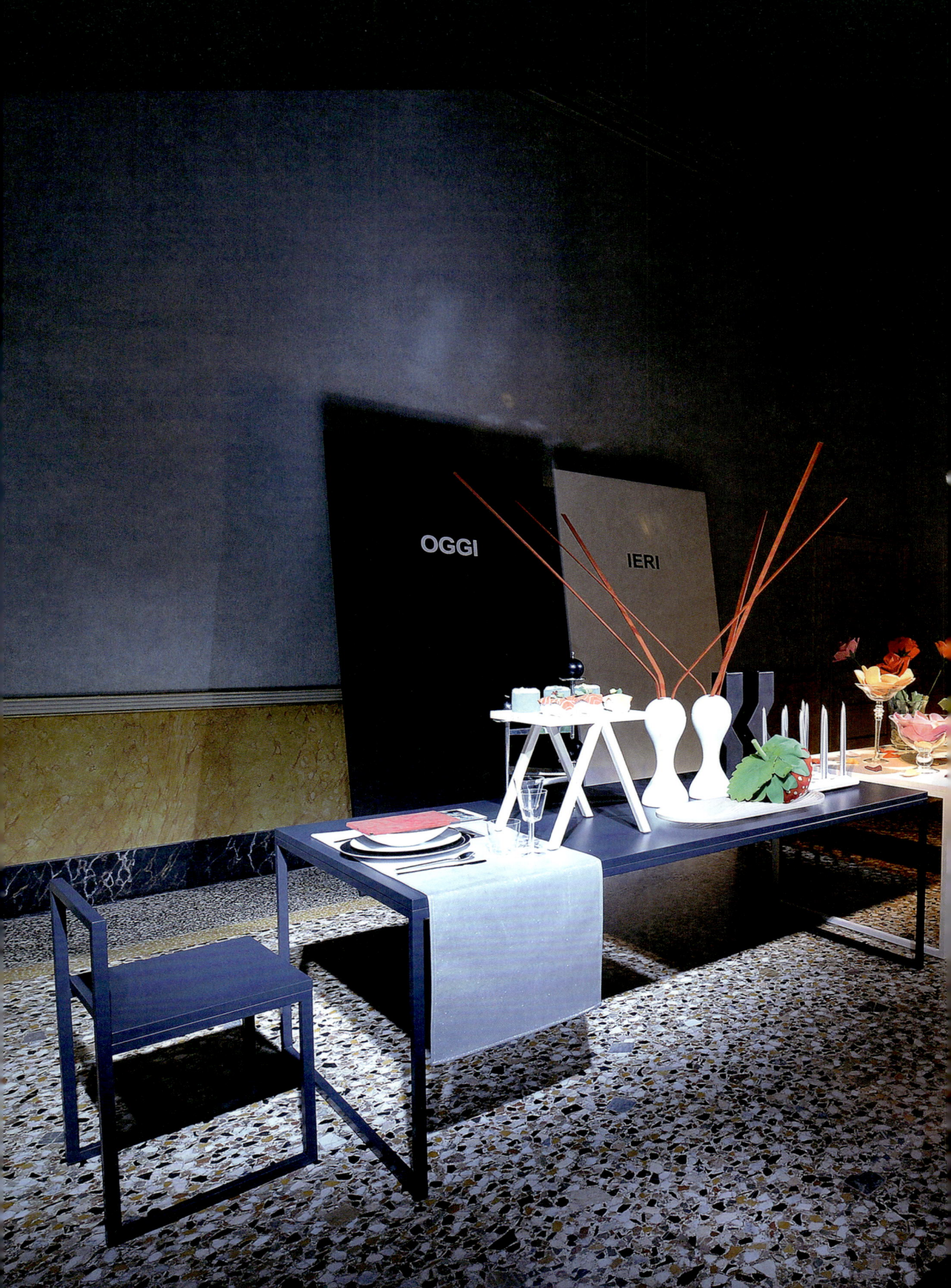

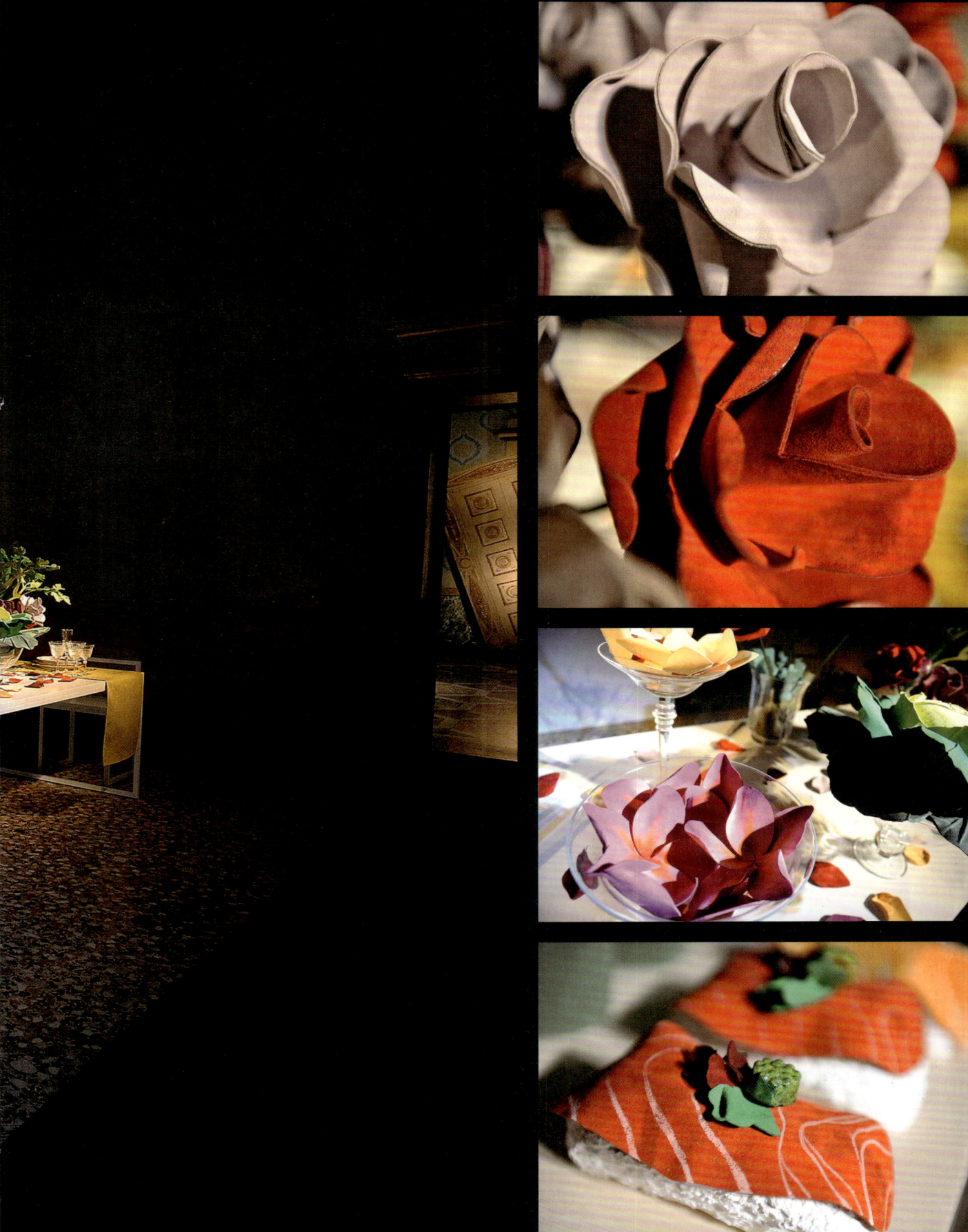

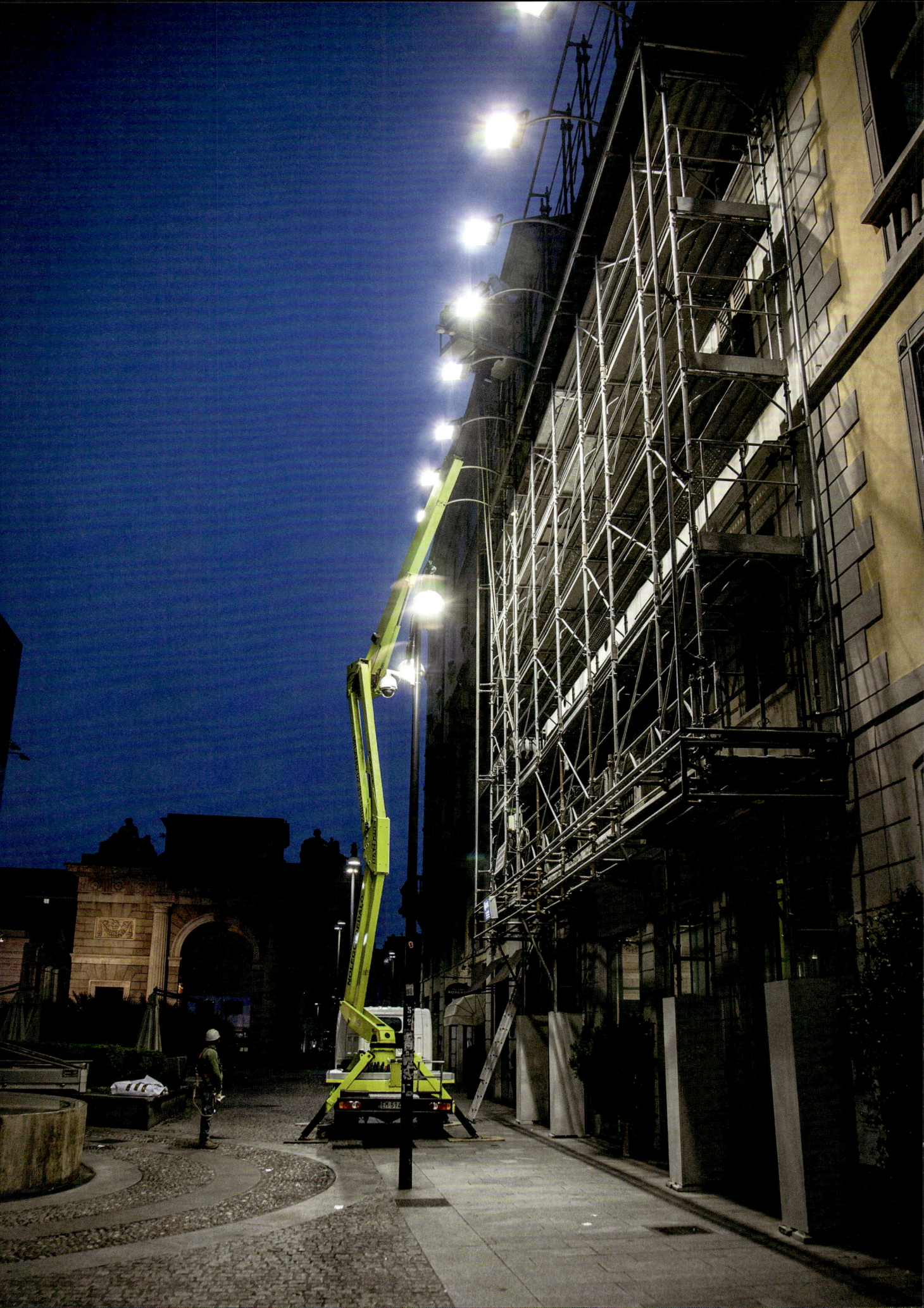

MAGIC HOTEL

The show began even before the curtain went up. There was a fine, period palazzo in Corso Como undergoing restoration work. The scaffolding covered all three storeys of the building, concealing the rigorous neo-Classical architecture of over a century ago. The narrow, elongated windows, the string-courses, two small wrought-iron balconies on each side on the second floor, and a double-length balcony in the central part of the building. The scaffolding covered up all this, but Alcantara was ready to bring it back to life, and to transform it. Passers-by gazed up at the facade of the palazzo. They realized that the on-site workers were different from usual: they were not builders but installers, set designers, specialist technicians with computers and projectors in tow. What was going on?

Gentucca Bini, "Alcantara Magic Hotel", Milan 2016

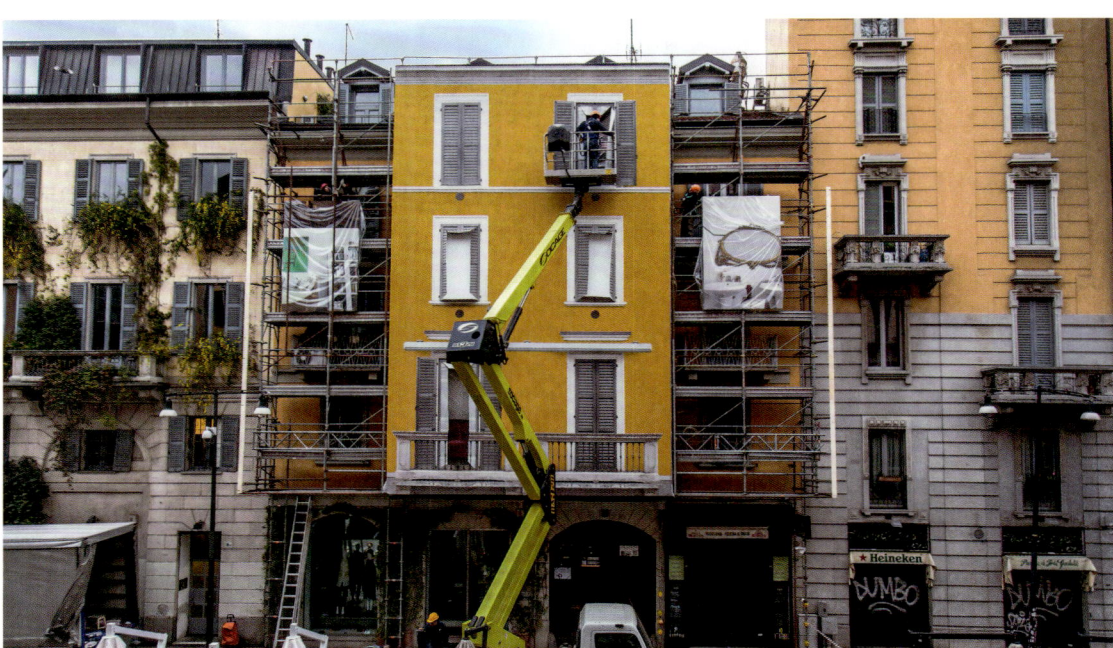

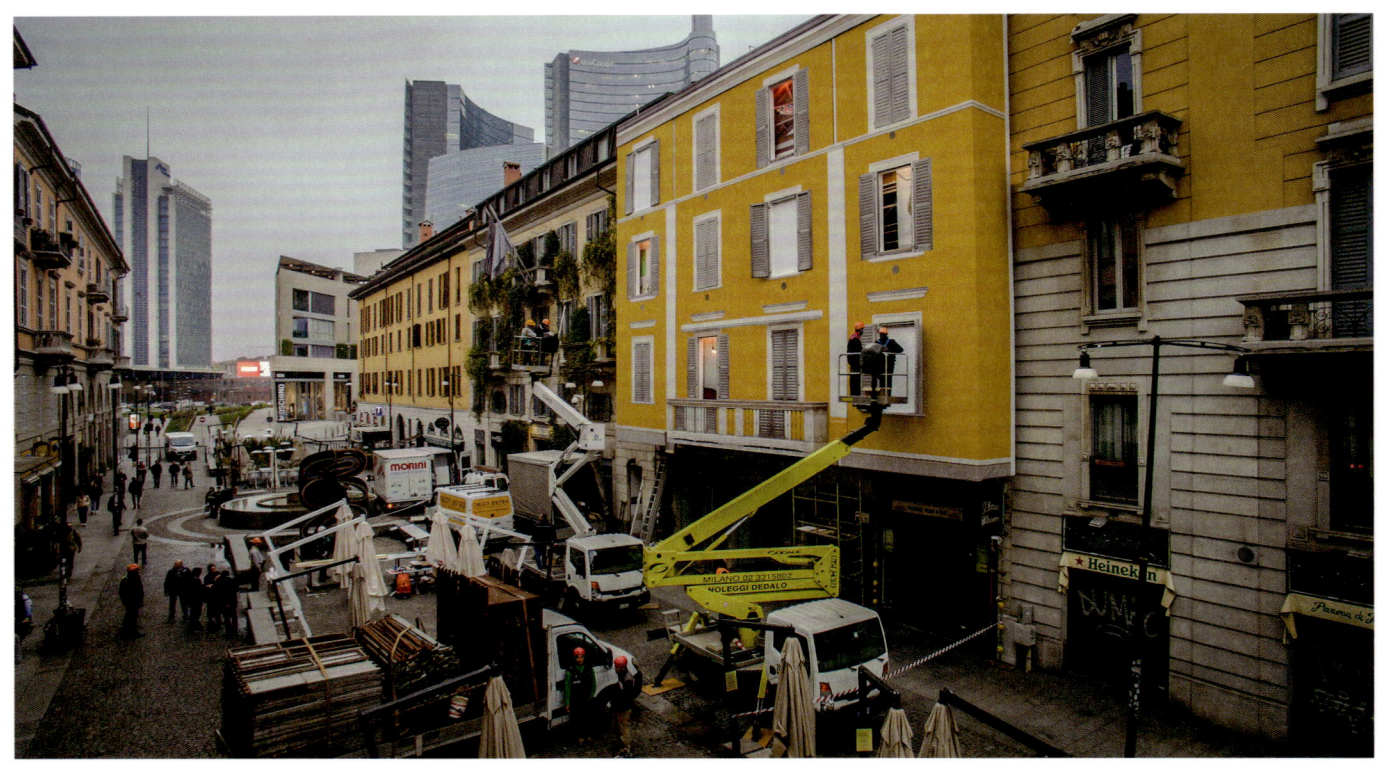

What was happening was that preparations were under way for Design Week 2016, and Alcantara was enjoying a new encounter with architecture, design, and art. This time, however, in a new, never-before-seen open-air version. In itself, the sheer size of the installation was thrilling to see: two hundred square metres of Alcantara, printed in high resolution, reproducing the facade of the building in exact detail, as it would appear when the restoration was complete. Every feature was there, as if it was real. An illusion, but a real one. It included the balconies with their wrought-iron decoration, the windows with half-open shutters, and everything else. Everyone below gazed up, open-mouthed. A wonderful sight.

    At dusk, the engineers checked the parameters of the projections. The video-mapping technology made it possible to project onto any surface with total precision. The technicians highlighted the windows, while a name appeared on the roof: Alcantara Magic Hotel.

    The rehearsal was a show in itself. Gentucca Bini had tested the ability of the Alcantara material to be transformed into a support for very high-quality printing in the Prince's Apartment at Palazzo Reale. Now he was pushing the material to its furthermost limits, in terms of its size, solidity, and response to natural light, which of course is impossible to control. The ability of Alcantara to absorb the rays of the light spectrum adds a new perceptual dimension to printing: it is as if the element which, by illuminating the material reveals its presence, was not there. Printing on Alcantara means making the reproduced material even more real and tangible. The effect at Palazzo Reale was surprising, but the scale of the Magic Hotel made it almost

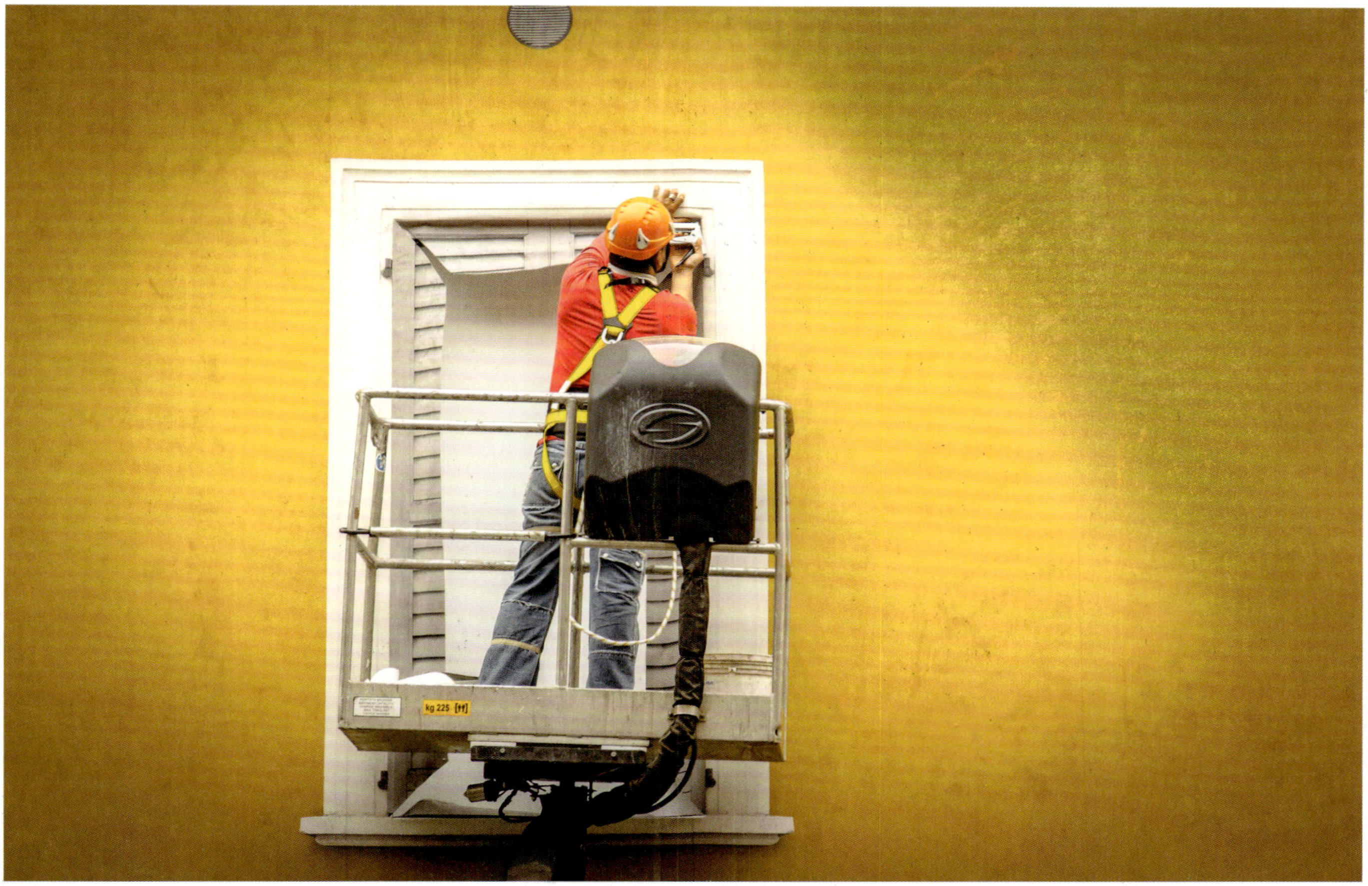

83

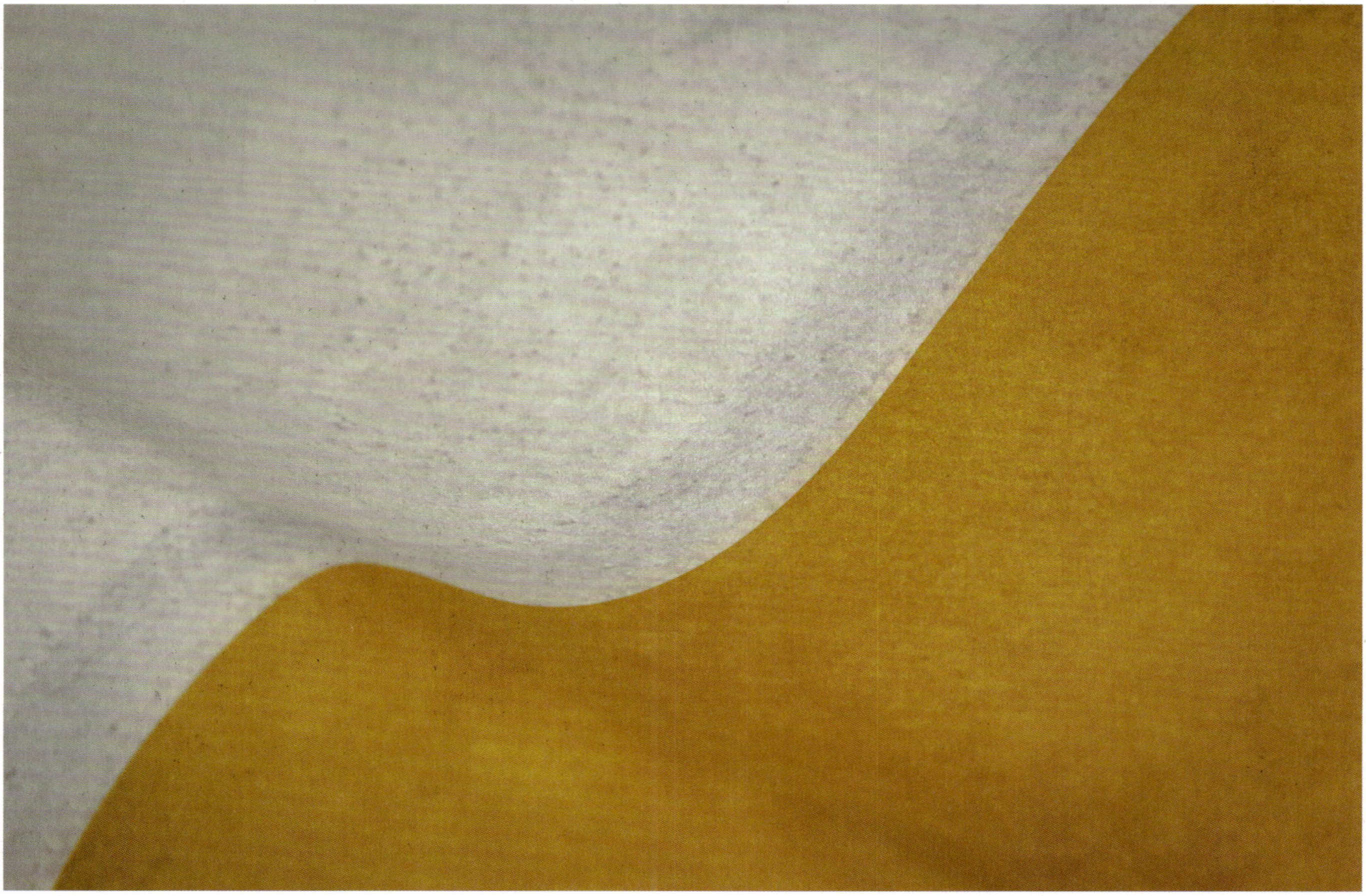

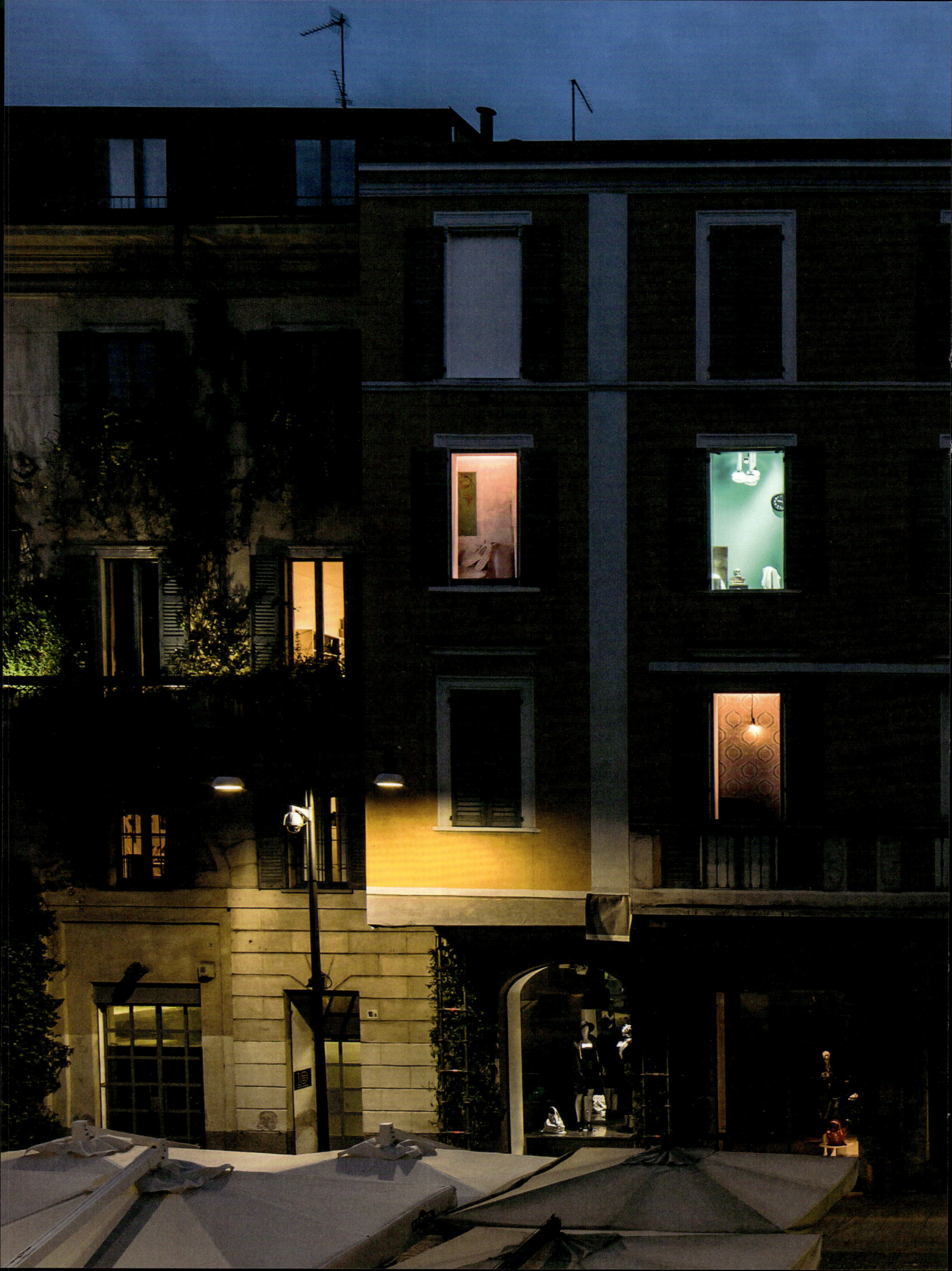

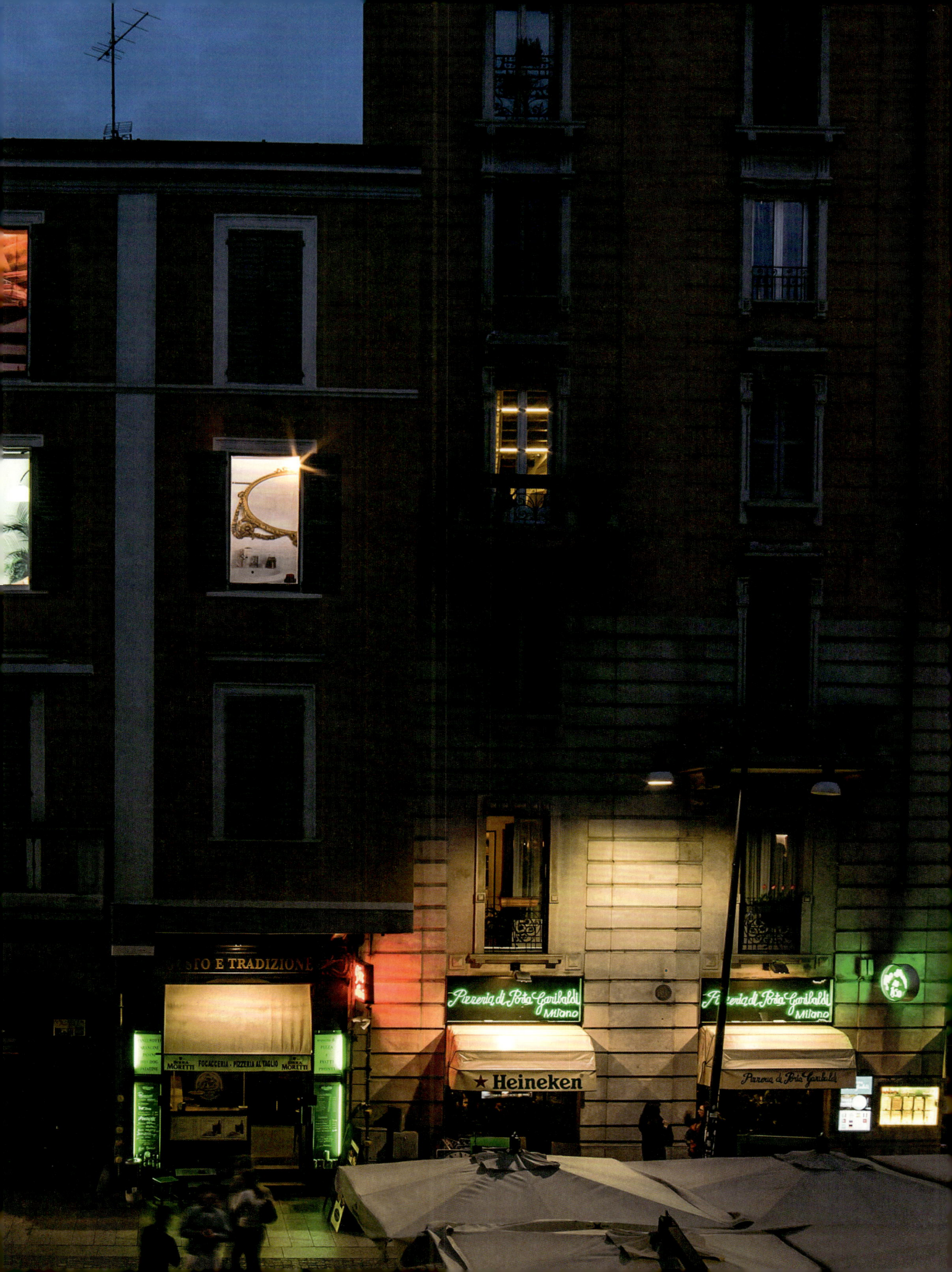

unbelievable. You had to see it for yourself, and, whoever actually saw it, couldn't help talking about it after the event.

People sat down on the benches opposite the palazzo and enjoyed the show. The installation had a dual aspect, a daytime and a night-time version. By day, the rigour of the architecture, represented in the form of a soft, seductive optical illusion; by night, an ironic look at the private lives of guests at the Magic Hotel of Alcantara. The building came to life with their stories. One person was having a shower, another was reading a book, someone else was dancing, another was watching television, and yet another was getting ready to go to sleep. Individual moments in people's daily lives that the passers-by observed. It was even more wonderful to look at them, as they looked up at the building instead of at the street. They would slow down, sit on a bench, and smile.

On the opening day, Andrea Boragno told the press that he was "very proud to present this incredible installation, celebrating the universal, contemporary features of Alcantara, showing all the material's extraordinary technical quality. At a time such as this, when Milan is standing at the centre of the international stage, Alcantara is using art, too, to reveal its ability to go beyond all limitations."

Gentucca Bini added: "I was fascinated by the photographic resolution of printing on Alcantara. It makes the material three-dimensional and magical. Also magical is this collaboration between the company and creatives from across the world. It is a precious thing, also for the evolution of design."

The Magic Hotel is fully booked, but there's always room outside. By day and by night, whatever the weather. You'll find Alcantara there, still holding on, and putting on a show.

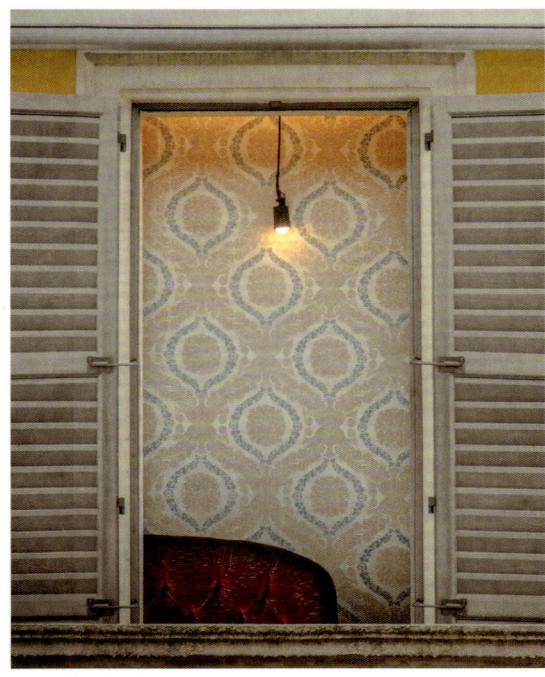
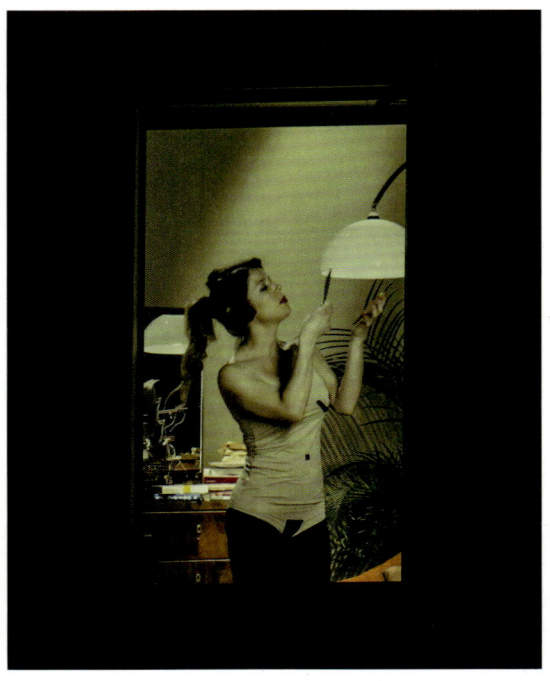

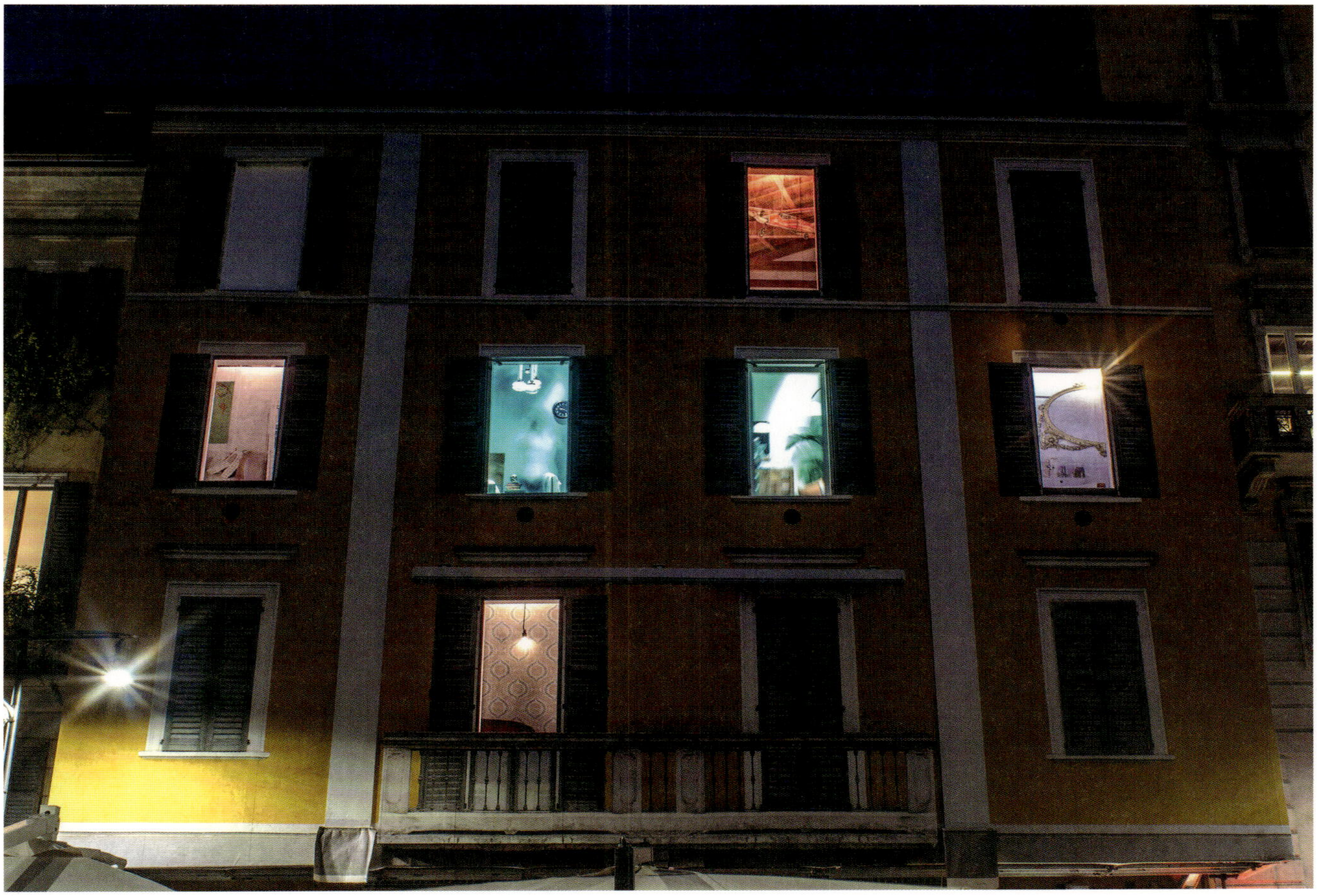

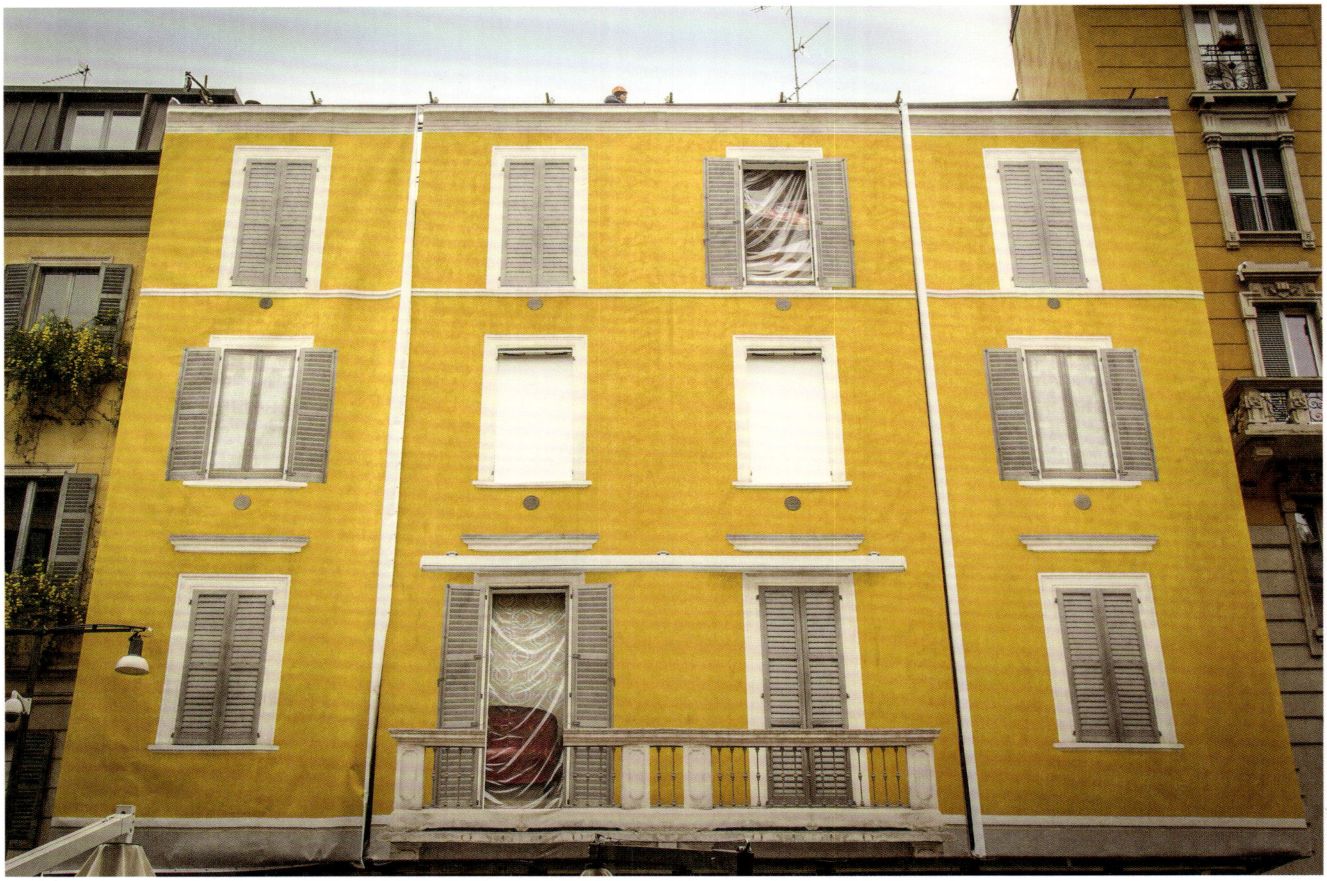

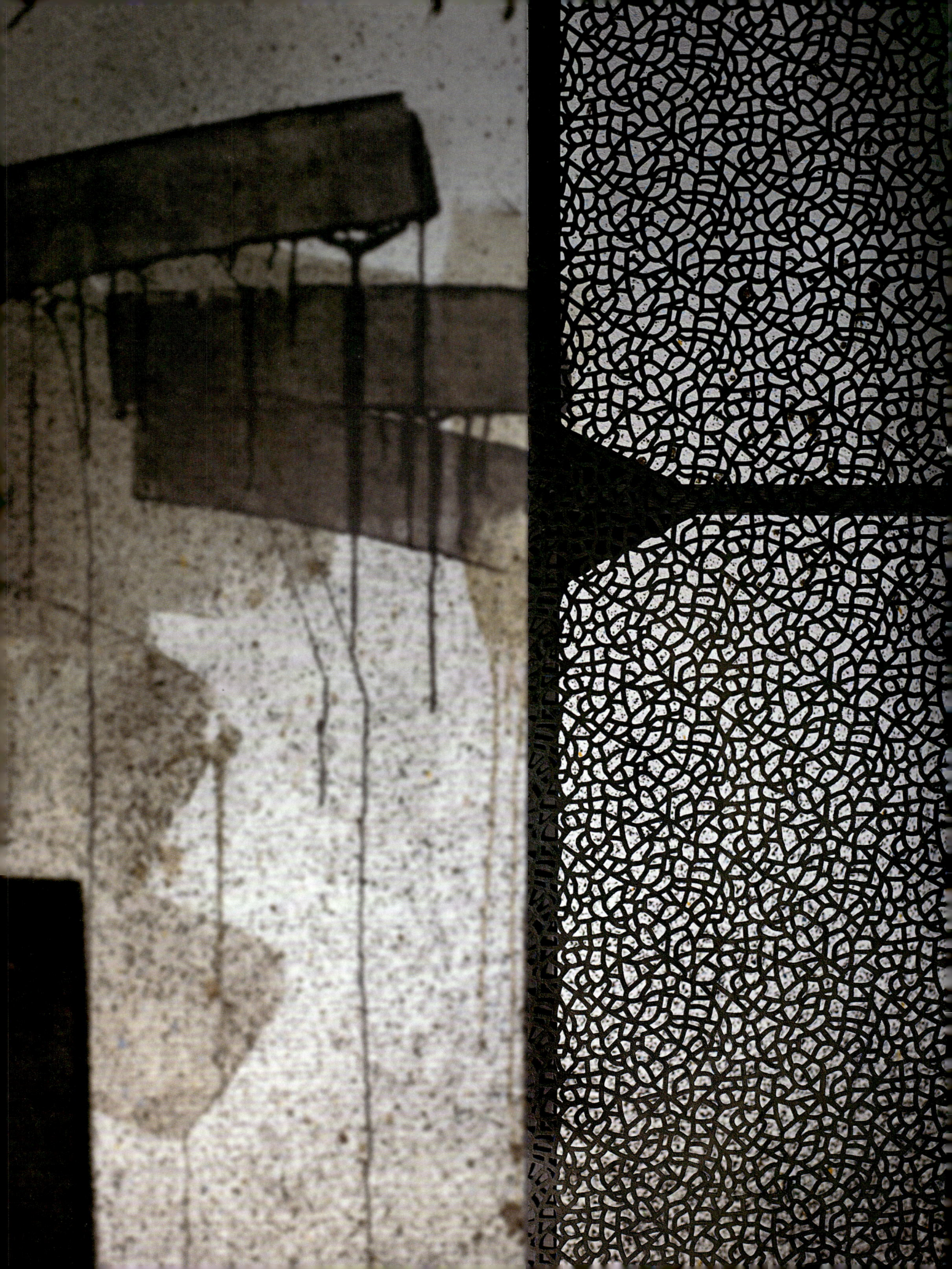

A COFFEE AT MOMUS

It was cold that winter in Paris, amid the attics and garrets in the Latin Quarter, without any wood to burn in the stove, or food to fill one's belly. Four artist friends enduring the chill. Four down-and-outs, we might say, but still young and alive. The writer decided to burn his manuscript, when there was a knock at the door: it was Mimì. Rodolfo opened, and instantly fell in love. "Che gelida manina", he managed to stammer, before joining the others at Cafè Momus.

La Bohème, Alcantara curtain, Teatro Regio Torino, Turin 2016

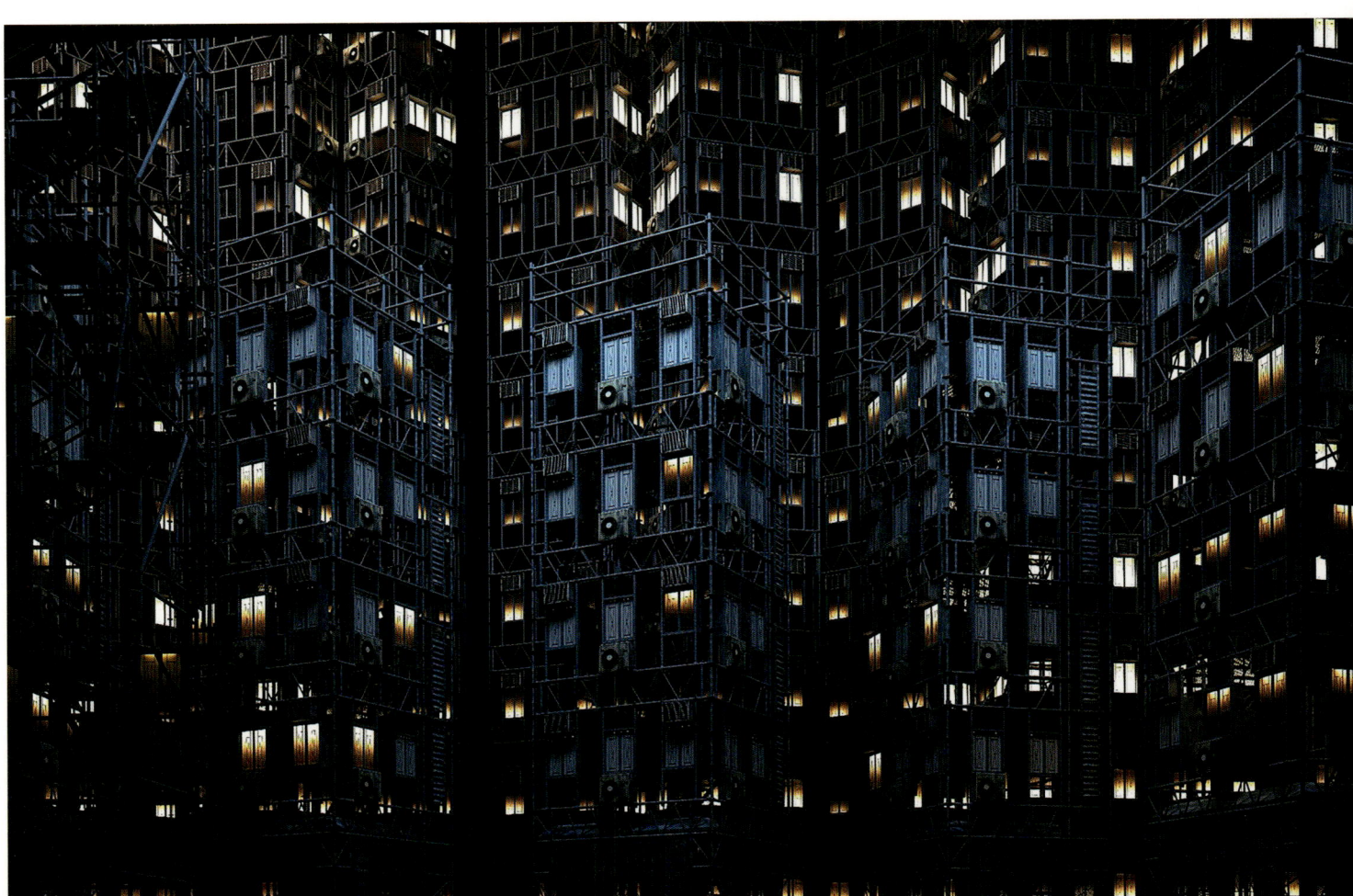

October 2016, on the stage at Teatro Regio in Turin *La Bohème* was performed, one of Puccini's first operas, and one of the last operas ever. Melodrama – at least the 19th century idea of a melodrama – ended with it. Puccini did not know about cinema (incidentally, while he was writing *La Bohème*, the Lumière brothers were shooting their first ever film), but he already had a very clear idea of it in his mind. Puccini *was* cinema.

This performance in Turin was conducted by Gianandrea Noseda, and directed by Àlex Ollè, from the Calatan group "La Fura dels Baus." One of the protagonists, on stage, was Alcantara.

The show began with the curtain itself: hundreds of square metres of Alcantara on which the set designer, Alfons Flores, had reproduced the main scene in the opera. A metallic architecture depicting the outskirts of a metropolis, with a jumble of pipes, stairs and suspended air conditioners. An endless number of modules repeated over and over again, like skeletons, a kind of urban wreckage.

The lights went off, the conductor strode through the orchestra pit and greeted the public. Applause. The curtain went up. Revealing yet more Alcantara: the entire rear wall was Alcantara, pierced with a deep blue highlighting the metal structures in the foreground, the lights of the houses drowned out in the city.

There was the garret, and there were Rodolfo and Mimì.

In Act Two, the scene switches to Momus. The cafe is overflowing with life, fun and opportunity. Musetta – the friend of Marcello, the painter – is wearing a tasseled Alcantara jacket, and there is an acrobat performing wearing a large turban made of the same material. Alcantara is so versatile that it managed to be everything that the director wanted it to be.

Then the lights in the cafe go off, and snow starts to fall again in the streets of Paris. After life comes the announcement of death. Time goes by, Rodolfo and Mimì love each other and abandon each other, they get together and then part again, they suffer the pangs of love. Musetta lives with Marcello, while the winter gets colder and colder, and life gets harder. All borderline existences, that are lived out a step away from a farewell. Spring comes, and then winter returns. Musetta and Mimì have made good matches with two rich and insignificant characters; the four artists have returned to their garret. They have one herring and a piece of bread to dine on, but they sing and dance as if they were at a banquet. This is another example of pure cinema: joy sprinkled over the surface of life, to cover up pain. By contrast, the melodrama is represented by Musetta, who knocks at the door and says that she has met Mimì in the street: she was alone, and sick, and wanted to go back to Rodolfo. And that is pure Puccini: Mimì wishing to die at Rodolfo's side.

In the doorway, behind Musetta, Mimì herself appears. She comes in and sits down. Their friends leave them to their memory of that first night, and their first kiss, and that cold hand. Then Mimì dies. You know this right

La Bohème, Alcantara fringed jacket for Musetta, Teatro Regio Torino, Turin 2016

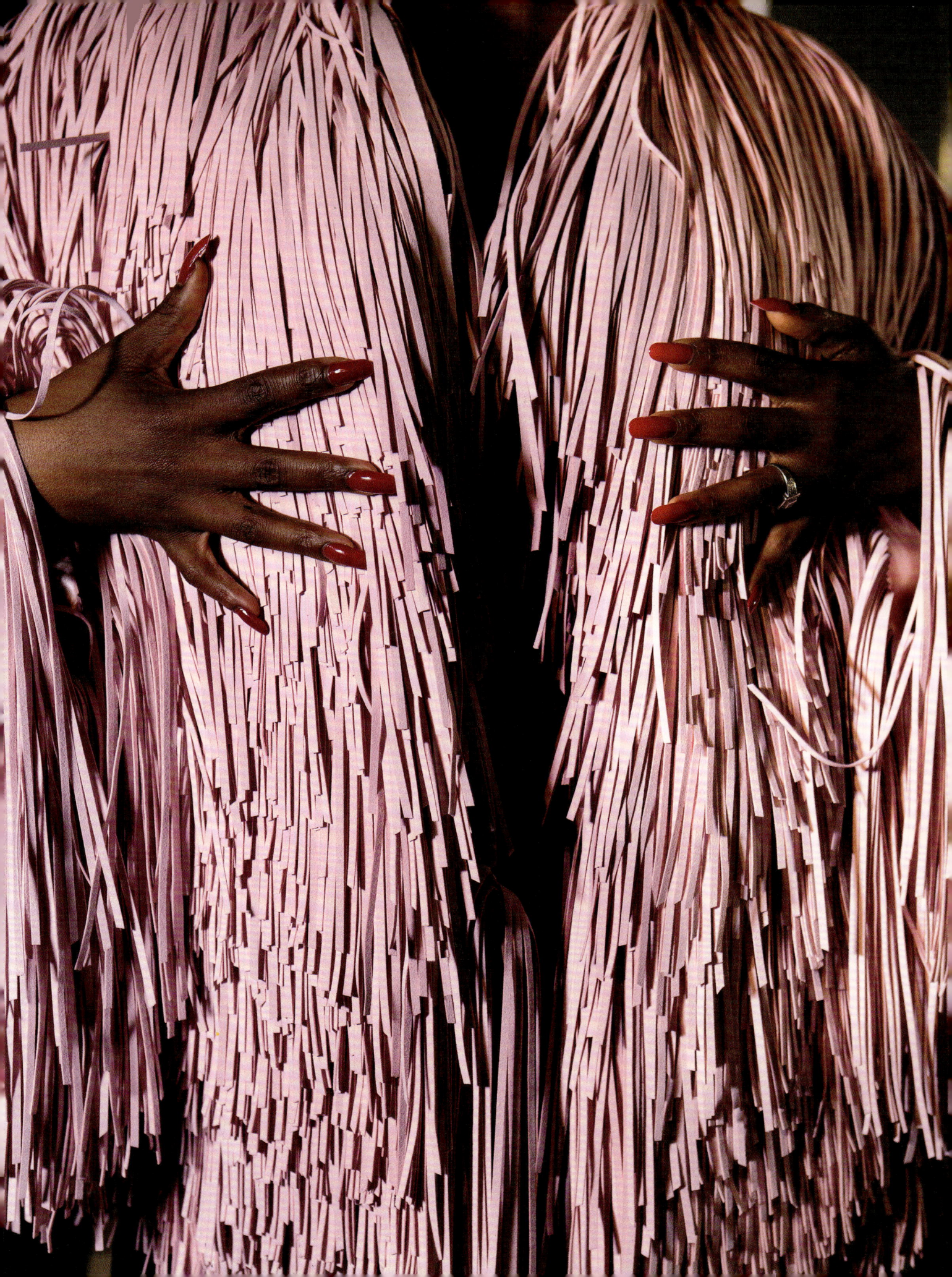

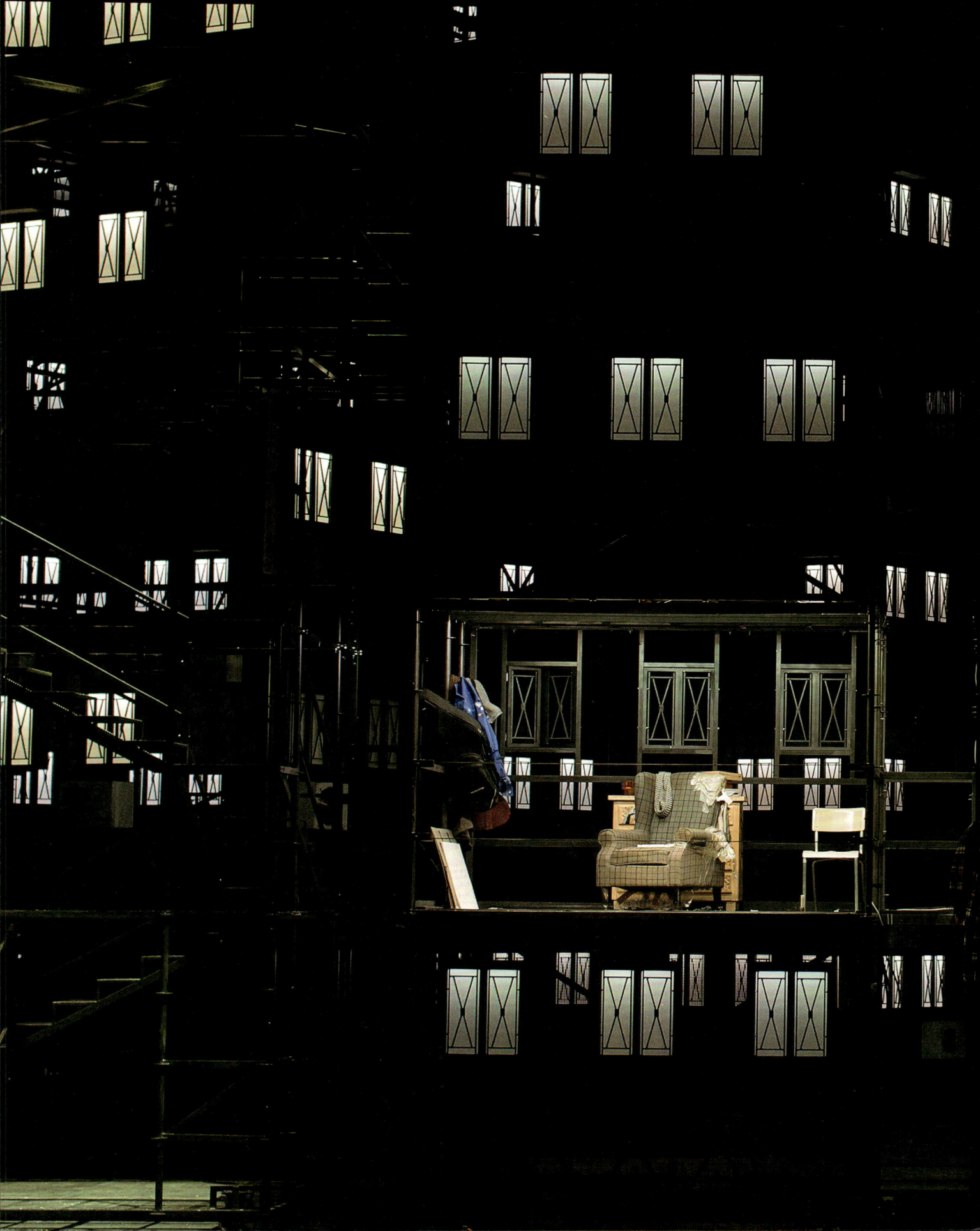

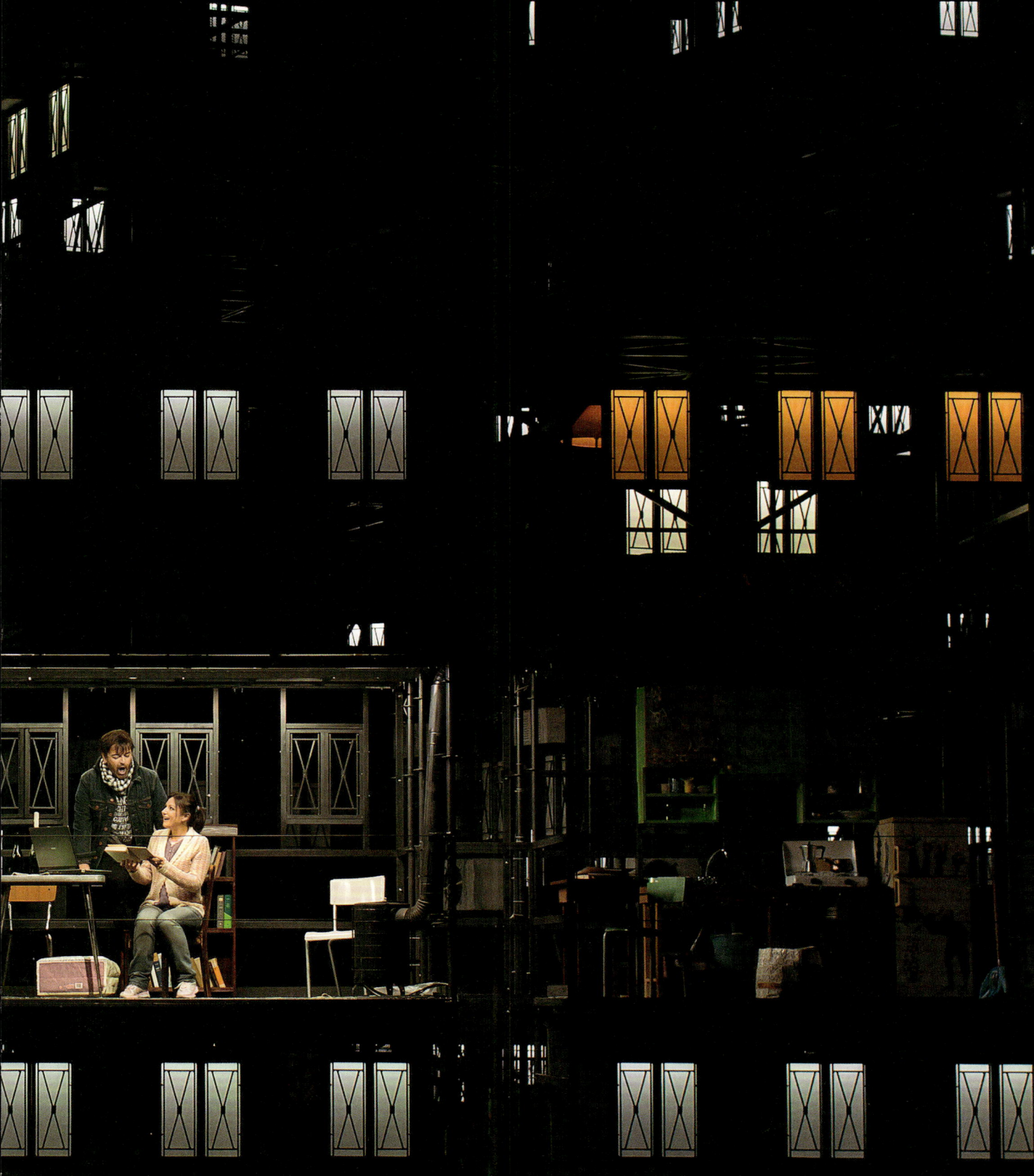

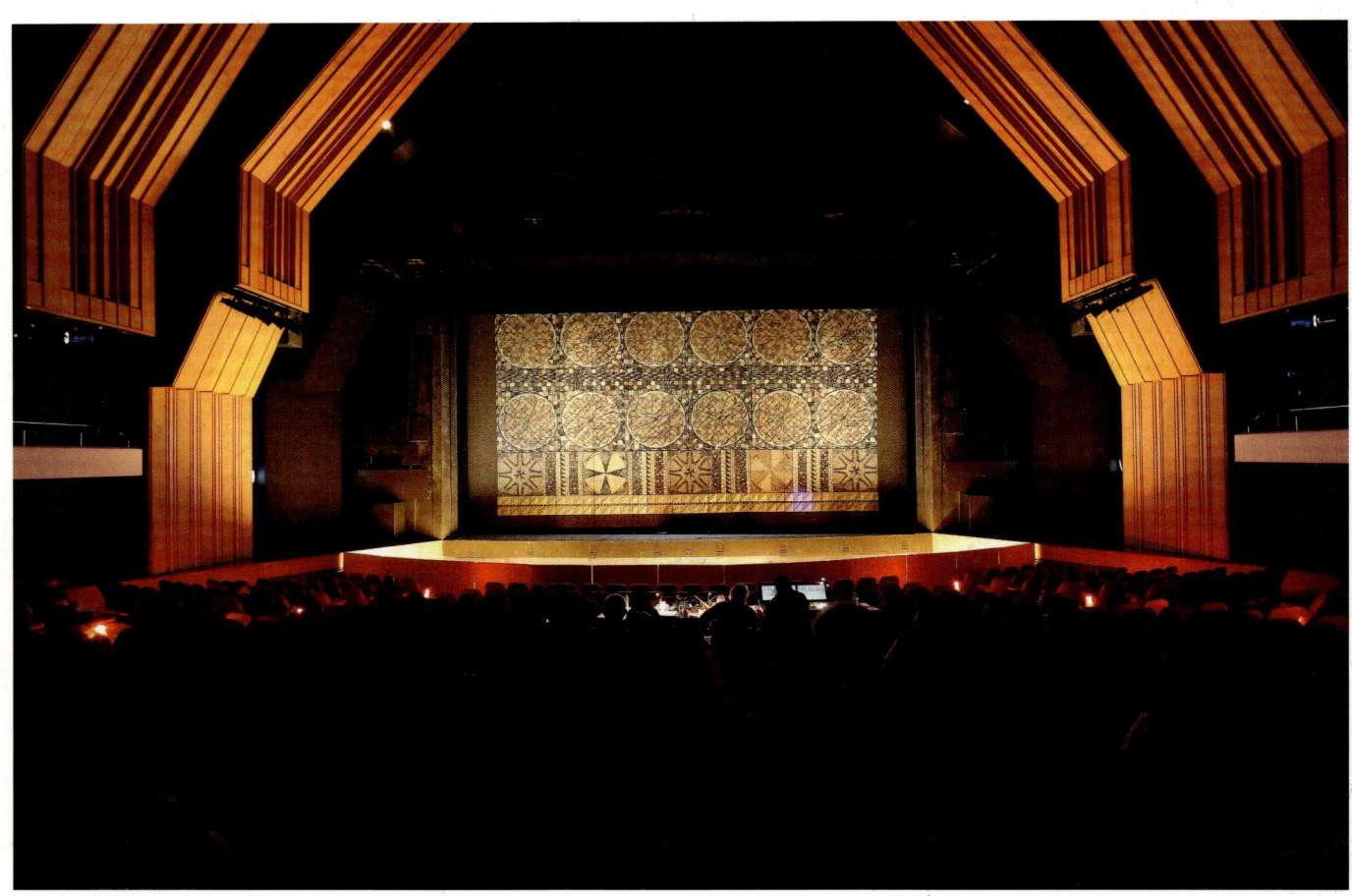

Simon Boccanegra, Alcantara curtain, Teatro Regio Torino production, Hong Kong 2016

from the start, but you cannot help crying. The Alcantara curtain comes down, the lights come on. Applause.

Before this première, Alcantara, the material, had already featured in Hong Kong with Verdi's *Simon Boccanegra*. After *La Bohème* it would appear again at the Regio in Turin with *Falstaff*, also by Verdi. In 2019 it would then go to Palermo, for a surprising production of *Turandot*. Puccini again, his last. Opera ending with melodrama, for real. If *La Bohème* was cinema, *Turandot* was the Internet, video games, and the metaverse. Written in Persia, set in Russia, reworked in Italy so as to be played out in China, *Turandot* is the modern fable of globalization. As the director, Fabio Cherstich, put it: "Ethnicity and nationality lose their meaning in the depiction of this fantastic, abstract and remote world, in which everything takes place at a distance of a *tweet*". The staging was an ongoing series of video installations creating a hybrid, virtual universe. Alcantara acted as a protagonist in the multifaceted, international dimension of reality, where every surface developed a narrative. The beautiful and sadistic Turandot loses her wager; the prince sings *All'alba vincerò*, and ends up winning for real. Love is the winner. A love that is eccentric, and as fluorescent as the Alcantara costumes made by the skilled hands of the costume department at Palermo's Teatro Massimo. Curtain down, house lights on, more applause.

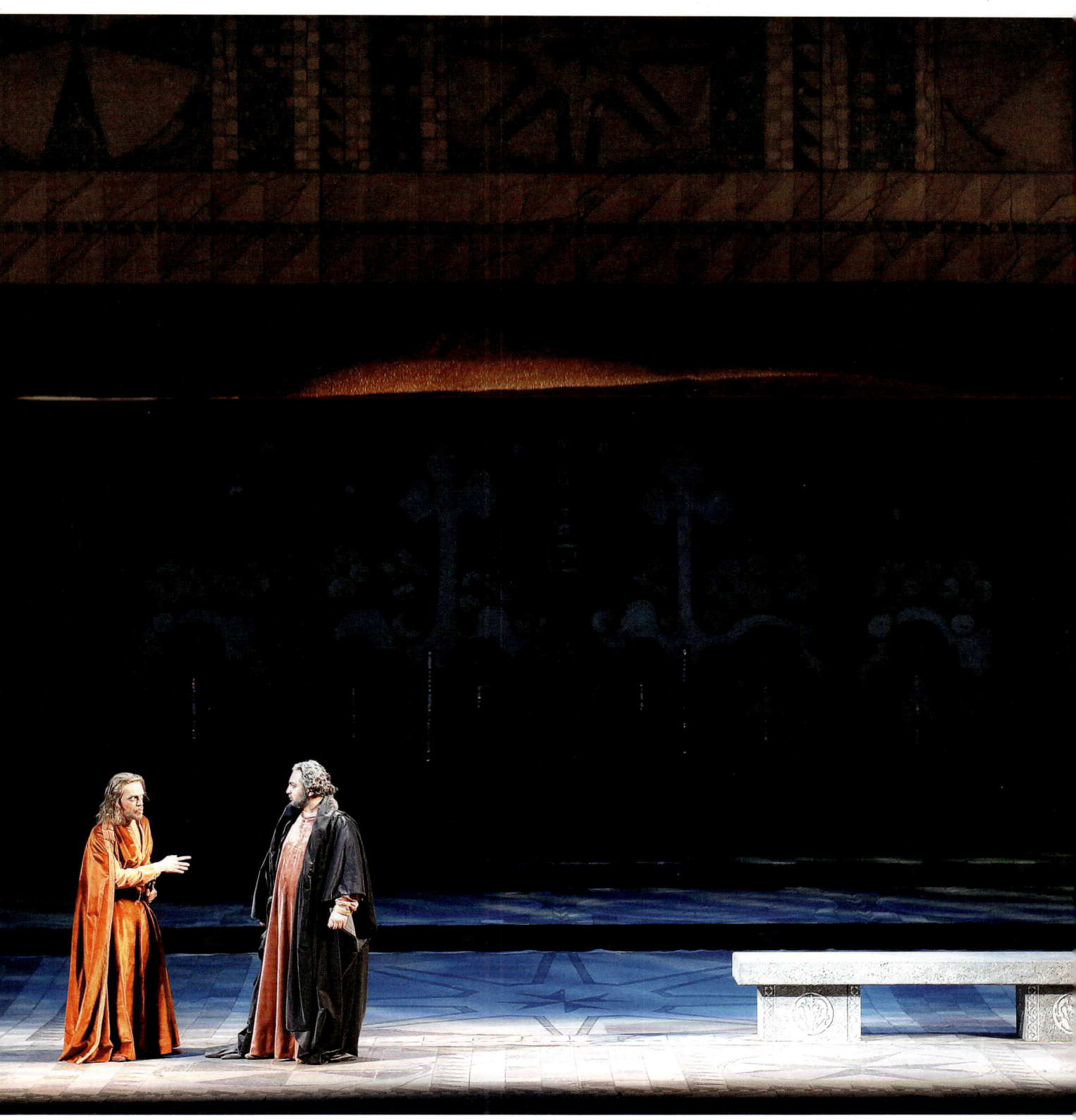

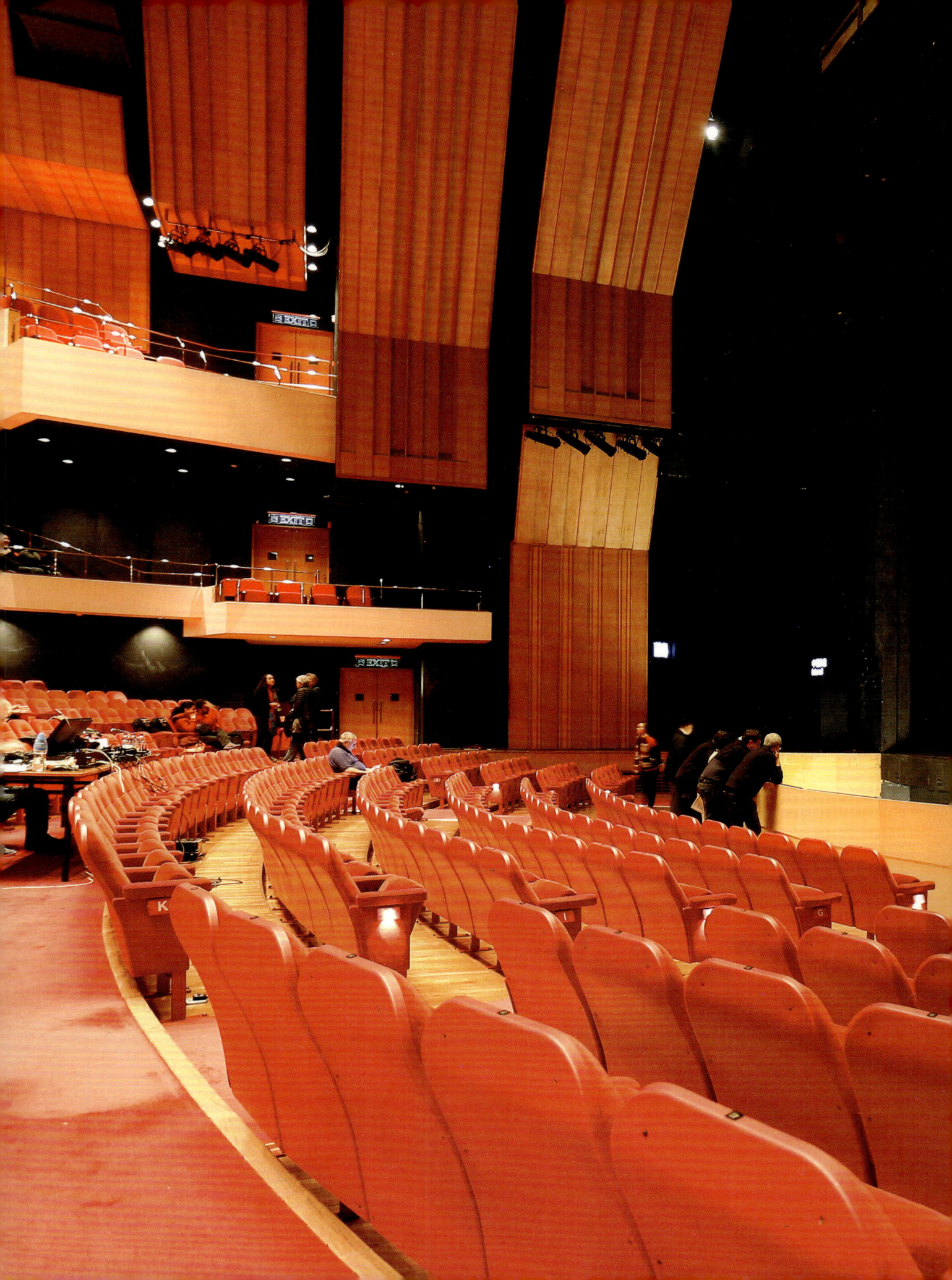

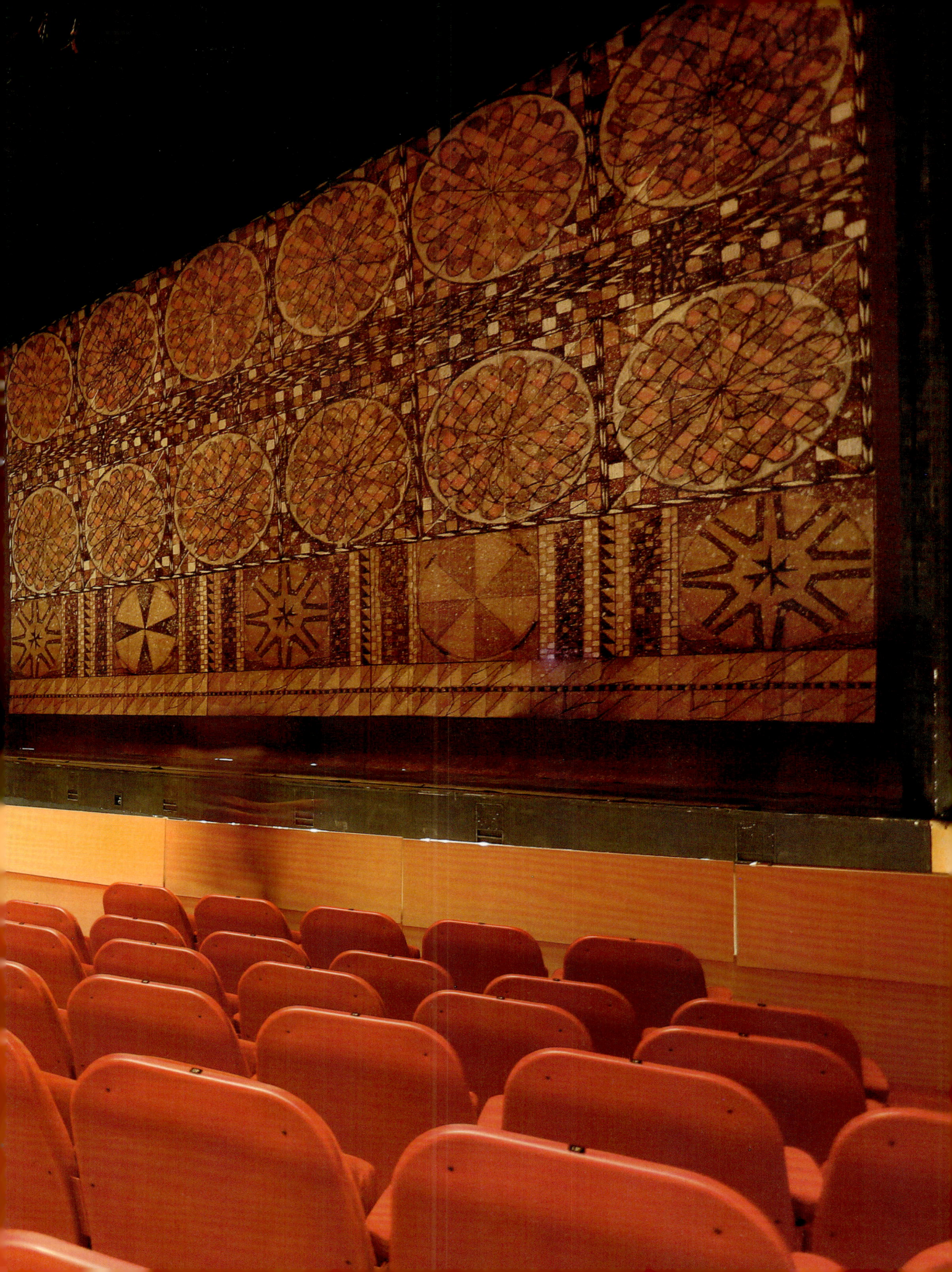

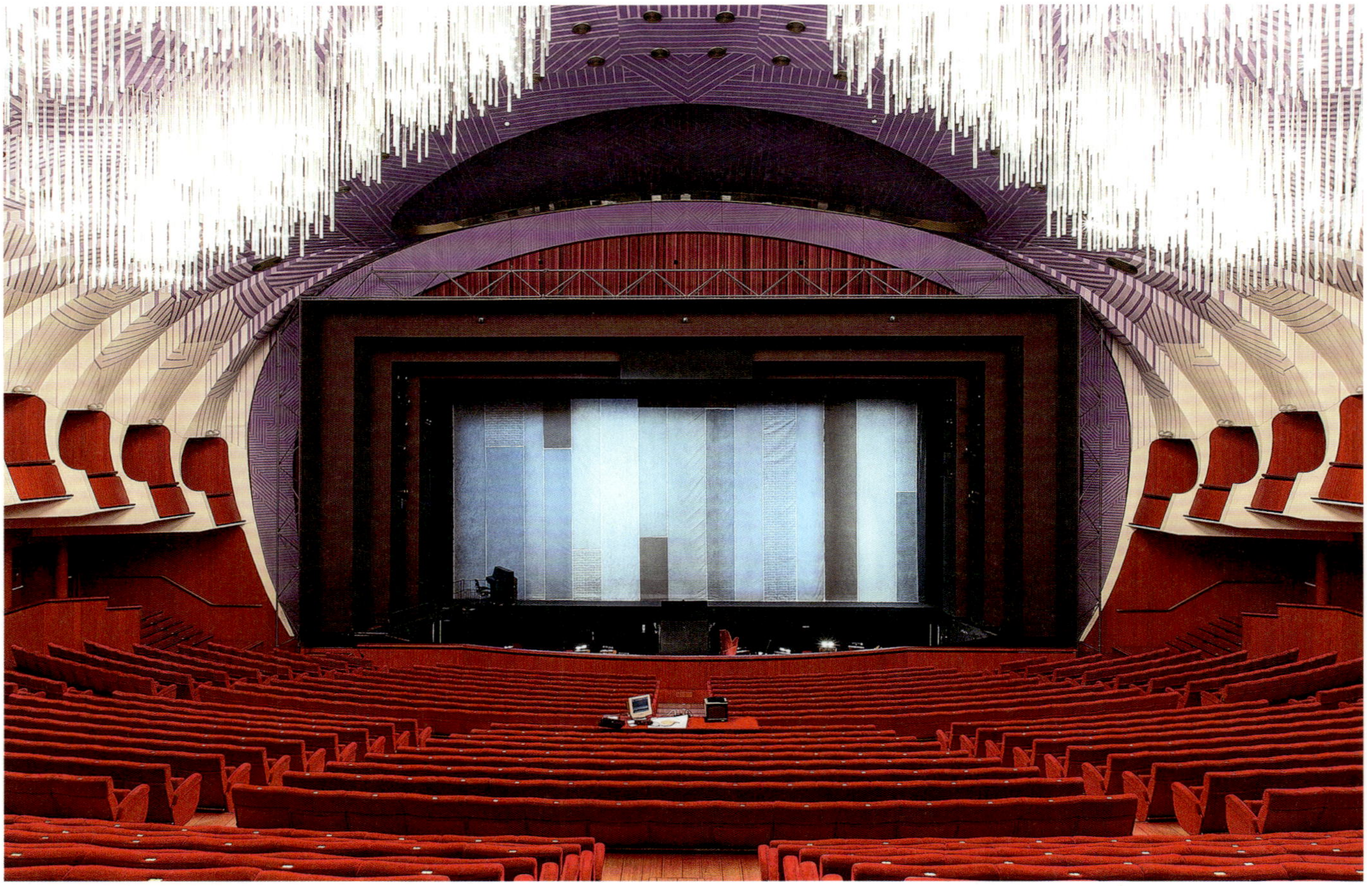

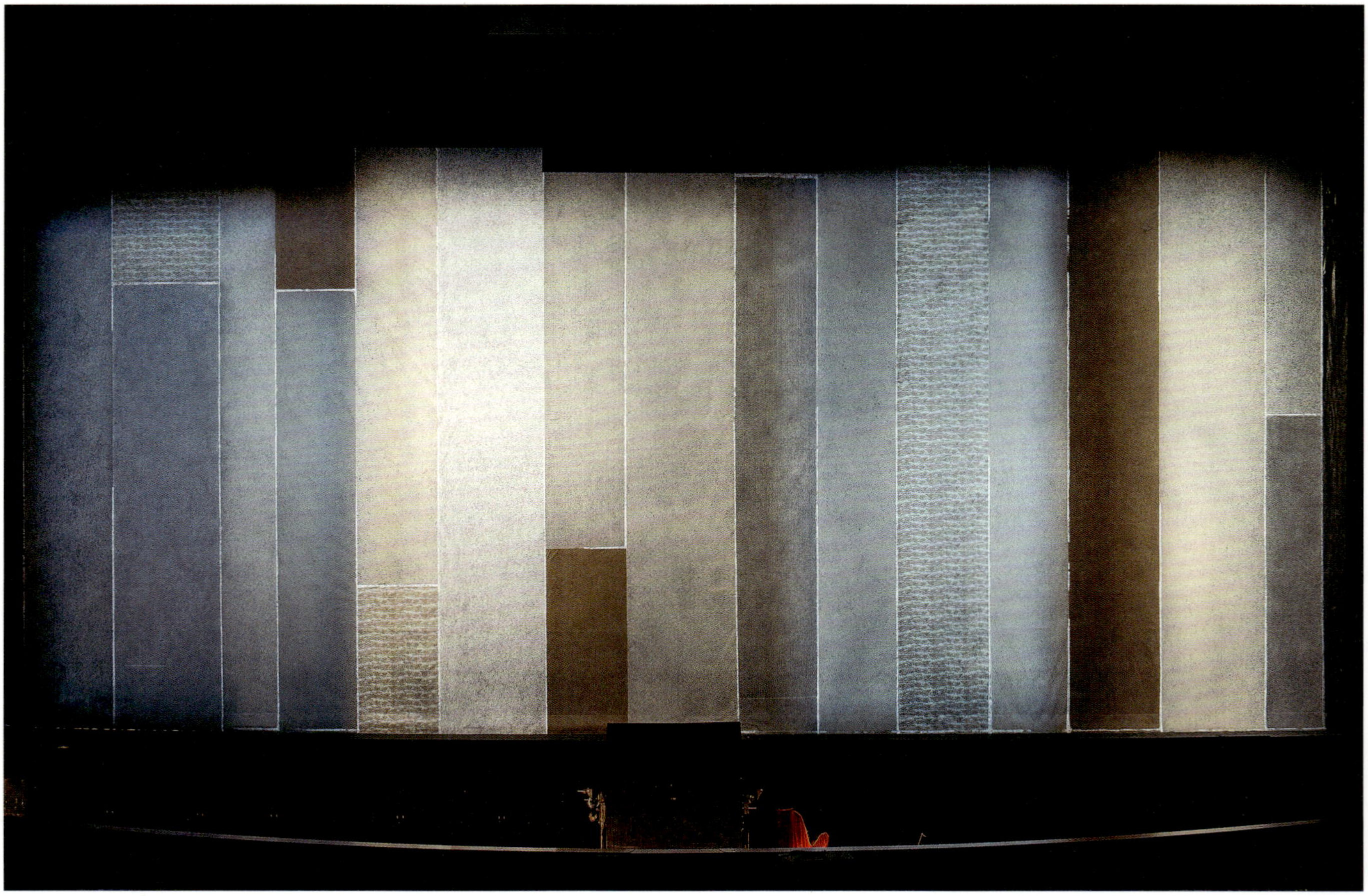

Falstaff, Alcantara curtain, Teatro Regio Torino, Turin 2017

Turandot, Teatro Massimo, Palermo 2019

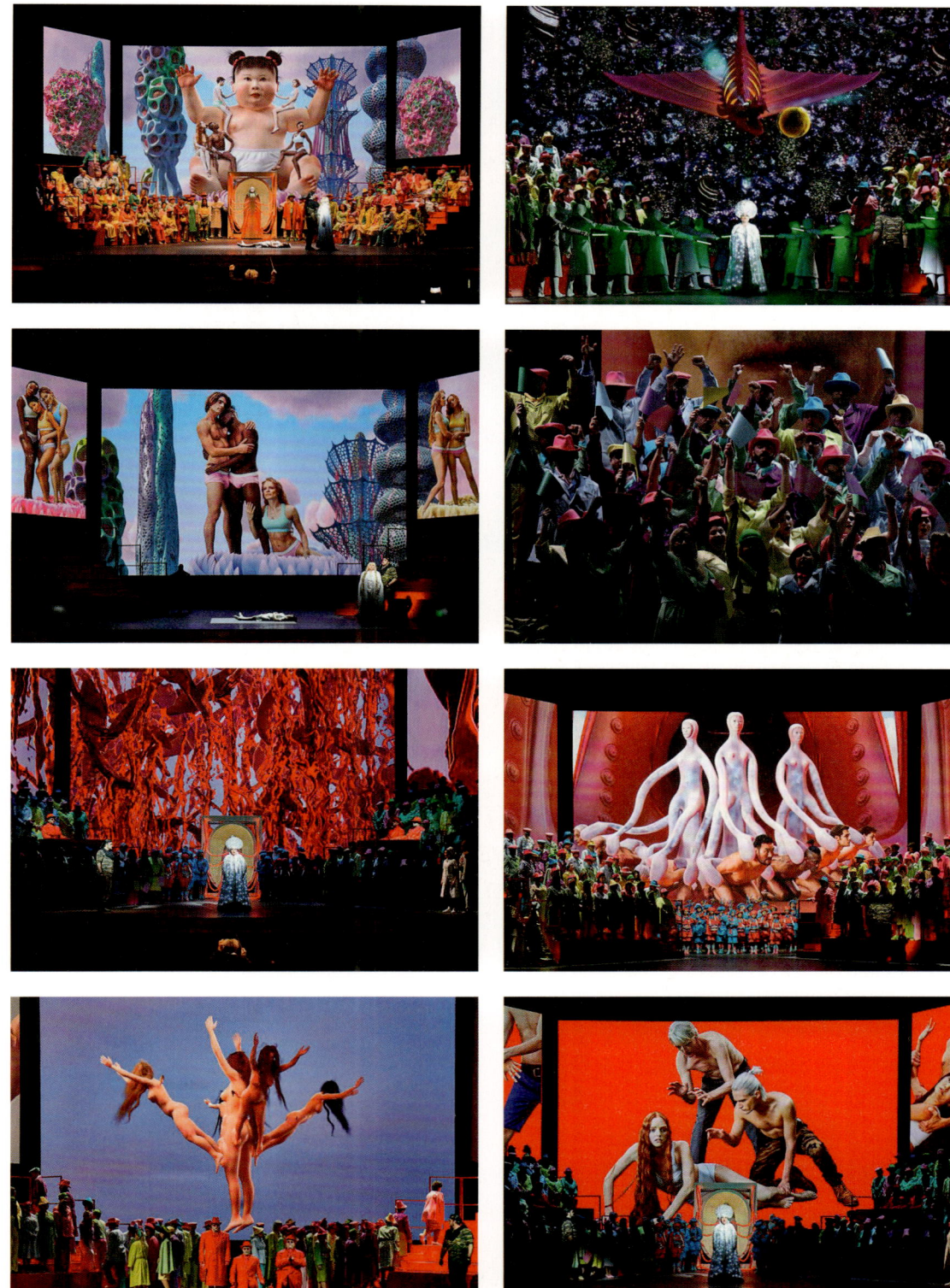

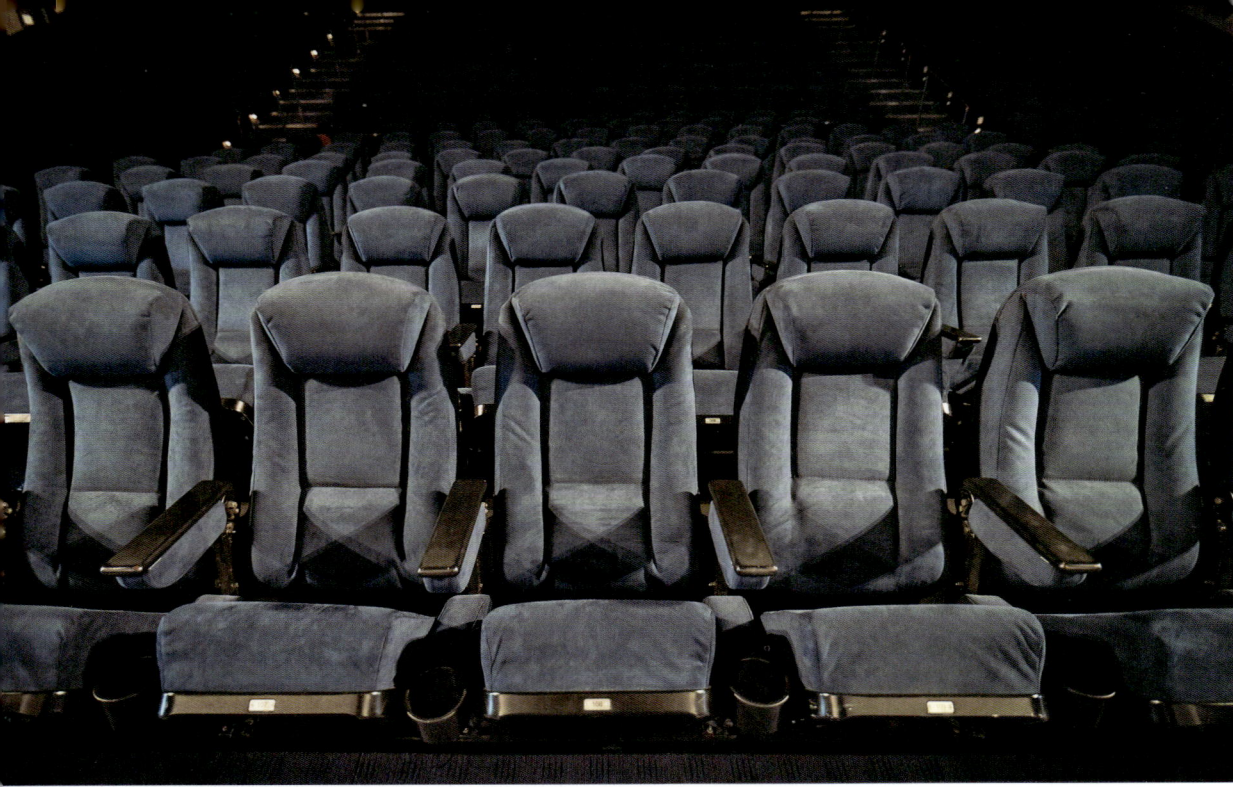

Egyptian Theatre,
Los Angeles 2016

*On the right and
following page*
Rebecca Moses,
"A Ride into Lifestyle",
Petersen Automotive
Museum,
Los Angeles 2017

Pagina 103
Rebecca Moses,
"Alcantara Drives
Dreams", Beijing 2018

These incursions into the world of opera might appear to be chance events, mere ad hoc collaborations. But instead they are further manifestations of Alcantara on its journey among the arts, and across the world. A versaltile material that inspires artists, designers, and directors. In opera and also in cinema. Indeed, also in 2016, Alcantara was in Los Angeles, for the refurbishment of Hollywood's legendary Egyptian Theatre. The company was responsible for the renovation of the stalls, creating new chairs in Alcantara for the 12th edition of the festival of Italian cinema. *Cinema Italian Style* was a tribute to Italy's very own film industry, in the temple of international cinema.

The following year, also in Los Angeles, Alcantara created an exclusive installation by Rebecca Moses at the Petersen Automotive Museum. A new event that once again marked a journey, into the worlds of cars, fashion and design, in an increasingly international dimension. The illustrator, designer, and artist Rebecca Moses created a series of large-scale objects that expanded Alcantara's infinite potential for expression.

Rebecca Moses' imagination gave rise to a maxi-car; the stiletto-heeled shoe wearing a steering wheel as if it was a buckle; the red carpet dress with train, on which rans a fairy-tale motorway leading to dreams.

In 2018 Alcantara and Rebecca Moses travelled to Beijing and created a new display in the prestigious setting of the Beijing Motor Show. An extraordinary international showcase, a never-ending source of inspiration for major auto designers. Alcantara asserted its status as an icon of Italian excellence in the world of international industry.

From opera to cinema, from art to fashion, the unlimited languages of Alcantara have adorned the most creative ideas.

House lights on. And, once again, more applause.

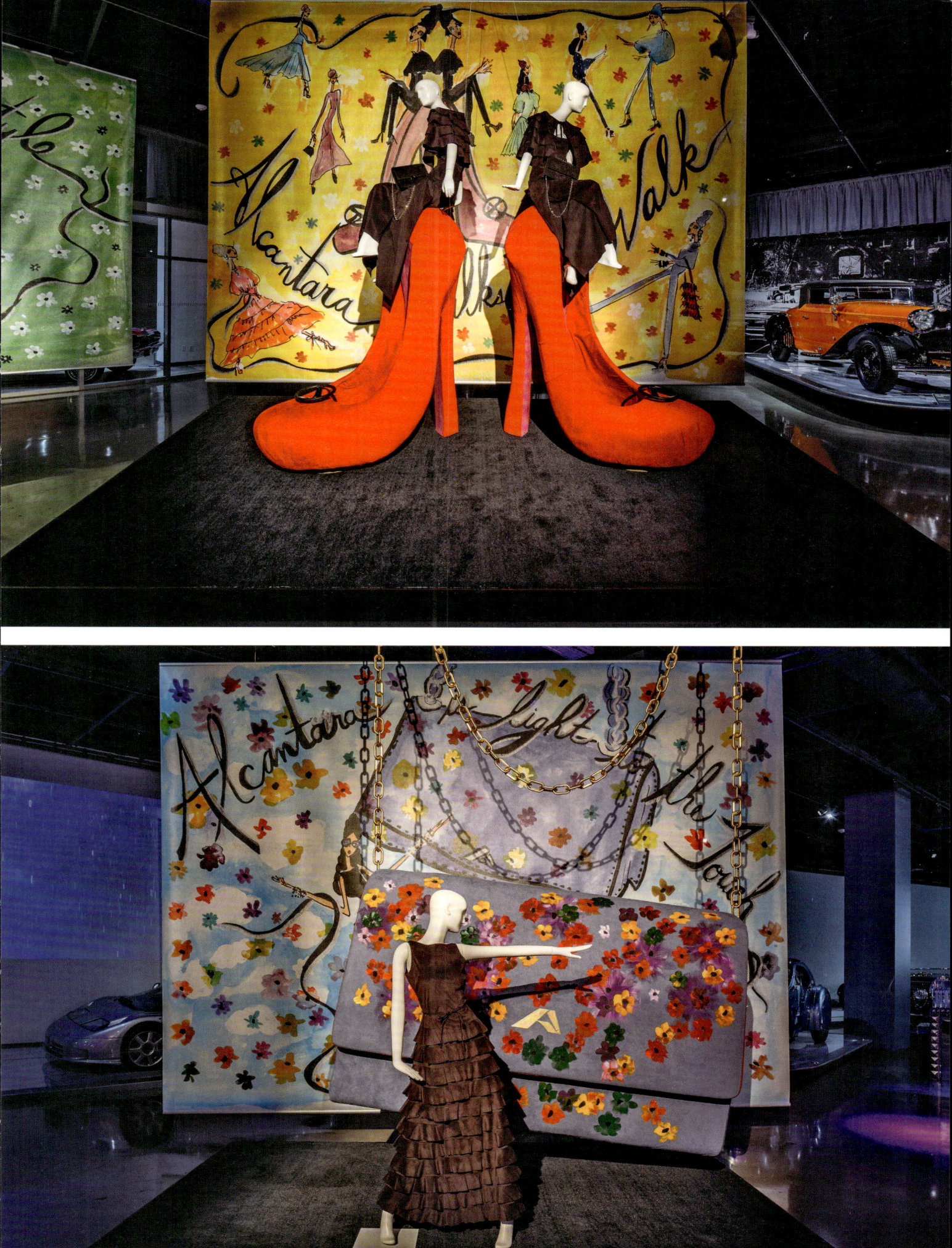

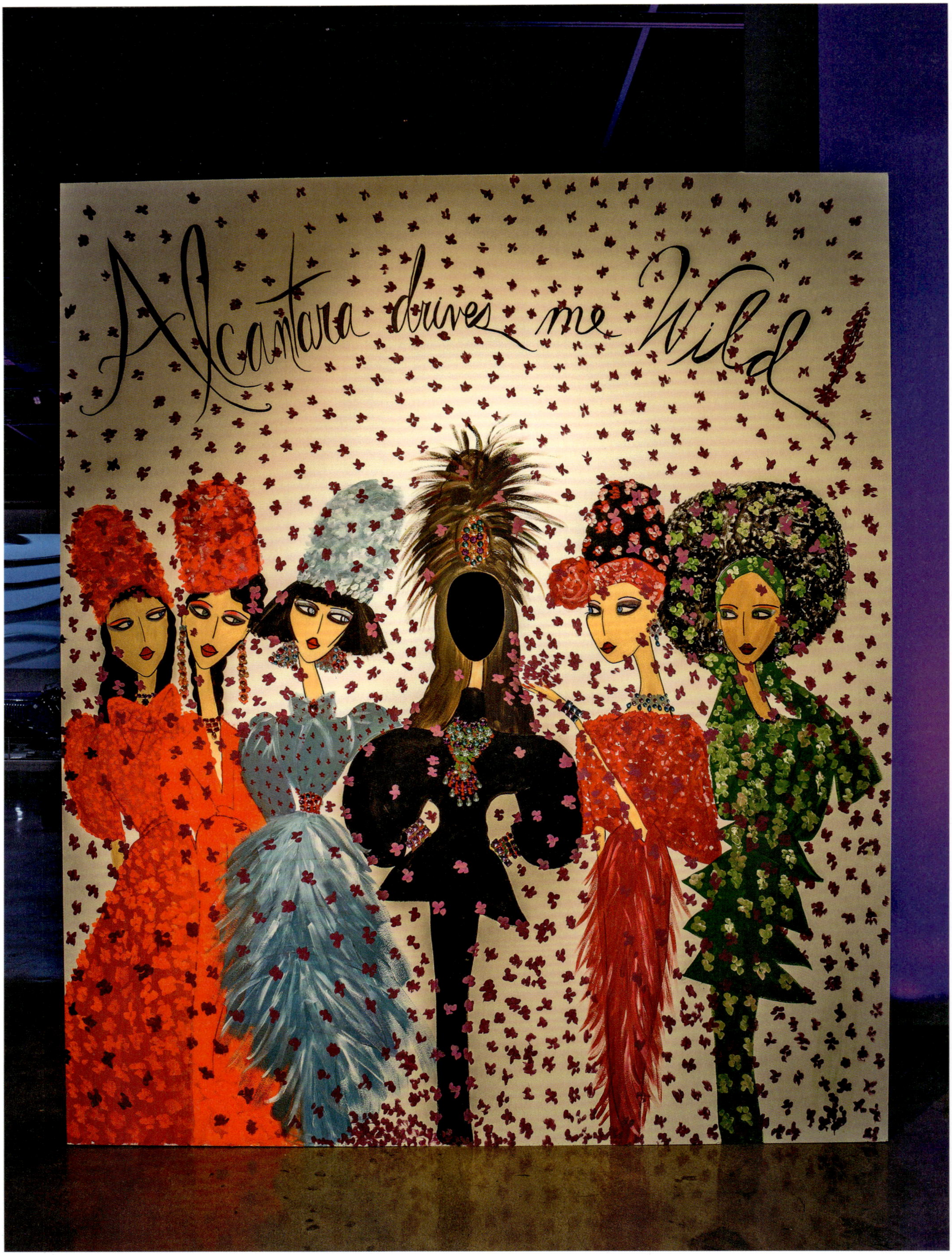

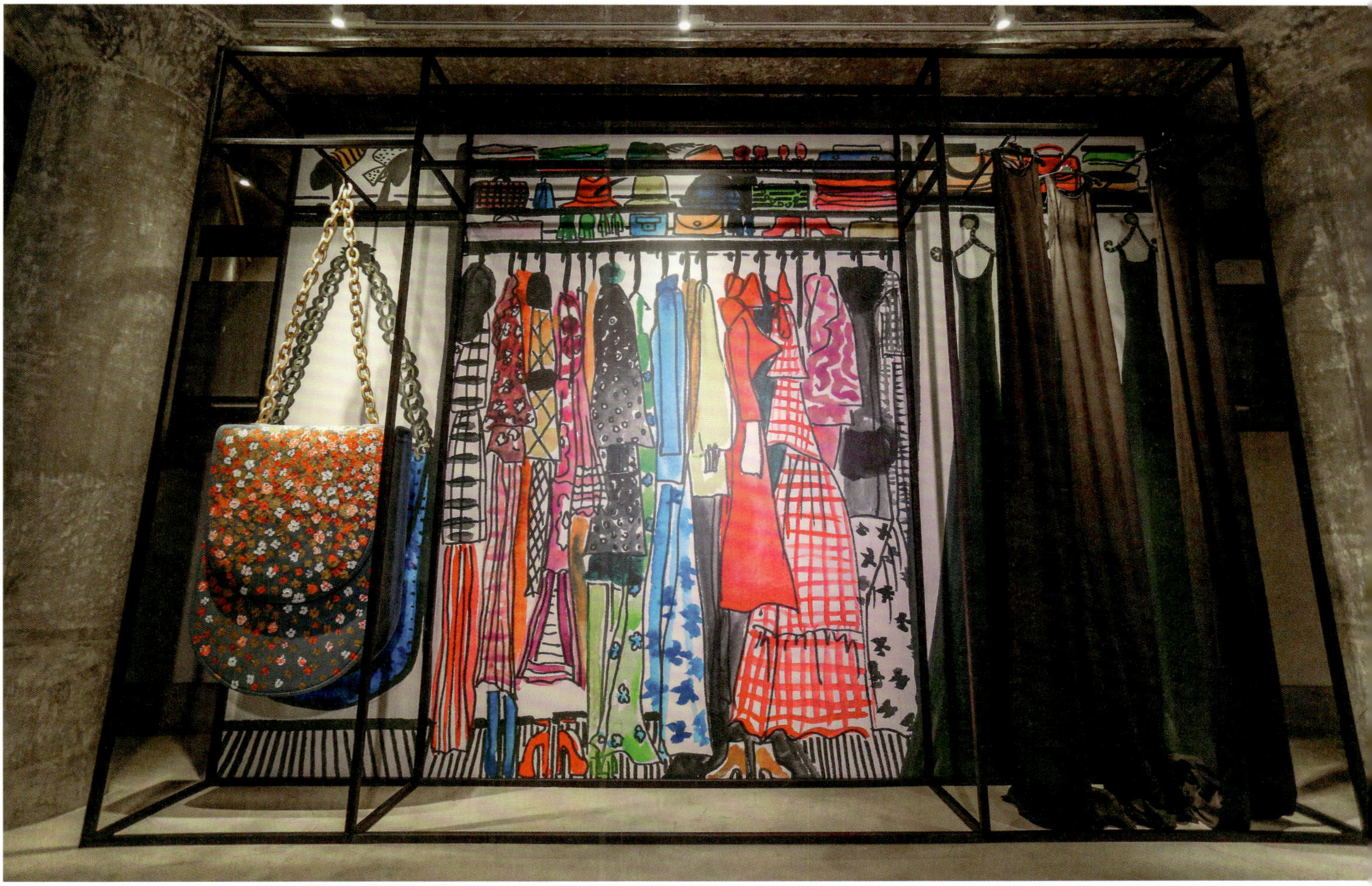

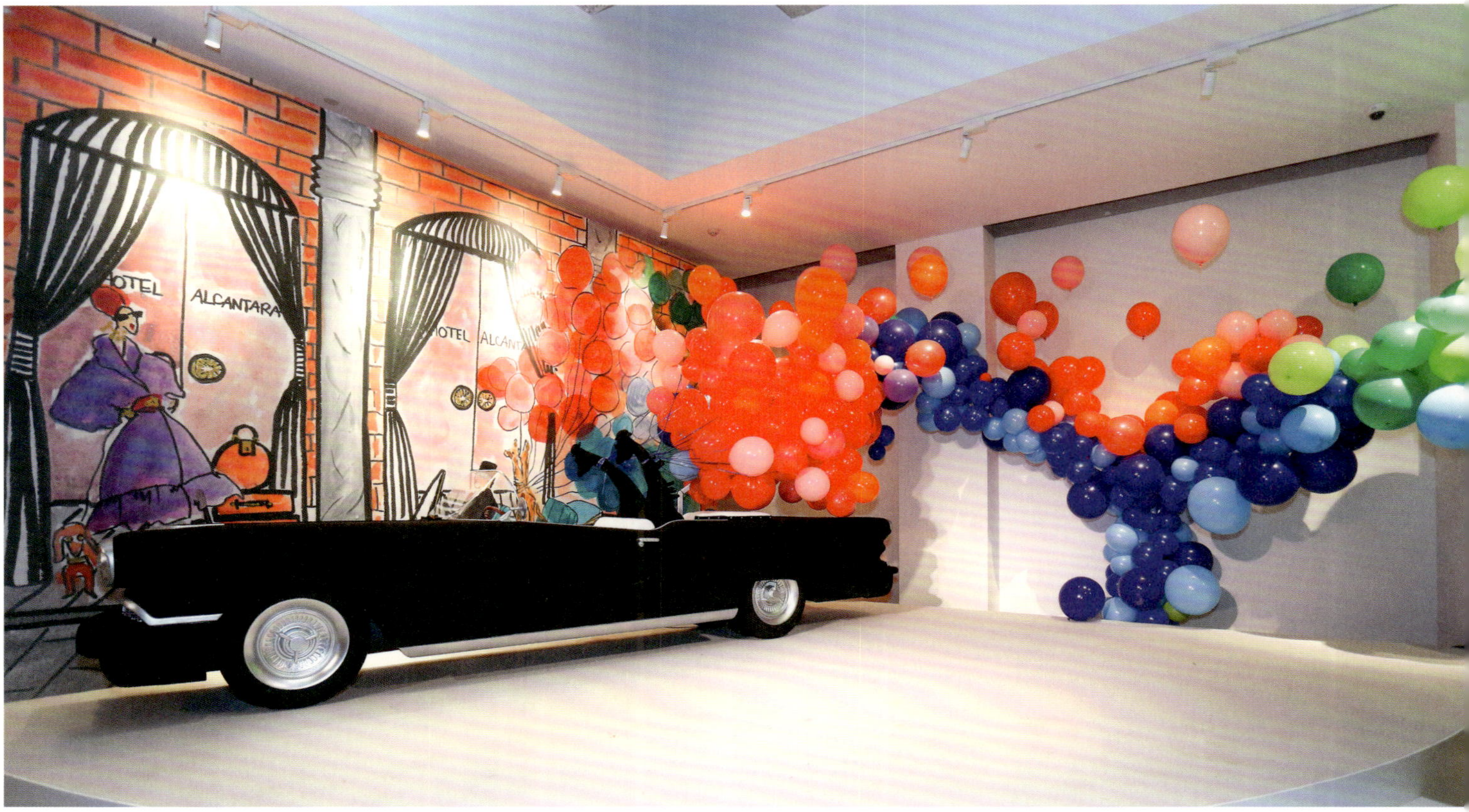

103

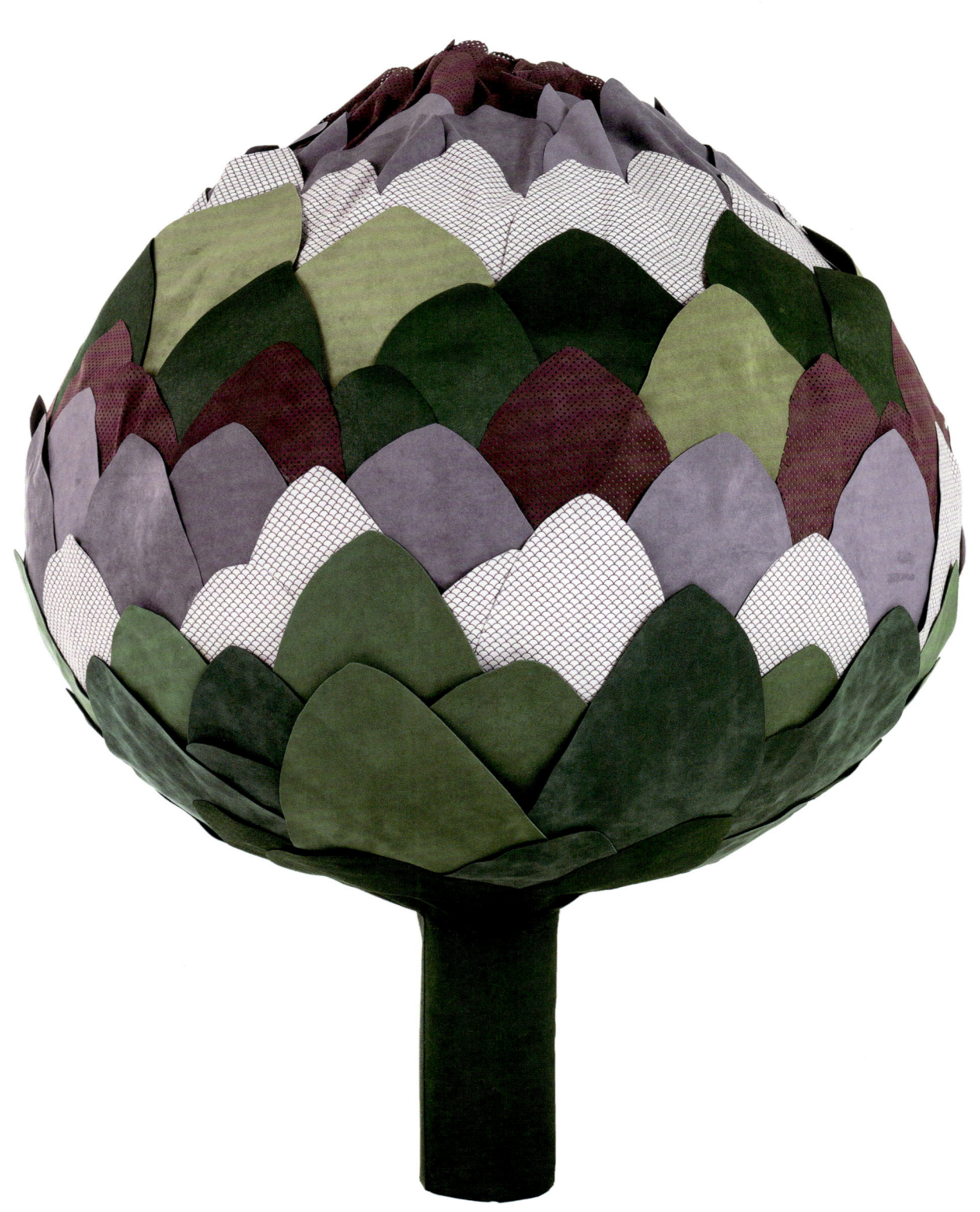

LOCAL ICONS

Roma caput mundi. From 2015 until 2017, Alcantara travelled across the world, setting out from Rome. It explored new routes from East to West, and from North to South.

In the first year, the designers' attention was focused on the capital, the hub of Italian style, and of the Italian way of life. In the Sala Scarpa at MAXXI, a huge merry-go-round was installed, with revolving objects in giant-size format redesigned in Alcantara. A huge artichoke and a wine flask – with the art material in place of the leaves and straw – referenced the aromas of typical restaurants in the Trastevere district, the kind that were very much part of the dolce vita. There are hand gestures, which in Italy often say more than words. If you don't understand them, you haven't understood anything.

Zanellato/Bortotto, *Carciofone*, "Local Icons", MAXXI Museum, Rome 2015

Paola Navone, *Dolce Vita*, "Local Icons", MAXXI Museum, Rome 2015

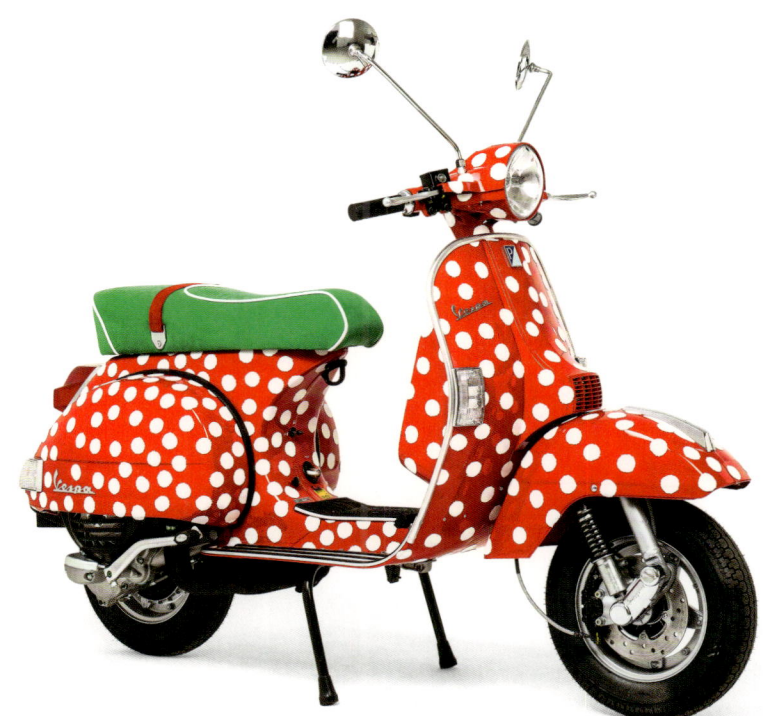

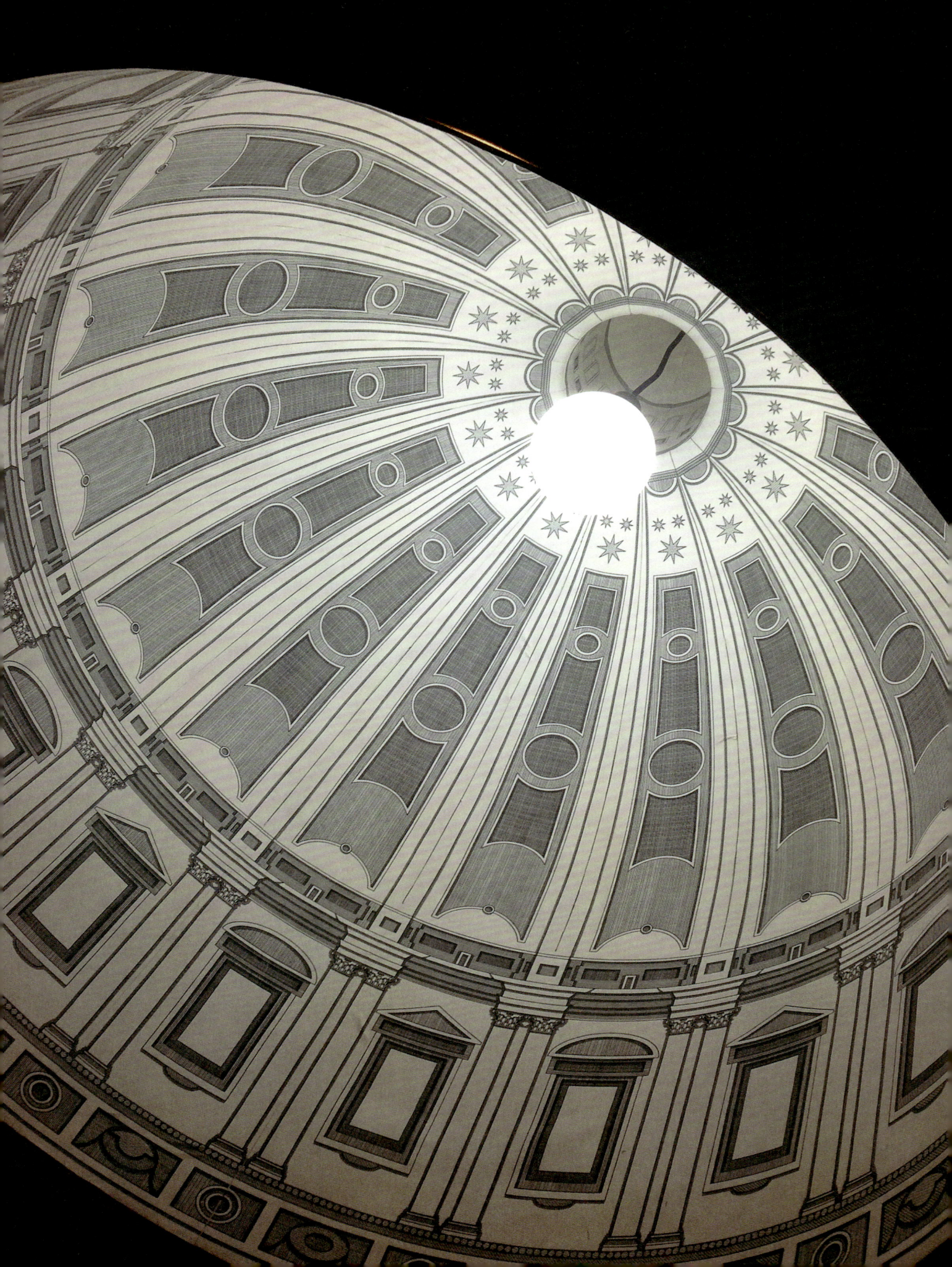

Lanzavecchia+Wai, *Cupolone*, "Local Icons", MAXXI Museum, Rome 2015

Neri&Hu, *Foreverhouse*, "Local Icons East/West", MAXXI Museum, Rome 2016

The Lanzavecchia+Wai studio created a series of lampshades in printed Alcantara, with architectural scenes from the Pantheon and St Peter's on the inside. As well as a Vespa in Alcantara in the colours of the Italian flag, and a manhole cover from Rome with the letters S.P.Q.R. – *Senatus PopulusQue Romanus*.

Are they crazy, these Romans? Maybe Obelix was right. Asterix found it very funny, like the public who played games and had fun, crowding around the carousel as it went round, round, and round again. Everyone held out their hands to touch the local icons. Alcantara works are made to be touched, just as cities are made to be lived in, and relationships experienced. Giovanna Melandri, the museum's President, told the press: "This project once again shows the validity of our creative collaboration. The public and private sectors must grow together, or else they perish. And we, together, have grown."

The following year the scenario became international, and followed the movements of the meridians, from East to West. It began with the rising of the sun, and ended at sunset. *Oriens* means the origin, rise, while *occidere* indicates a journey downwards. Whereas the sun rises on one side, on the other side it descends. And in the middle is the day. The lives of billions of people, languages, cultures. Conceptually, Alcantara overlays the world, and inspires designers and artists from Shanghai, Singapore, Hong Kong, Taipei

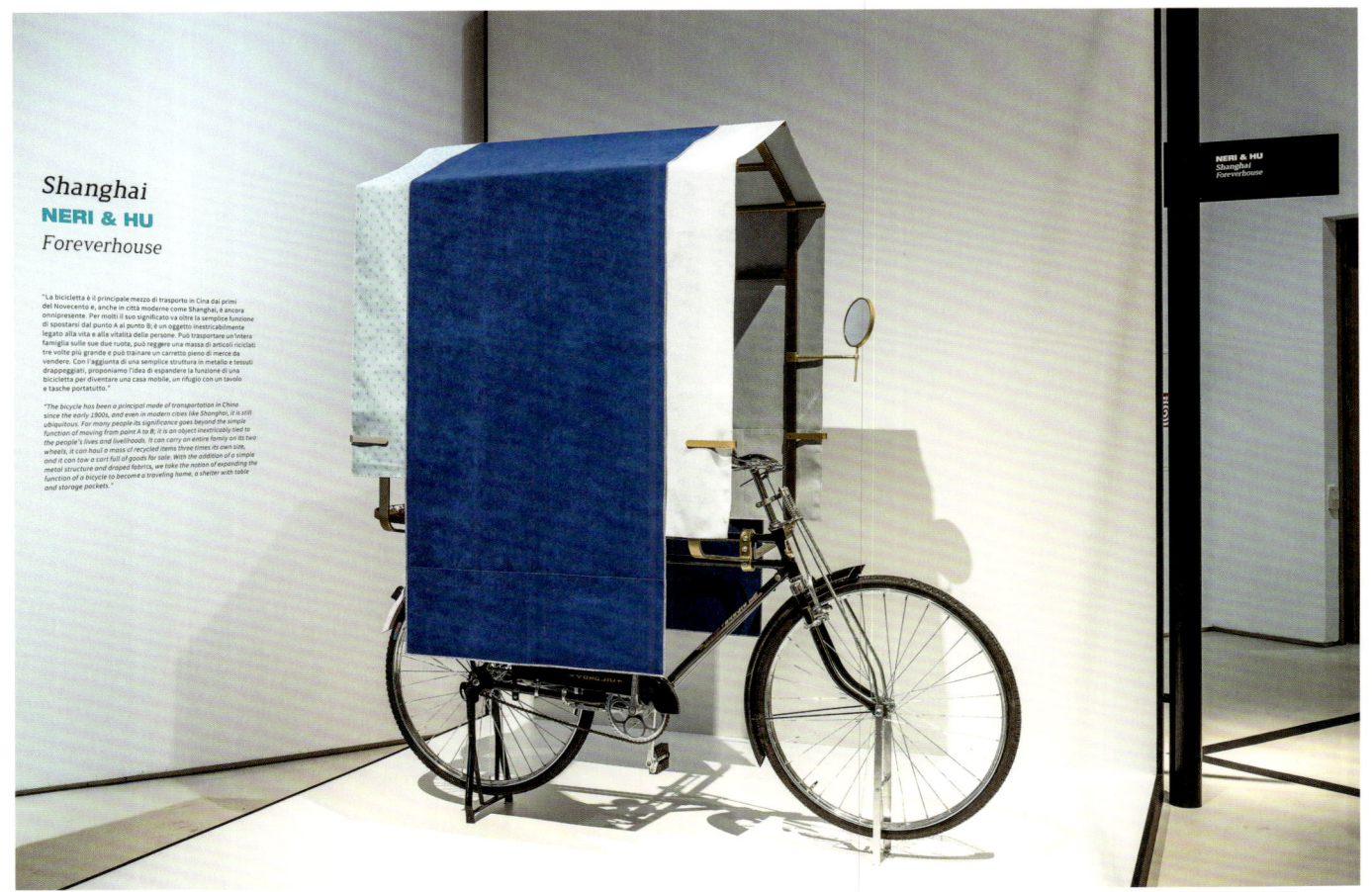

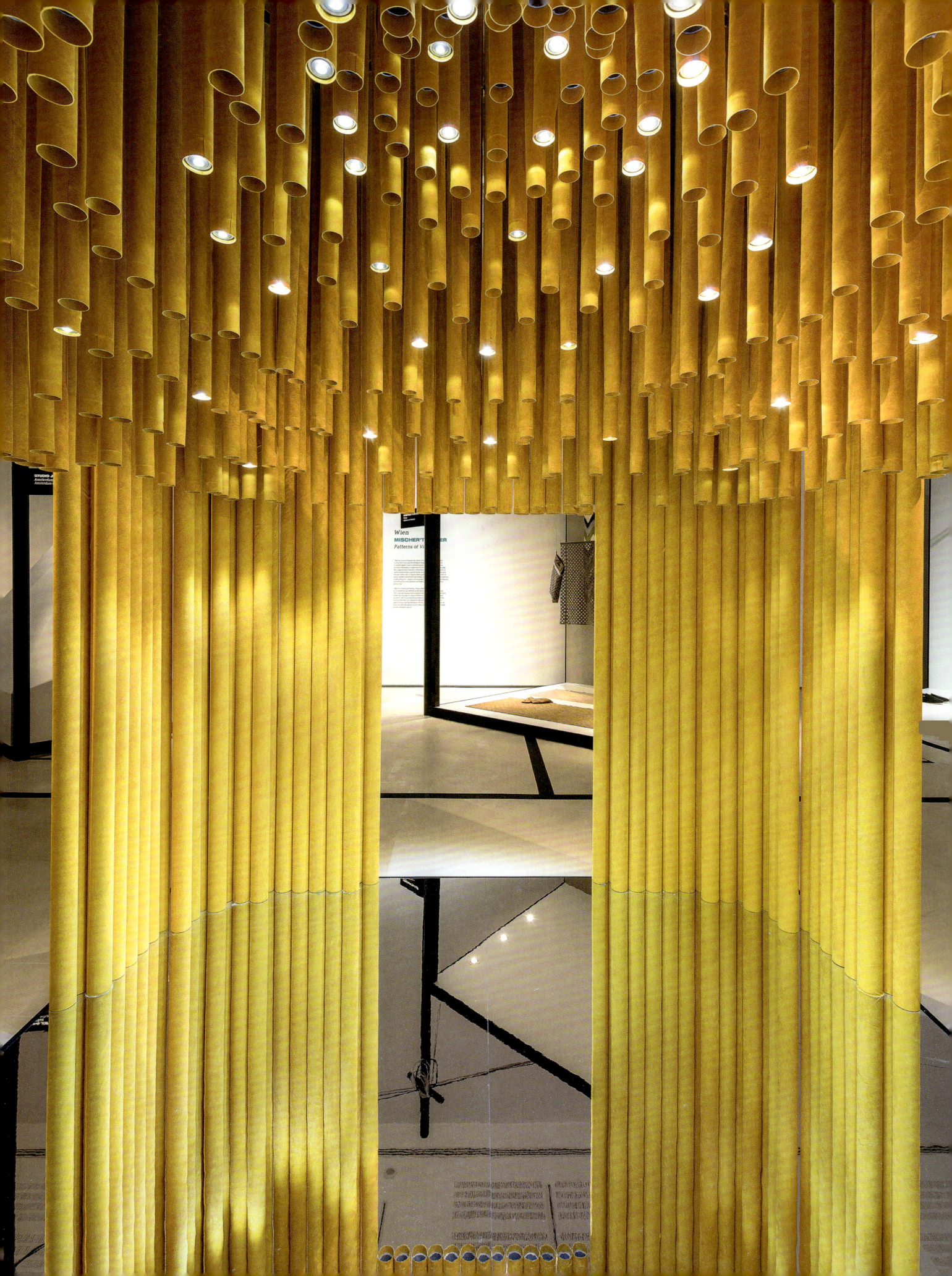

Poetic Lab, *London Tube Chandelier*, "Local Icons East/West", MAXXI Museum, Rome 2016

Steven Haulenbeek, *Chicago/City of the Big Shoulders*, "Local Icons Urban Landscapes North/South", MAXXI Museum, Rome 2017

and Jakarta, extending all the way to Paris, London, Amsterdam, Vienna, and Copenhagen. One is struck by the vision of Neri&Hu, who devised an Alcantara version of the bicycle, that mode of transport that continues to hurtle to and fro through the streets of Shanghai. Today it is still everywhere you look: a travelling home, an office, an object totally bound up with peoples' lives and their vitality. On a frame they assembled a self-standing structure that they covered in Alcantara. It really was a home, with walls and a roof. Pockets everywhere to contain objects. A bicycle can also become a refuge. It offers shelter from the rain, it can carry a whole family, it bears an enormous weight. A contemporary icon, as it was centuries ago. The London installation was also stunning, featuring an Alcantara lampshade subdivided into a myriad light tubes. These were the countless eyes that look at the city and its underground rail system. Millions of people who note the old and the modern. Each person sees with their own eyes; the meaning of each thing changes with the changing point of view of the observer. Thus, viewed side-on, the Alcantara lampshade created an abstract, ever-changing profile of the city; viewed from below, it became an avalanche of tubes of light spilling out straight from the bowels of the metropolis, like the trains that emerge from out of the darkness and approach the station; they break out of the map of the London Underground, a graphic icon of the British capital.

The third year, the journey ended along the parallels, from North to South. The cities were Stockholm, Helsinki, Chicago and New York, and then down towards Santiago, Rio de Janeiro, Mexico City and Dakar.

The Alcantara Friesian cows advancing in front of the city of Chicago become fixed in one's memory. One of the most modern American

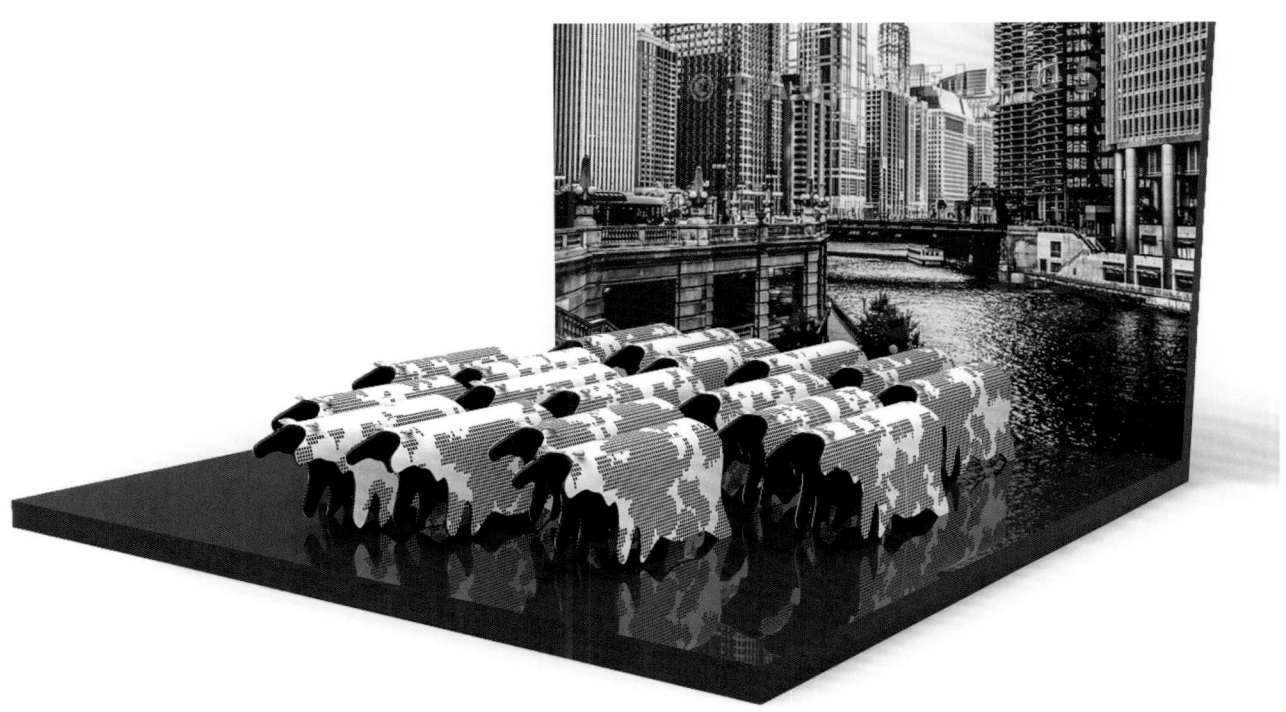

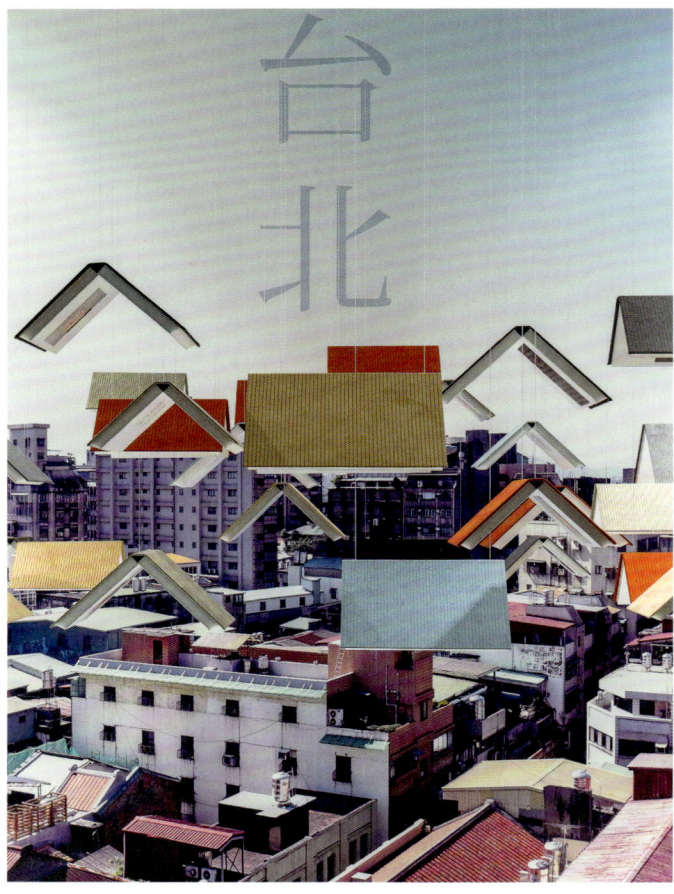 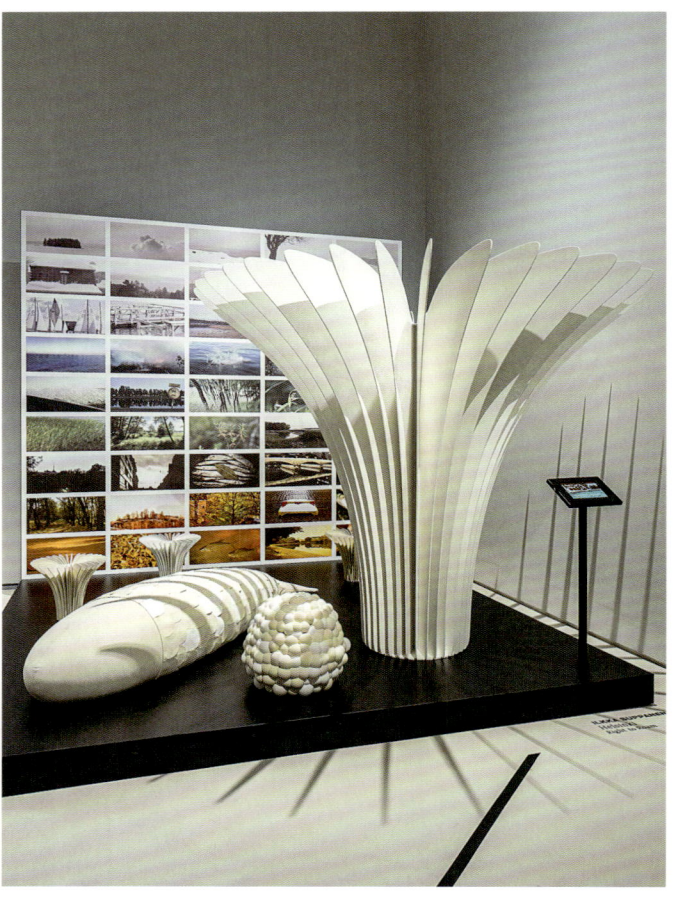

Poetic Lab, *Taipei Roofs*, "Local Icons East/West", MAXXI Museum, Rome 2016

Illkka Suppanen, *Helsinki/Right to Roam*, "Local Icons Urban Landscapes North/South", MAXXI Museum, Rome 2017

metropolises owes its image to the reconstruction following the great fire at the end of the 19th century. Legend has it that it was caused by the cattle themselves, after they tipped over an oil lamp. *Ex malo bonum*, one might say, to return for a moment to Rome and the Latins: Chicago was reborn, the first city in the world to develop by discovering the vertical dimension, with its skyscrapers designed by Louis Sullivan, icons of urban modernity.

The cultures of the world, viewed through the lens of Alcantara, become one great visual and conceptual cue or prompt, an invitation to discovery, and inclusion.

"Local Icons" are watchwords in a universal vision which only a material as adaptable as Alcantara, able to speak an unlimited number of languages, manages to express through art and design.

Gustavo Martini, *Rio de Janeiro/Altinha*, "Local Icons Urban Landscapes North/South", MAXXI Museum, Rome 2017

Liliana Ovalle, *Mexico City/Underlay, overlay*, "Local Icons Urban Landscapes North/South", MAXXI Museum, Rome 2017

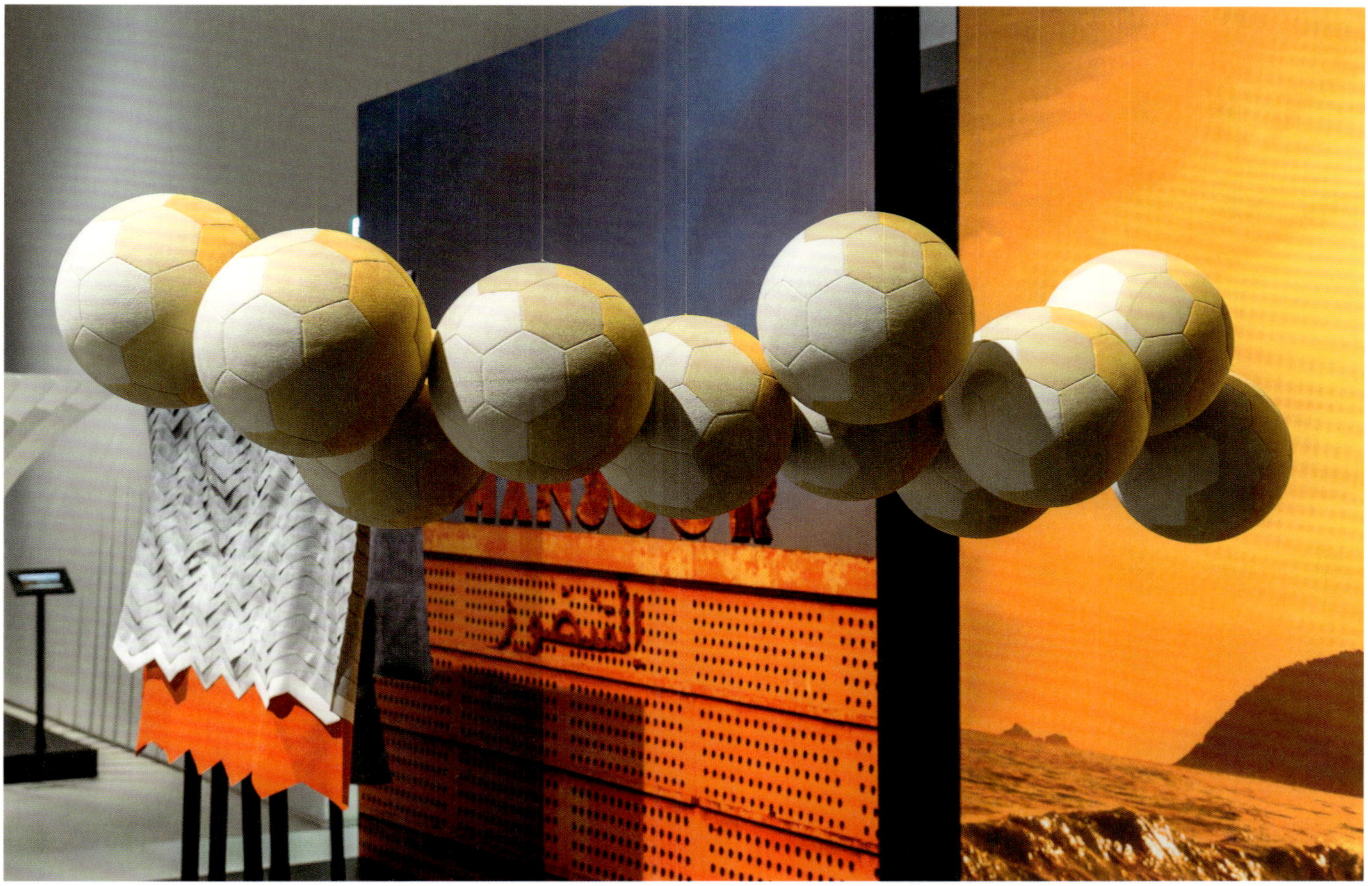

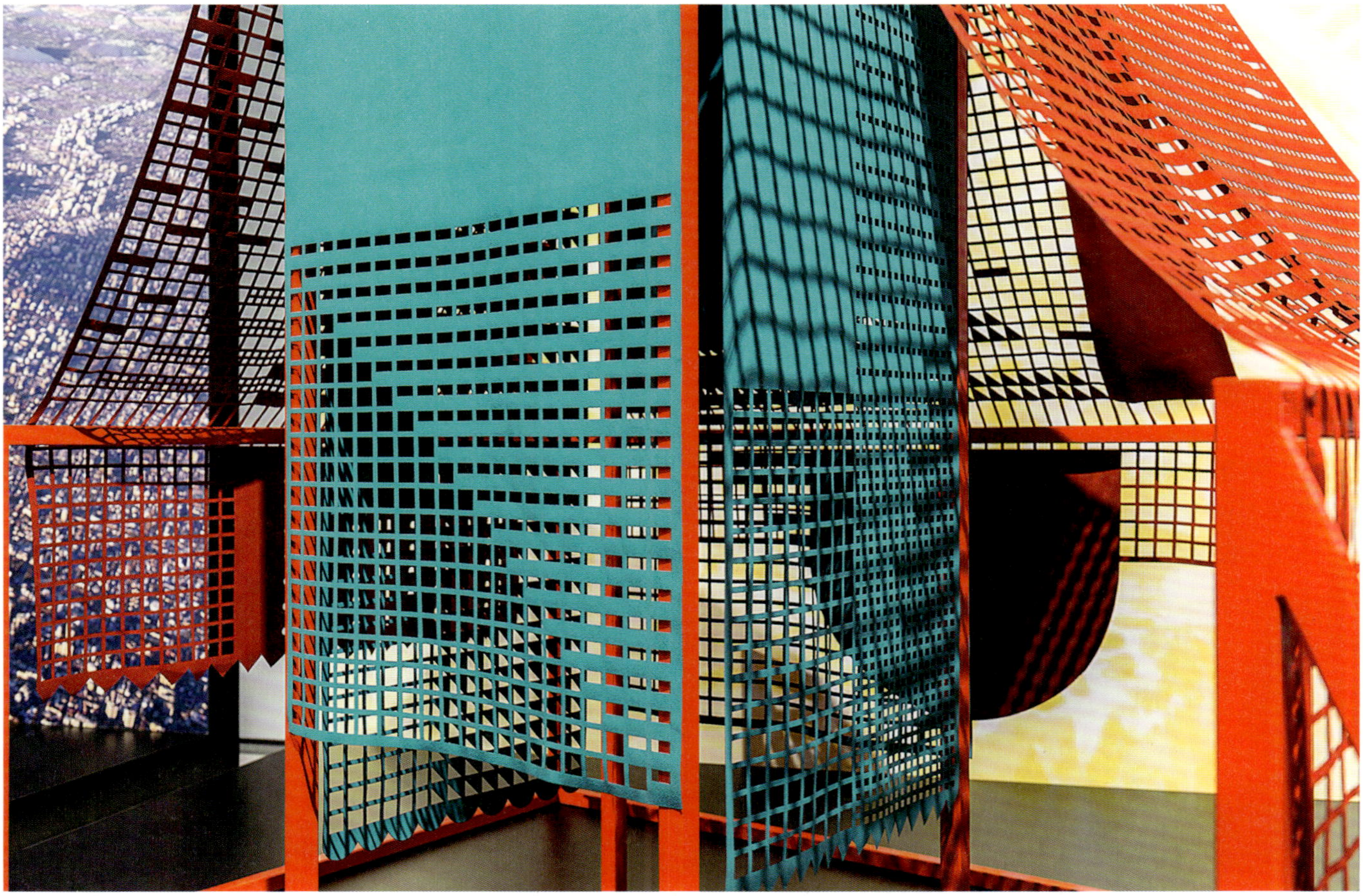

111

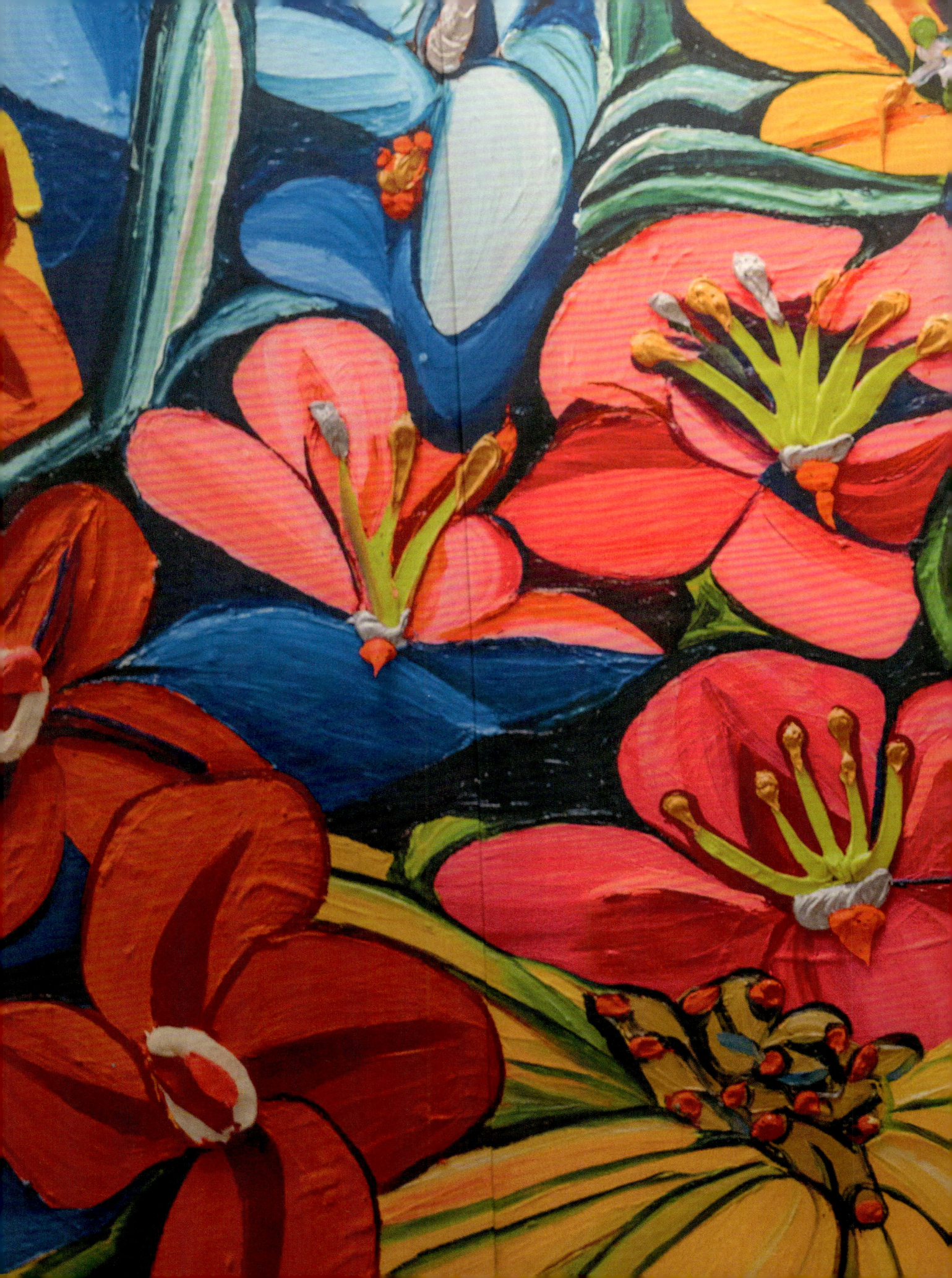

THE SOUND OF ALCANTARA

Alcantara returned to Palazzo Reale. Instead of lightly ascending the grand staircase, it erupted into the Prince's Apartment. Conceptually speaking, it broke down the walls and landed in the form of a spacecraft. An Alcantara spaceship, created by Nanda Vigo, and equipped with devices capable of extracting the extraordinary from everyday life. The exhibition, curated by Massimo Torrigiani and Davide Quadrio, was entitled "Fantasy Access Code". An explicit reference to the words of Gianni Rodari, when he taught people how to construct stories by connecting thoughts, realities, and dreams together. The Palace interiors are not simple settings, they are veritable narrative environments. As the visit unfolded, surprising worlds came to light, generated by the relationship between the locations and the works. Brand new glimpses into time and space.

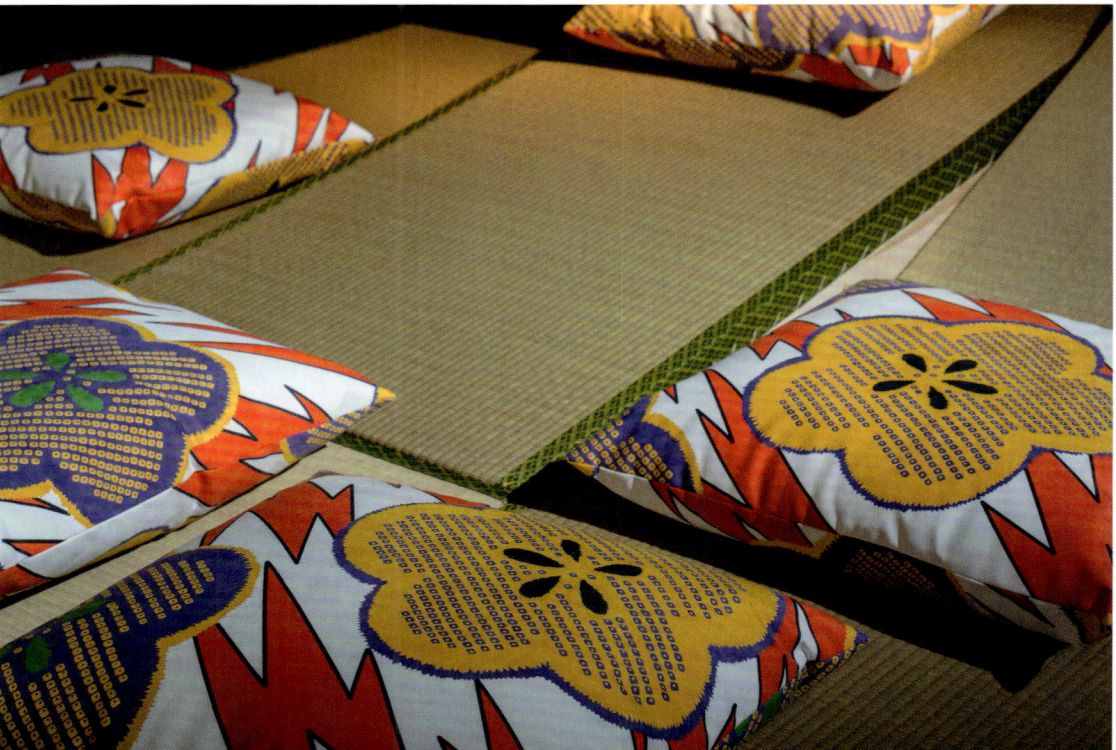

Aki Kondo, *Time Limit*, "Codice di avviamento fantastico", Palazzo Reale, Milan 2017

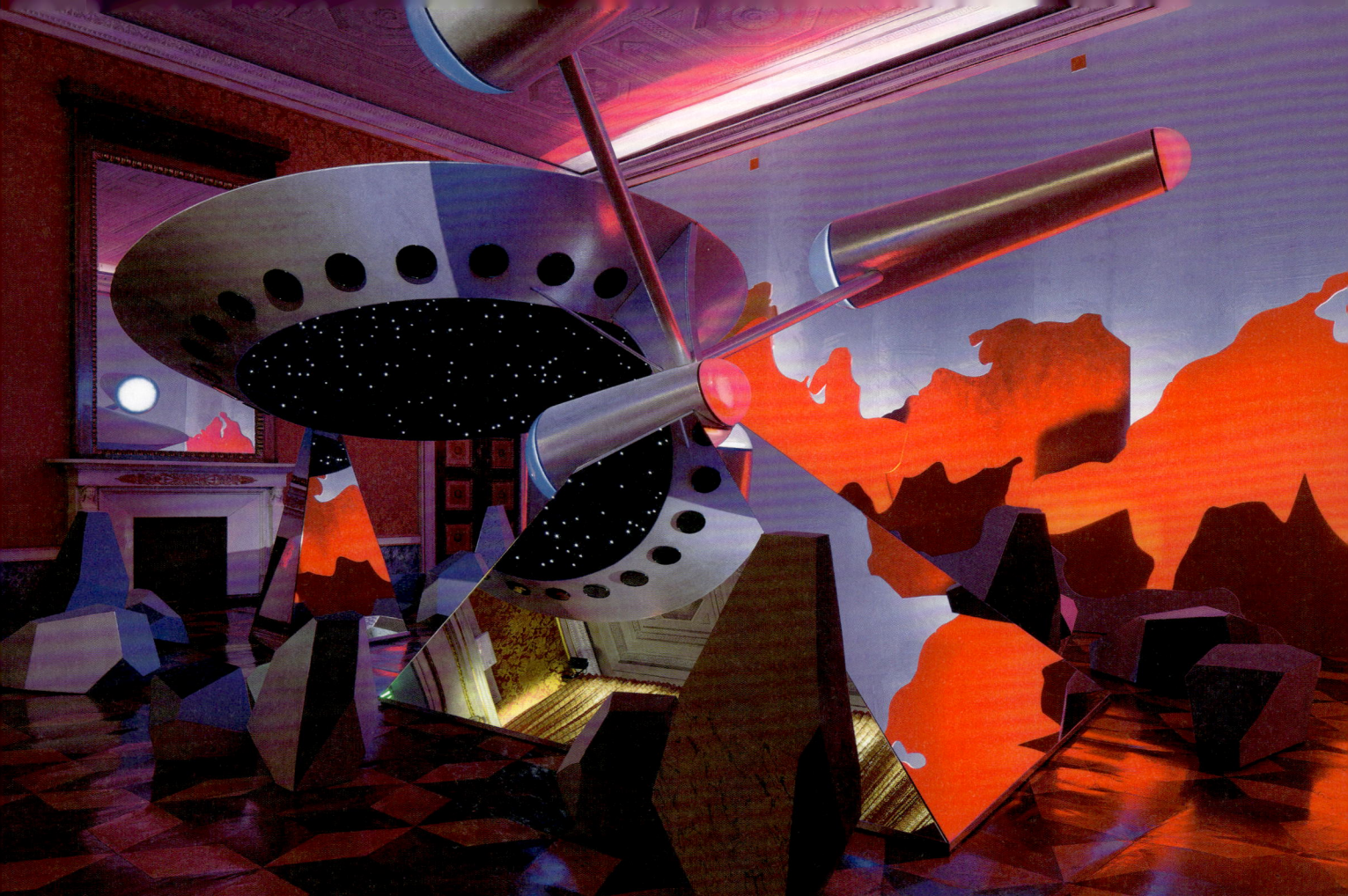

Nanda Vigo's spaceship got the ball rolling in a game in which all one's senses were involved. The public was invited to look, and touch, but also to listen, and perceive. Aki Kondo painted a garden of primordial dreams, Lorenzo Vitturi created a psychedelic jungle, and Georgina Starr invented an interactive time machine that engaged visitors in a powerful piece of theatre. Then you entered the room of the Soundwalk Collective, where listening was a different way of seeing.

    The collective came into being in New York, almost symbolically in the year 2000, just as the third millennium was getting under way. It makes compositions that announce a timeless world: sounds of the present that meld with the memories of an ancestral past. The future that can be seen in the nooks and crannies of uncontaminated places, or overpopulated metropolises. These artists create soundscapes that begin life from an observation of nature, and from an exploration of living and working environments, anthropological and ethnographic narratives. Their projects require intense periods of study in the field. Patti Smith collaborates with them, as does the choreographer Sasha Waltz and, in the past, the film director Jean-Luc Godard.

    On the floor, in the Prince's Room, a perimeter was marked out resembling a boxing ring. Standing all around were a dozen or so pieces of

Nanda Vigo, *Crash*, "Codice di avviamento fantastico", Palazzo Reale, Milan 2017

Aki Kondo, *Time Limit*, "Codice di avviamento fantastico", Palazzo Reale, Milan 2017

Following pages
Lorenzo Vitturi, *The garden inside the thread*, "Codice di avviamento fantastico", Palazzo Reale, Milan 2017

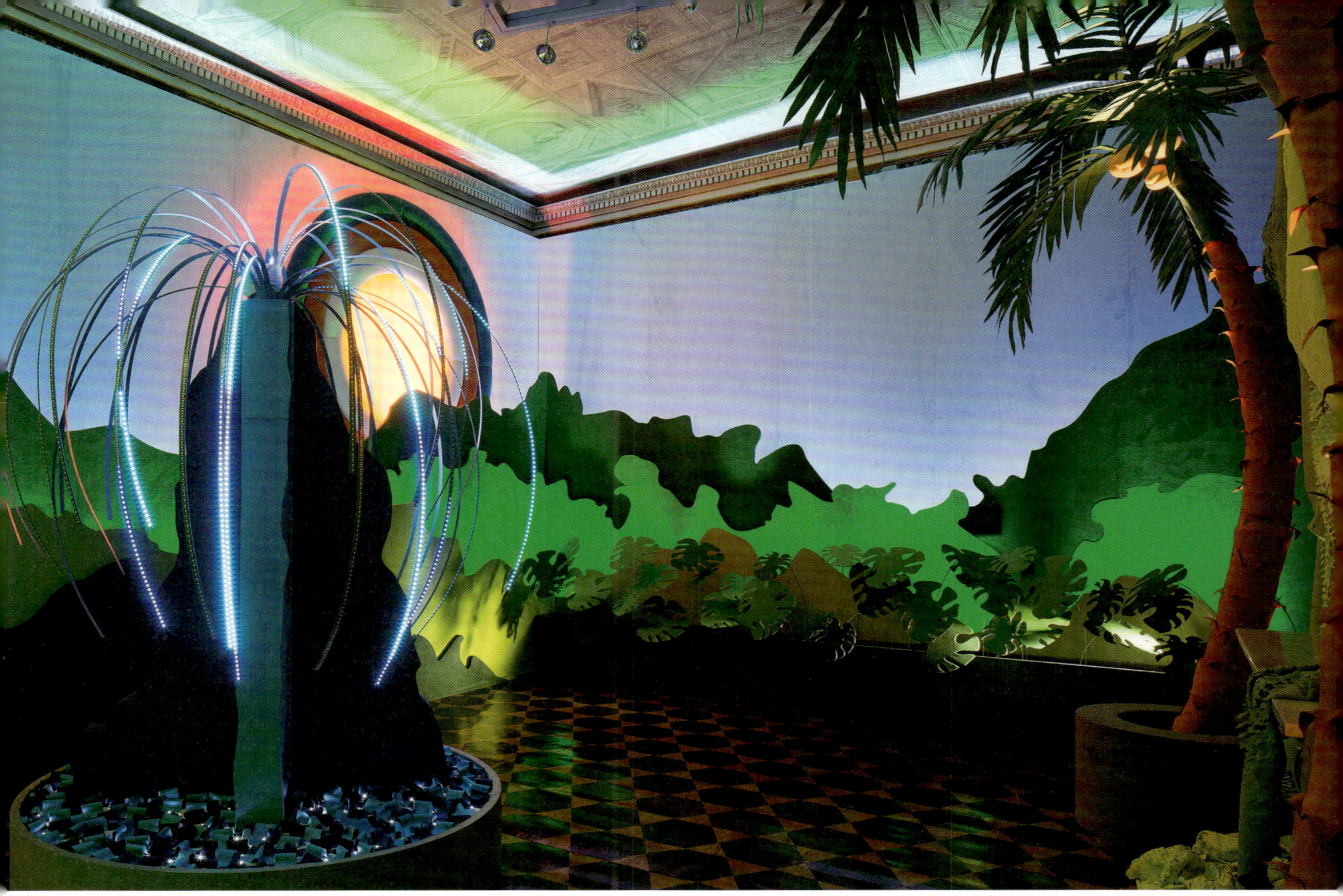

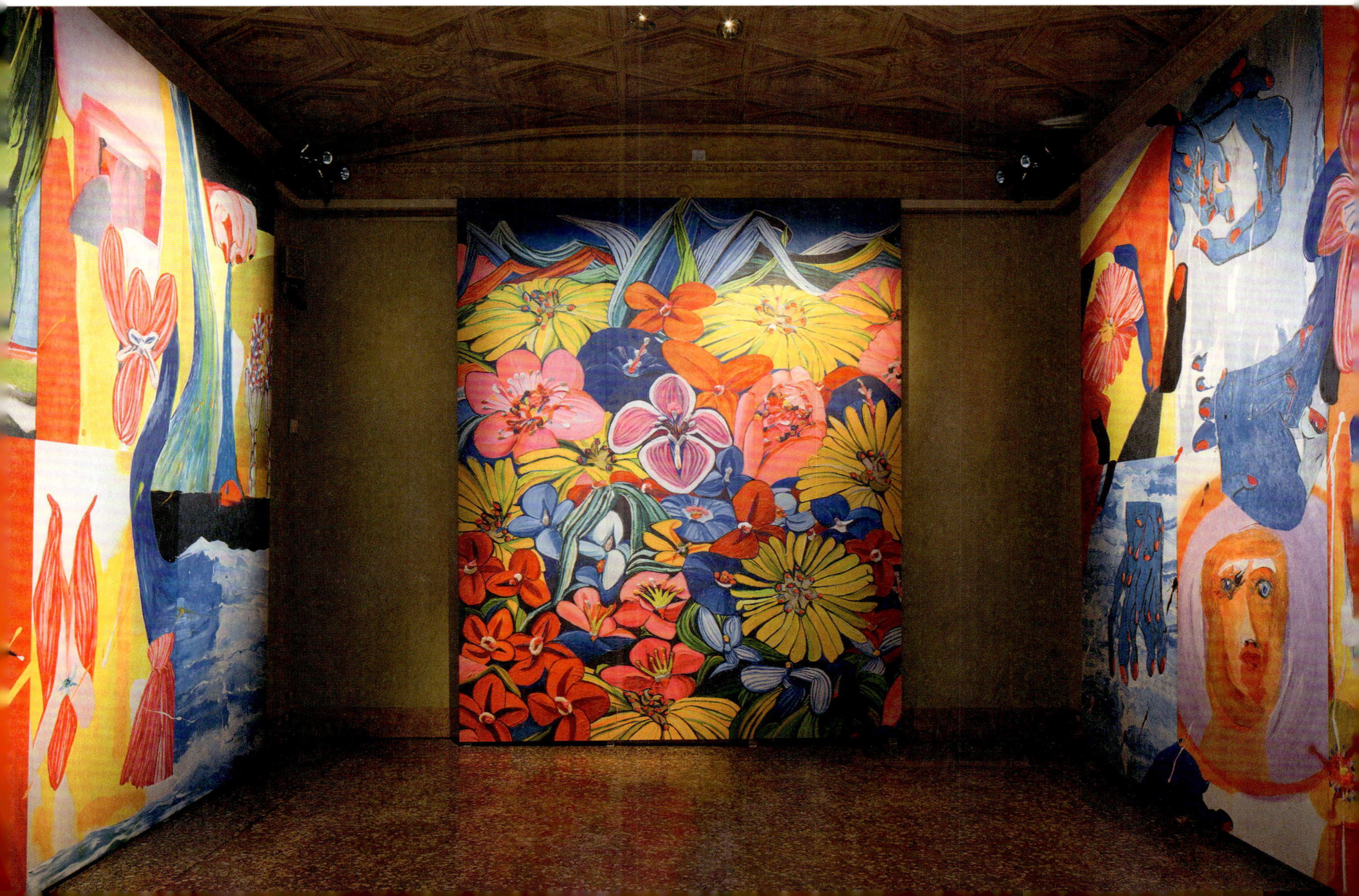

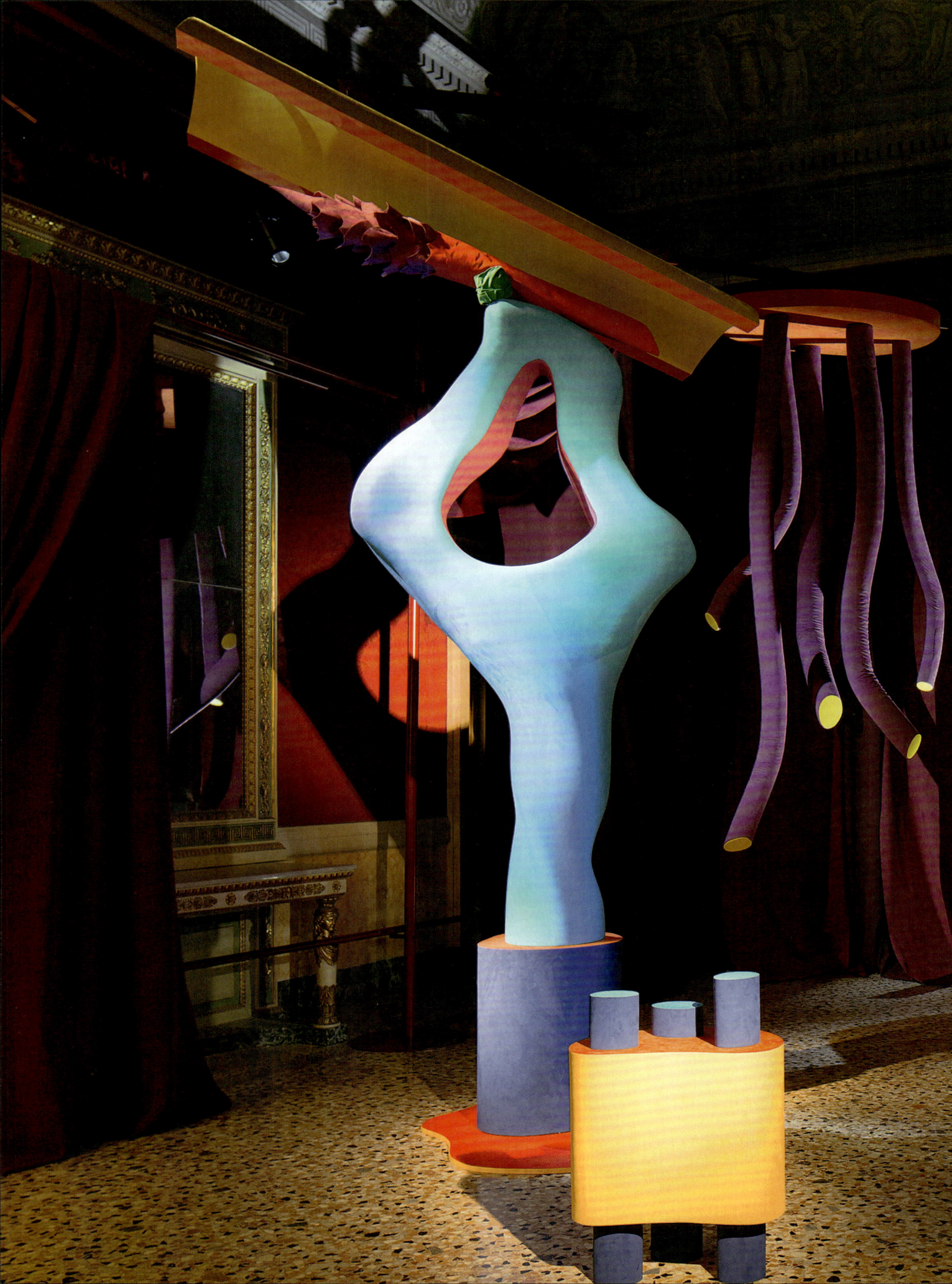

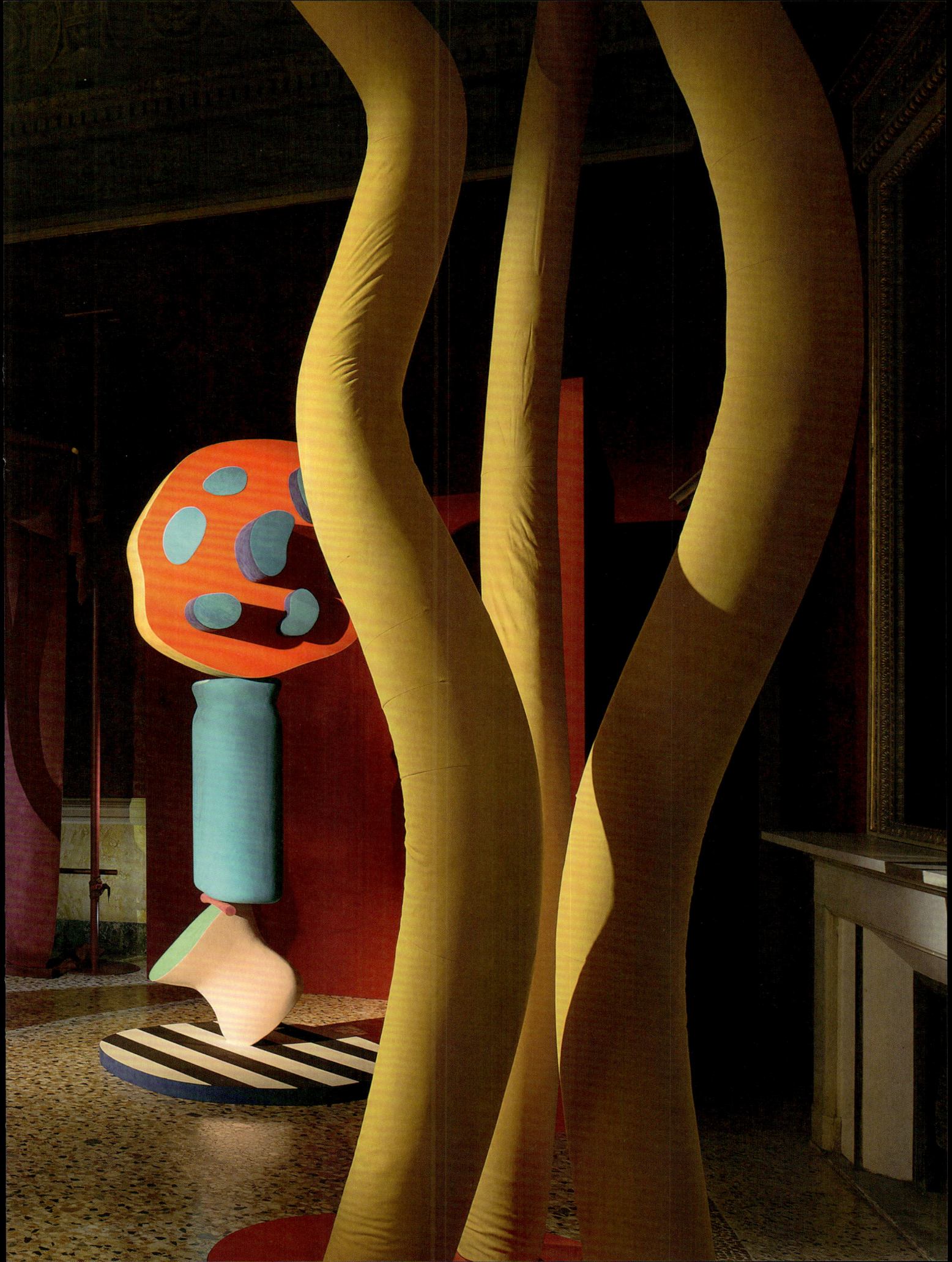

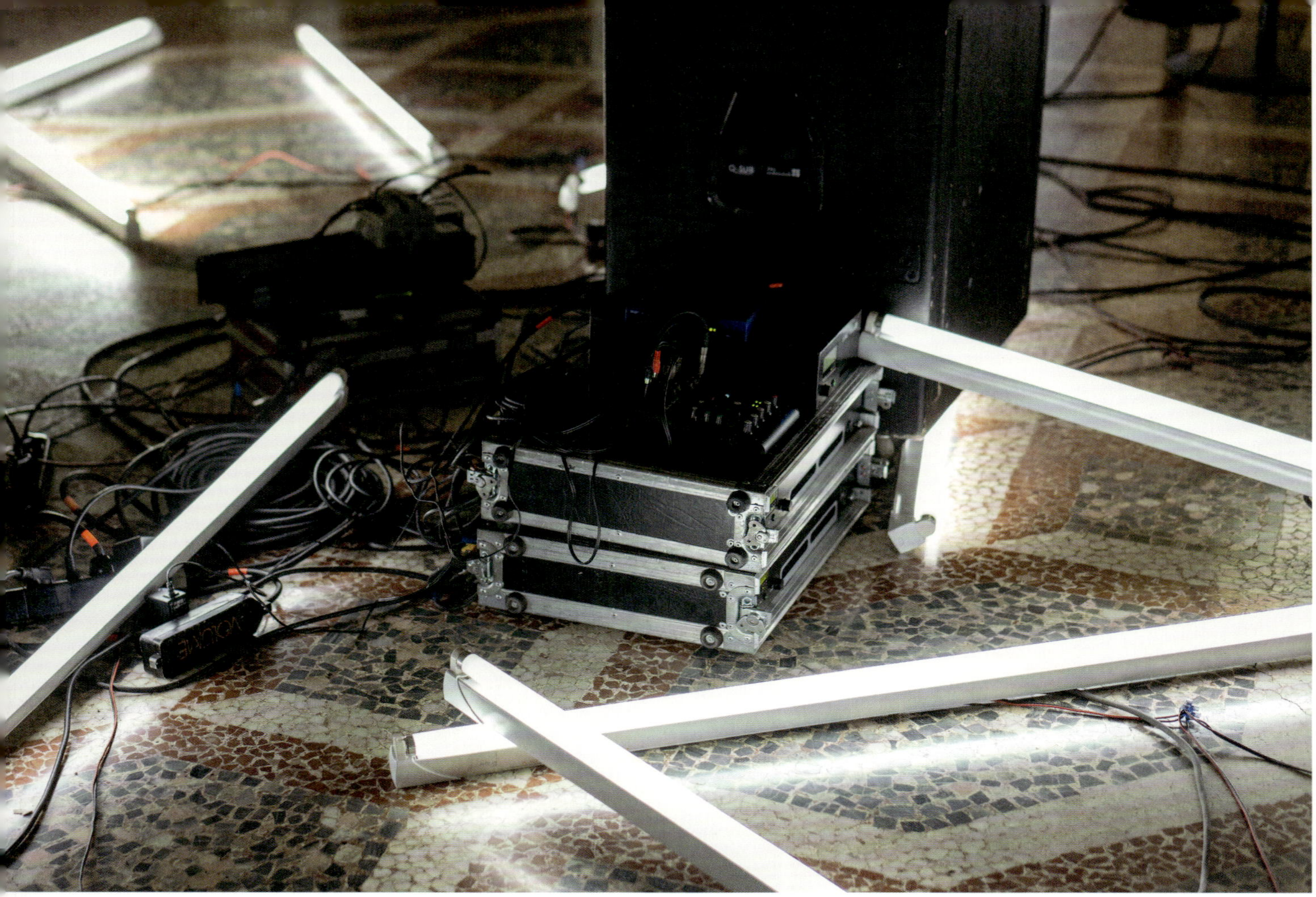

Soundwalk Collective, *Resonance*, "Codice di avviamento fantastico", Palazzo Reale, Milan 2017

equipment looking like guards protecting some kind of treasure. In the middle of the space were light tubes arranged apparently at random, a tangle of electrical cables and metal cases. All very technological, and appearing to be jumbled up. Overall, the work seemed akin to a hacker's computer: very powerful, but bare, devoid of the shop window-style glamour of modern electronic equipment. You might have wondered where Alcantara was. The answer is: everywhere. The art material was floating freely in the air, in the form of a sound composition. A musical abstraction that led the public into the heart of Alcantara's manufacturing process, at the Nera Montoro factory, from the moment when the synthetic fibres look like islands floating in the sea, all the way down to the dyeing process, and beyond.

    The Soundwalk Collective had also visited the factory, in common with all the artists involved in Alcantara's creative projects. Later they went back to Nera Montoro, with their sophisticated sound recording equipment. They sampled the sounds of the machinery, the ambient sounds of the various parts of the site. In the Prince's Room, the final arrangement represented the dialogue between the human elements engaged in manufacturing Alcantara, and the artificial ones.

    The installation was entitled *Resonance*. The sound atmosphere derived from a sequence of repetitive loops switching from the natural world

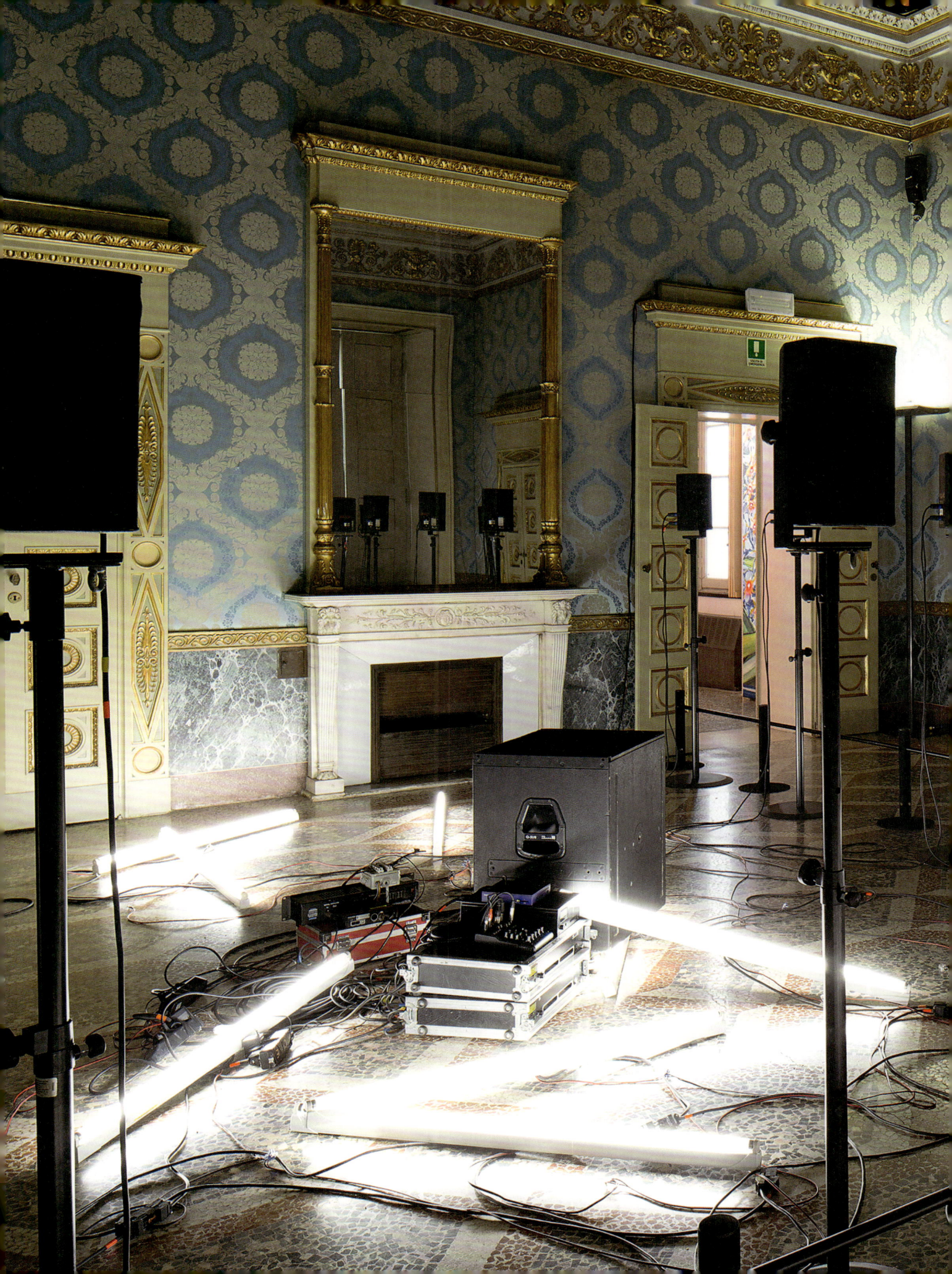

to the world of industry, the real and the virtual. An immersive experience involving all the senses. Especially one's imagination. What you heard was music, but it was also an idea. You perceived the creative buzz that leads to the creation of Alcantara. You listened to it, and you were also part of it. To some extent, by means of sounds, you took part in the magic.

The musical cell was a circular module. The underlying beat featured occasional sound vibrations which could have been the springs of a piece of mechanical machinery, or a detail of the working of some hydraulic component. Then there was a very swift musical break, like cymbals clashing. It could have been the trolley of a transportation device. Slow timing, precise metre, infinite time. You couldn't stop it, it was hypnotic. Who knows, perhaps this was music you could dance to on Nanda Vigo's spaceship. Over here, it resembled the sound of the Earth breathing, the secret beat of the world. Or the kind of music that is in our heads when we think, and don't even notice it. One thing's for sure: it was Alcantara, which becomes everything that we wish it to be.

Georgina Starr, *Momento Memoria Monumento*, "Codice di avviamento fantastico", Palazzo Reale, Milan 2017

Nanda Vigo, *Crash*, "Codice di avviamento fantastico", Palazzo Reale, Milan 2017

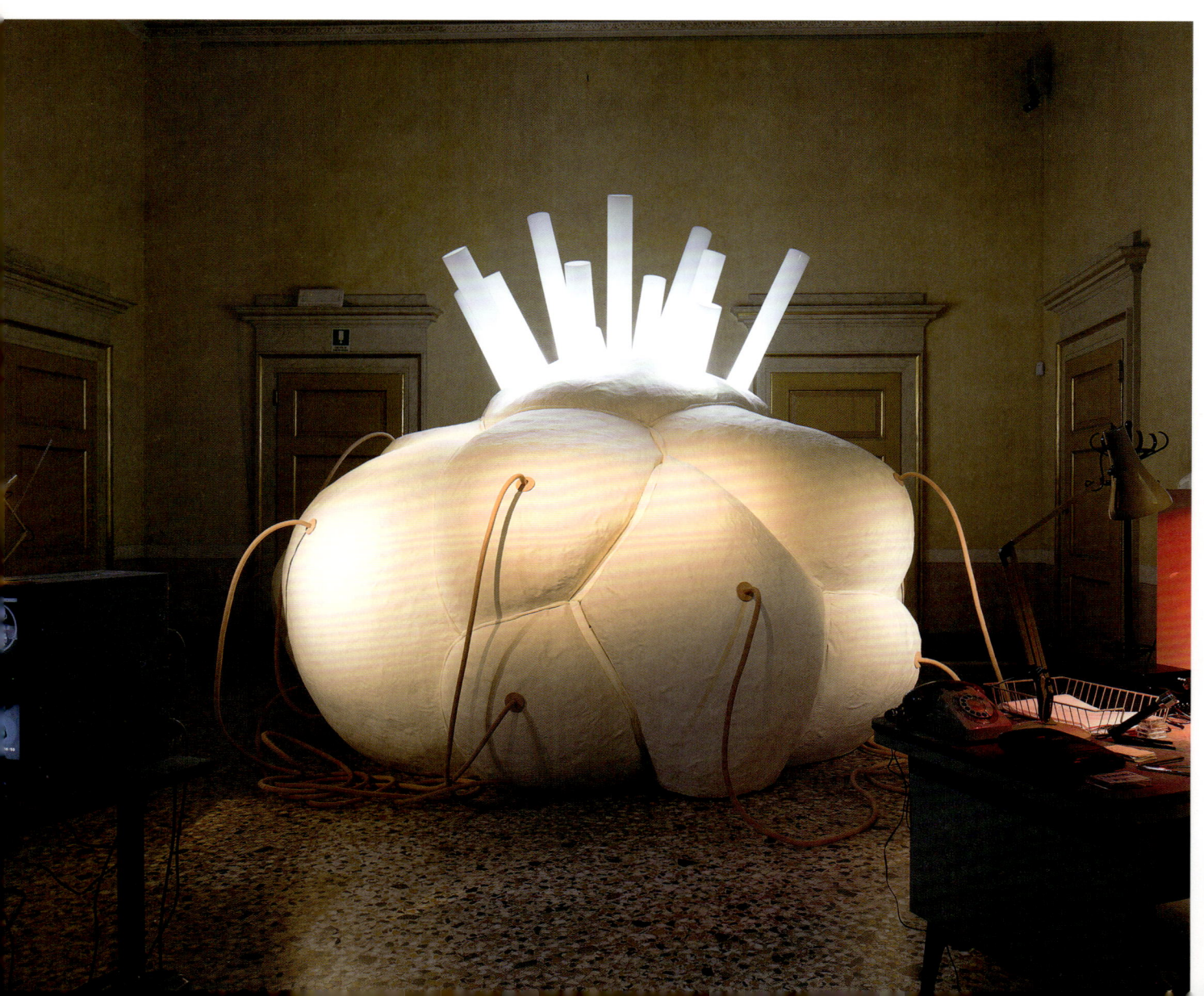

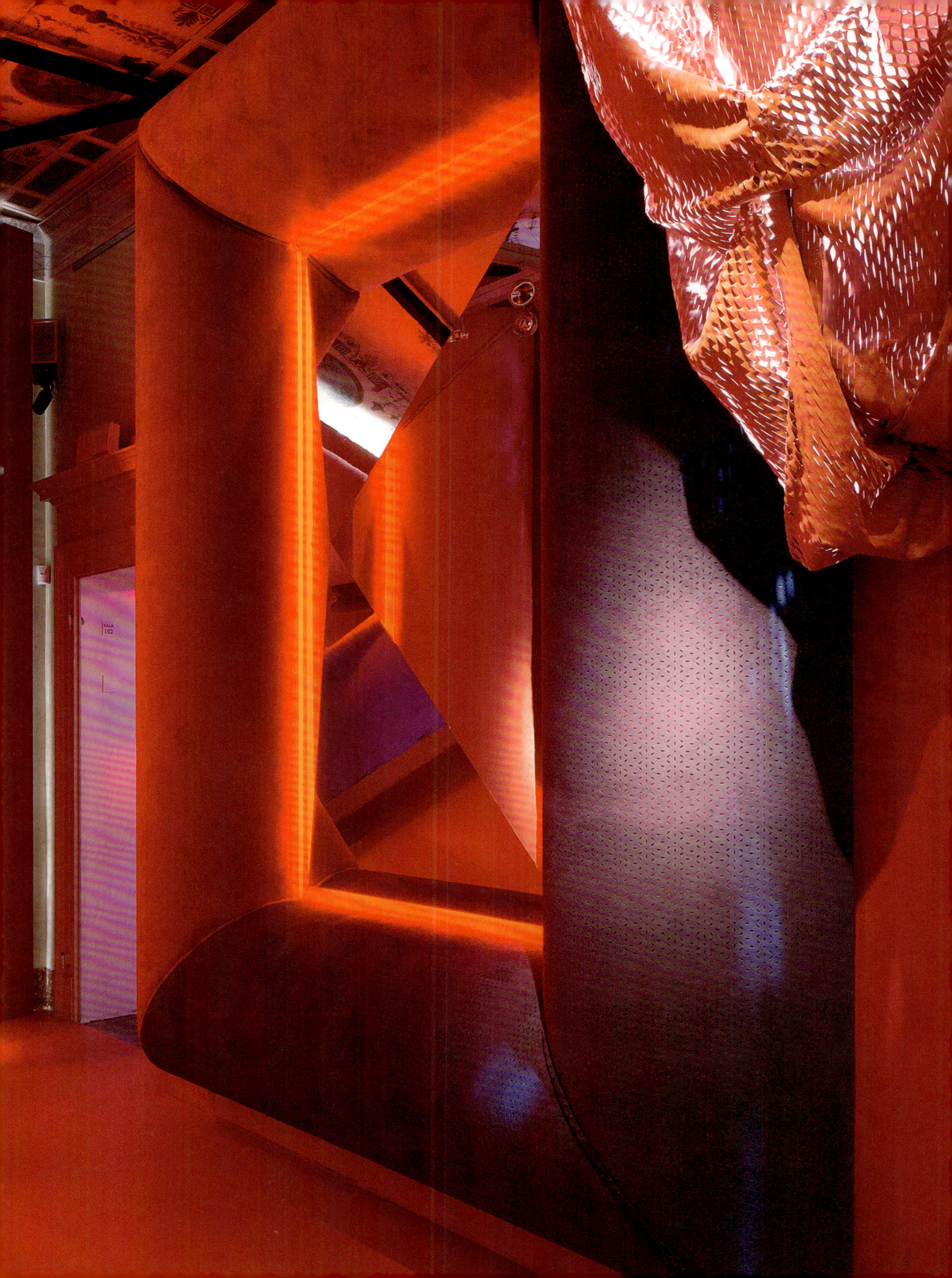

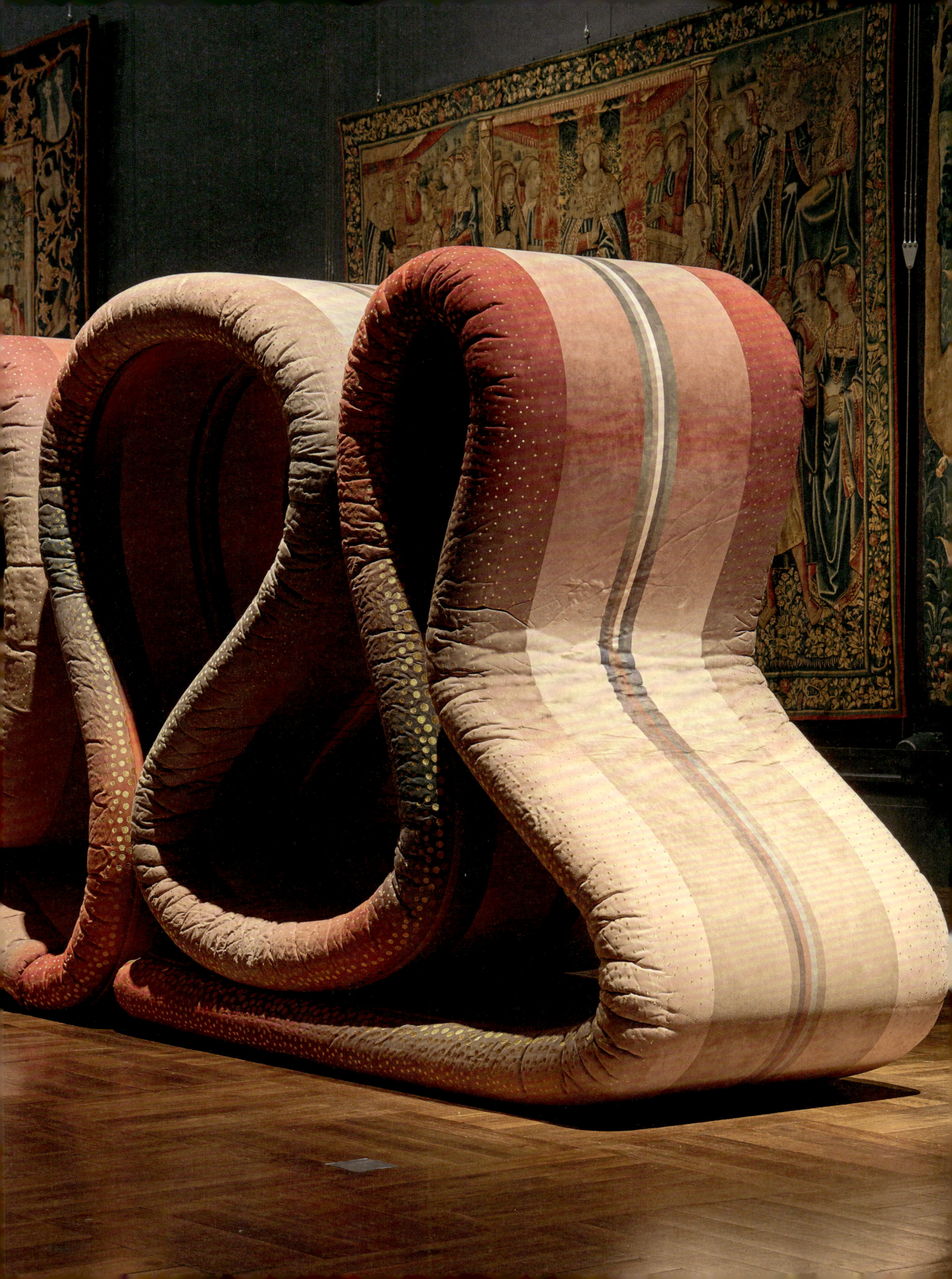

WAVES OF ENERGY

Ross Lovegrove, *Transmission*, Victoria and Albert Museum, London 2017

London, Victoria and Albert Museum. The year was 2017, and the event was the London Design Festival. The museum, named after Queen Victoria and her consort Albert, is one of the most important museums in the world devoted to the applied arts. It holds almost five million pieces, telling 5,000 years of human history.

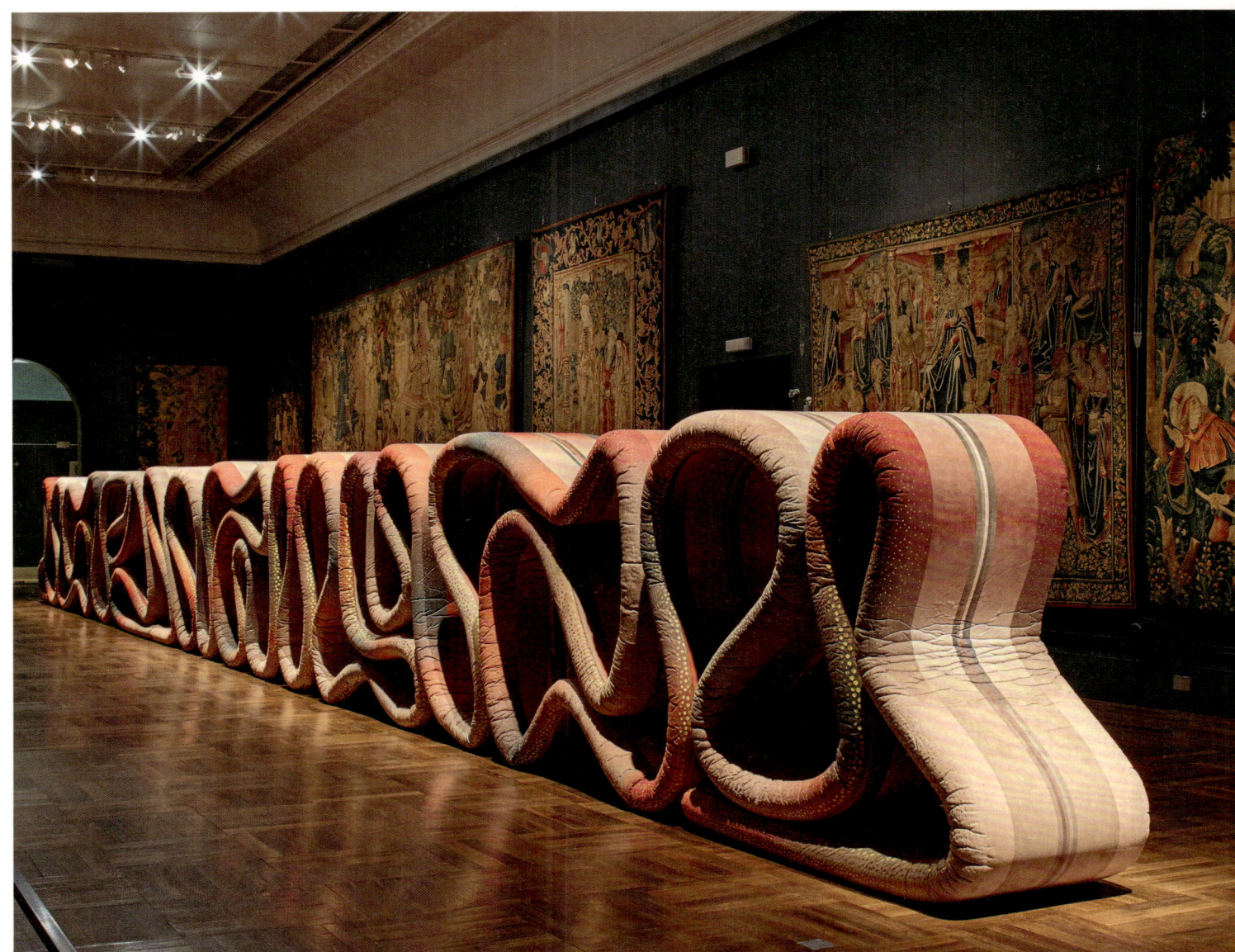

The Tapestry Room, with the Devonshire hunting scenes, is one of the most prestigious rooms. Large-scale medieval works, originally designed to be hung on walls. They were used to decorate the coldest rooms in castles, and they warmed them up. With the warmth of their material, and with the narratives in the stories they told. Court anecdotes and military feats, tales of love and the hunting of bears, boars, and deer. The richly adorned ladies' dresses, the finely woven decorations in shades of red, blue and gold. The hats and turbans, the weapons of the hunters on horseback, the hunting dogs, and falcons on the arms of falconers. Each of these tapestries tells of social relations, romantic escapades and feats of courage. Each point is a precious fragment of life.

As in the installations at Palazzo Reale in Milan, Alcantara was present with an innovative work, which, in its contemporary form, engaged in a dialogue with the past that played host to it. The tapestries with the hunting scenes in Devonshire, hanging on the walls, looked on with an air of curiosity.

The designer Ross Lovegrove works above all on the size and scale, colour associations, and scenic presence of forms and volumes. He made a self-standing Alcantara structure more than 20 metres long, running through the middle of the room. It resembled a gentle wave of energy. The title he chose for it was: *Transmission*. The installation featured colour saturation of Alcantara material, with digital printing reproducing embroidery, and echoed the ancient dyeing process of the tapestries. The light and dark areas were translated into the gently undulating folds of the work. The gold and silver threads captured the light, and traced the line of the structure in space.

The energy contained within the stories of the tapestries was unfurled as in an ancient scroll. A treasure-trove of events that rolled away and resembled the notes of a ballad. Alcantara captured fragments of tapestries, and fixed them in the energy wave. The almost liquid movement of the work harked back to the voices of bards, the rhythmic undulation of the rhymes that attune themselves to the music, to one's breathing, and the slow procedere of the narrative.

The combined effect of Alcantara's *Transmission* and the *Devonshire Hunting Tapestries* offered a moment of peace, calm and a space for listening. "I want to show the public that art and design do not exist just to be looked at," said Ross Lovegrove. "I invite everyone to visit the room, admire the tapestries and then touch the installation, and play with the tactile nature of the Alcantara material."

Andrea Boragno added: "Alcantara is the point where emotions, beauty, and technology intersect. A material that knows no bounds, an increasingly international brand…"

Art and design told of hundreds of years of history and of life, emotions that detached themselves from the walls of the room, painted on the frame with intertwining threads, and reached all the way to us, nestling in the gentle folds of the Alcantara wave. The tactile experience also became visual, when

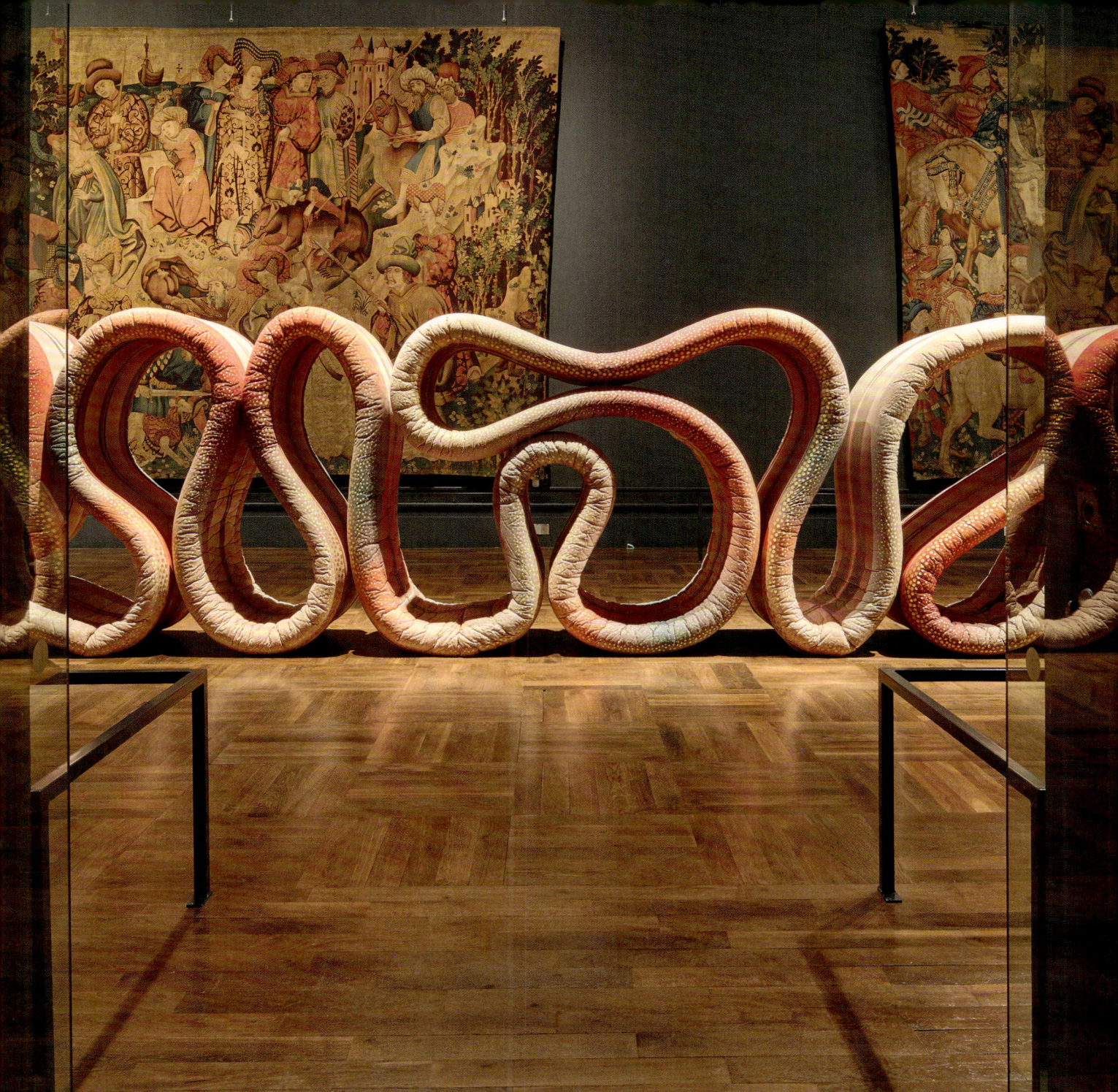

sections of the ancient tapestries could be spotted among the coils of the modern installation. It was wonderful to walk around it, to allow your mind and your gaze to wander, your senses activated by the suggestions of a time that is forever, woven by hand with skill and patience. Underlying all this was man, speaking of himself through the quality of his work. The creative passion behind the tapestries was reflected in the courage in design and construction seen in a material like Alcantara.

    A material of the future, a material that is timeless.

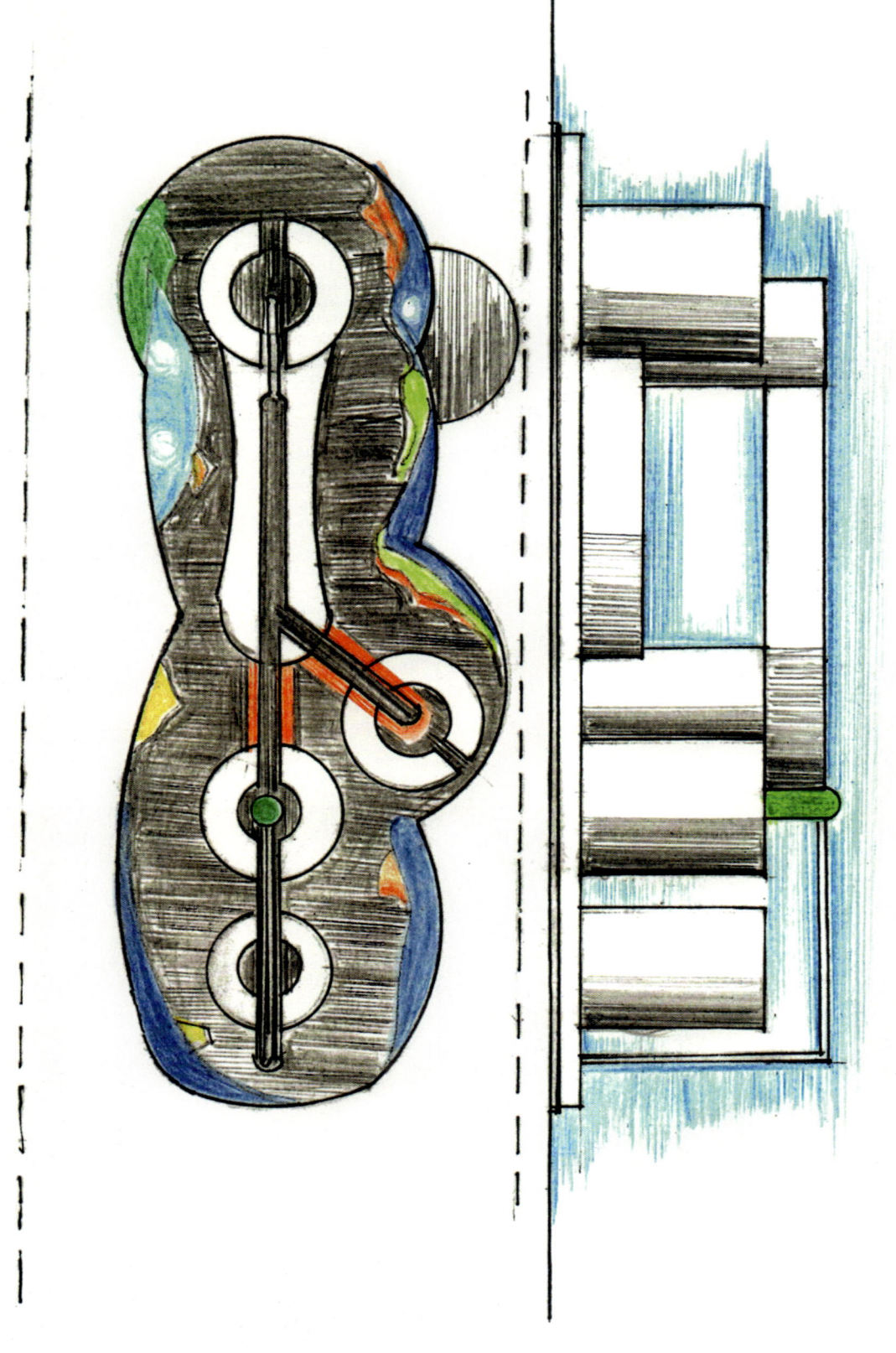

STUDIO VISIT

It may have been Battiato's voice in the background, or the beams of white light tinged with blue and azure when they glided over the colours of the sky as it turned into space. Perhaps it was the bright dots in the background, looking like stars, or Alcantara itself, that made everything so soft and gentle. What you felt vibrating was the lightness of a suspended time, like a feeling of anticipation. Your body, enraptured, was stolen away and led into a different dimension. With lightness, indeed, to use that word again.

Nanda Vigo, *Arch/Arcology*, "Studio Visit", MAXXI Museum, Rome 2018

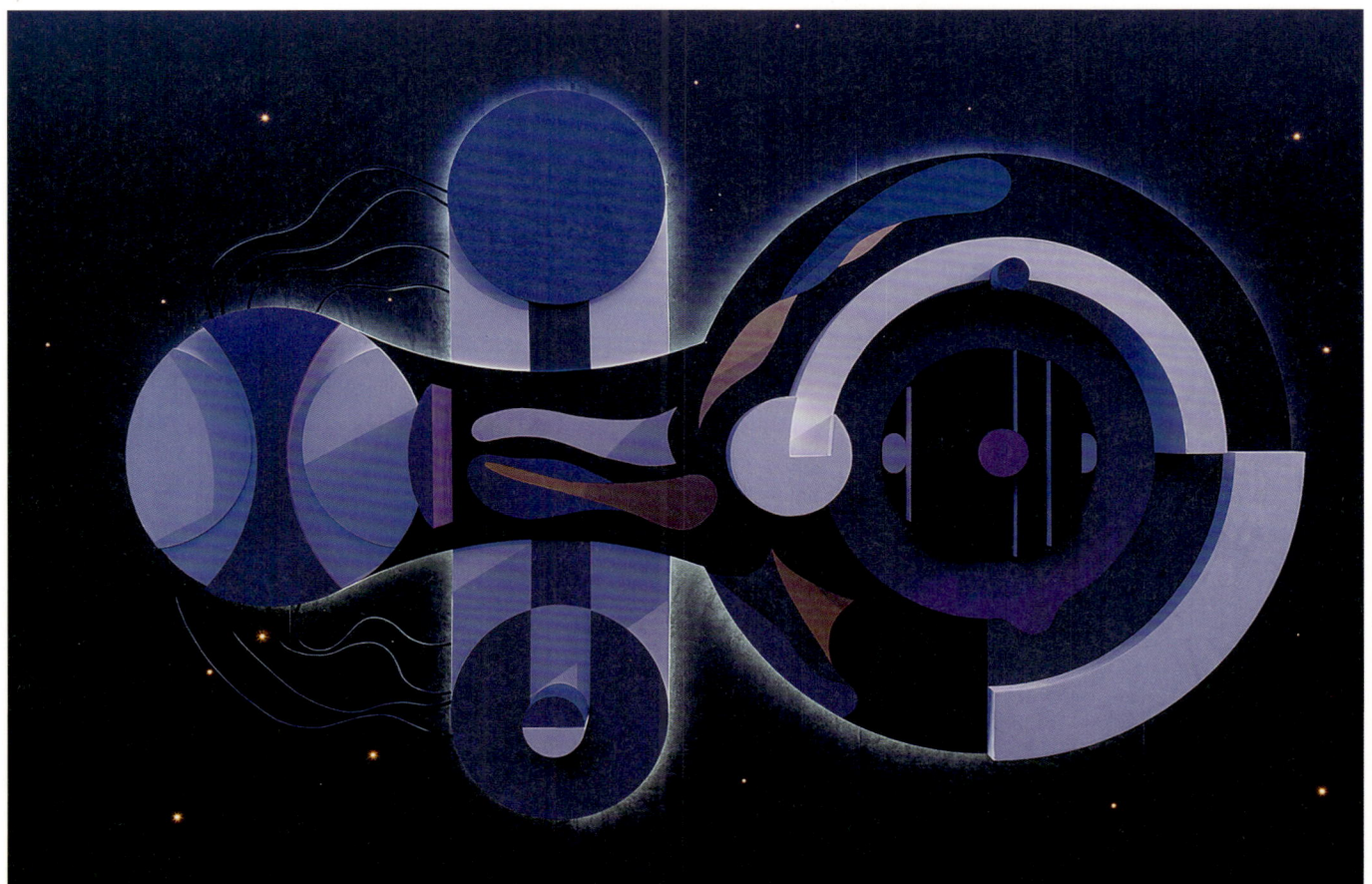

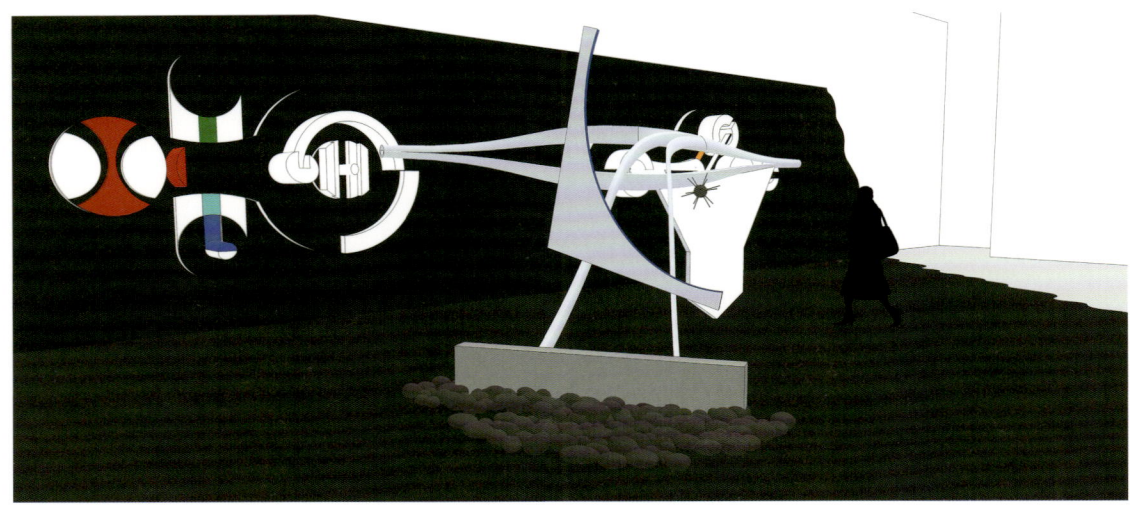

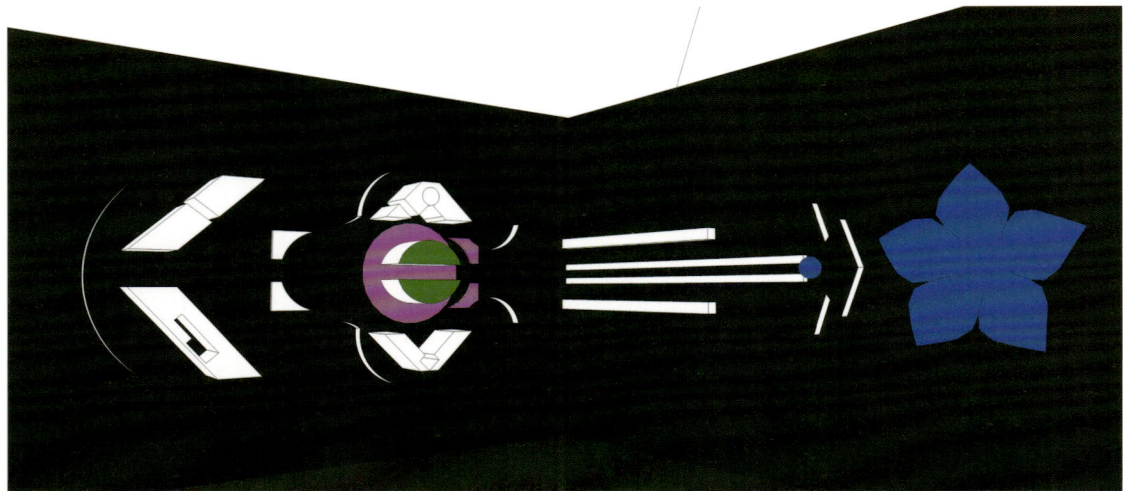

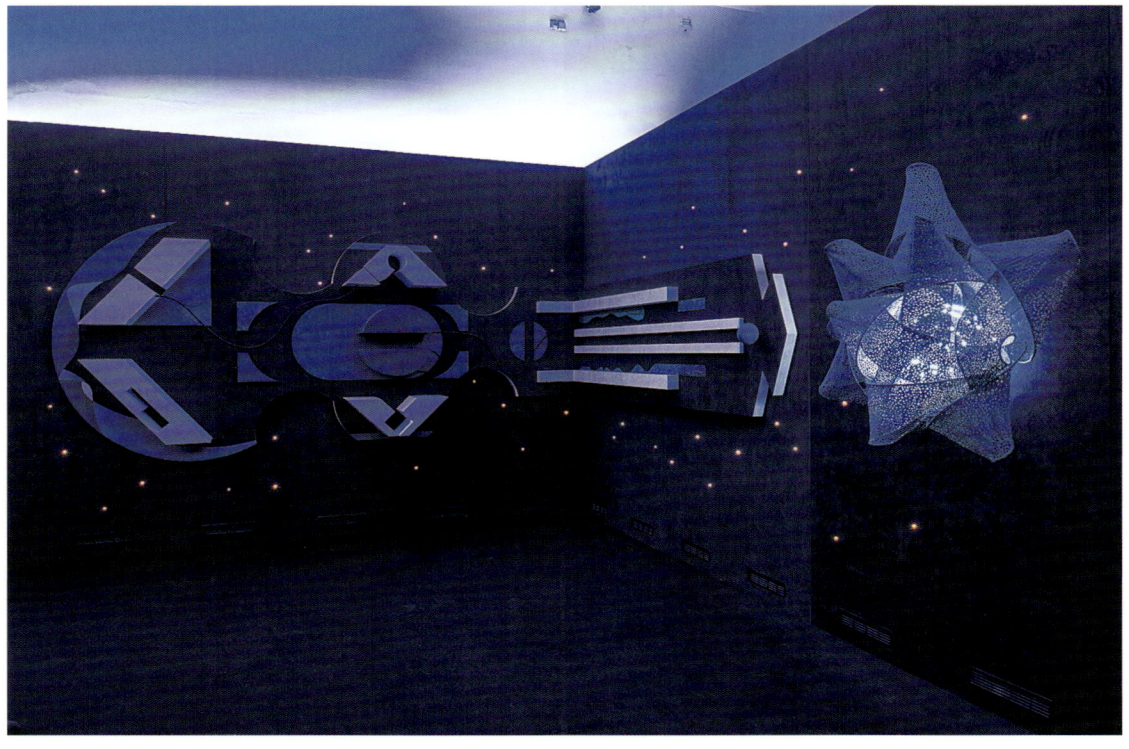

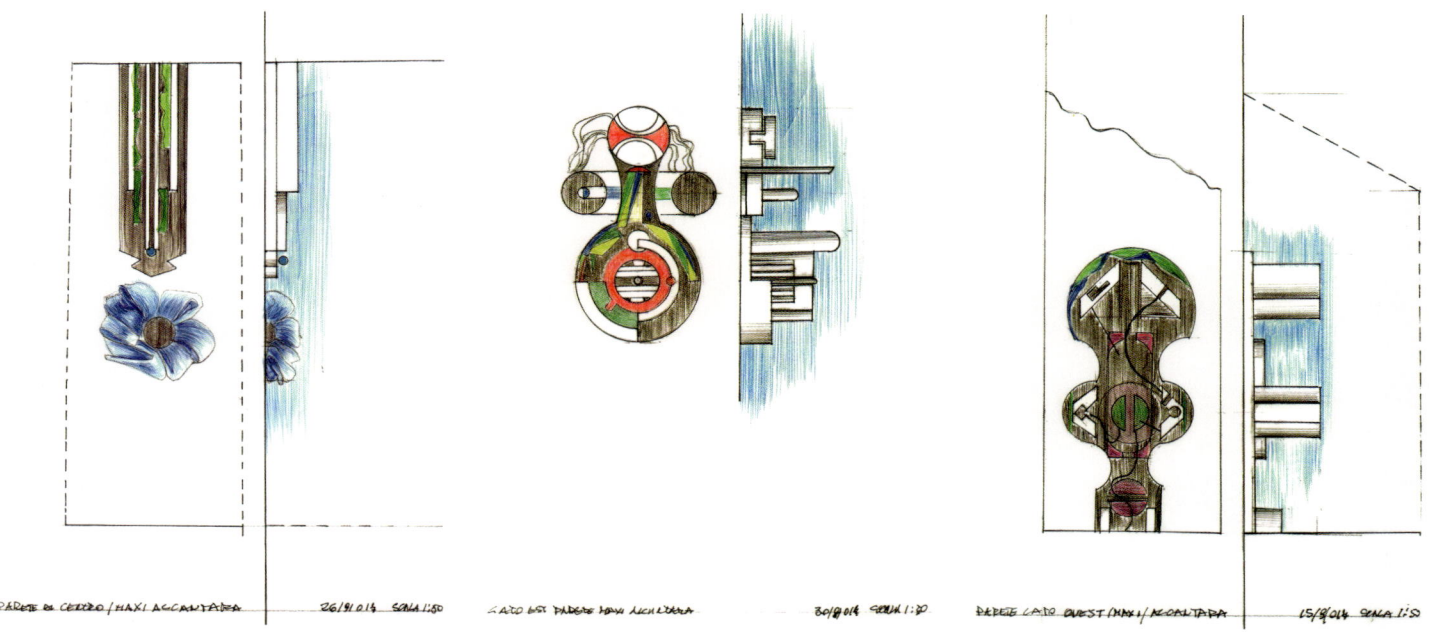

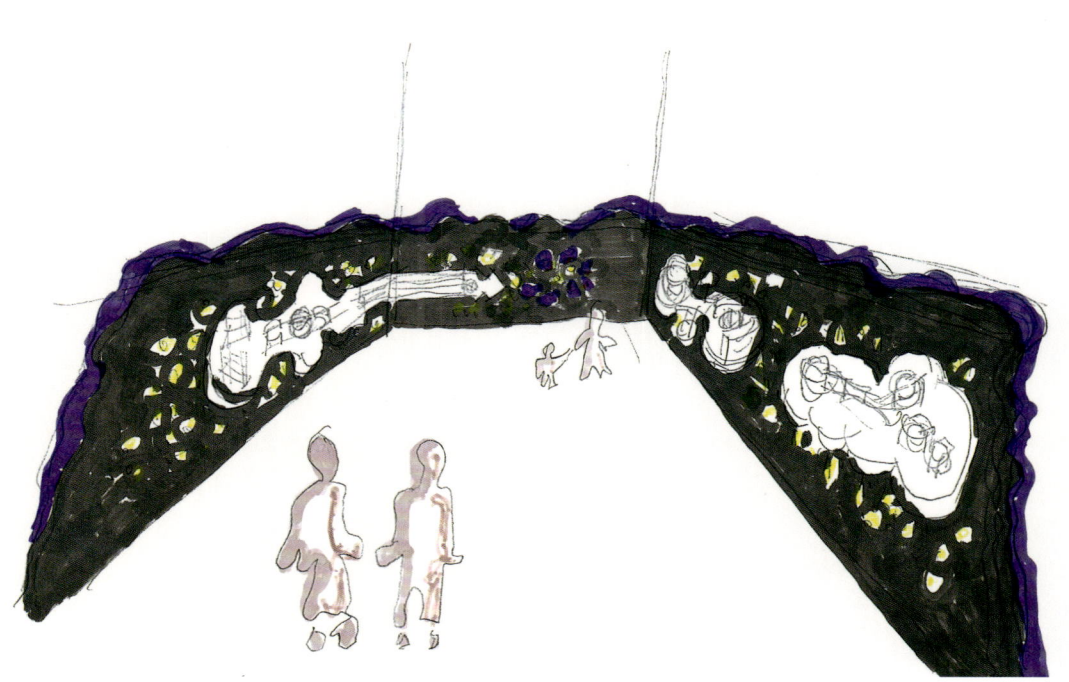

The year was 2018, the place: MAXXI. The installation created by Nanda Vigo enabled us to float in space, particles of a future time that we will not be able to see for ourselves, but which we have an urgent need to imagine. And to plan, even.

But let's start at the beginning. After six years of collaboration, the working relationship between Alcantara and MAXXI continued, and extended even further. By setting out from their own identities, as always. The idea was

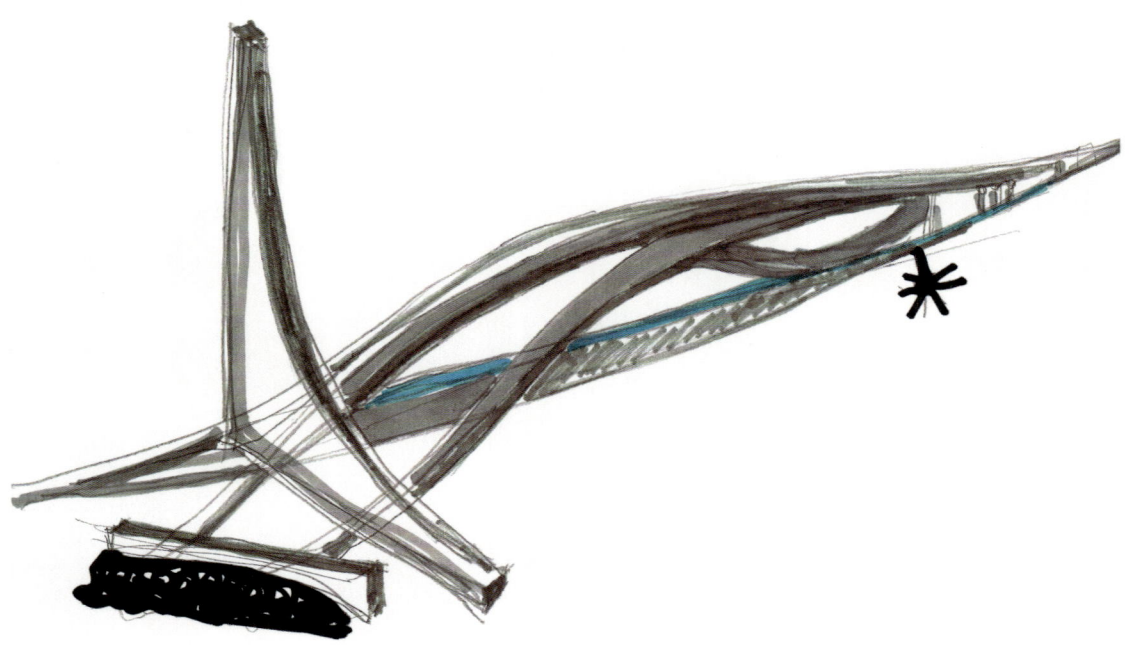

to ask contemporary creatives to come up with a response to the masters of old. The museum opened the archive of its permanent collections, and invited the artists to interact with their own most precious material. A sort of dance, a *paso doble* between great figures in art. Imagine that project culture is music, and they were the dancers. The best ones in existence. They got up on stage and began to circle around. They were weightless, they never tired. You watched them, and you lost yourself in them. Lightness can go to your head.

    The archives of a museum such as the MAXXI are a treasure-trove of ideas, jealously guarded by historians and archivists, who handle works with gloves and tweezers. The artist approaches those same materials with the liveliness and freshness born of sheer talent. The new journey embarked upon by Alcantara and the MAXXI was entitled "Studio Visit", and it was just that, a dialogue – a dance – between artists who held the reins of time in their hands, who travel beyond time, and talk to each other using the words of creativity and innovation. In presenting the project, the curator, Domitilla Dardi, said: "When an artist's work is placed in a museum archive, it is studied, analyzed, and re-evaluated, but a part of its original vitality is also removed, because it is stripped of the context of life. "Studio Visit" points to the horizon of an reverse process: it brings thoughts back to life, in the form of new projects."

    We could call it a new, bold exercise in memory: making things of the past present, for the purposes of the future.

    The first invitation in the "Studio Visit" cycle was extended to Nanda Vigo. A poetess of light, an eclectic artist, able to embrace design, architecture and the environment in her vision. In the MAXXI archives she

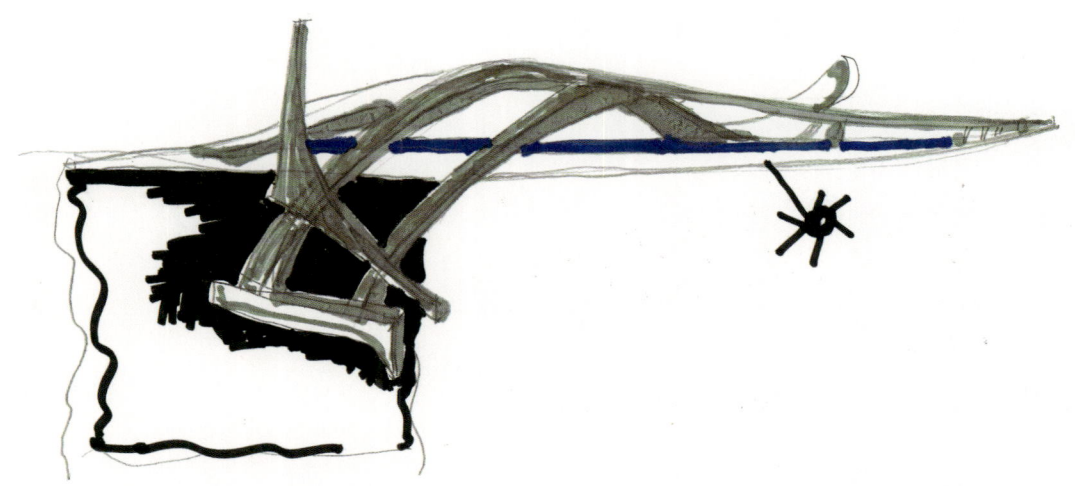

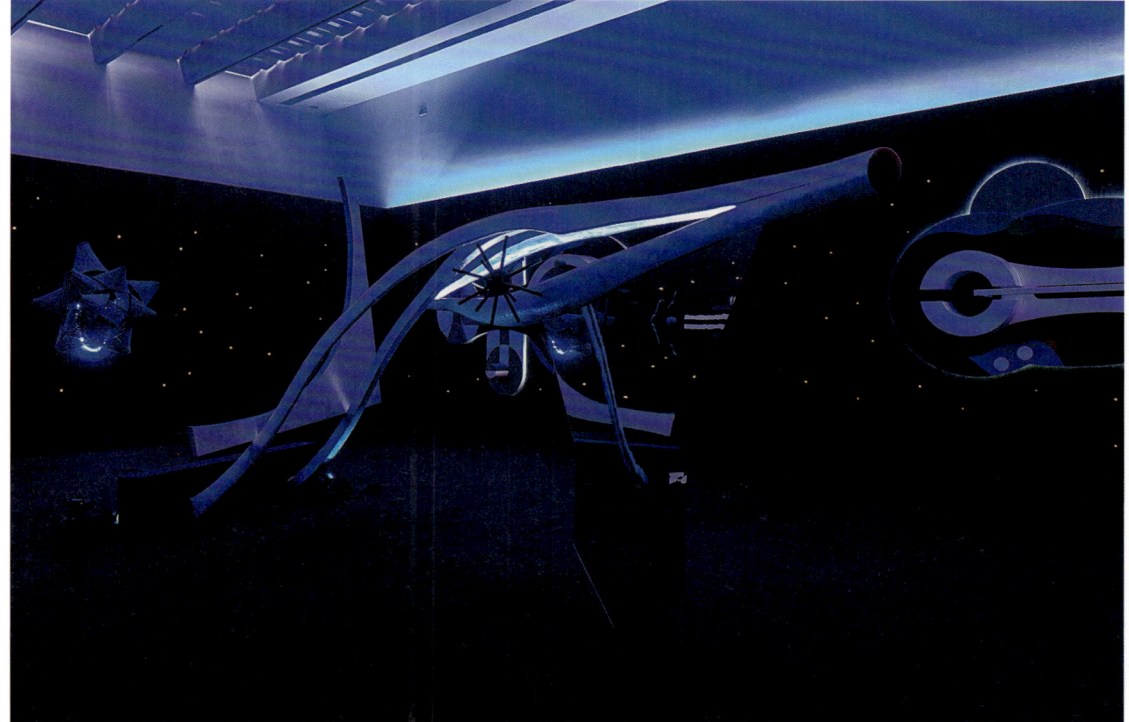

came across the work of Paolo Soleri, the architect who, as long ago as the 1950s, devoted himself to designing the cities of the future. He considered these solutions to be real and possible, in what was the only possible future. Soleri designed homes floating in space, where people would live in zero-gravity. The Earth would be regenerated, after all the human beings had left it, and it would be loved and respected as the generator of food and life.

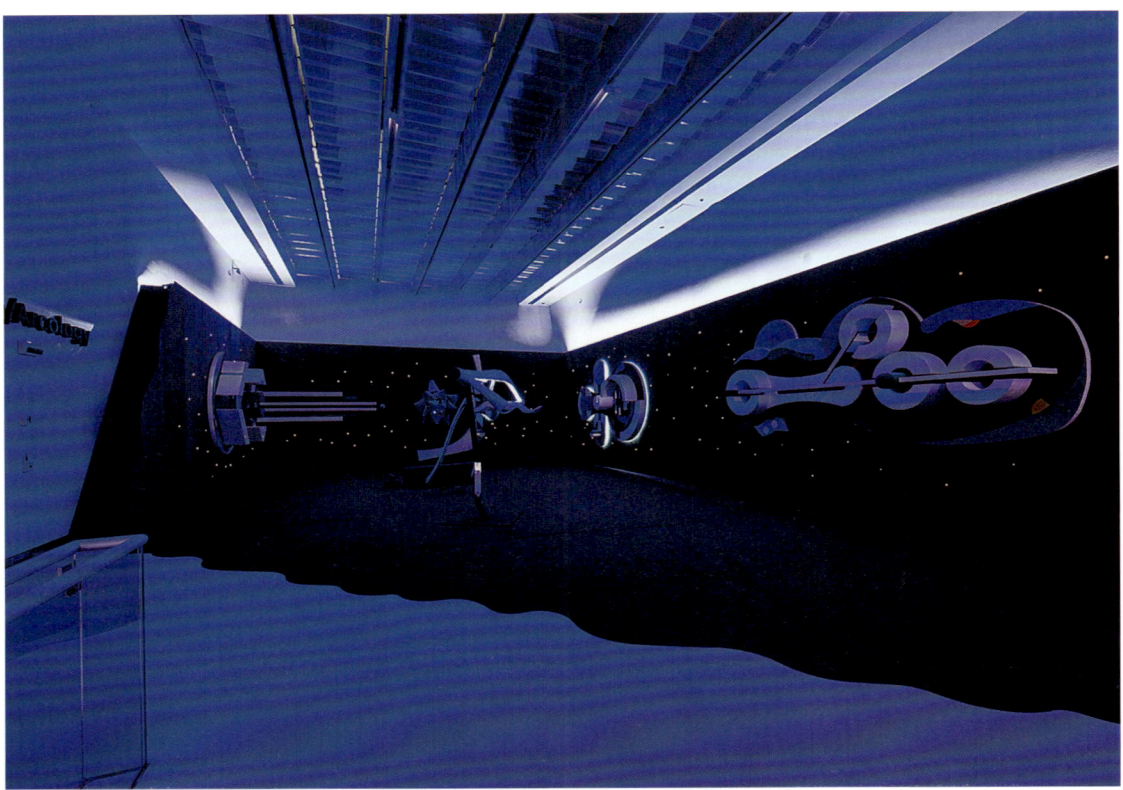

Soleri's visions have also taken material form in the world of science fiction. In the Arizona desert he built the eco-sustainable city of Arcosanti, which George Lucas once visited in the 1970s. The *Star Wars* saga is full of Soleri's ideas, which took shape in the form of film sets. Nanda Vigo, who used to read *Flash Gordon* when she was a girl, and imagined living on the planet Mongo, approached the master's work with the enthusiasm of those early dreams she once had.

The museum staged a major project by Soleri. It was large-scale, in the literal sense of the word: eleven metres of plan drawing of a city suspended in outer space. A fascinating work, being by its very nature projected into the third dimension of space, and yet anchored to a terrestrial past, bound to the two dimensions of an architectural plan. There were no walls, no light, or vertical development that would make it intelligible in the eyes of the public, too. That was what triggered it all. Nanda Vigo created that missing dimension, which stemmed from the plan itself, but that became an entirely new vision, her vision. And she framed this vision in Alcantara, the material of the future. The only material capable of giving a lightweight solidity to a "space poetics, in which life is played out within cosmic spaces, at zero gravity." Nanda Vigo took advantage of Alcantara's softness to the touch, its ability to absorb light and to act as an echo chamber for sounds, the way it can be cut perfectly, enabling it to cover surfaces and eliminate the perception of corners. As Nanda Vigo herself put it: "I was able to turn this dream into a reality with the help of a material as versatile as Alcantara,

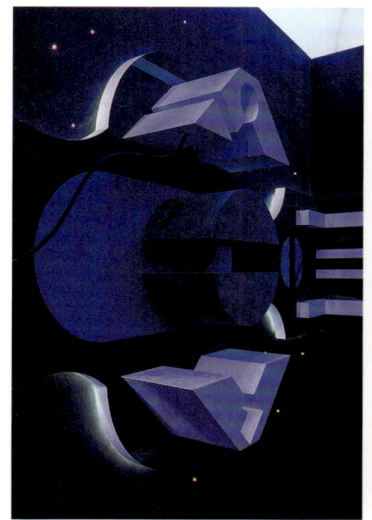 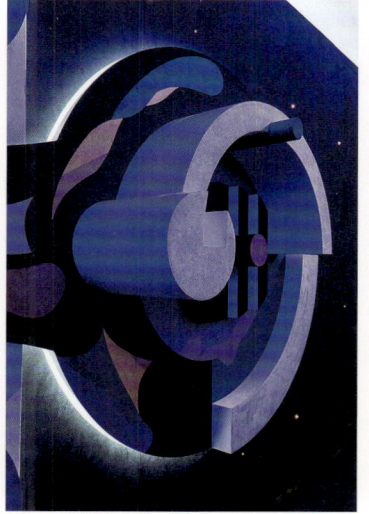 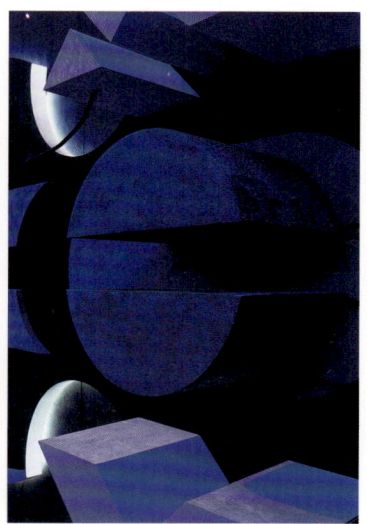

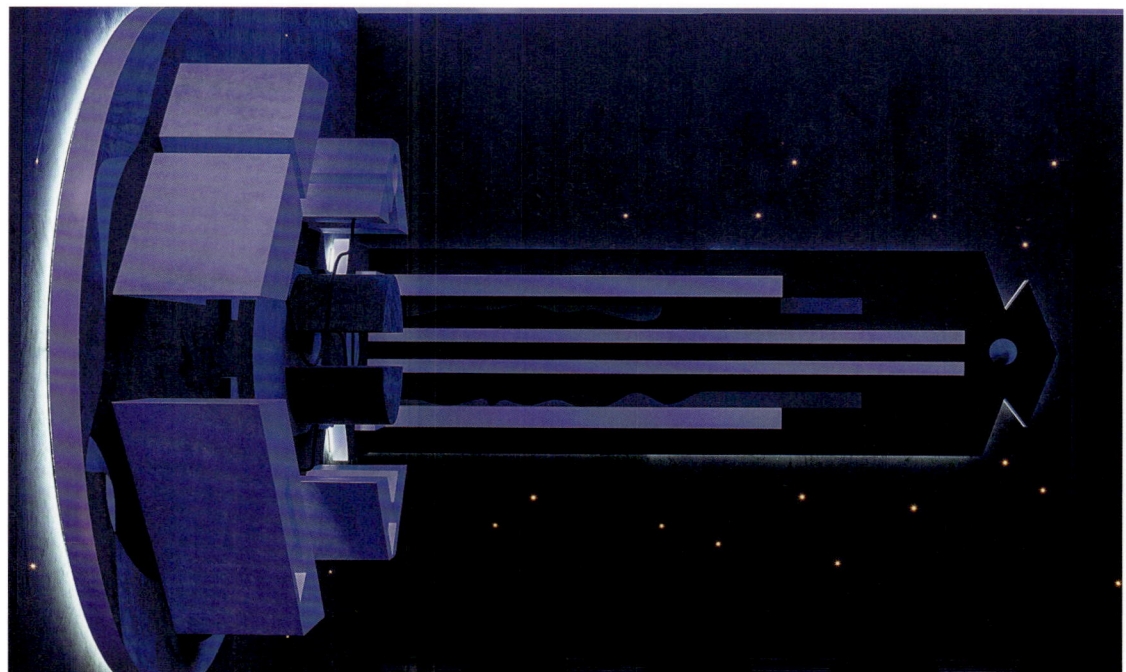

which allowed me to come up with daring solutions, and a very soft, continuous evolution."

The installation was entitled *Arch/arcology*. A pure, immersive space, a unique opportunity for the public to physically get inside a project. The term *arcology* was coined by Soleri to convey the concept of harmony between architecture and ecology. Andrea Boragno, Chairman and Managing Director of Alcantara, stressed that: "Our material is a versatile medium, which allows a dialogue between artists in a truly international dimension. What's more, this reflection by Nanda Vigo on Soleri's ideas, and his concept of *arcology*, underlines our pioneering, constant efforts as regards sustainability."

A dance, indeed. A three-step: two artists plus Alcantara.

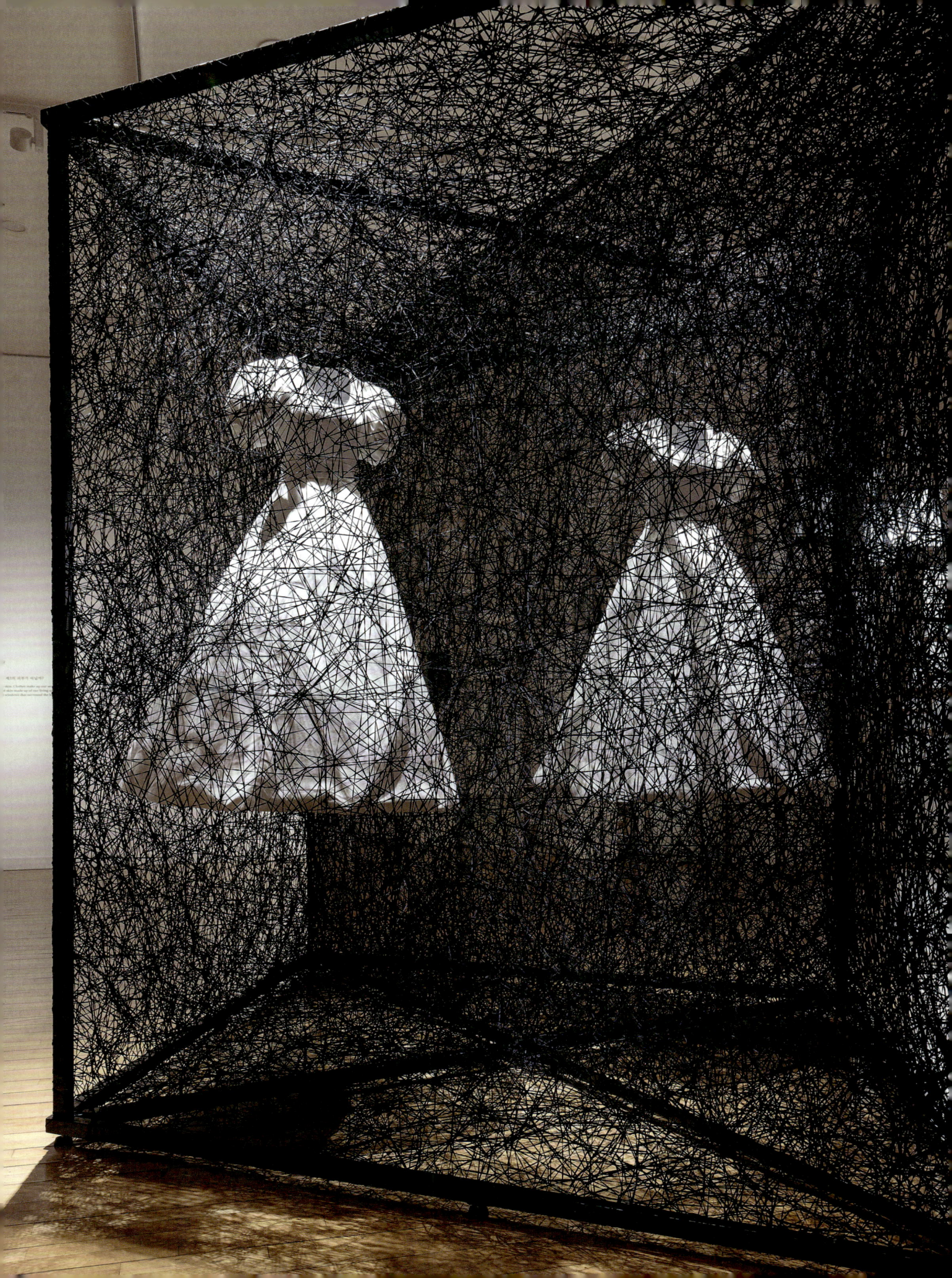

BEYOND THE BODY

Chiharu Shiota, *Reflection of Space and Time*, "Nove viaggi nel tempo", Palazzo Reale, Milan 2018

Zeitguised, *Oltre il giardino nucleare*, "Nove viaggi nel tempo", Palazzo Reale, Milan 2018

Alcantara's new exhibition in the interiors of Palazzo Reale in Milan, in 2018, was entitled "Nine Journeys in Time". A fluid, highly subjective time. Inspired once again by the rooms of the Prince's Apartment, made possible by the characteristics of Alcantara as a tool for artistic creation. A material that can take an endless number of forms: from painting to fashion, from digital design to music. Ten artists explored Alcantara in every direction, exploiting its full potential. They succeeded in going beyond material substance. Beyond the body.

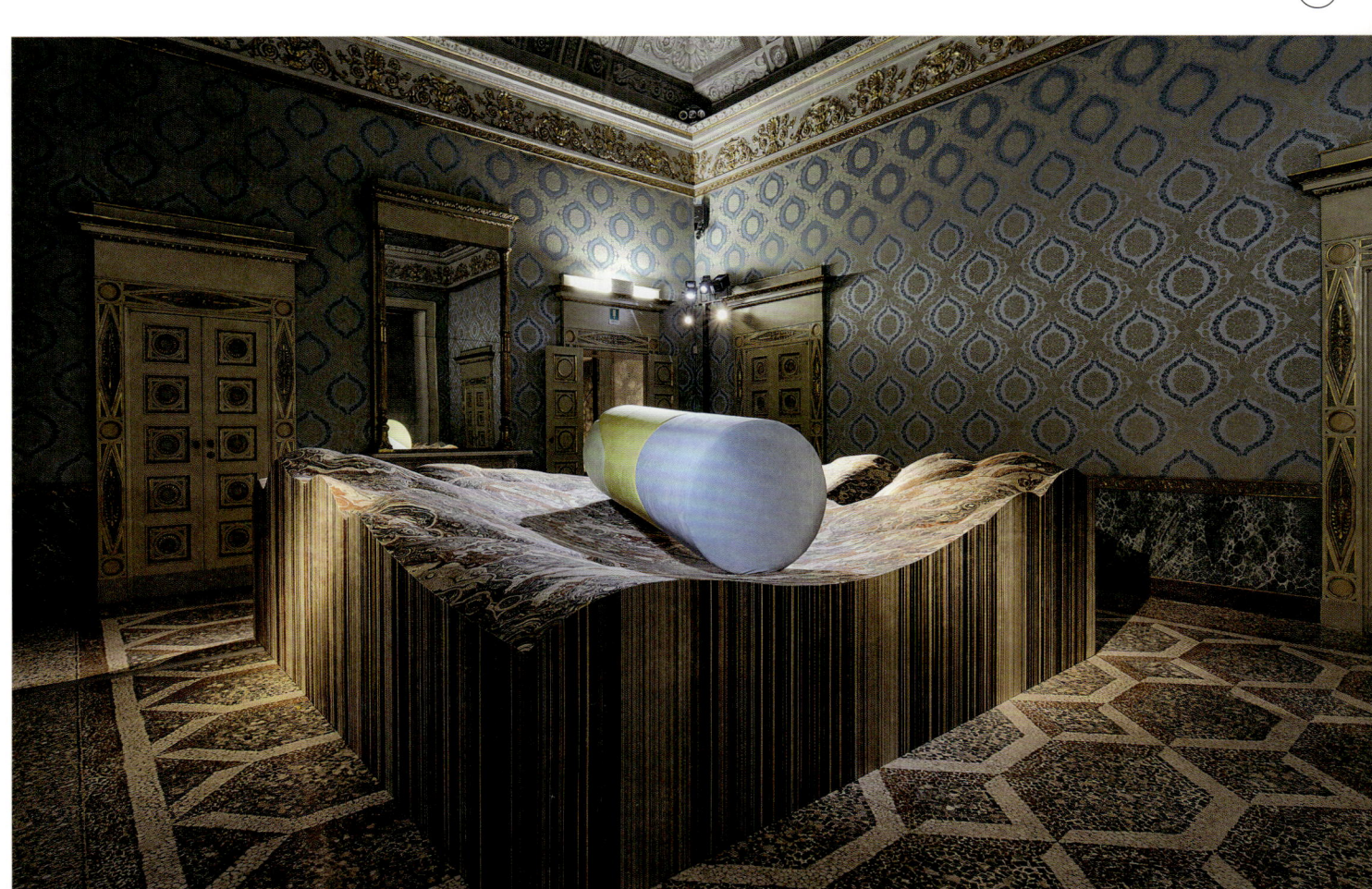

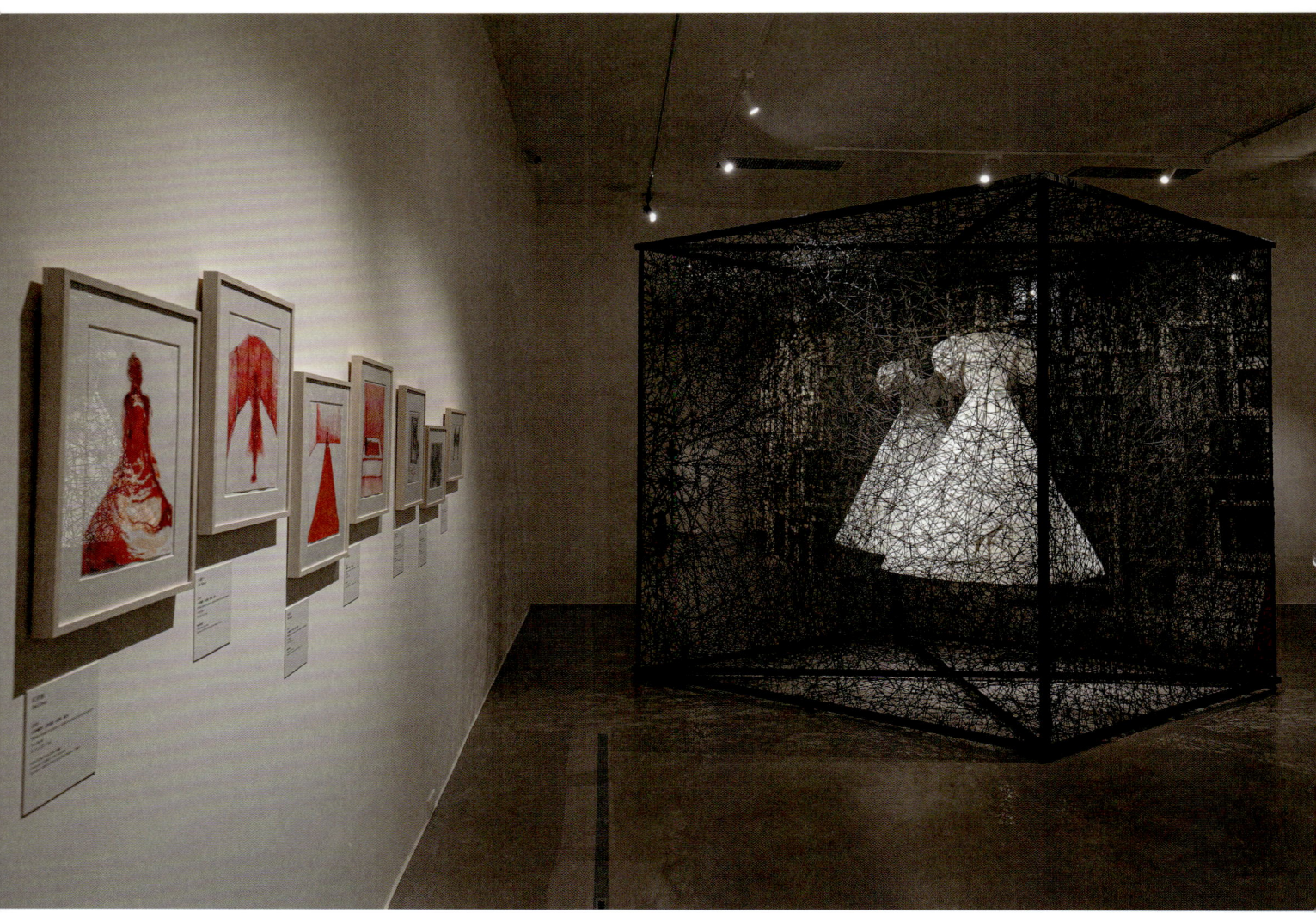

One of the nine rooms played host to a project by Chiharu Shiota, the artist from Osaka who has based her entire poetics on the relationship between space and time, in relation to the body. The installation was entitled just that: *Reflection of Space and Time*. To turn it into a reality, she used more than 100 km of Alcantara thread. One was slightly awestruck by the physicality of this intangible language. You looked at it, and you were put in mind of a maze-like trap, a regression of the mind that imprisons thoughts, and turns them into nightmares. You think of the cocoon of some primitive insect, infinitesimally small but tenacious, a tireless worker, able to gather up that whole mass of threads, and to withhold emotions, and compress feelings. This was a work that played with the idea of anxiety. Fascinating. A powerful gravitational pull.

    You went up to it, taking one small step at a time. The Alcantara threads floated freely, but how heavy they were! You felt the need to touch them, all those threads tied by hand, one by one. They were impassive to light, they were patient: they seemed eternal. Chiharu Shiota created complex worlds with the simplicity of a single thread. She attached

Following pages
Esther Stocker and Iris van Herpen, *Extended indefinitely*, "Nove viaggi nel tempo", Palazzo Reale, Milan 2018

cobwebs to the walls, and these moved in space like swarms of filaments, and wrapped themselves around objects. A fire-damaged, silent piano, or chairs that could not be sat on. Things of that nature. For the exhibition in the Prince's Apartment, the Japanese artist created the dark metal structure of a cage. The Alcantara threads moved around chaotically inside the regular volume of the form. They sought their own internal rhythm: infinite movements within a finite space. Like thoughts in the human brain, when they described curves, and leapt hither and thither. Sometimes their constant movement made you feel like you were losing your mind: our head is incapable of containing the infinite.

Chiharu Shiota's work was devised as a universal place, a custodian of memories. The monochrome web had a specific symbolic meaning, referring again to the body: the red threads, a colour that she often uses, represented blood that reaches every part of our organism, and that forms a line, a plane, a volume. The other key colour is black, which featured prominently in the Palazzo Reale installation, depicting the cosmos, the expanse of the universe. Chiharu Shiota placed a mirror at an oblique angle to the metal structure. The threads drifted around the reflective surface and were multiplied. Then they enveloped a white dress, a kind of cocktail dress, in Alcantara. The dress was suspended, without a body. The reflection created an illusion, another source of confusion. The Alcantara threads were flows of material, pockets in space and time in which one could go looking for the remains of the individual, of humanity.

It was not easy to leave this room. You had to overcome a sense of dizziness, the tale woven by all those kilometres of black Alcantara neatly tied up, the empty dress hanging in space, and its reflection. But the effort was worthwhile, for you then entered another room in the exhibition, also projected beyond the body. This room featured Iris Van Herpen, the designer who creates garments on the bodies of celebrities. Using Alcantara she made another sculpture, shaping the material by means of a meticulous, craft-inspired process. The dress, which was real, looked like a virtual image. Fragments of white light floating in the dark space of its surroundings, and resting on the gentle curves of a female body, which was absent. The only thing there was a dark, almost invisible mannequin. The slender strips of Alcantara created a constant movement intercepted by light beams: a choreography of lines resembling contour lines on a topographical map. A map. Yes, Iris Van Herpen's dress was reminiscent of a map, a way of finding oneself again after getting lost in the landscape of the body. To exist, we cling to art.

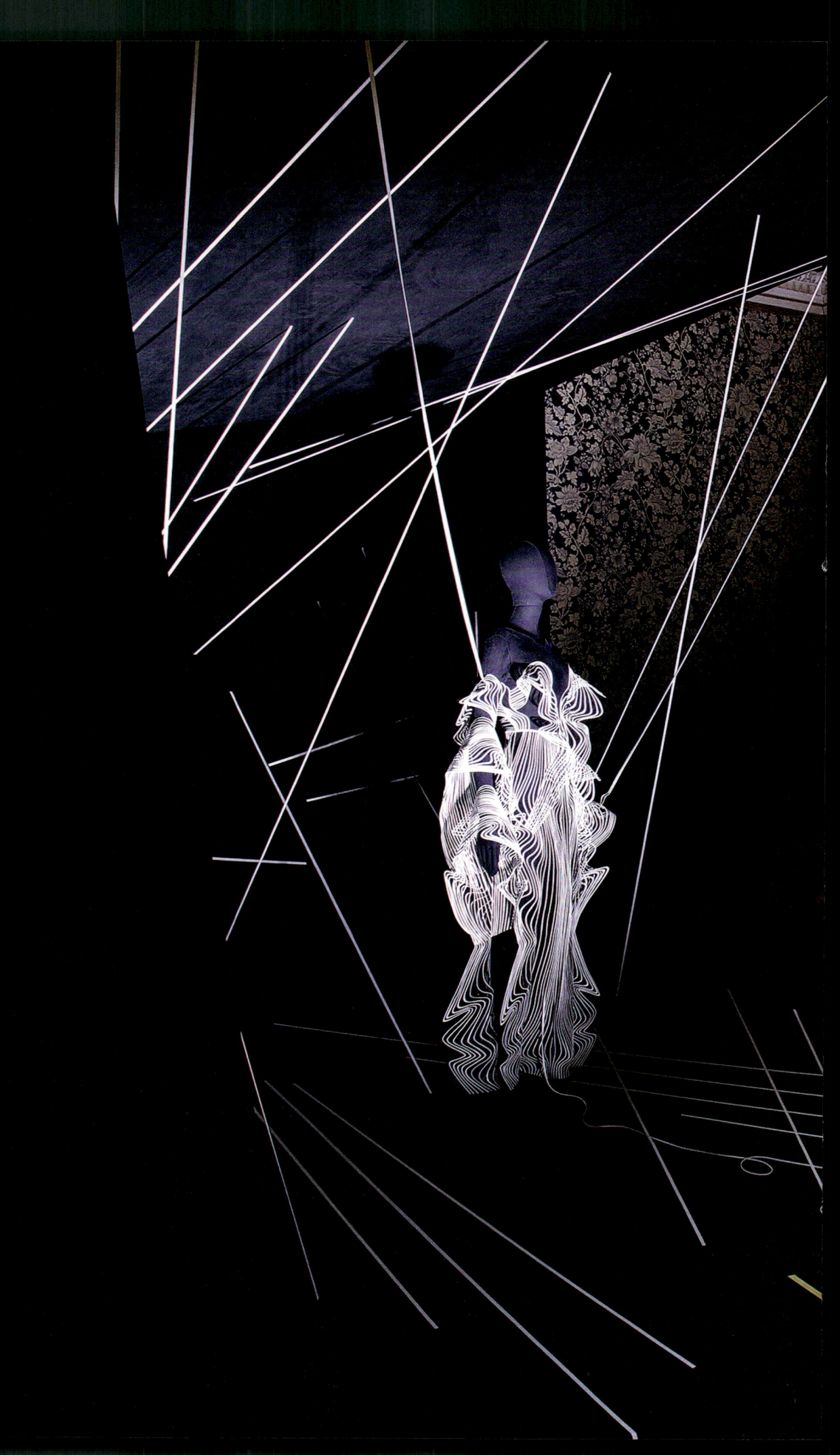

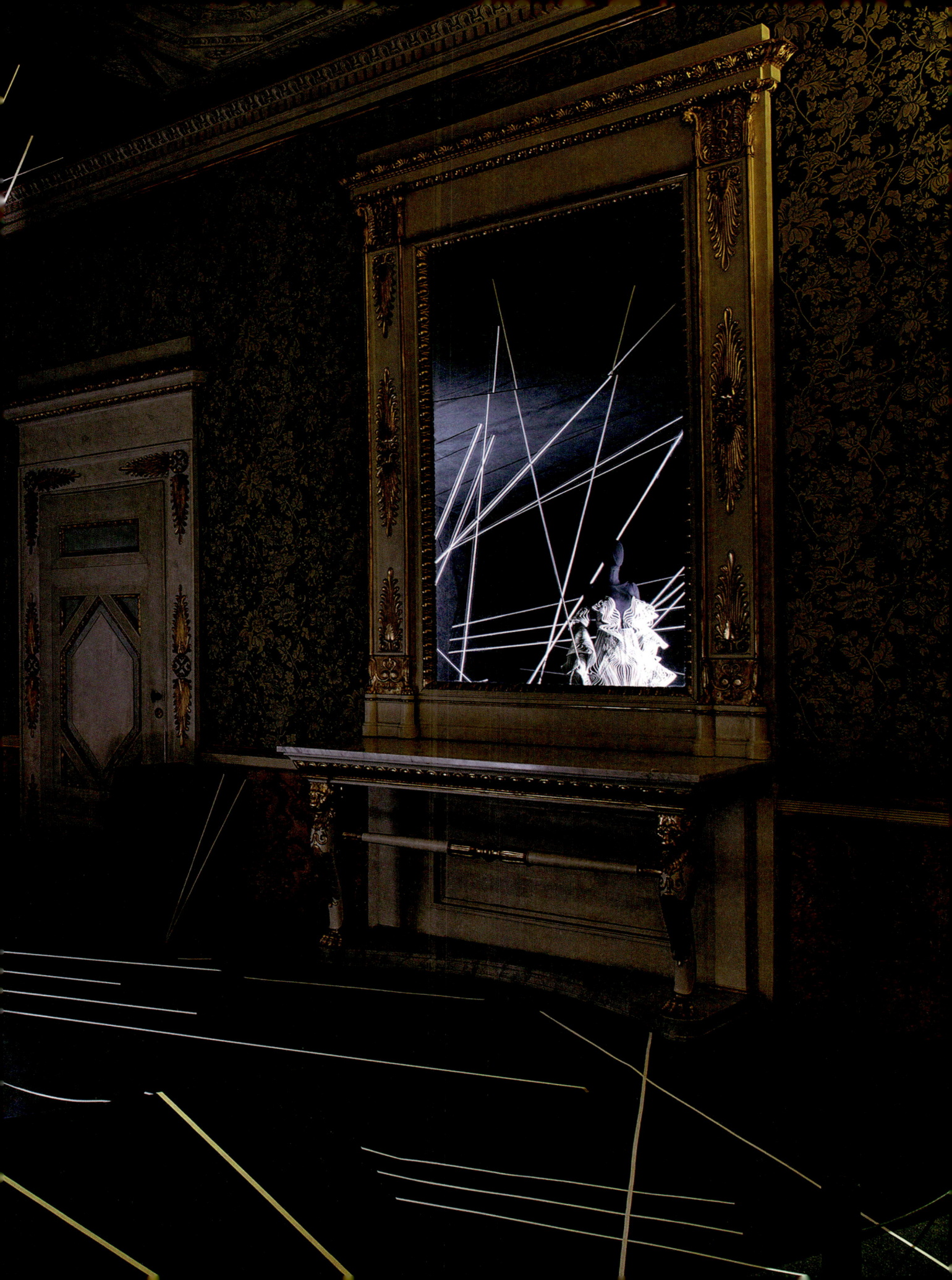

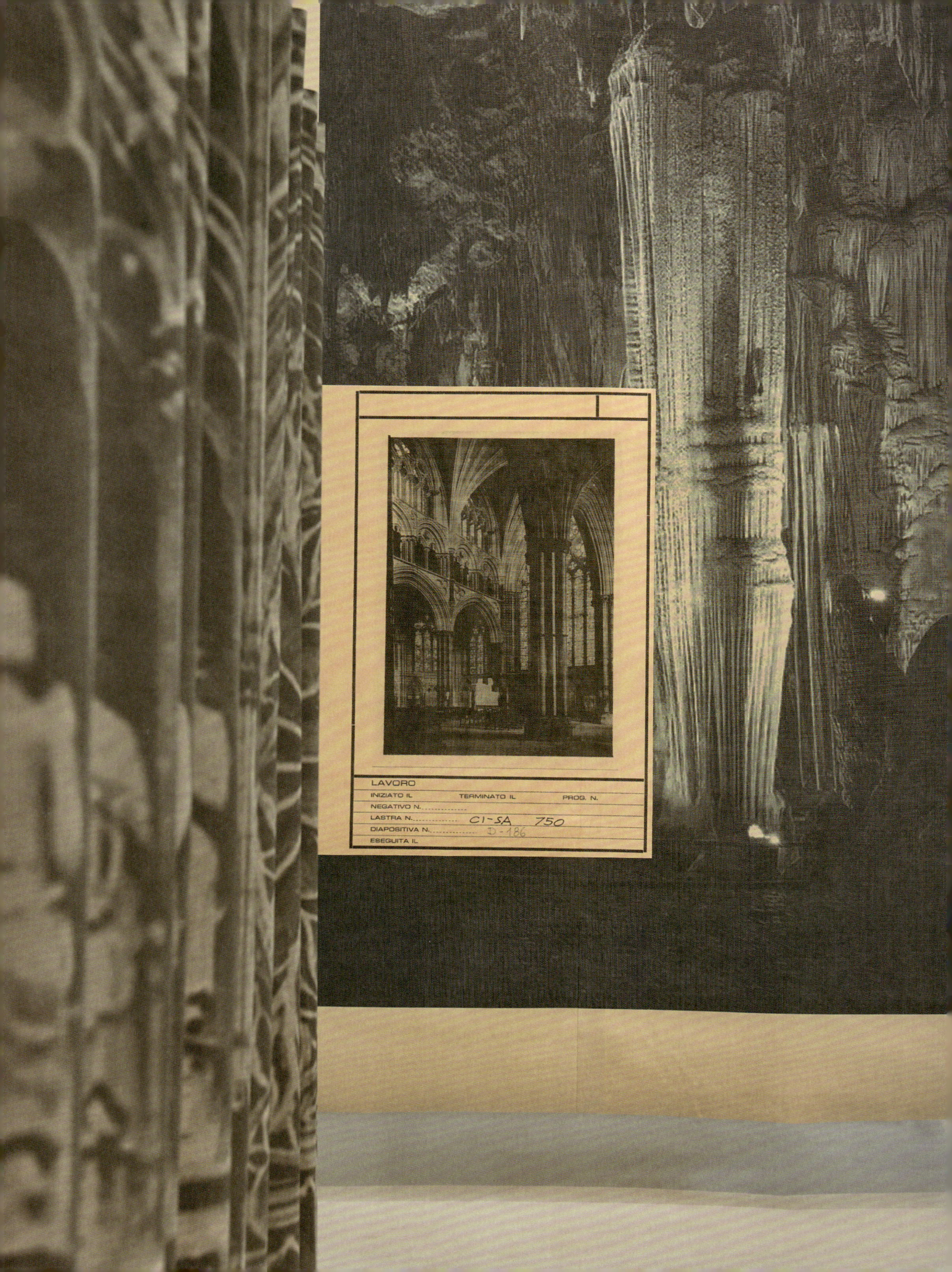

MOBILE STRUCTURE

"Studio Visit", the themed cycle dedicated to the dialogue between contemporary creatives and masters from the past, continued at the MAXXI. In 2019, the museum's archive welcomed the Formafantasma studio to its premises. Italian designers with an international culture: Andrea Trimarchi and Simone Farresin work by mixing scientific knowledge with an instinct for project design. They operate in a space straddling industry and craft skills, between the object and the end user; design as a critical form of the interpretation of reality.

Formafantasma, *Nervi in the making*, "Studio Visit", MAXXI Museum, Rome 2019

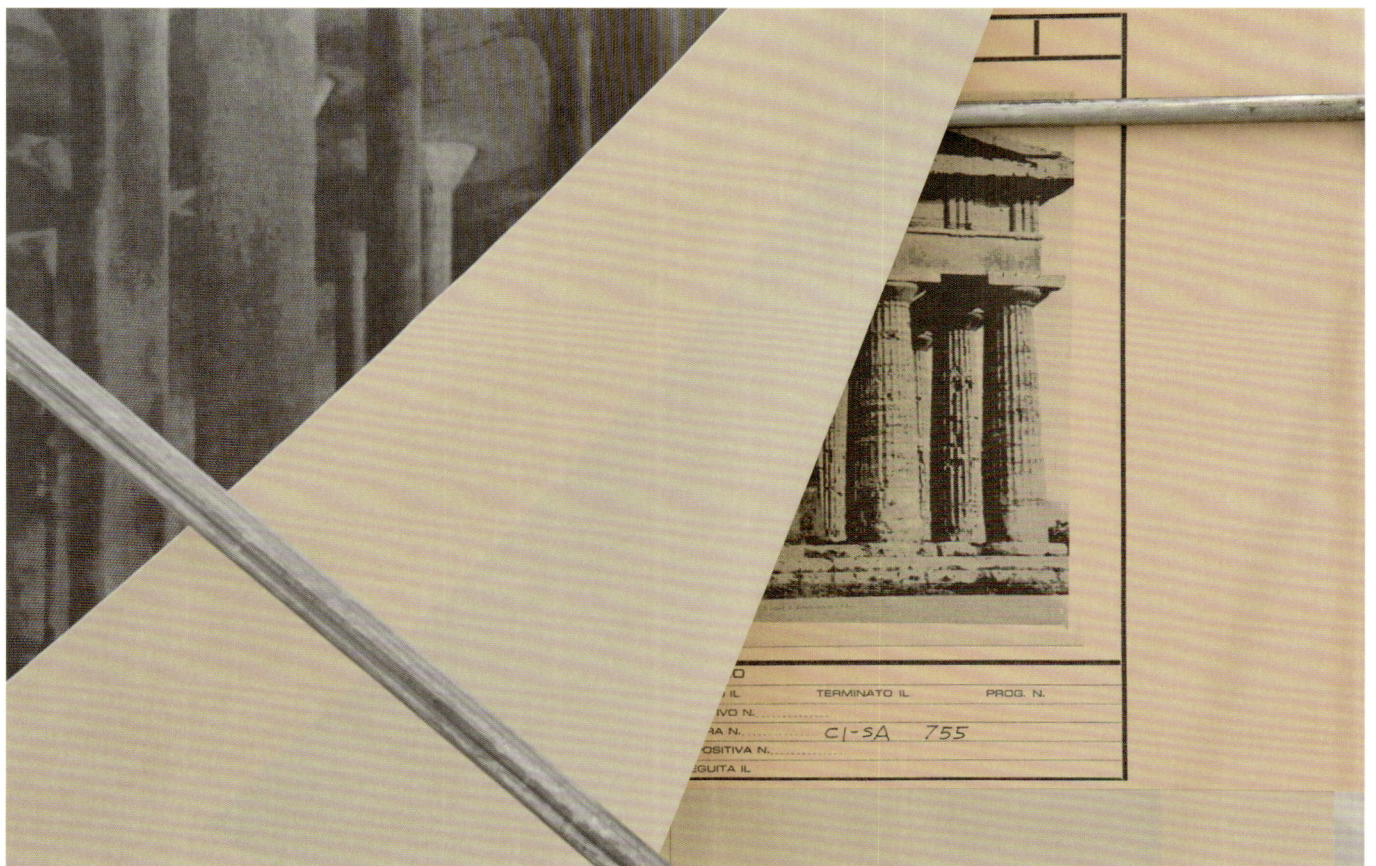

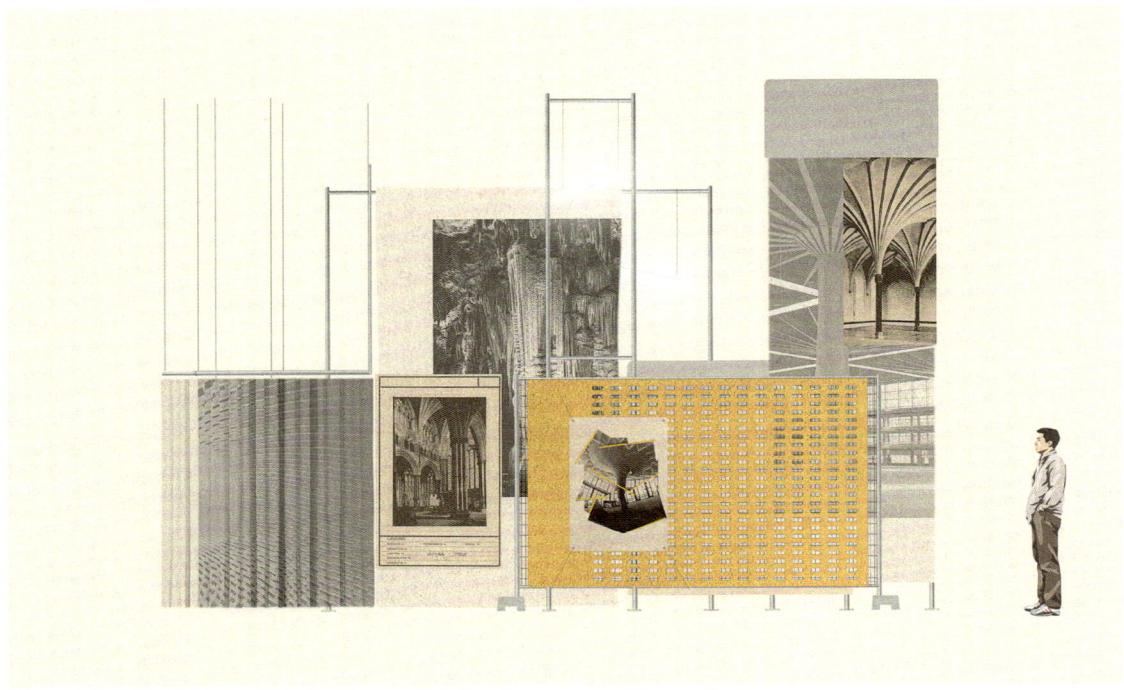

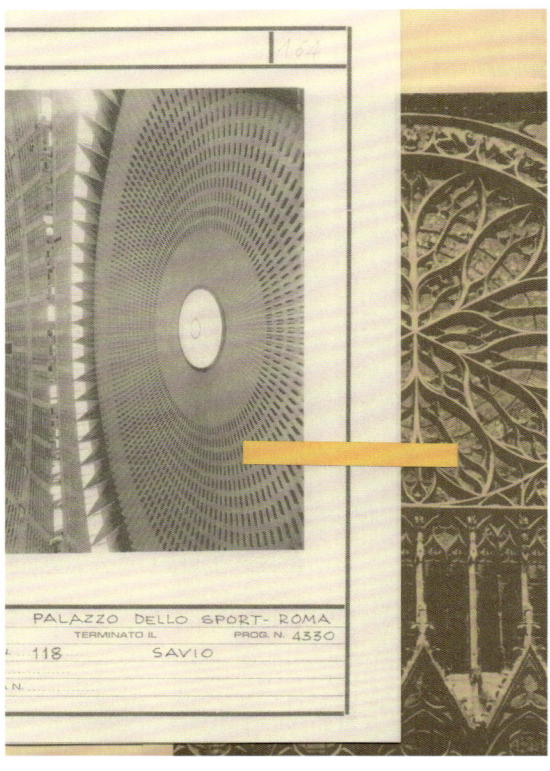
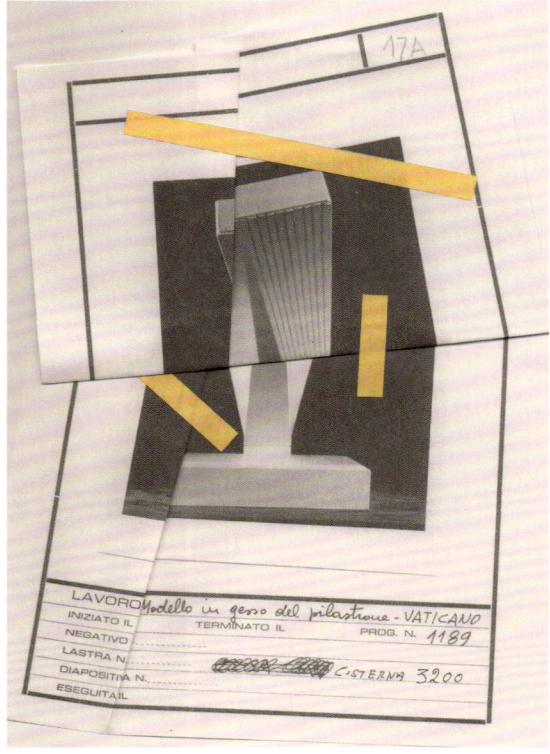

They decided to take a look at Pier Luigi Nervi, and reread the master's immense work on reinforced concrete, attracted as they were by Nervi's mental rigour, and the calatoguing criteria that he himself devised. An all-round engineer, he had compiled a record of his research in the form of file cards, complete with pictures and technical notes: large box inserts with a black outline on the white background of paper that had now yellowed with age. Placed in sequence, those paper records are like an archaic, conceptual version of Instagram. Neat and elegant configurations of solids and empty spaces, framing the memory of what was a revolution in architectural design. Reinforced concrete changed the world, and the way buildings were imagined, enabling bold solutions that play with new static equilibriums. Creating structures that cling to the air, but that are solid and stable. In this area of applied research, Nervi wrote works of fundamental importance to modern architecture. He carried out and documented an astounding number of experiments, backed up by calculations and experimental trials. A far-sighted work, the very work that made our country's post-war reconstruction possible.

The language that facilitates dialogue between creatives from different eras is Alcantara. Indeed, Formafantasma's research into Pier Luigi Nervi and reinforced concrete gave rise to extraordinary points of contact between the two materials. Both are versatile, functional, flexible, adaptable to the most differing applications, and able to collaborate with other materials. "Alcantara expresses itself with extraordinary adaptability in every context in which it is applied," said the designers, "as if it was governed by an artificial intelligence of its own."

The result was an installation recreating a building site environment. Scaffolding and tubes and metal grilles supported tables from Nervi's archive, accompanied by audio recordings from his university lectures. "Structure," the people from Formafantasma went on to explain, "is the keyword which, more than any other word, brings out the affinity between reinforced concrete and Alcantara."

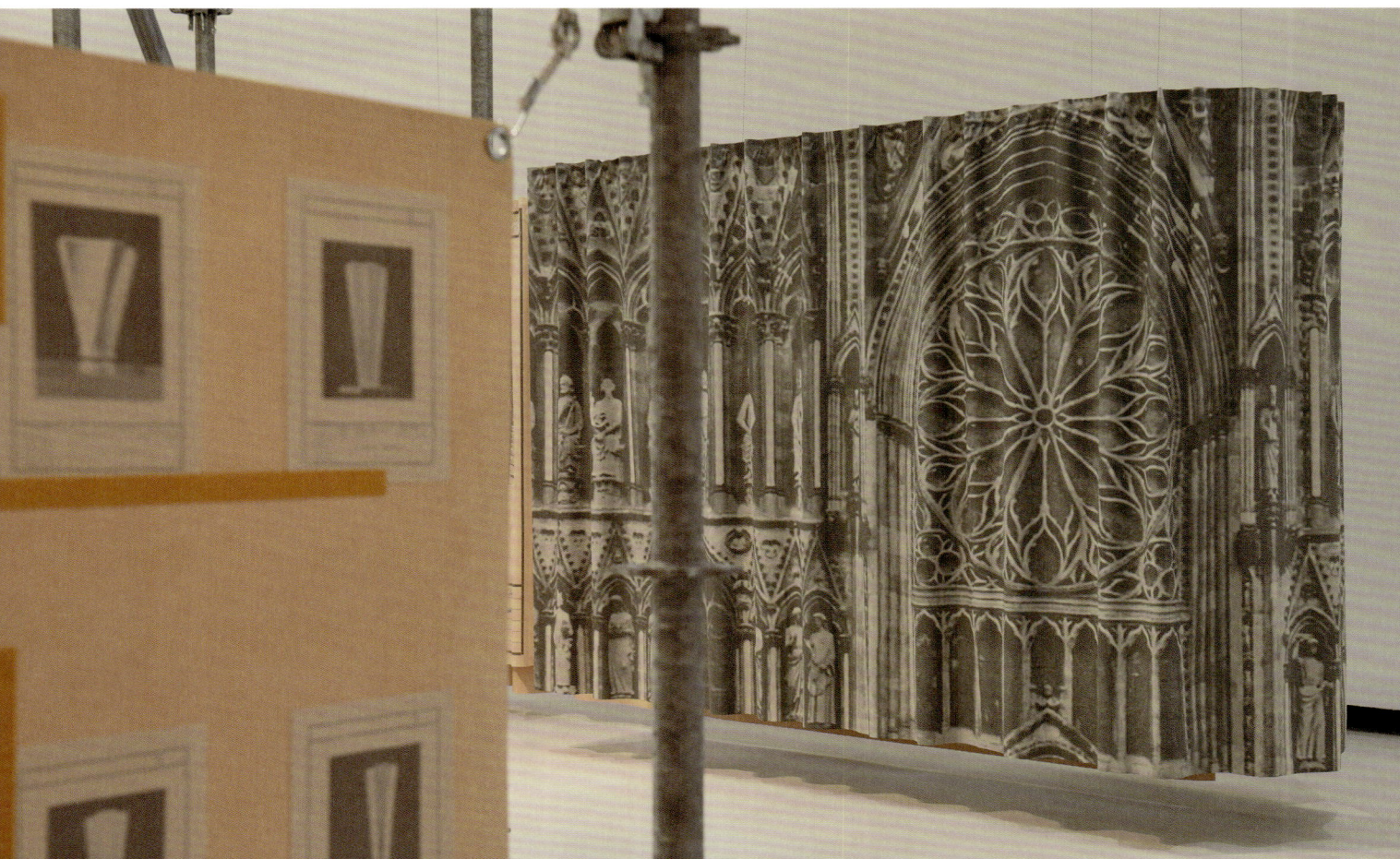

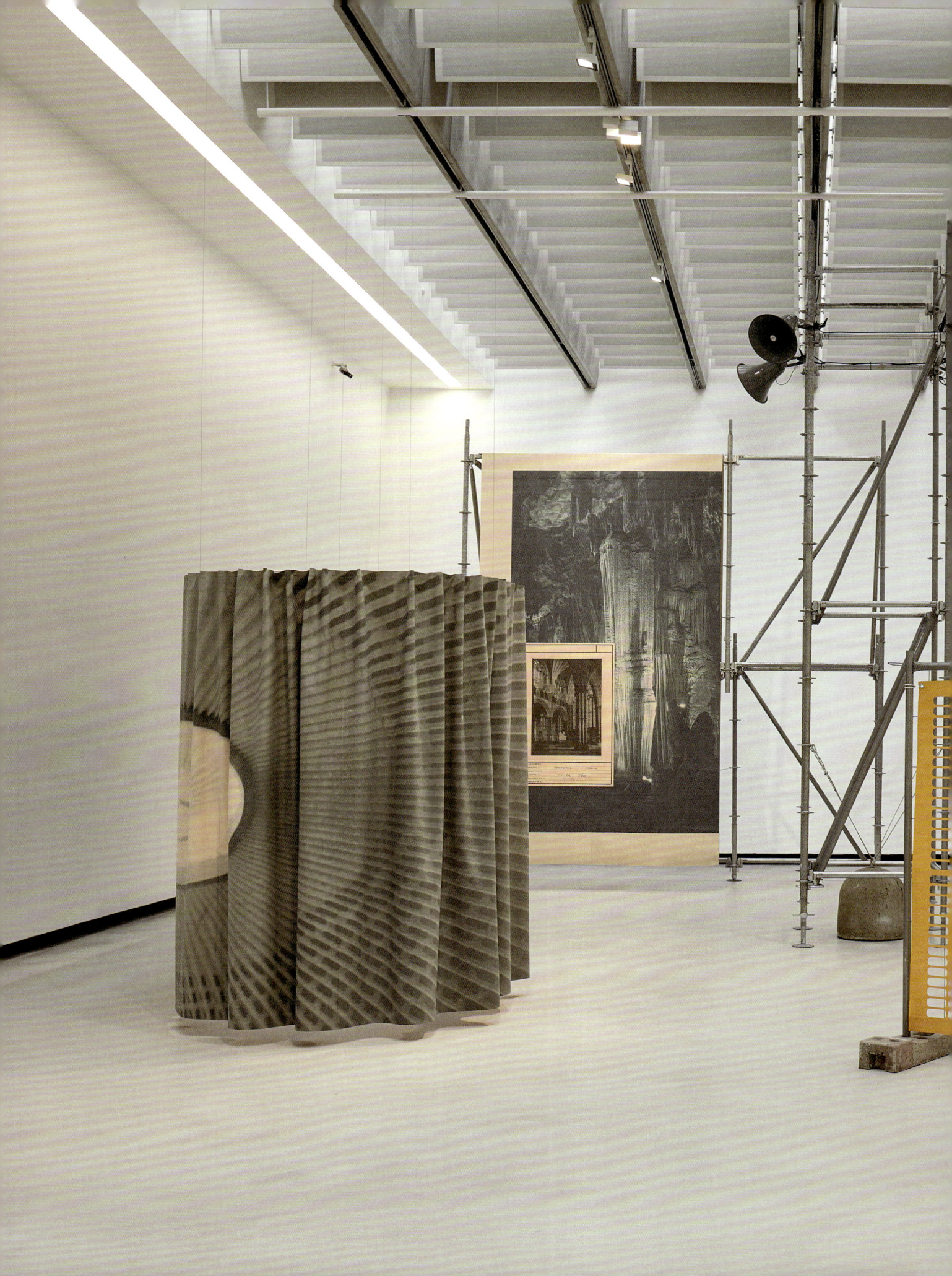

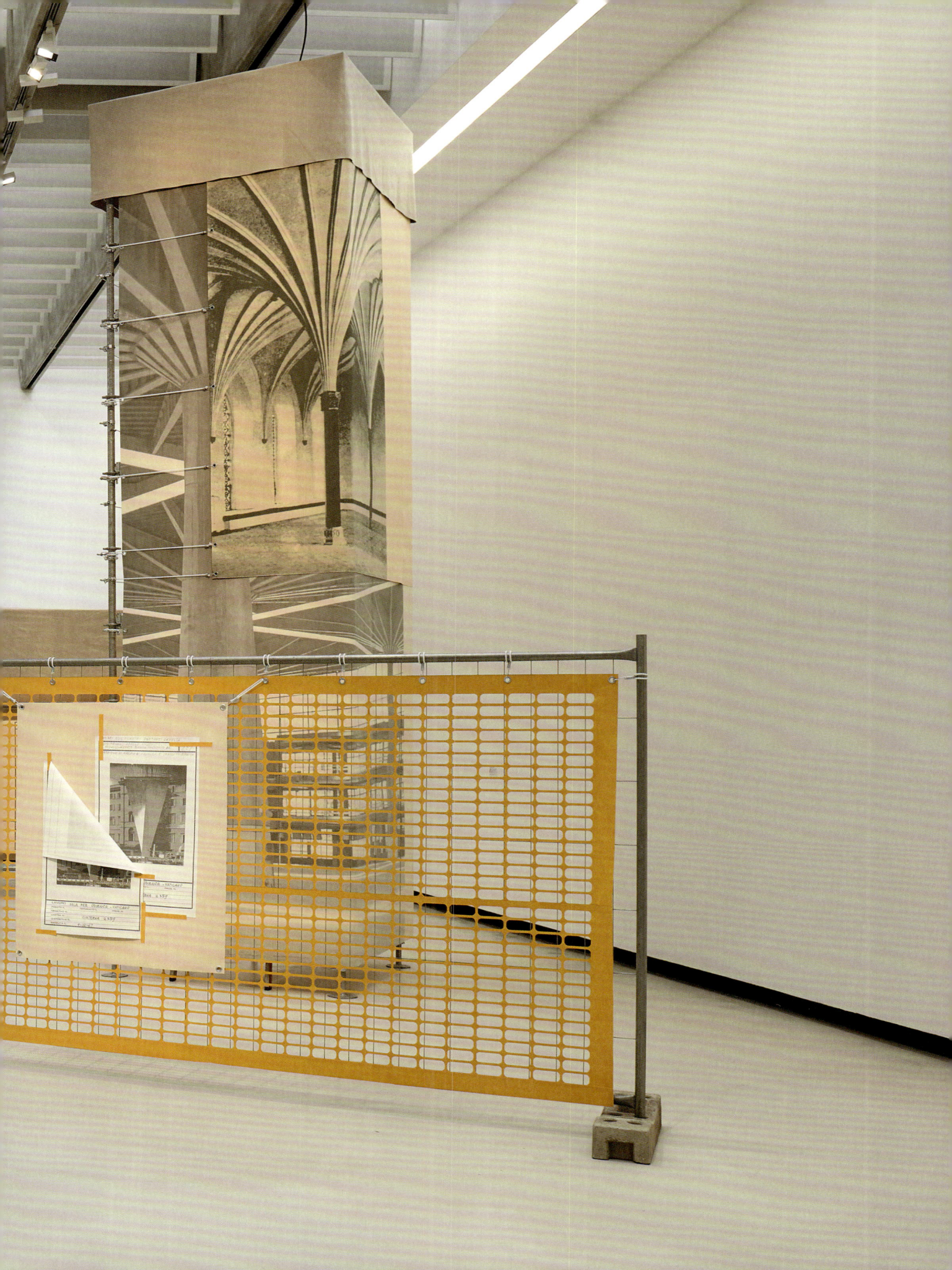

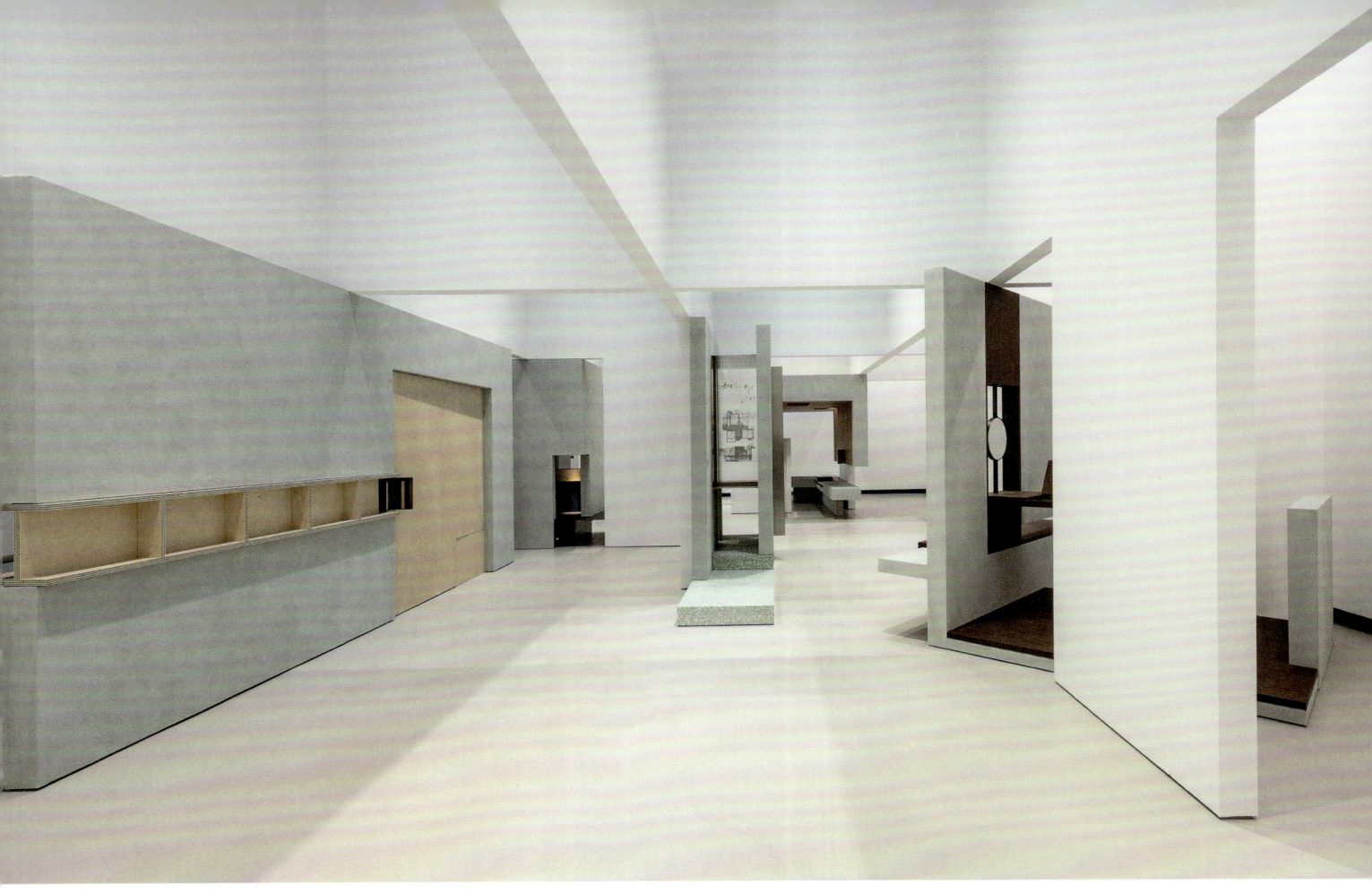

Neri&Hu, *Traversing Thresholds*, "Studio Visit", MAXXI Museum, Rome 2021

    Mobile structures in the material also featured two years later, in 2021, when the MAXXI played host to Neri&Hu engaging in a dialogue with Carlo Scarpa. A research process that explored new horizons, in Alcantara's customary international dimension. Neri&Hu interpreted Scarpa's work by setting out from the notion of "threshold," an architectural concept that identifies spaces that are adjacent but contrasting, such as indoor and outdoor, public and private.

    "The threshold is a space," said Lyndon Neri, "but it is also time." Rossana Hu added: "I think of it as the space of an interval, a void that gets filled up, like silence between notes in music." Guided by this view, the creatives reread key themes in Scarpa's work: emptiness, suspension, angled perspective, and slippage in structural axes. Pure lessons in architecture that were the inspiration for plans for new interiors: six views where the public was invited to look for Scarpa's original message. All created in Alcantara, which proved to be an extraordinary building material, with huge potential in terms of versatility, tactile quality, softness, and elegance.

    The possibilities of use for the creation of new materials knows no bounds. New Alcantara forms, such as the beautiful multi-layer panel created by superimposing material in place of particle board.

    The keyword remains: structure.

    A structure that is mobile, malleable and versatile, like Alcantara itself.

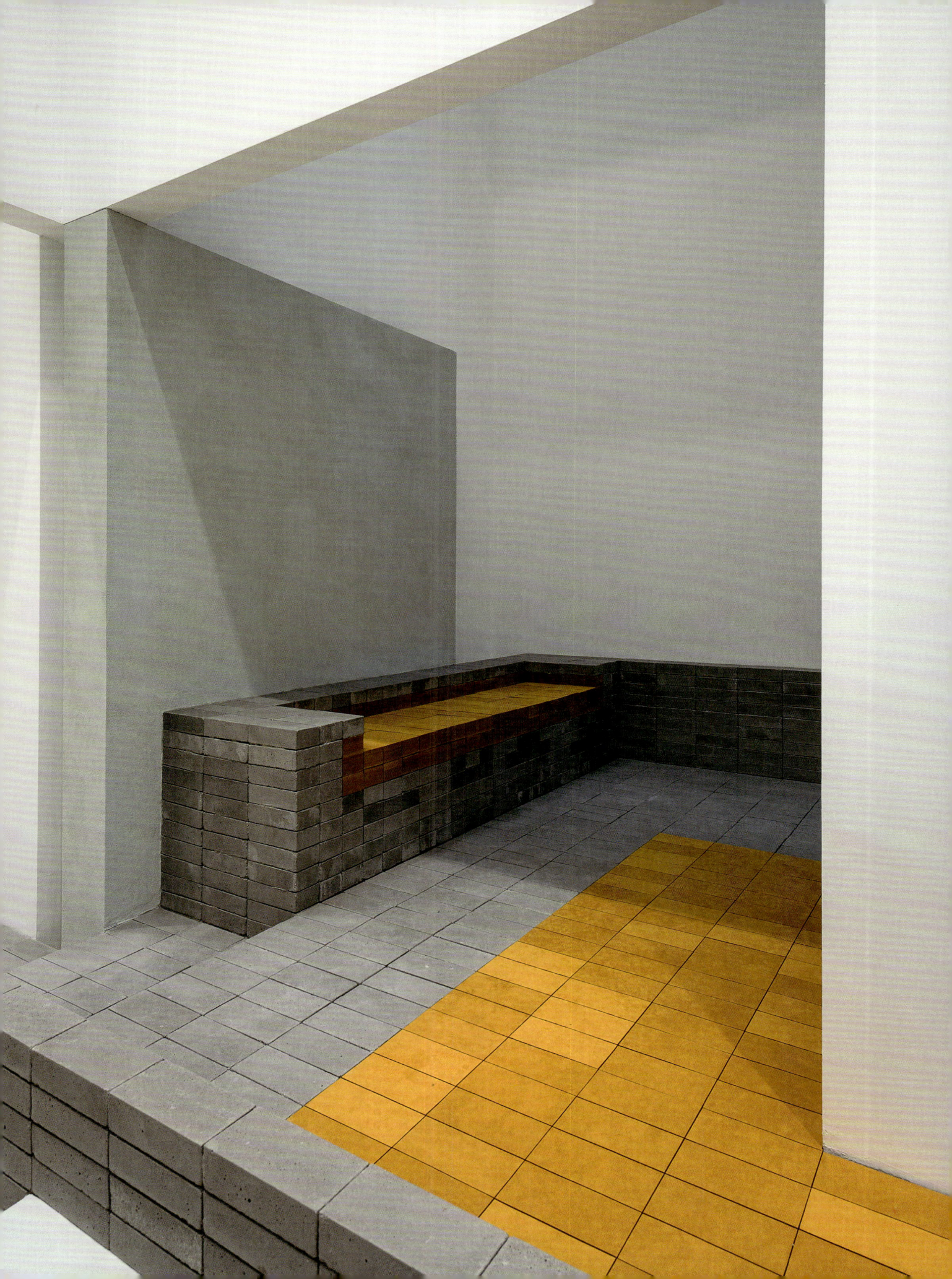

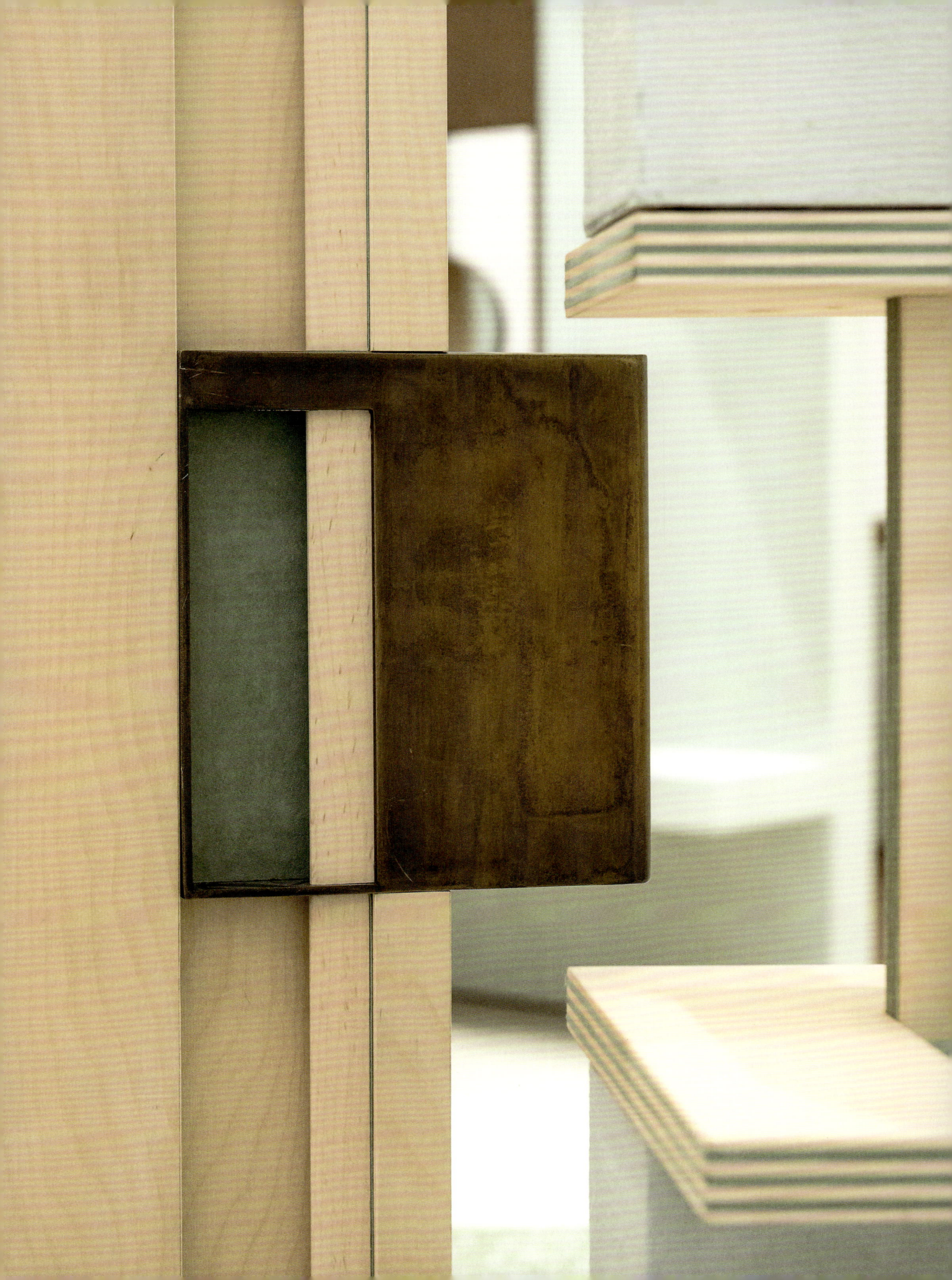

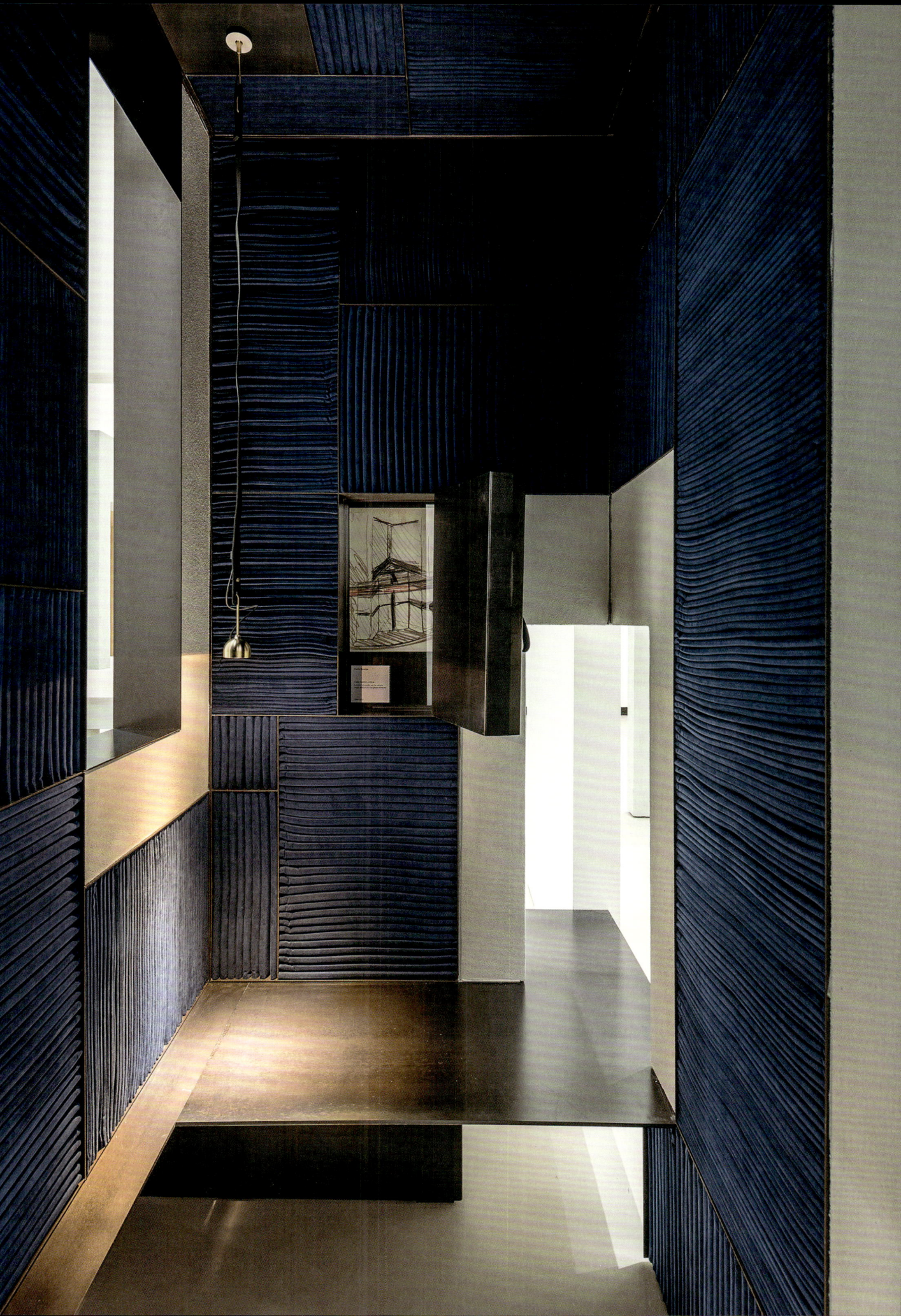

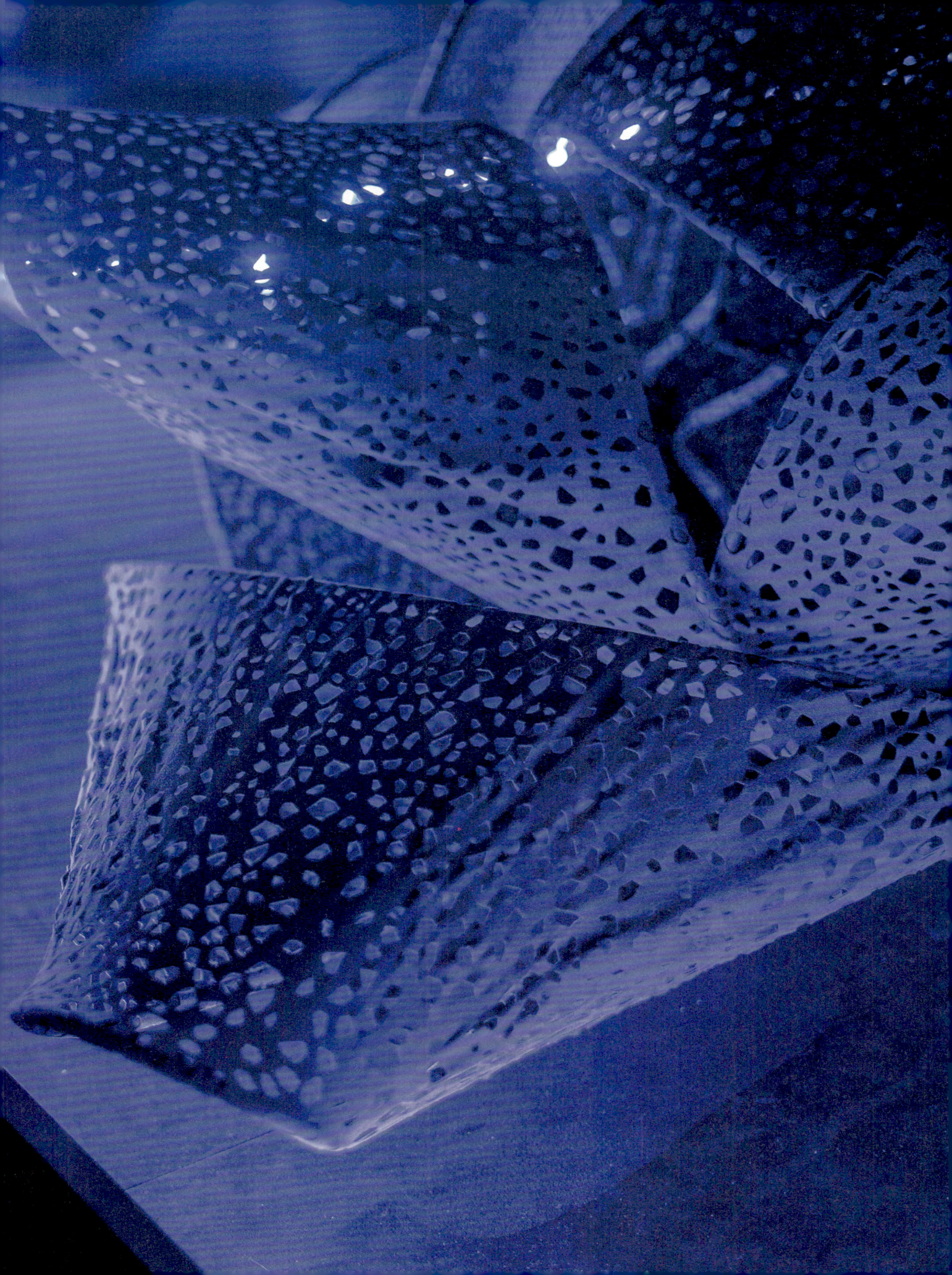

FLUID SPACE

The works travelled. They left the Prince's Apartment at Milan's Palazzo Reale, and the collections of the MAXXI Architettura museum in Rome, and found themselves in a famous lagoon, floating rapidly over the water among the canal ferries and fishermen's boats. They sailed along the Grand Canal, and moored at the private jetty of Palazzo Rocca Contarini Corfù. In 2018, the 16th Architecture Biennale was under way, and the Alcantara works were ready to catch up with the people visiting Venice for the occasion. The works had already been created and exhibited, and were now having a change of venue, offering new manifestations of Alcantara as an art material. Venice is not just a city, it is a container of meanings. Seen as an exhibition space, it alters the perception of works. Especially those chosen for this initial exhibition, entitled "Multiforms". Variations on the Alcantara theme that define new spaces to be lived in, and to be experienced.

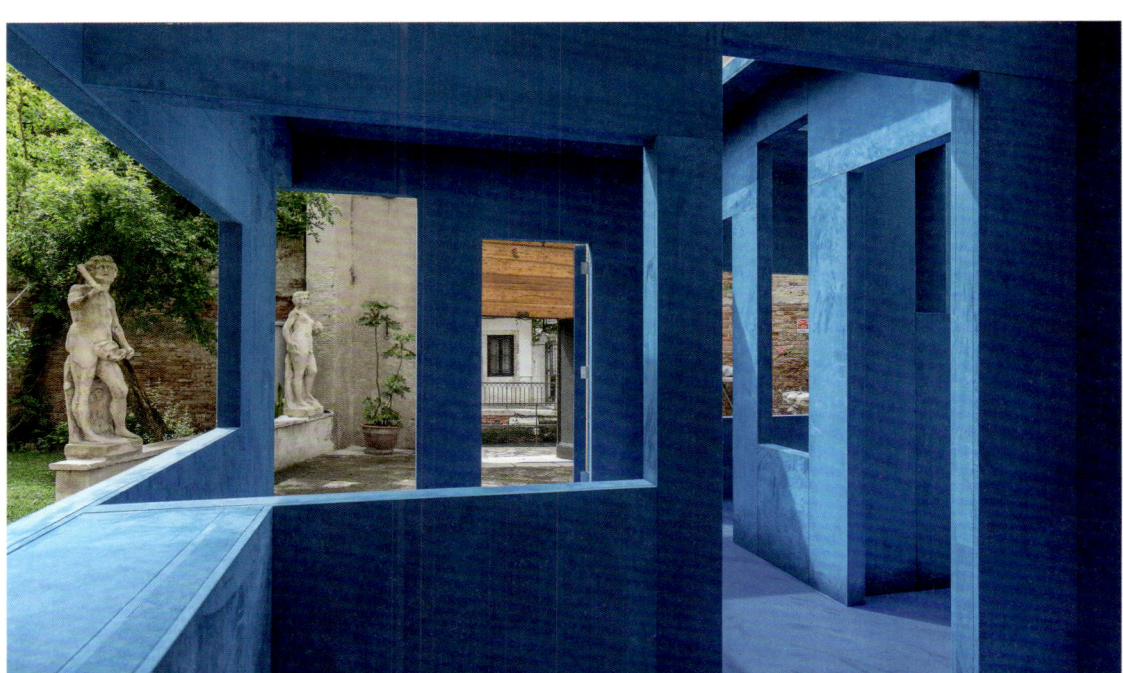

Krijn de Koning, *Work for Alcantara*, *Blue Chair*, "Multiforme, declinazioni tra spazio e tempo", Palazzo Rocca Contarini Corfù, Venice 2018

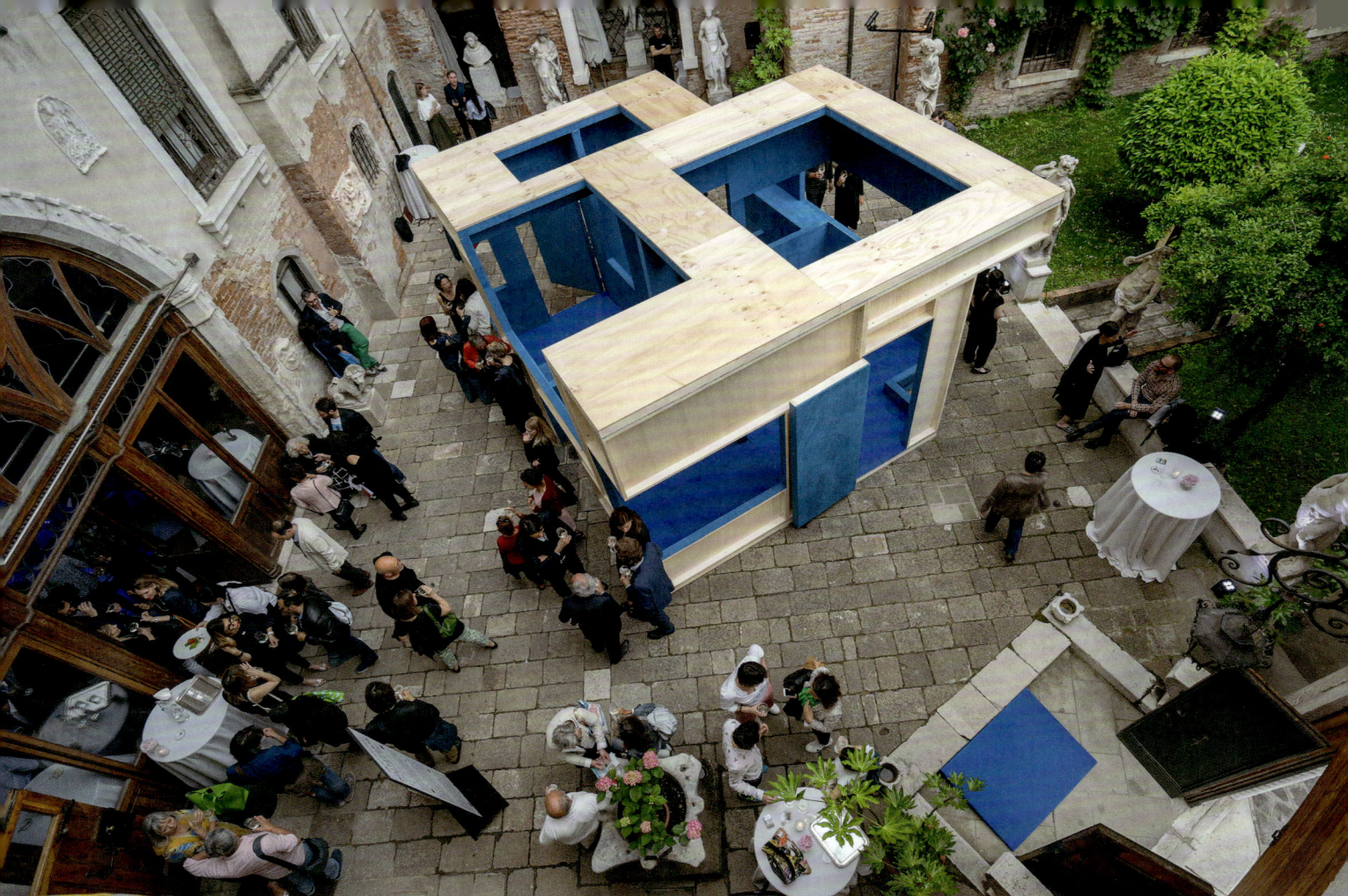

The setting was prestigious. And multiform, too. Actually, there were two palazzi, dating from different periods, which the Contarini family built and joined together in order to have the kind of space suitable for social life in medieval and Renaissance Venice. The location was in the Dorsoduro district, looking out over the Grand Canal. The older palazzo, on the right, is 15th century, in Venetian Gothic. The left-hand building is 17th century, the work of Vincenzo Scamozzi, a pupil of Palladio. The perspective scenery of the city of Thebes at the Teatro Olimpico in Vicenza is by him. An architectural master, whom Scamozzi himself regarded as: "exact science."

    Previous guests at the palazzo, prior to Alcantara, included: emperors of Austria and Prussia; poets, musicians and inventors such as D'Annunzio, Mascagni and Marconi; and members of the royal Savoy dynasty and princely couples such as Charles and Diana, accompanied for the occasion all the way up to the panoramic turret. On this occasion, Alcantara found lodgings lower down, in the wonderful internal courtyard and in the large rooms on the ground floor, barely above water level. An ideal horizon for *Arch/arcology* by Nanda Vigo, *Work for Alcantara, Blue Chair* by Krijin de Koning, and *Beyond the Nuclear Garden* by the German collective Zeitguised.

    The city of the future invented by Nanda Vigo, to plans by Paolo Soleri, gained an entirely new charm in the setting of the Venetian palazzo.

Krijn de Koning, *Work for Alcantara, Blue Chair*, "Multiforme, declinazioni tra spazio e tempo", Palazzo Rocca Contarini Corfù, Venice 2018

Nanda Vigo, *Arch/arcology*, "Multiforme, declinazioni tra spazio e tempo", Palazzo Rocca Contarini Corfù, Venice 2018

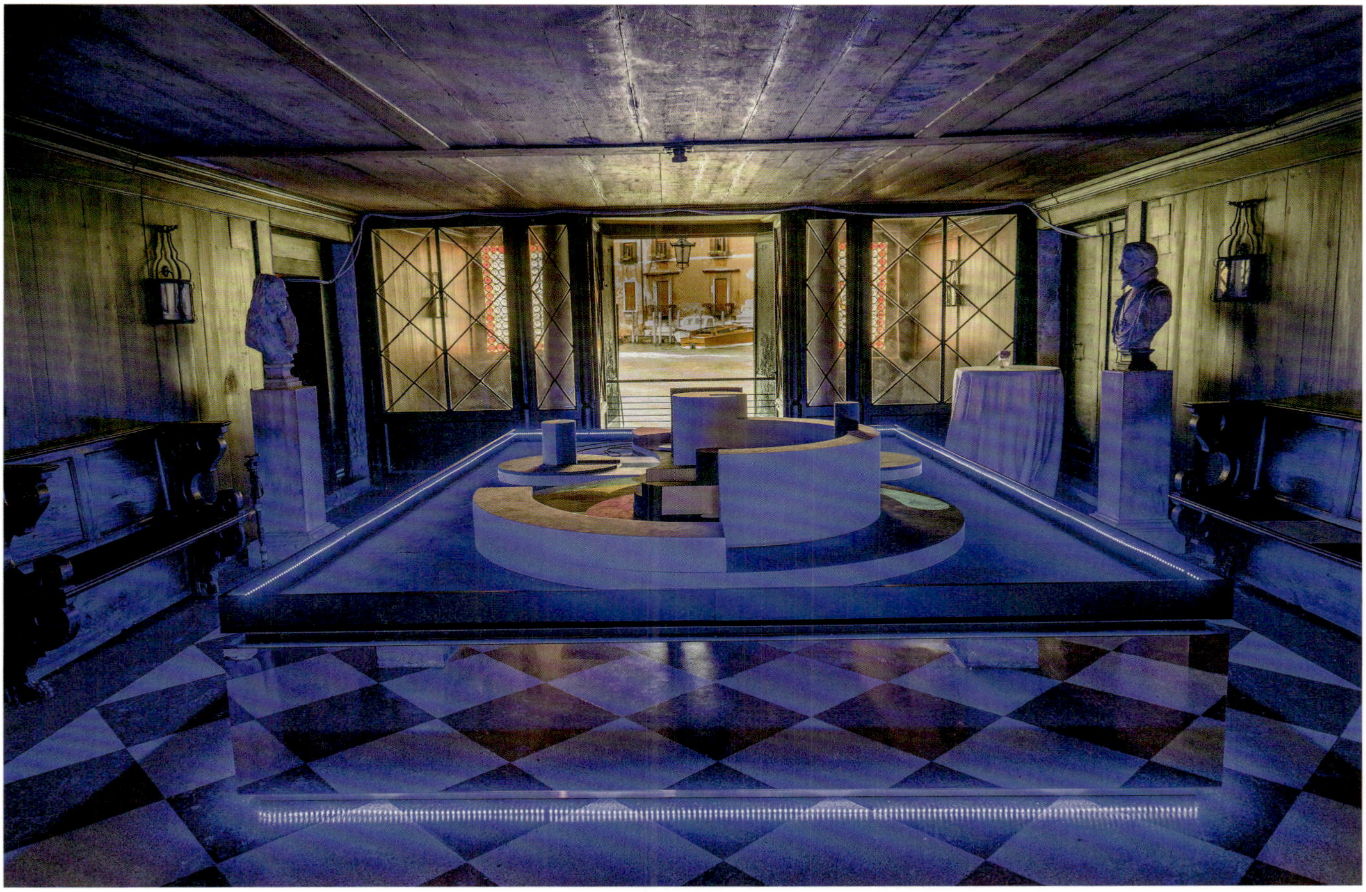

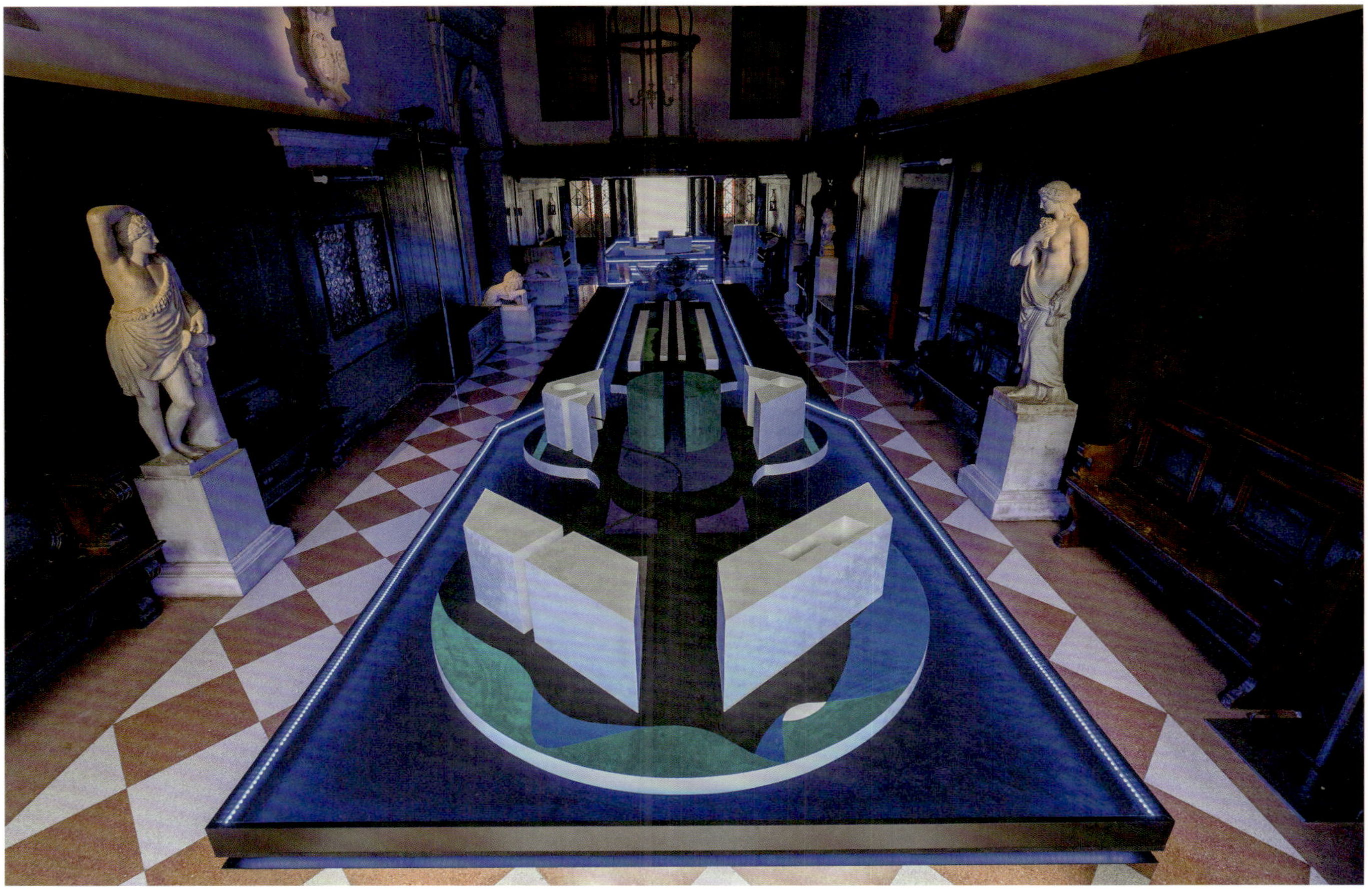

153

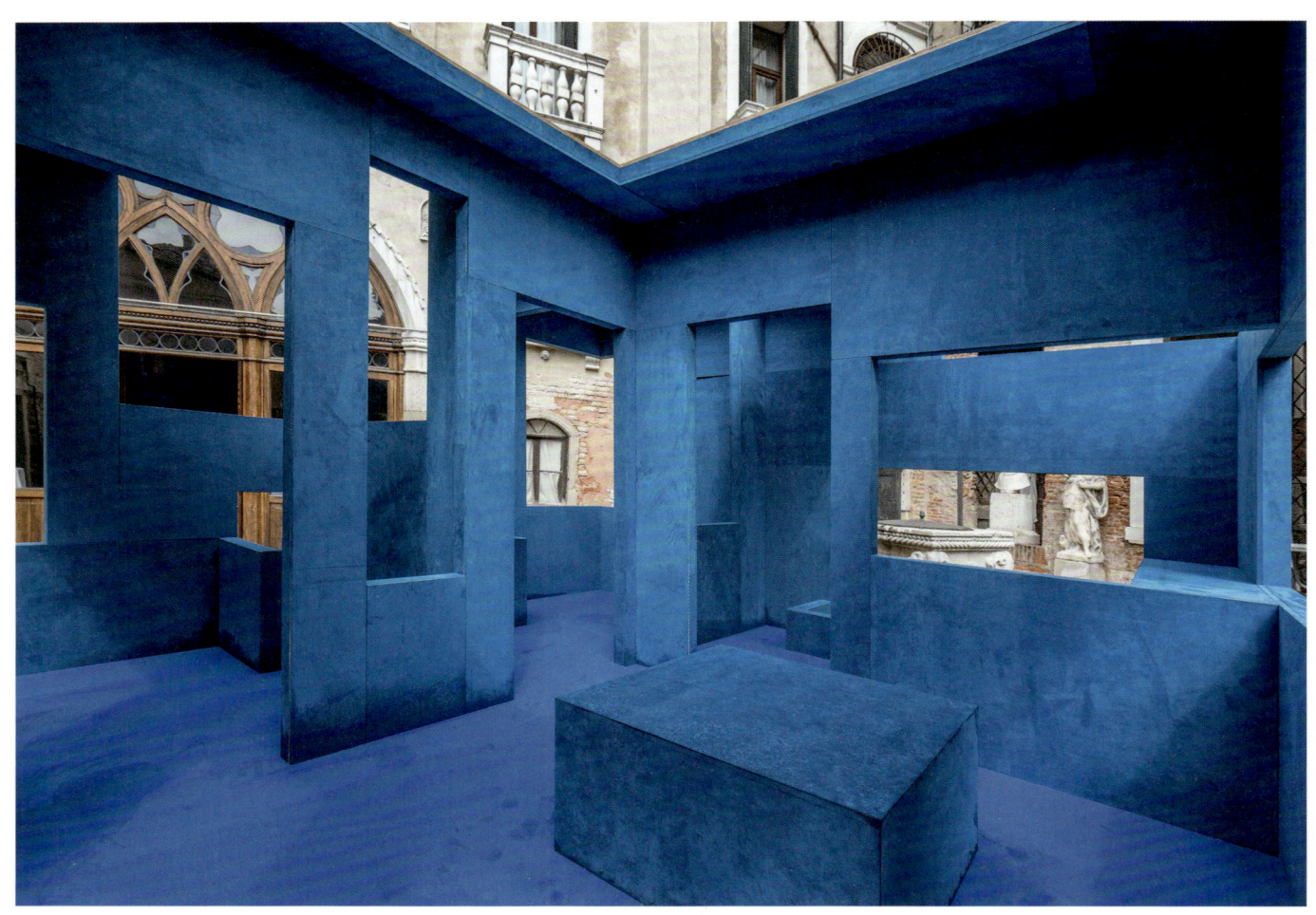

Krijn de Koning, *Work for Alcantara, Blue Chair*, "Multiforme, declinazioni tra spazio e tempo", Palazzo Rocca Contarini Corfù, Venice 2018

The Alcantara components that were hung on the walls at the MAXXI in Rome, were here arranged in the middle of the room, over the timber foundations. As stated earlier, the vanishing point is water. A fluid horizon, that by definition is ever-changing in its forms and state, which is always in active motion. The statues of the palazzo, along the sides of the room, eyed the volumes of the Soleri-Vigo city. They seemed to be forging new connections across time. A surprising, breathtaking dramatic effect.

Krijin de Koning, on the other hand, exhibited the structure that he had created for Palazzo Reale in Milan. In this case, too, the new and different setting stimulated new meanings in the Alcantara work. The horizon, which was absent at Palazzo Reale, became a prominent feature here, in the dimension that only Venice can provide. The "room without a room" was assembled in the palazzo's internal courtyard. A blue box, made entirely of Alcantara, where an effect of perceptual alienation is produced, due to the lack of traditional spatial reference points. The public strolled around between the walls, without managing to determine what spaces were designed to be occupied. The monochrome architecture suggested the colours and hues of the waters of Venice, and its skies, it enveloped and embraced, but at the same time it fragmented the spectator's vision.

Nanda Vigo, *Arch/arcology*, "Multiforme, declinazioni tra spazio e tempo", Palazzo Rocca Contarini Corfù, Venice 2018

Following pages Zeitguised, *Oltre il giardino nucleare*, "Multiforme, declinazioni tra spazio e tempo", Palazzo Rocca Contarini Corfù, Venice 2018

The focal point of this Alcantara space was a stylized chair, also blue. An invitation to stop, to give a new sense of balance to one's perceptions.

Finally, the offering from Berlin's Zeitguised was *Beyond the Nuclear Garden*. Art and digital design, constructed on the foundations of algorithms. Digital textures and volumes were projected onto the ancient walls of Palazzo Rocca Contarini Corfù, and these moved in virtual space. A sequence of colours that produced organic and anthropomorphic shapes. A visual dance, stimulated by rhythmic, tribal sounds. Acting as a counterpoint to this were two comfortable Alcantara chairs, produced by the graphic breaking down of the waves that rippled through the space. It was all highly complex, innovative and technological, but at the same time so simple that it resembled a children's playground; an explicit urging to touch, listen, and joyfully revel in the sensory experience of the material.

After a decade of activity in the world of contemporary arts, staging almost a hundred exhibitions, and involving dozens of artists, Alcantara continues to travel across the world, and to lay down bridges between places and cultures. The fluid languages of art material go beyond barriers, they cross space and time, and they reach new and unexplored territories in a dimension that is ever more international.

Venice is a stop-off on a journey: the gateway to the East.

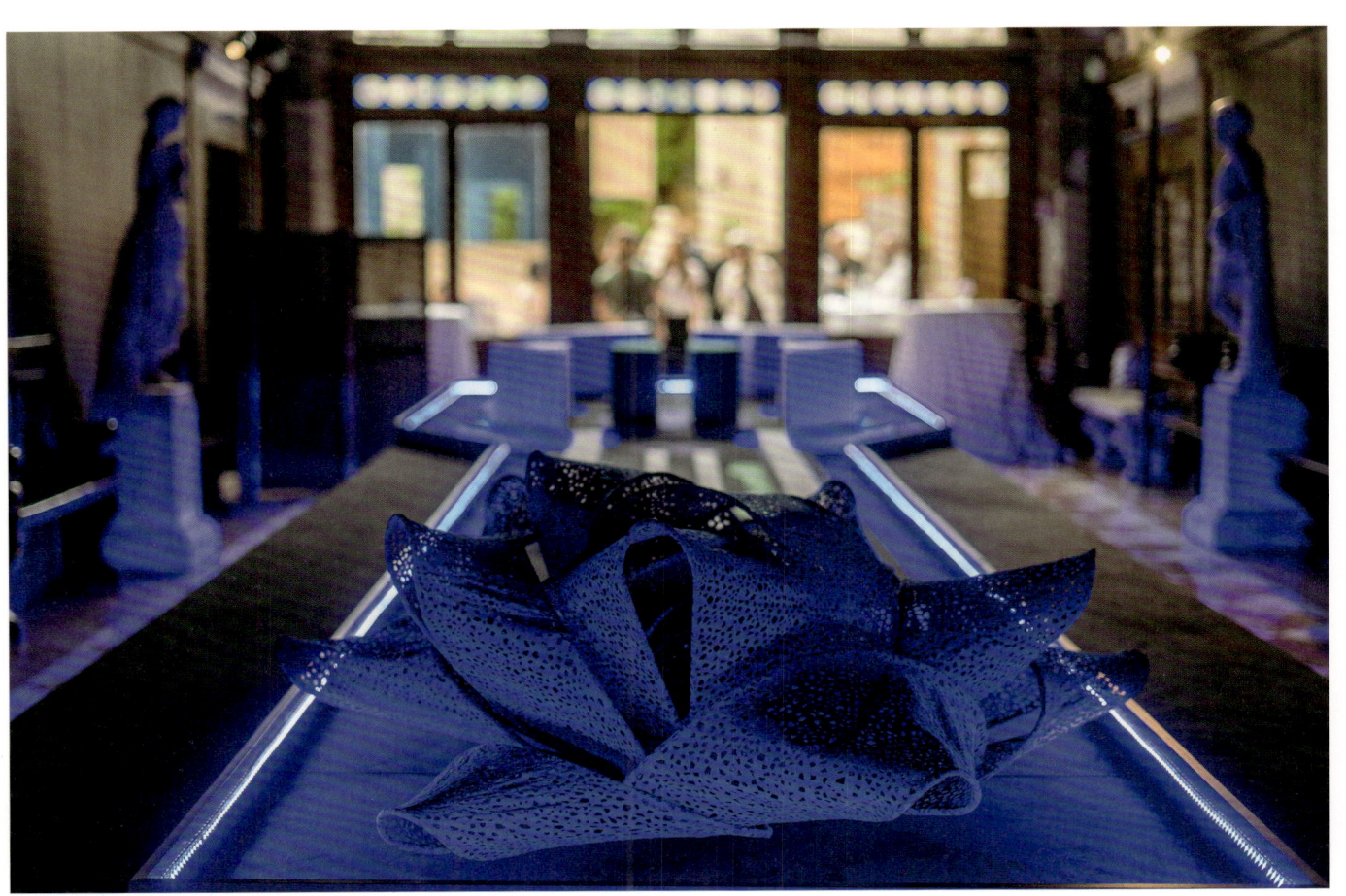

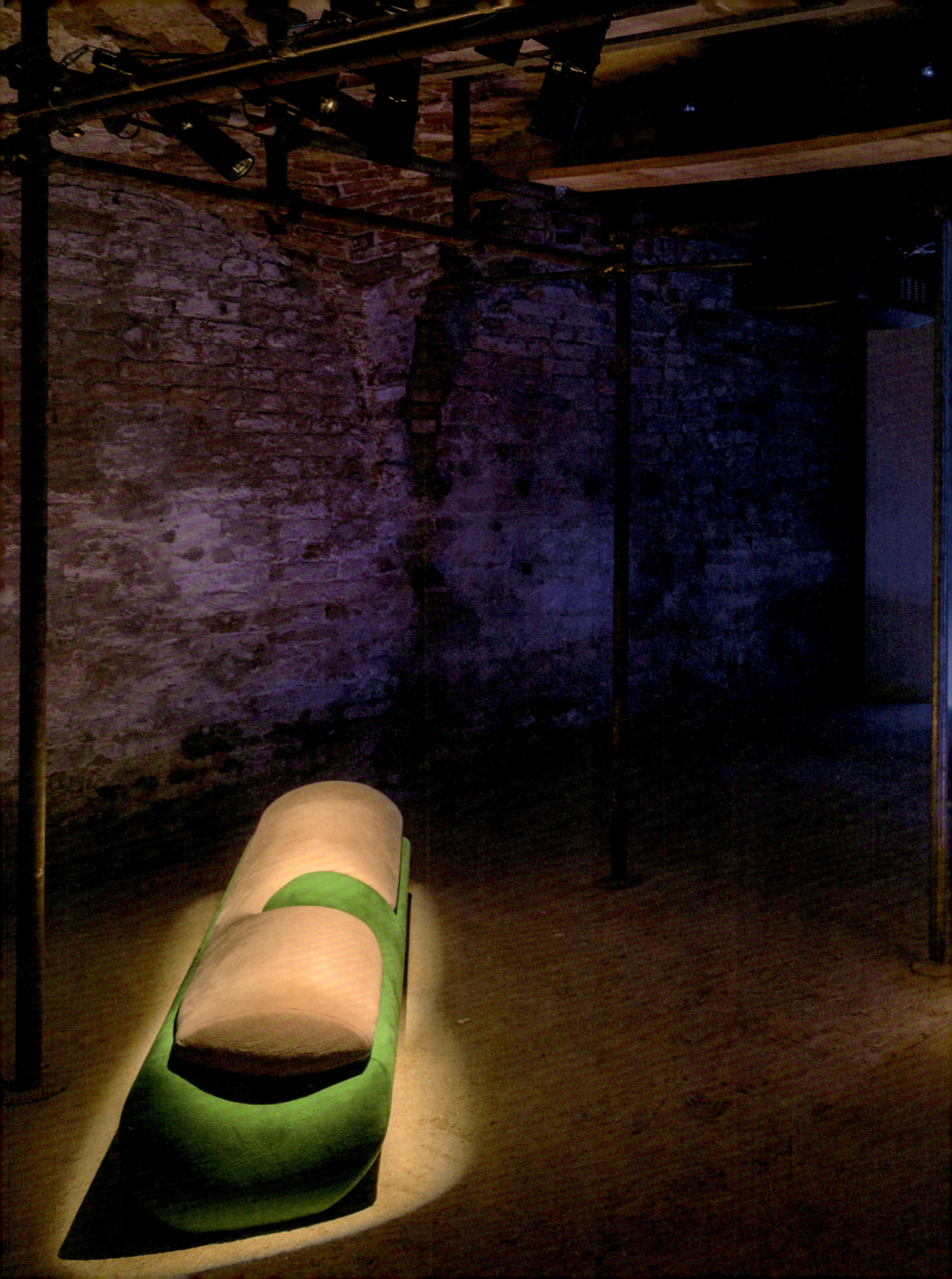

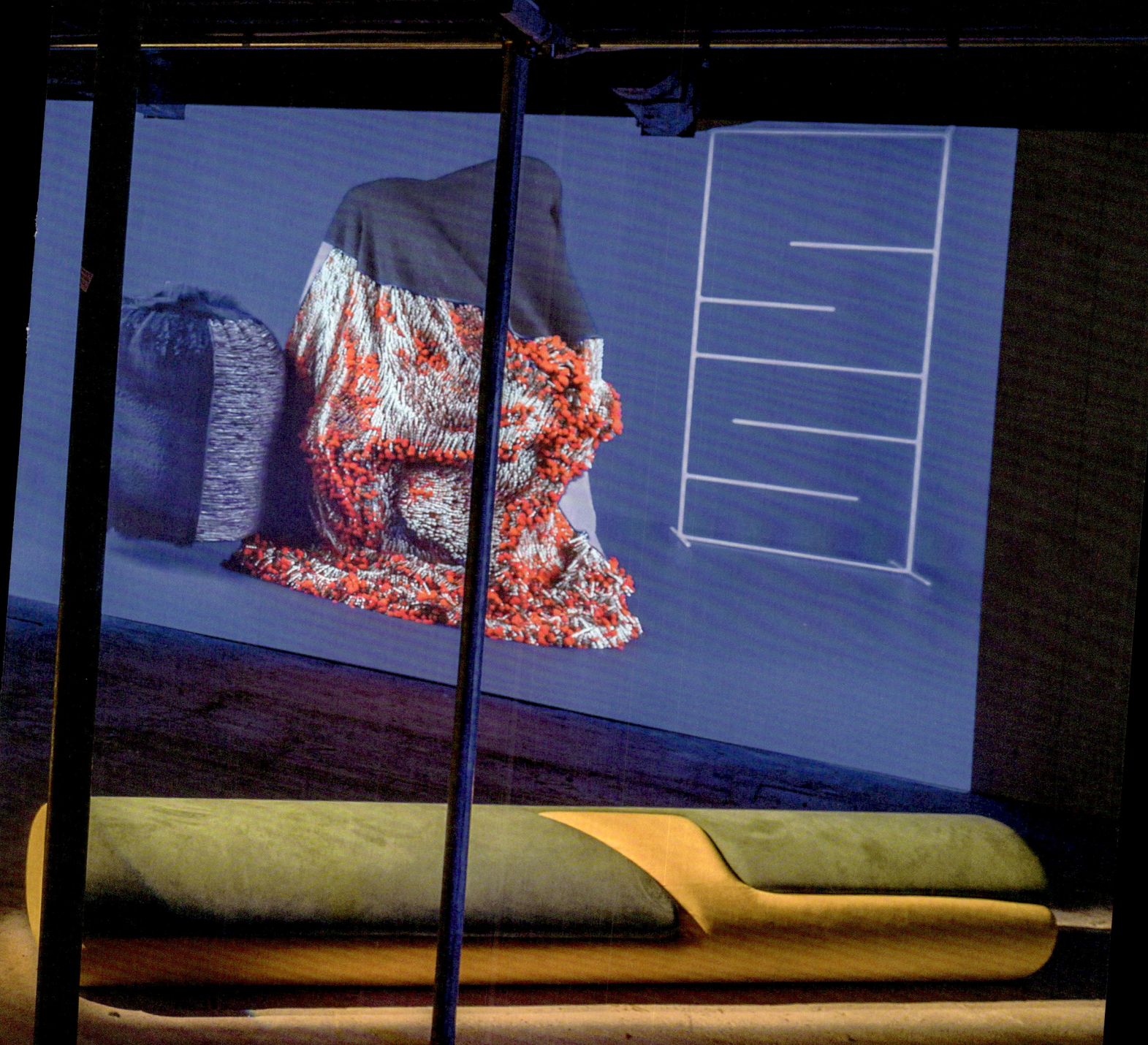

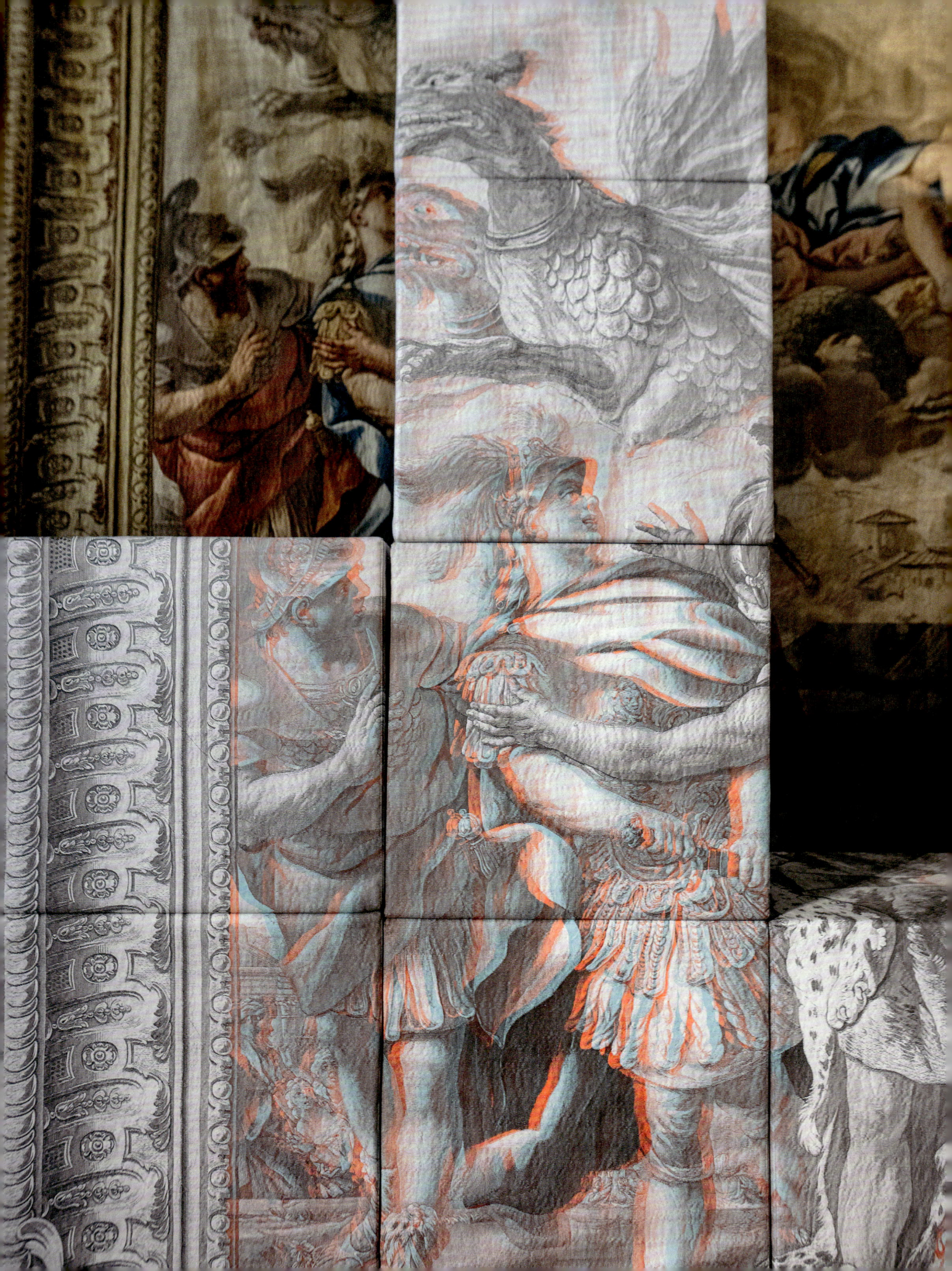

REALITY, IMAGINATION

It could be a Hollywood film, only the place names and the names of the characters would need to be changed.

Act One: Jason is determined to take back the throne that once belonged to his father. However, he has to win a wager: if he manages to bring back the Golden Fleece, the throne will be his.

Act Two: Jason summons his friends, his best friends. He puts together a team of characters such as Castor and Pollux, Peleus (the father of Achilles), Hercules and other heroes. He puts them all aboard a ship, and sets sail. On board with him there is also his bride, Medea: a sorceress, a niece of Circe. The ship is called the Argo, and the crew are the Argonauts. The voyage of the Argonauts is transformed into a series of adventures that make the Odyssey look like an ocean cruise. All goes well in the end, in the sense that Jason and Medea and the Argonauts reclaim the Golden Fleece, and the throne. But…

Sabine Marcelis, *Dimensions of Medea*, "De Coding", Palazzo Reale, Milan 2019

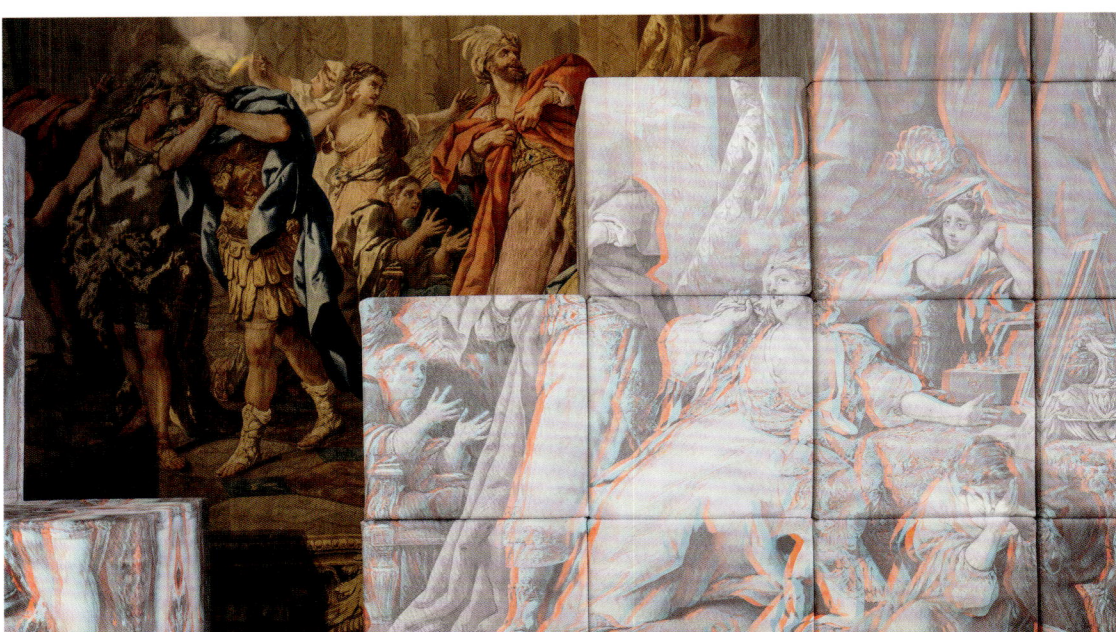

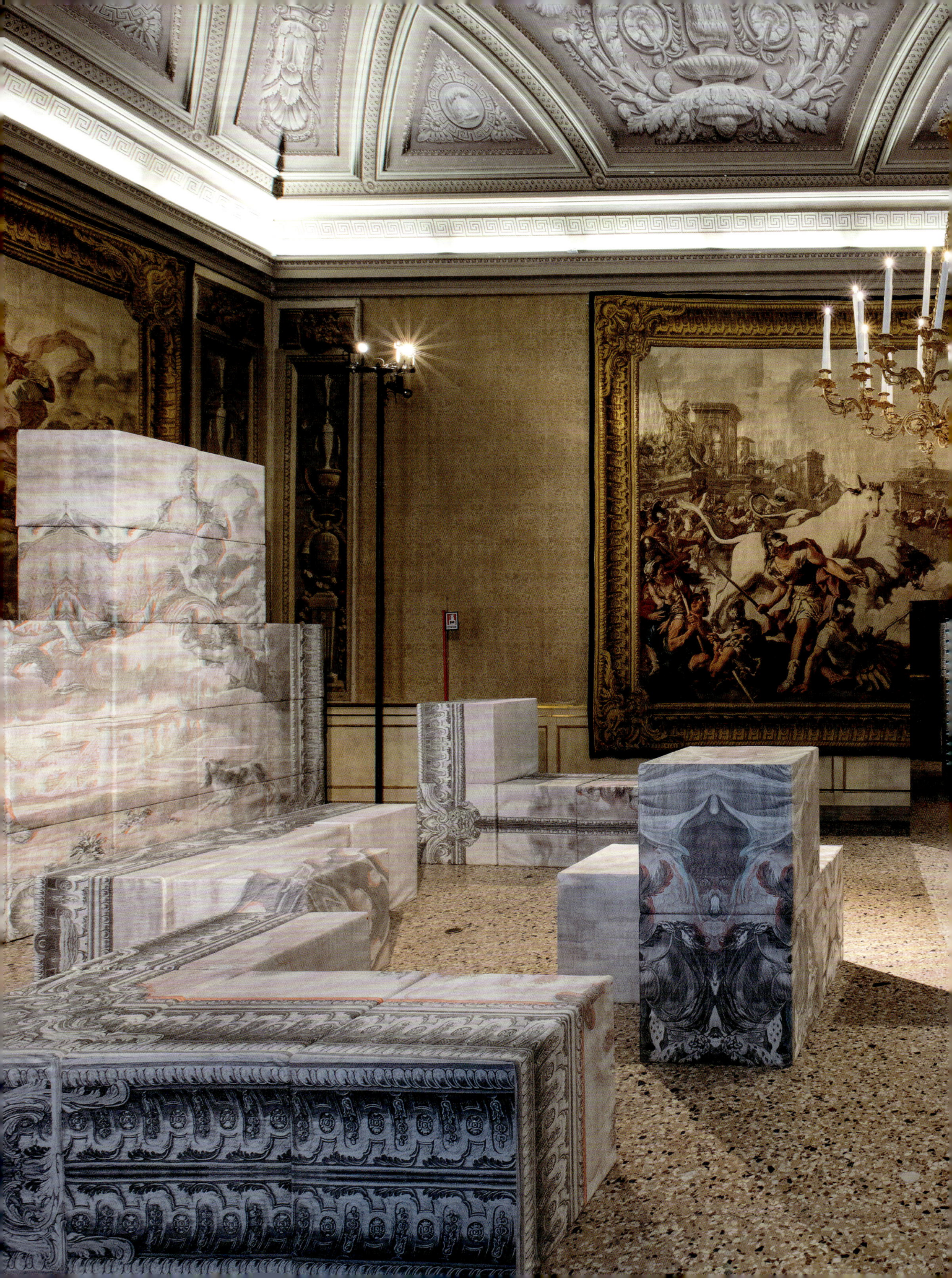

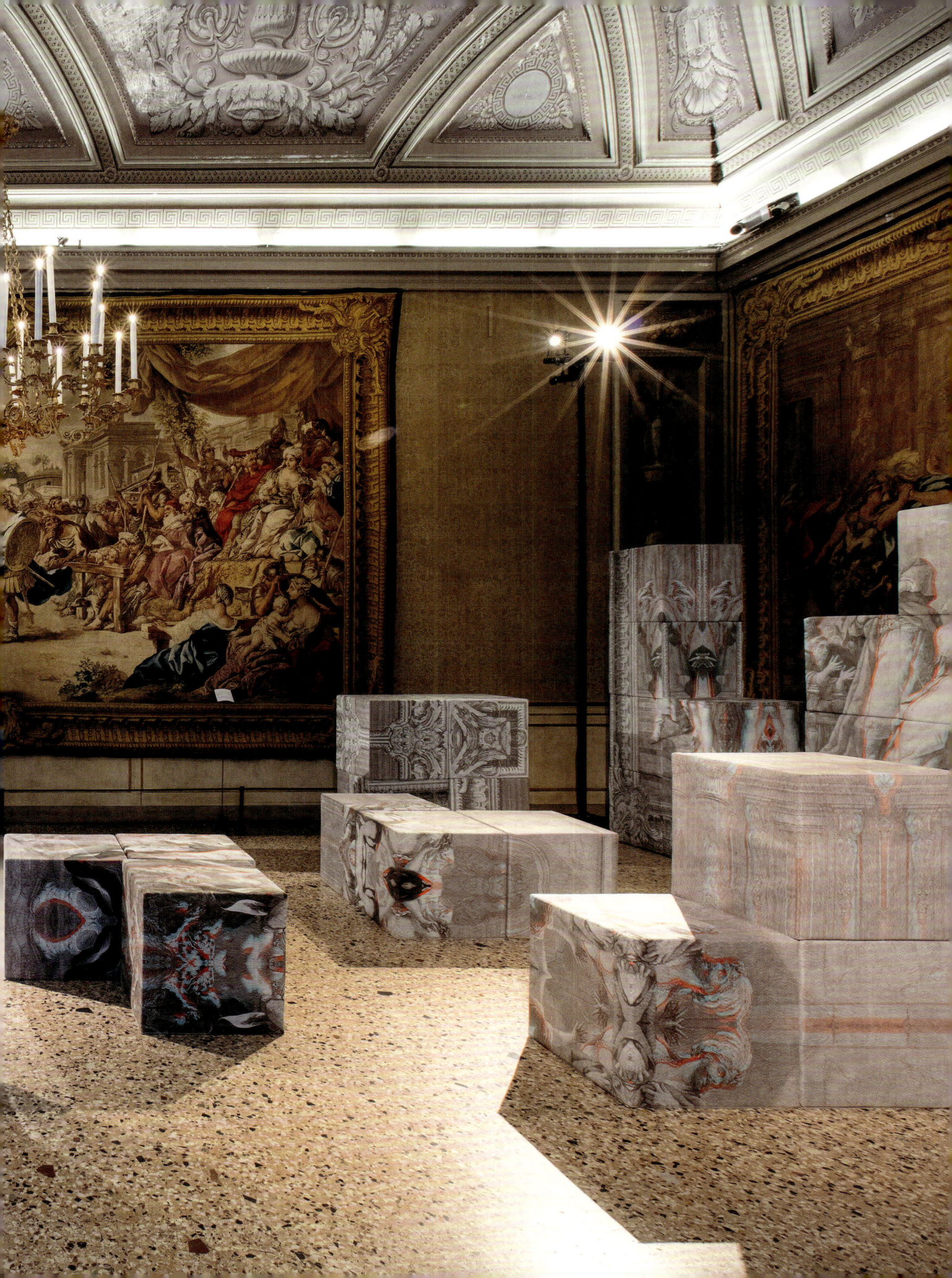

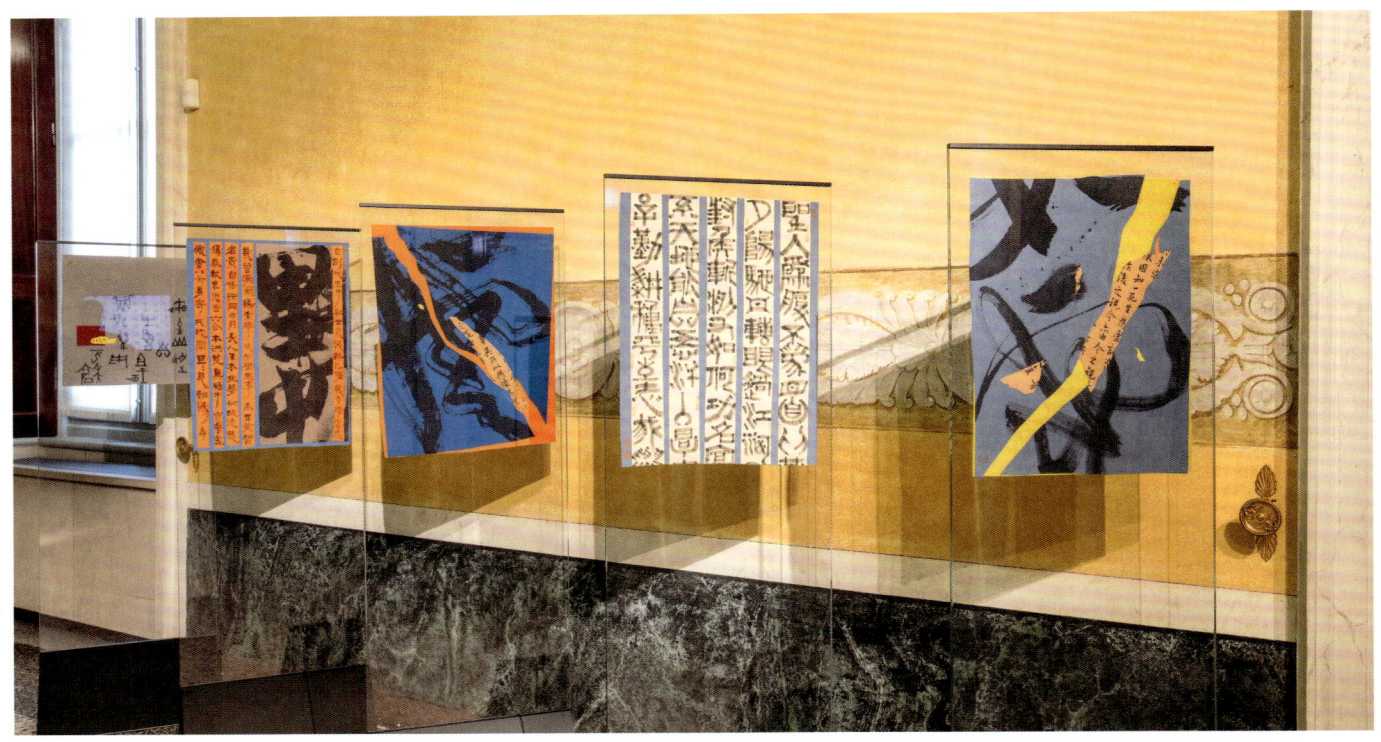

Qu Leilei, *Signs, Symbols and Scripts*, "De Coding", Palazzo Reale, Milan 2019

Act Three: Jason falls in love with another woman, and Medea is enraged. She is a sorceress, and can be very persuasive. In the end everyone dies, including the sons of Jason and Medea, who took no hand in proceedings. She is the only one who survives. But there is no injustice. It's not that the Greeks were not overly fond of happy endings. It's just that they used mythology to talk about the world, and, in this world of ours, there is also much grief and pain.

The story of Jason and Medea has been told over the centuries by poets in the form of poetry, by painters in the form of paintings, and by weavers' tapestries. In the interiors of Palazzo Reale, in Milan, there are tapestries that recount the version given of it in Ovid's *Metamorphoses*. Medea's anger is a story involving a metamorphosis. Jason falling in love is also a metamorphosis. In life everything changes, this is what the myth tells us. In 2019, Alcantara renewed its acquaintance with the interiors of Palazzo Reale, and encountered the tapestries that recount the metamorphosis of Jason and Medea. "De Coding", the Alcantara exhibition curated by Domitilla Dardi and Angela Rui, illustrates "the process of decoding a system of signs in relation to a changed form of support." The episodes narrated by the wall-hangings are de/coded and re/narrated via Alcantara, the art material, the malleable medium, with its ability to convey multiple, different expressive languages.

The exhibition displayed four pieces, that became ludic machines, with which the public was invited to interact by activating their senses, especially their sense of imagination. Which does not exist, of course, but which is the most powerful sense of all.

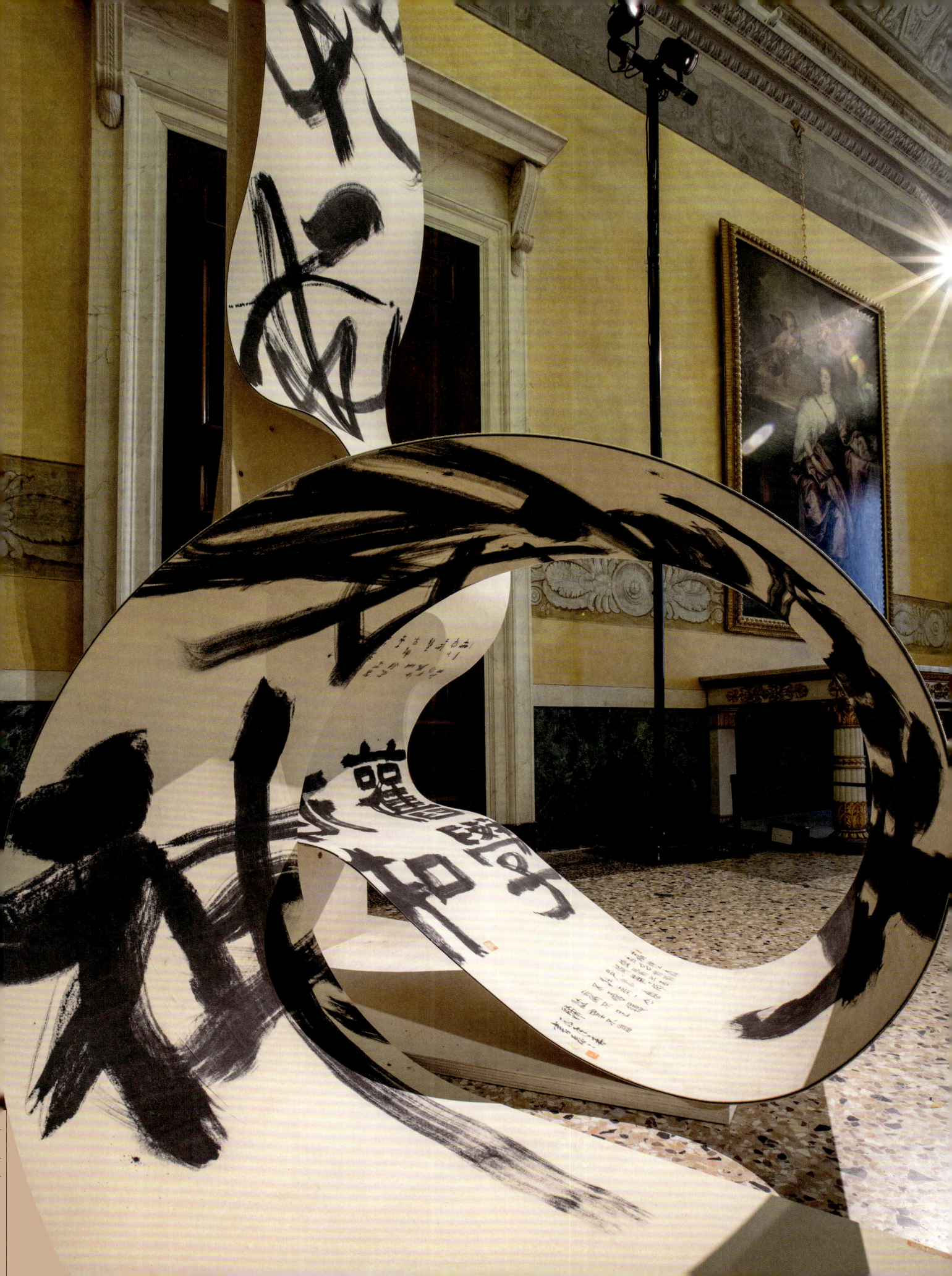

Room one: Qu Leilei is a master of calligraphy who painted on sheets of Alcantara. The codes of his language are ideograms that become art in the conceptual dimension of writing.

Room two: Sabine Marcelis captured the elements of the myth, and reworked them so that the public themselves could rethink and reshape them, in accordance with the process of them becoming three-dimensional.

Room three: Constance Guisset brought about a metamorphosis, creating giant tentacles belonging to a fantastic creature that grew out of the tapestry, invading the whole room, and coming to rest among the public. A colourful and playful image: scales of Alcantara just made to be stroked and caressed.

Room four: the *Wardian Case* by Space Popular. Let us imagine that this Alcantara shell, invented in order to transport ecosystems, is Argo, the Argonauts' ship. Accordingly, the public becomes a hero, and experiences what it is like to go on a mythological voyage. The ship literally travelled through the stories of the tapestries: the experience became a coexistence between the real and the virtual. You climbed aboard, put on the glasses, and allowed yourself to be carried away by the wind of perceptions, which become emotions. Your fingers grazed the Alcantara surfaces, but what you saw with your eyes was not the same thing that you touched with your hand. It seems

Constance Guisset, *Scylla*, "De Coding", Palazzo Reale, Milan 2019

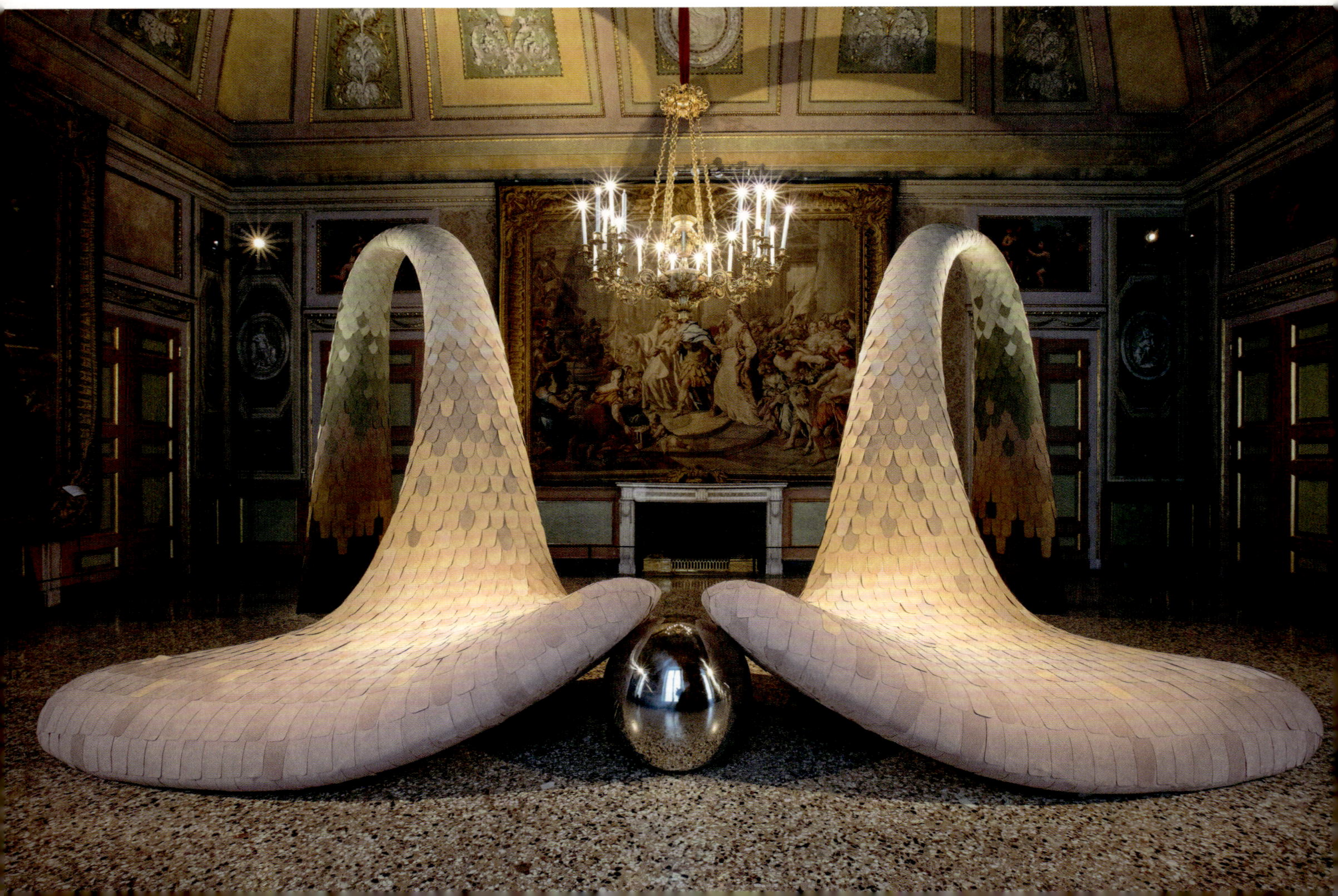

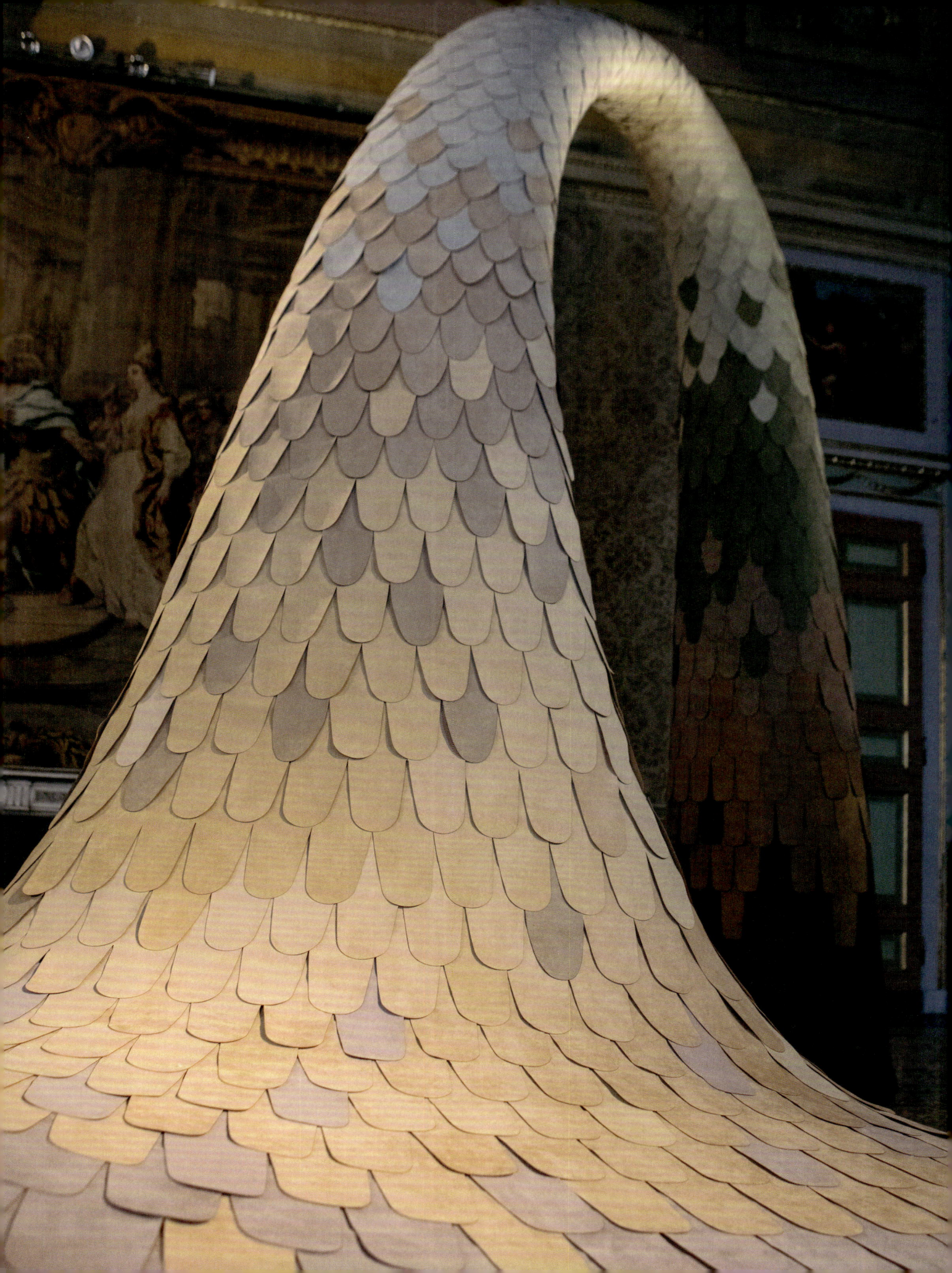

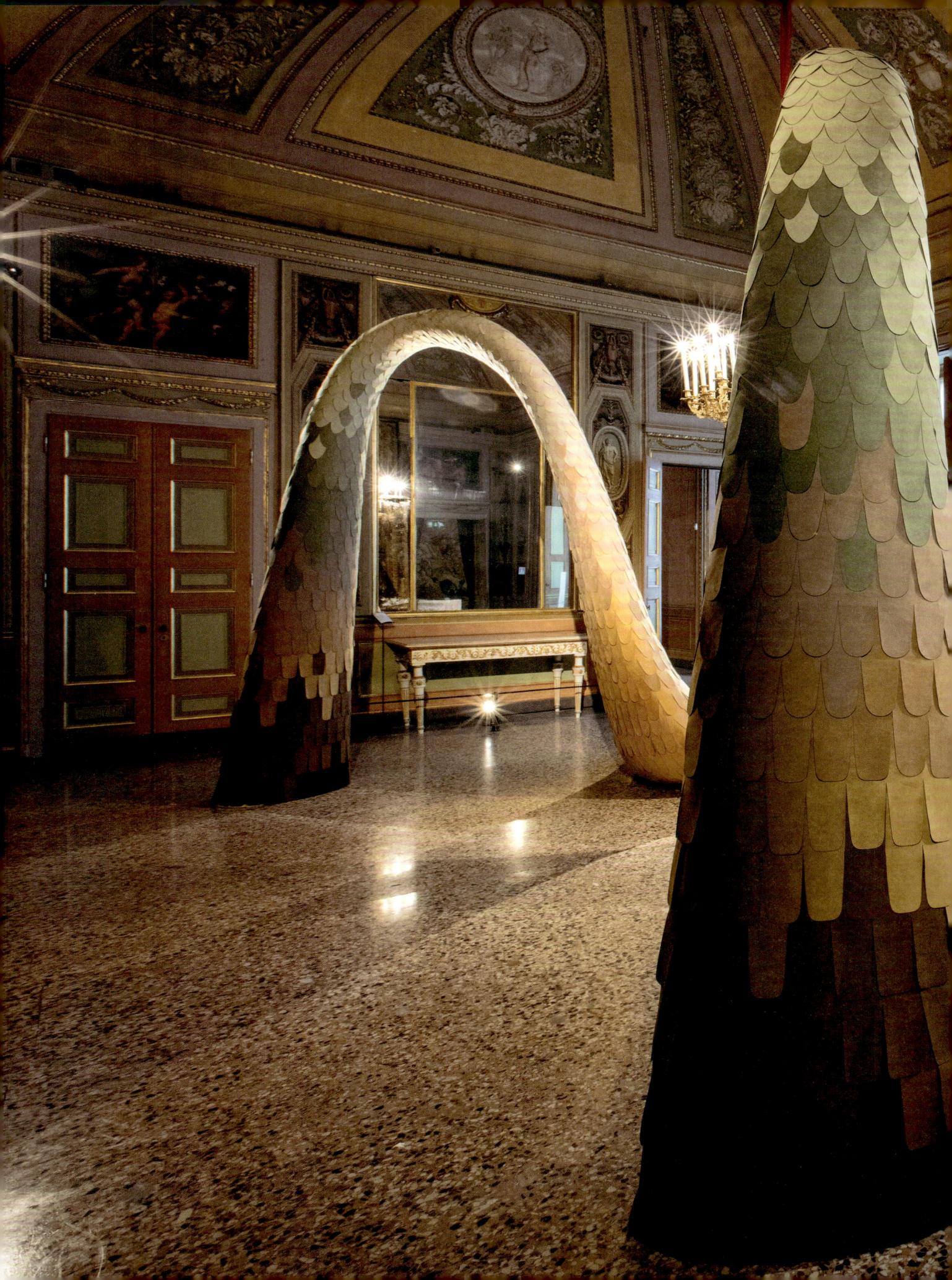

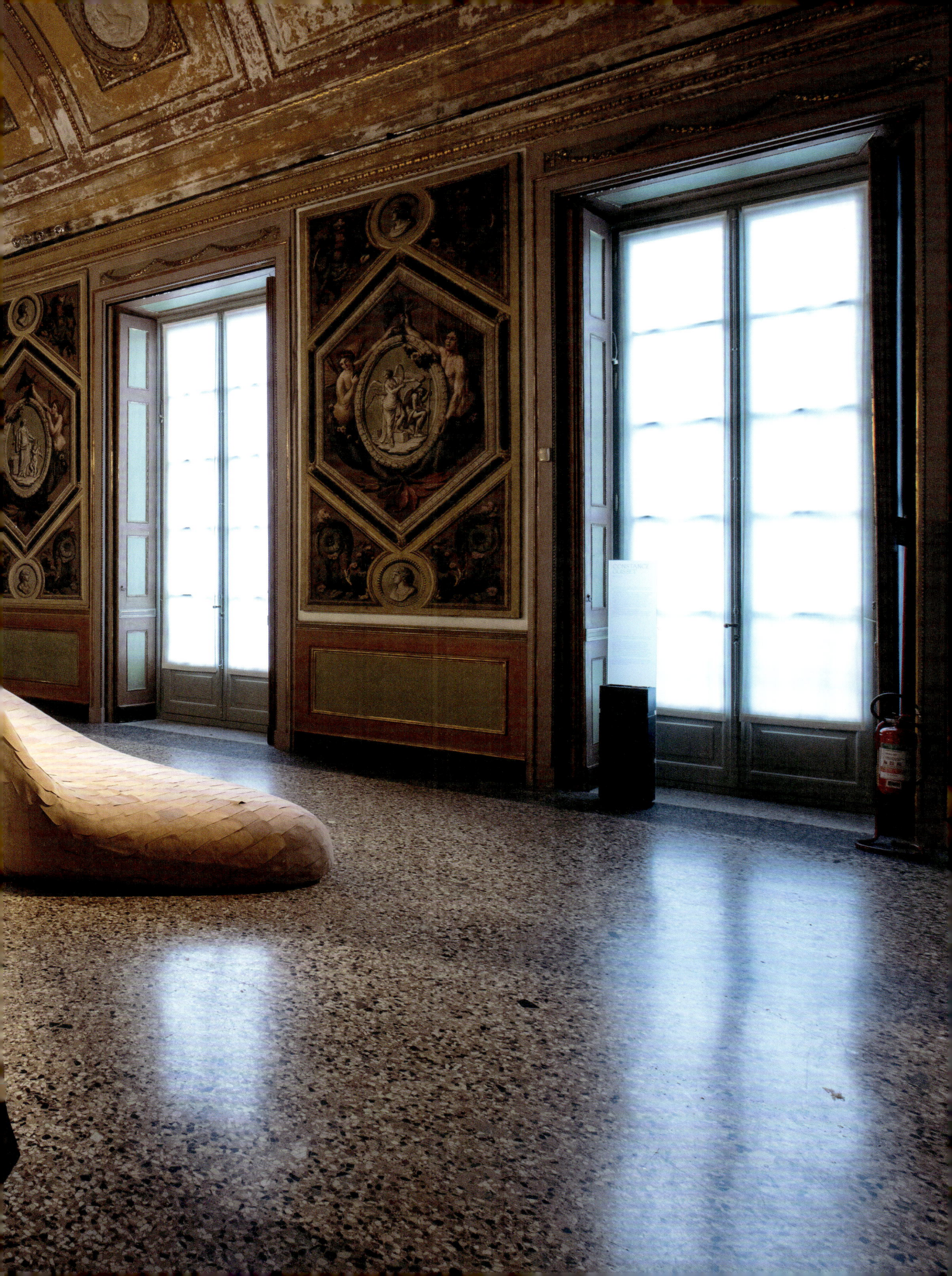

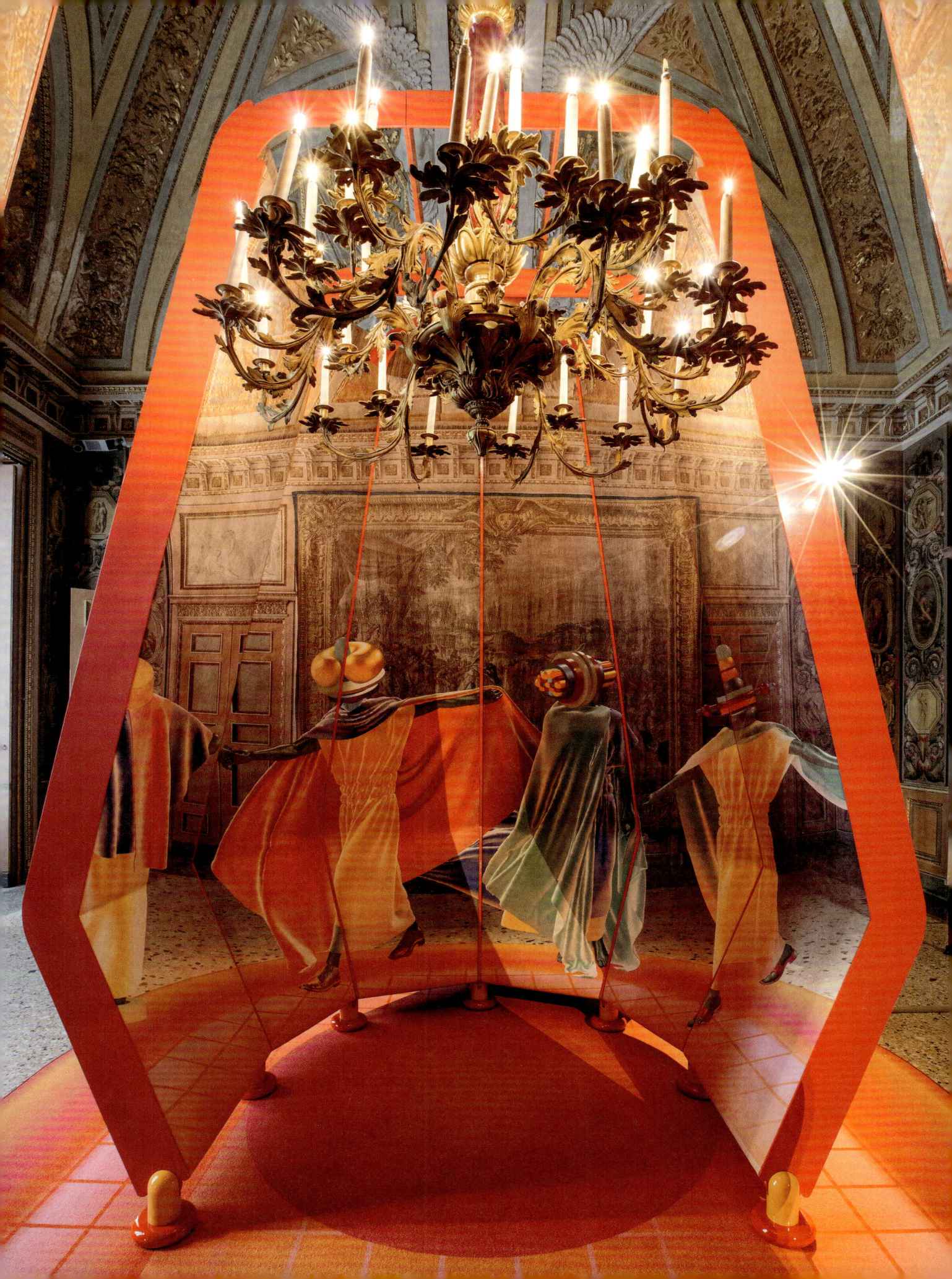

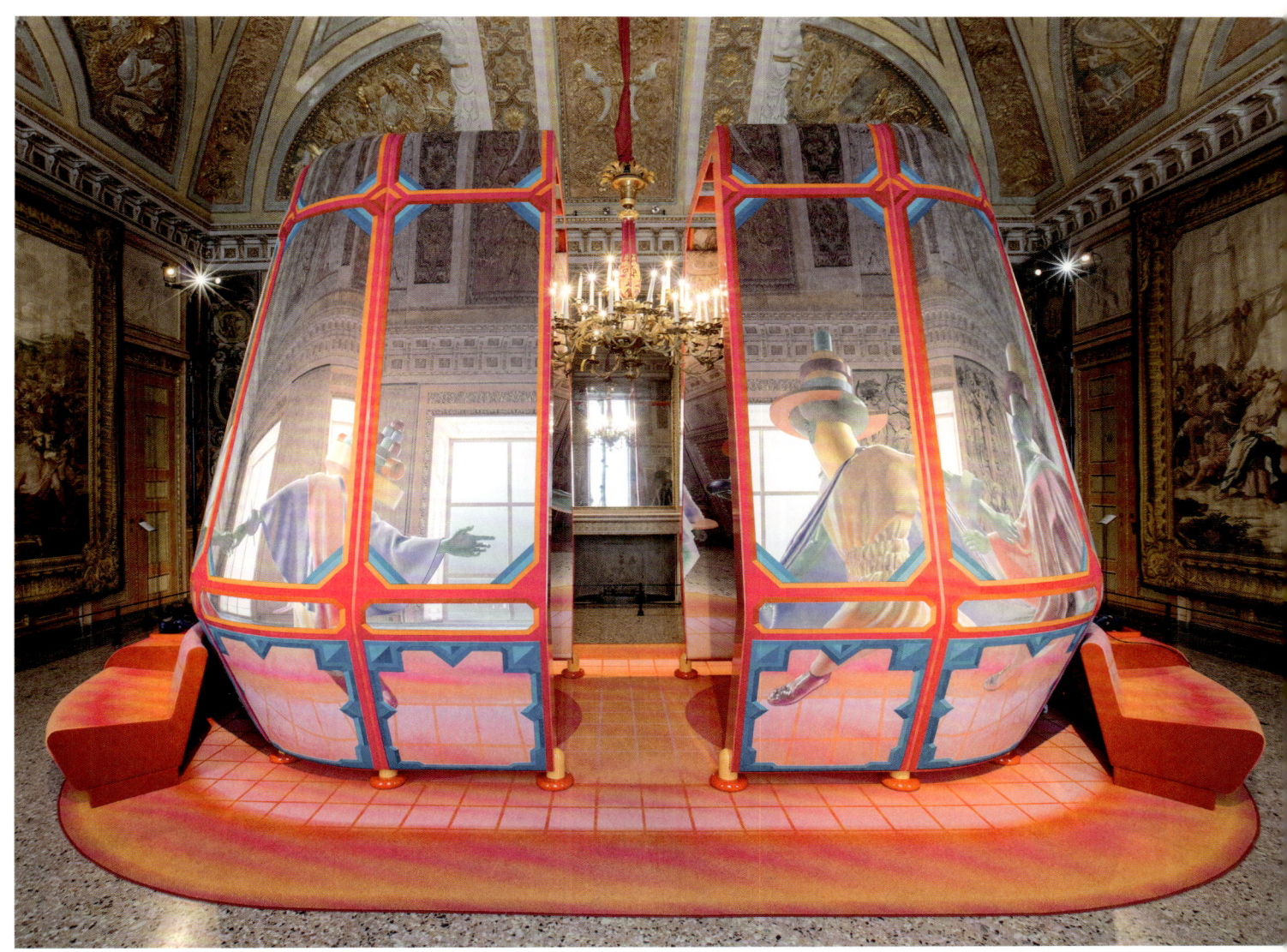

Space Popular, *The Wardian Case*, "De Coding", Palazzo Reale, Milan 2019

crazy, and indeed it was. A sort of augmented synaesthesia was created, combining the reassuring tactile experience – earthly and mortal, like Jason – with a dream-like dimension which was the magical world of Medea. Emphasized by contact with the various Alcantara surfaces, the mythological stories sprang to life in the minds of the public in a sequence of experiences. A new, individual narrative, generated by the apparent incongruity between what was perceived by touch and what was understood from seeing.
Talk about the future, indeed.

The cinema industry, and Hollywood, recently made a film called *Ralph Breaks the Internet*. It is about us, and the way we experience the world through the Internet. It explains that the web is a map that we explore by moving a cursor, by means of a mouse. Imagine what would happen if we could get inside that map: experience it, inhabit it.

Well, Alcantara became the map: as soon as you came into contact with it, you were immediately on the bridge of the Argo. And you became an Argonaut, in the metaverse.

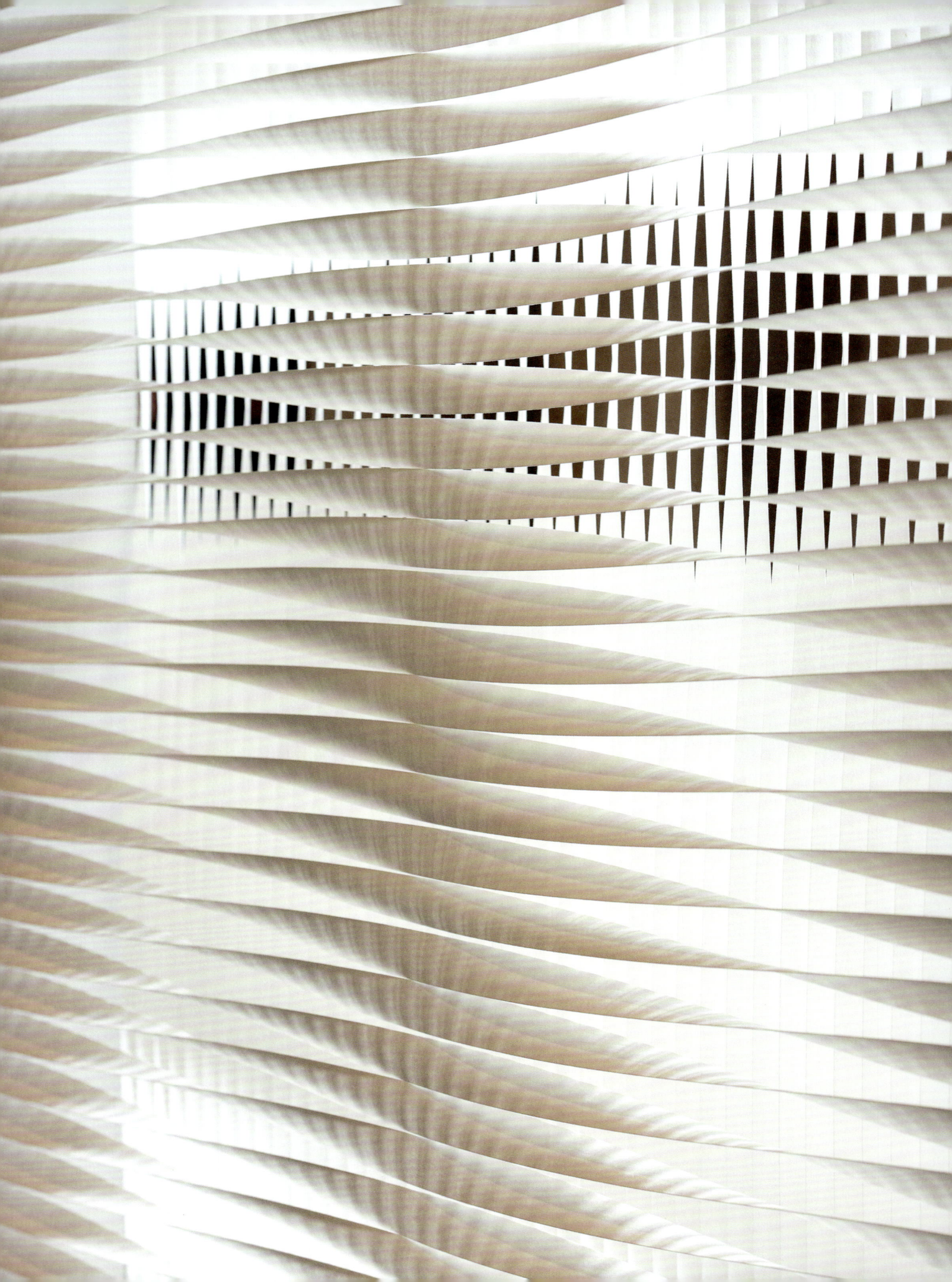

THE MATERIAL OF VISION

There are two trains in the station. They are stationary, one standing alongside the other. Aligned, but facing in opposite directions. Two young people are looking out of the windows, a boy and a girl. They do not know each other, but they look at each other, and smile. Suddenly the boy's train departs, he has the impression that he is moving further away from her. The carriages of the other train pass by in front of him. All of them, down to the last one. Only then does he realize that he had been still and unmoving all the time. It was the girl's train that had moved off. She was the one who was moving away from him. Yet the boy had clearly perceived motion; he did not see it only with his eyes, he felt it within him. A kinetics of the heart? No, a simple optical illusion, the material of vision. The perception that objects at a standstill are in motion: immobile forms that the eye registers as being in evolution in space.

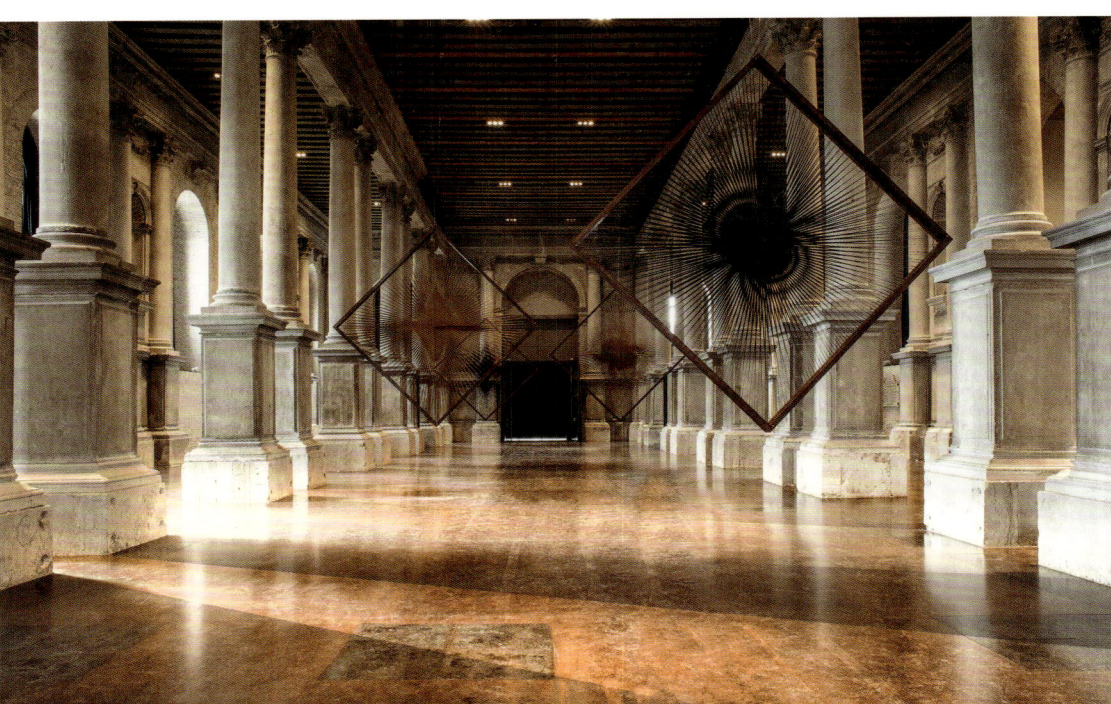

Alberto Biasi, "La Materia della Visione", Scuola Grande della Misericordia, Venice 2019

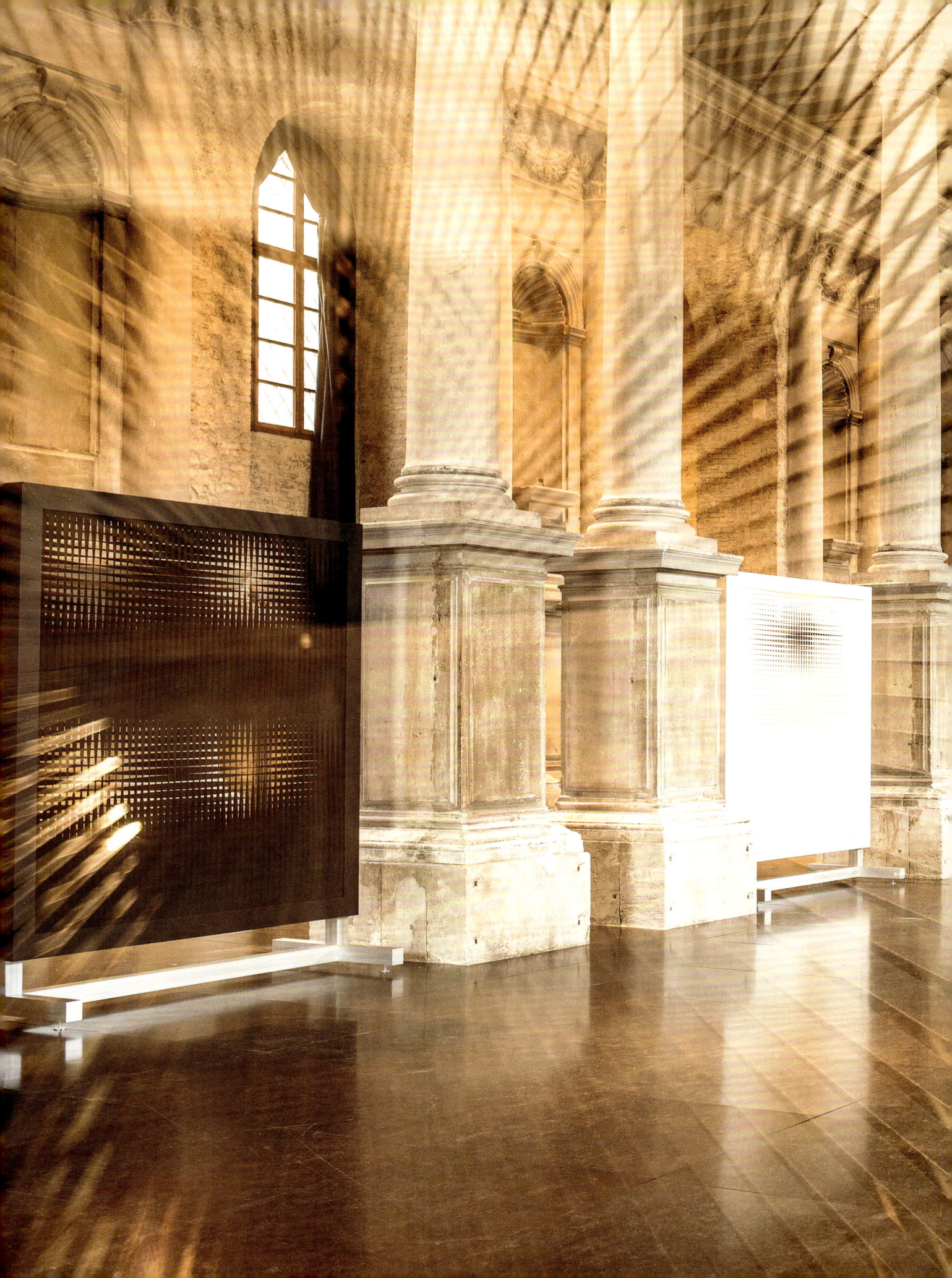

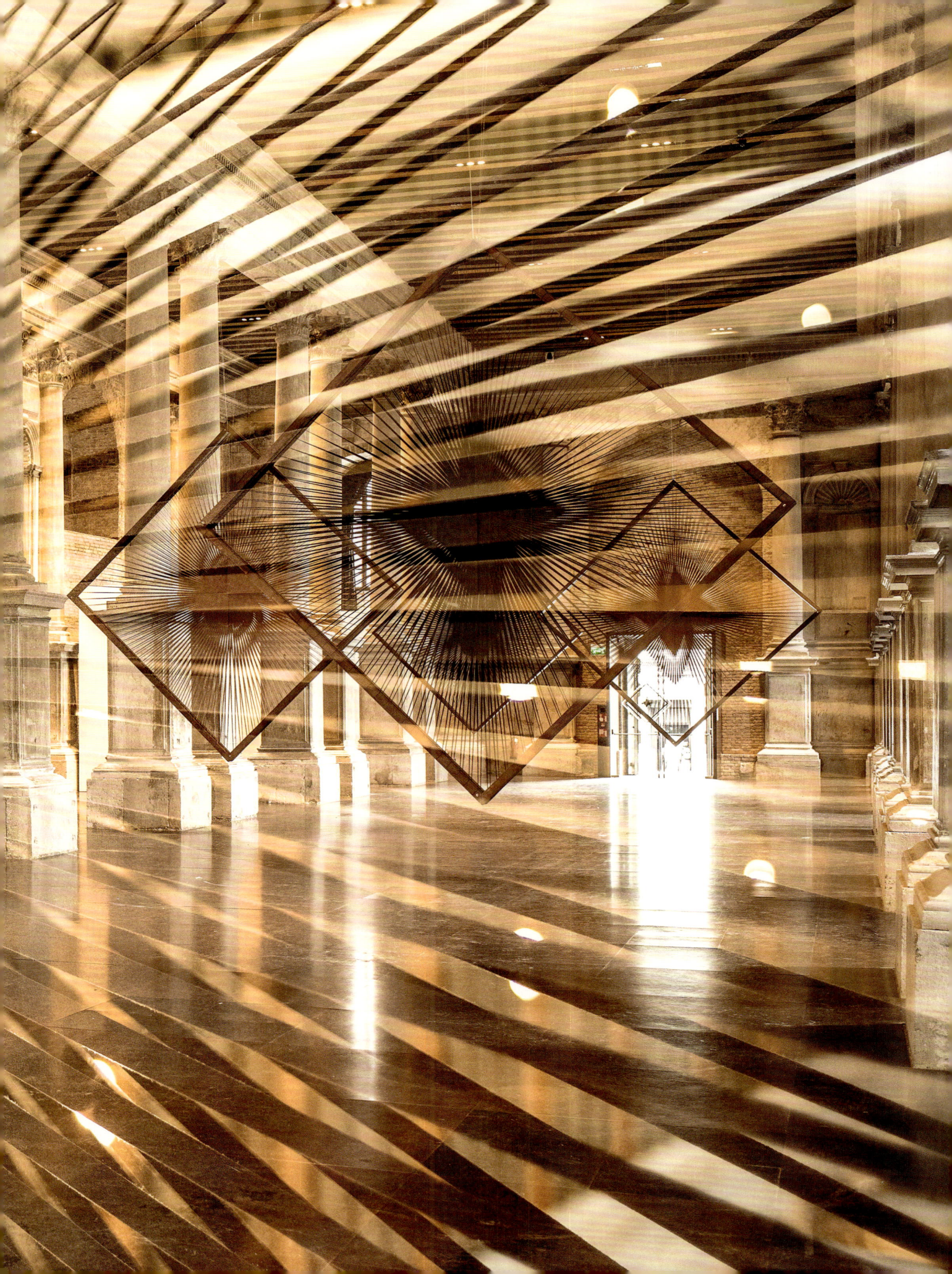

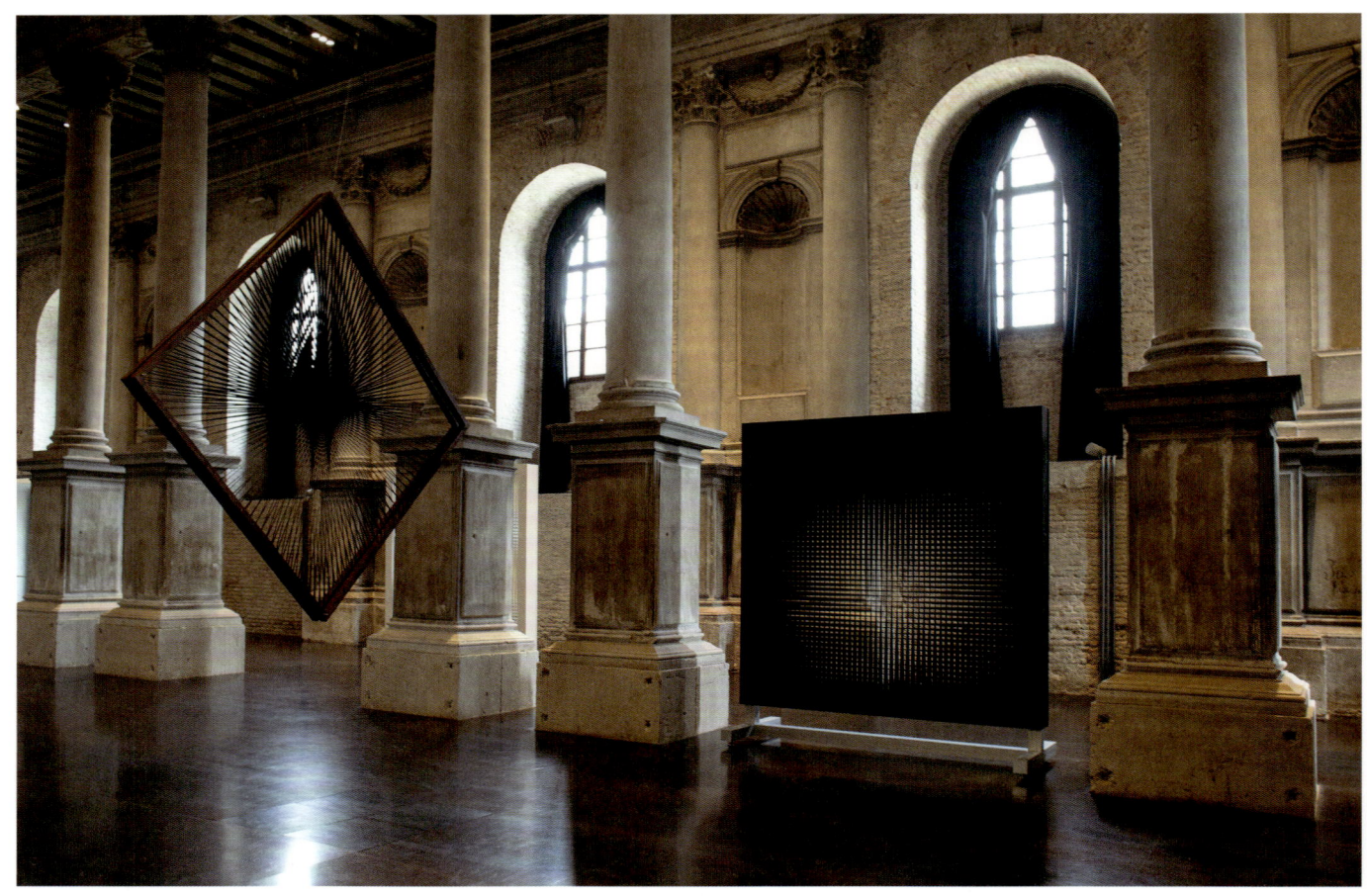

Alberto Biasi, *Ottico dinamico*, "La Materia della Visione", Scuola Grande della Misericordia, Venice 2019

Setting out from vision and seeing, as the preferred object of his artistic research, Alberto Biasi has been working for over 60 years. It all began almost by chance, while he was still a teacher of technical drawing at school, and he noticed the *moirè* effect created when punch-cut cardboard designs are placed next to each other. This led to his idea of creating his earliest patterns, by cutting the flat material into pieces, and making inlays, creating an interplay between light and shadow to produce the effect of movement. Then his research became more complex, with large-format works, made using slats of various materials, especially PVC. And after exploring all the aspects of plastic materials, the idea occurred to him to try Alcantara. The material of art became: "The Material of Vision". This was the title of a major exhibition dedicated to Alberto Biasi in 2019 in Venice, together with Alcantara, in the prestigious setting of the Scuola Grande della Misericordia. A one-man show that retraced the main events in a life devoted to constant artistic research, forever centred around illusory motion in human vision. When science was art, and artists were scientists, the rigorous study of natural phenomena was the inspiration for works. Biasi locates himself within that fertile tradition. His works are often complex, all it takes is the slightest mistake in the regularity of one thin strip, in the angle of inclination of another, and the kinetic effect disappears.

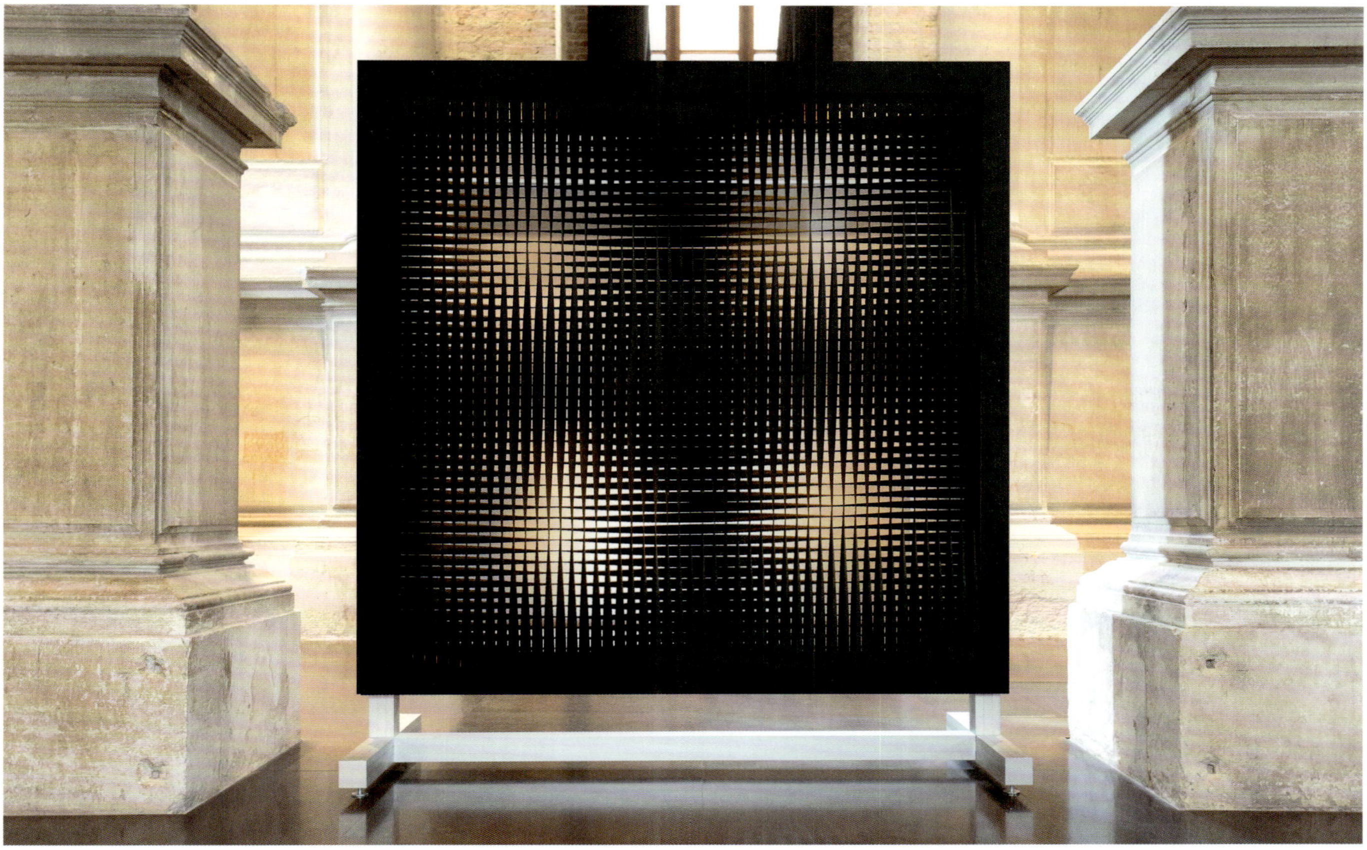

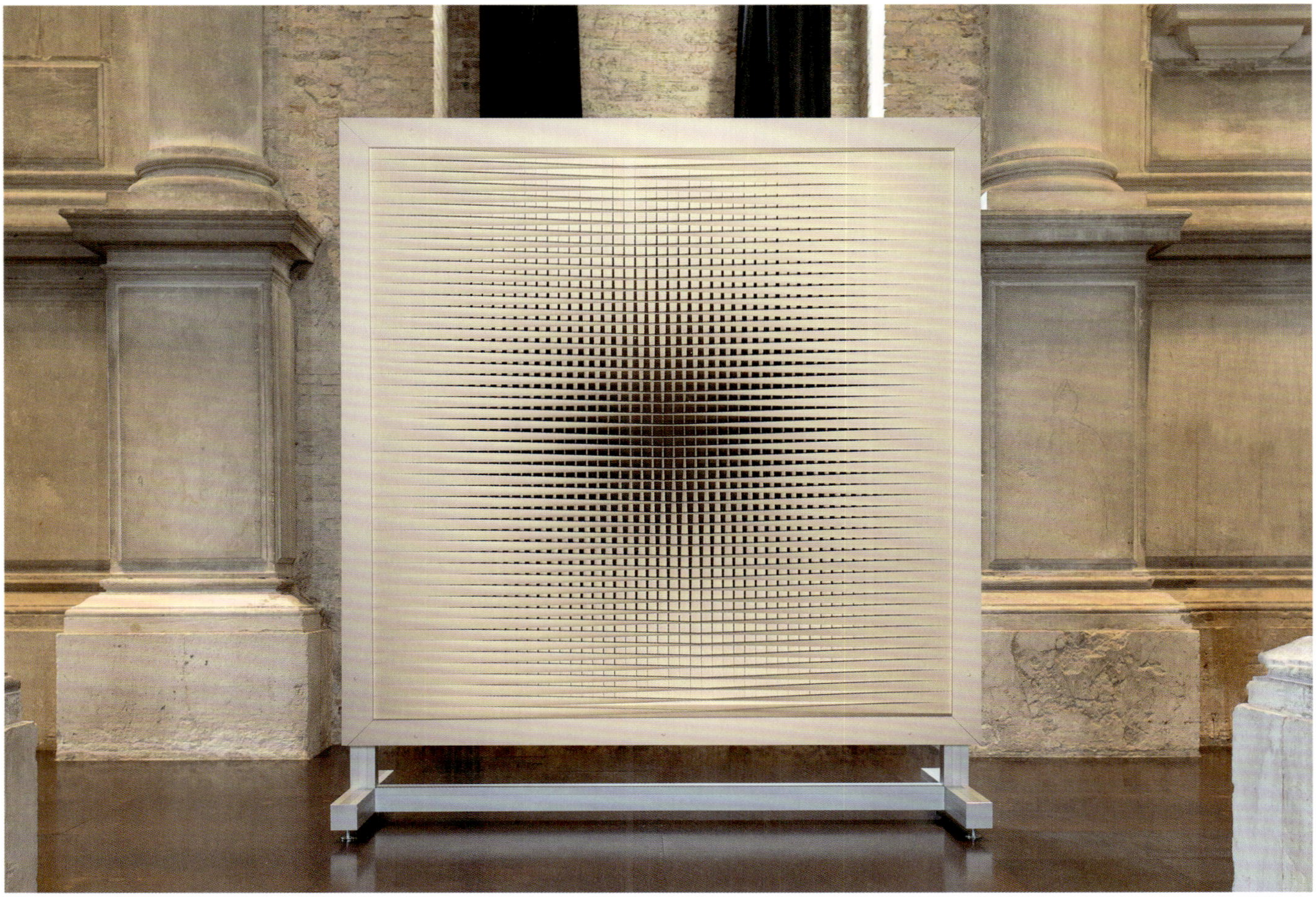

175

Biasi creates works that are combinations of narrow coloured strips folded back on themselves, and assembled so as to radiate away from the centre, or aligned along parallel lines. The key often lies in the way the material is twisted, creating areas of unpredictability. The relationship between the parts of the work produces the illusion of movement of the figure or of the background, in relation to the observer's point of view. Everything moves because it is human vision itself that is moving, even if imperceptibly. Biasi often asks the public to interact with his works, walking around them in order to create new and surprising kinetic effects. "For some time I had wanted to try out a new material," the artist said on the occasion of the Venice show. "I was looking for something softer and less three-dimensional, but still able to resist the strong tension to which I subject the strands that make up my works. I've known Alcantara for ages, and I wanted to try it. The company was very amenable, sending me samples, and cutting up the surfaces to be tried out. This material is not just soft on the eye, and to touch, and resistant to tension, it is also changeable. When taking apart a prototype, I noticed thin strands of the same piece of Alcantara that seemed to be made of different colours. The material processes light, and the effect changes depending on how it is observed. This specific aspect is my kind of thing, and I like it a lot. That is how my latest works in Alcantara, my new material, came into being."

Andrea Boragno, the company's Chairman and CEO, added: "Over the years we have tried out a way of interacting with artists, and this has created a virtuous circle. In the beginning, with the support of out technical departments, we were the ones who invited them to explore the material's adaptability and versatility; today what happens is that it's artists themselves who seek a relationship with us, and who choose Alcantara as a tool to express their poetics. Not just in Italy, but throughout the world."

In the spacious interiors of the Scuola della Misericordia, among marble columns and frescoes, the public moves in synchronicity with Biasi's works. Everything is in motion, even when it remains motionless. There are two young people holding hands. They met on a train: every day she would go one way, and he the other; they met in the middle. One day they got off their trains, while the trains were moving off. The carriages filed past rapidly, and they were stationary, on a bench, embracing.

Who was moving more? The moving trains or those youngsters, immobile, sharing a kiss? The kinetics of affection, a material of vision.

Alberto Biasi, *Torsione sovrapposta* (details), "La Materia della Visione", Scuola Grande della Misericordia, Venice 2019

Bottom right
Alberto Biasi, *Ottico dinamico* (detail), "La Materia della Visione", Scuola Grande della Misericordia, Venice 2019

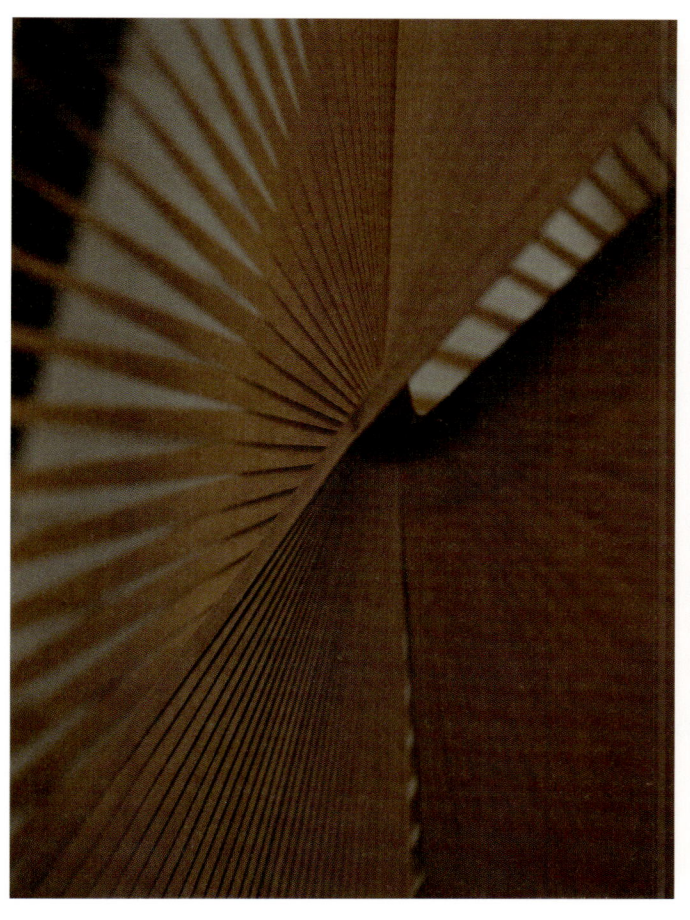
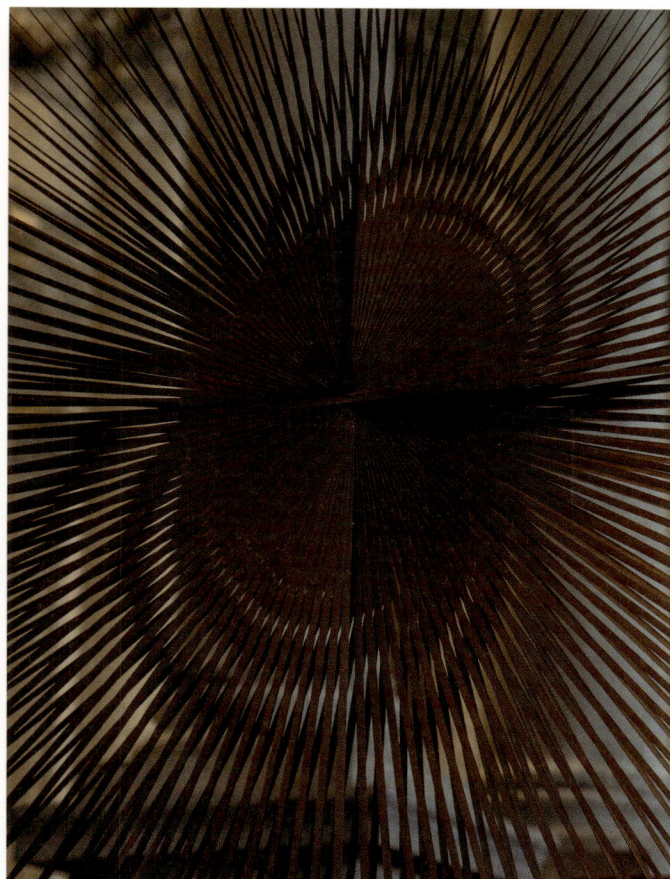
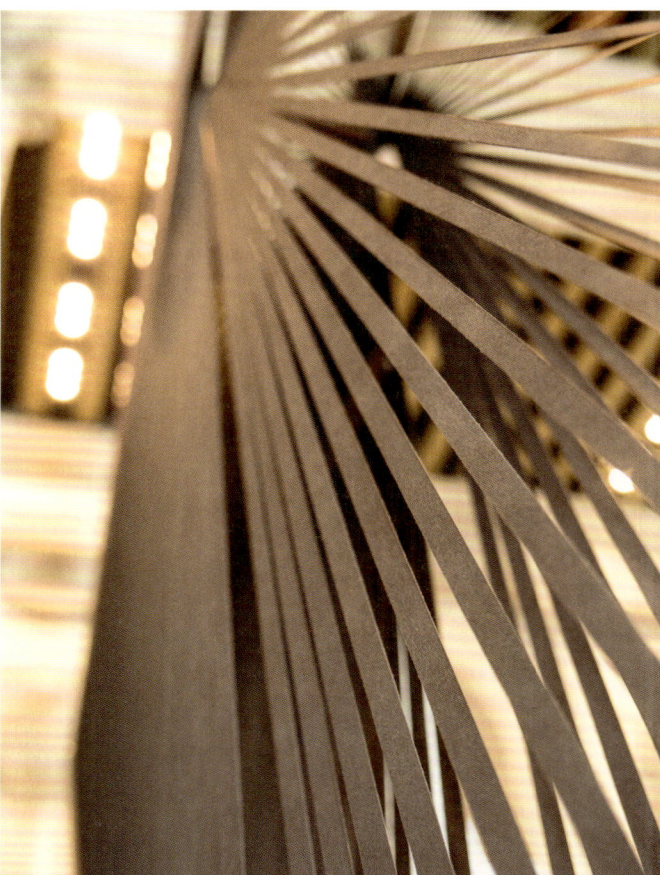
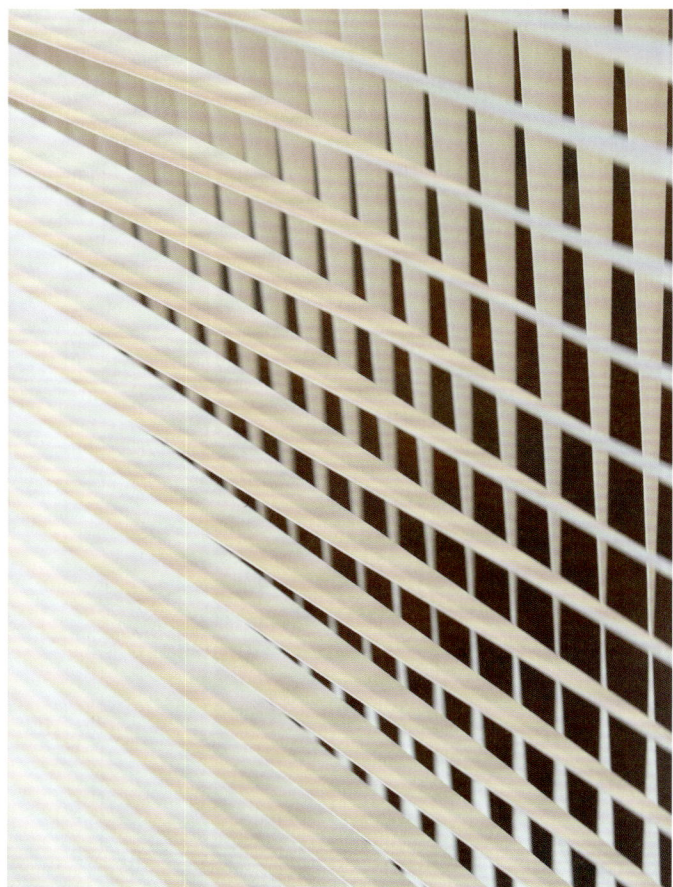

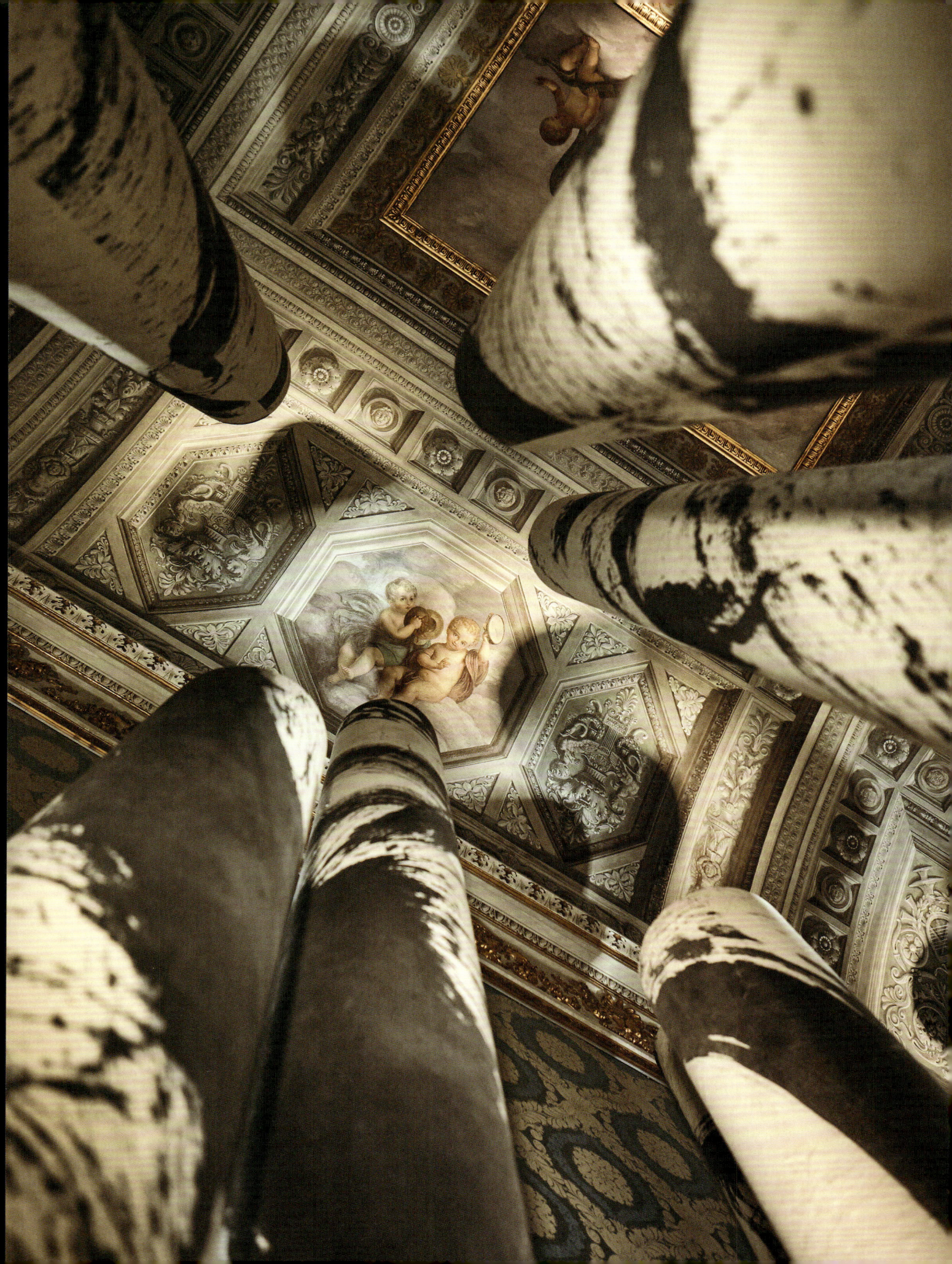

OUT OF THE BLUE

The artist is in his studio. A large room, full of light and bereft of objects: the mirror of the calligrapher's mind. On the floor he has laid out a long strip of Alcantara. He has already prepared the ink, as liquid as it needs to be, as dense as necessary. He has put it in a bucket. The brush is very large, twice as big as he is. To the casual eye, it might look like a floor cloth, but actually it is an object of disarming precision. He stands there, motionless, on the sheet of Alcantara, for a time that seems never-ending. Then he dips the brush in the bucket, and holds it over the material. A few drops of ink fall. The artist waits a little longer. Suddenly he firmly applies the brush to the Alcantara surface, and presses with all his weight. It looks as if he is wrestling with the material.

Qin Feng, "Out of the Blue", Palazzo Reale, Milan 2020

Mao Lizi, "Out of the Blue", Palazzo Reale, Milan 2020

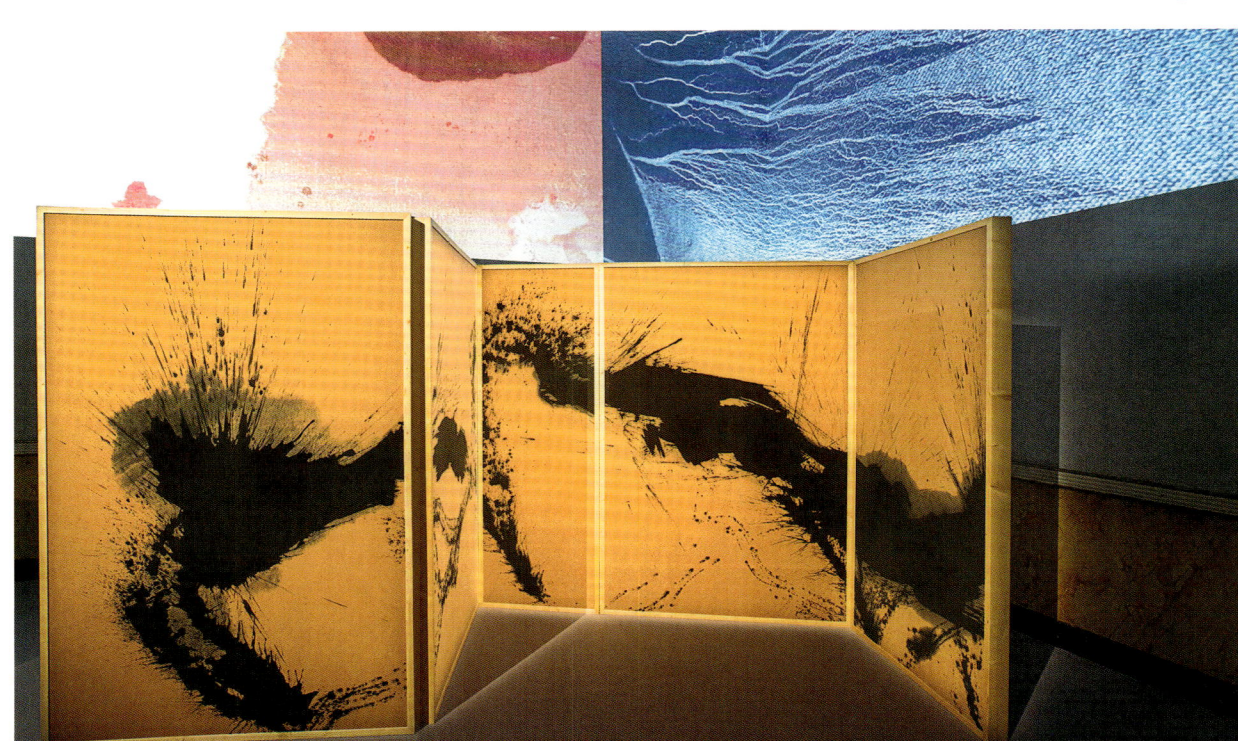

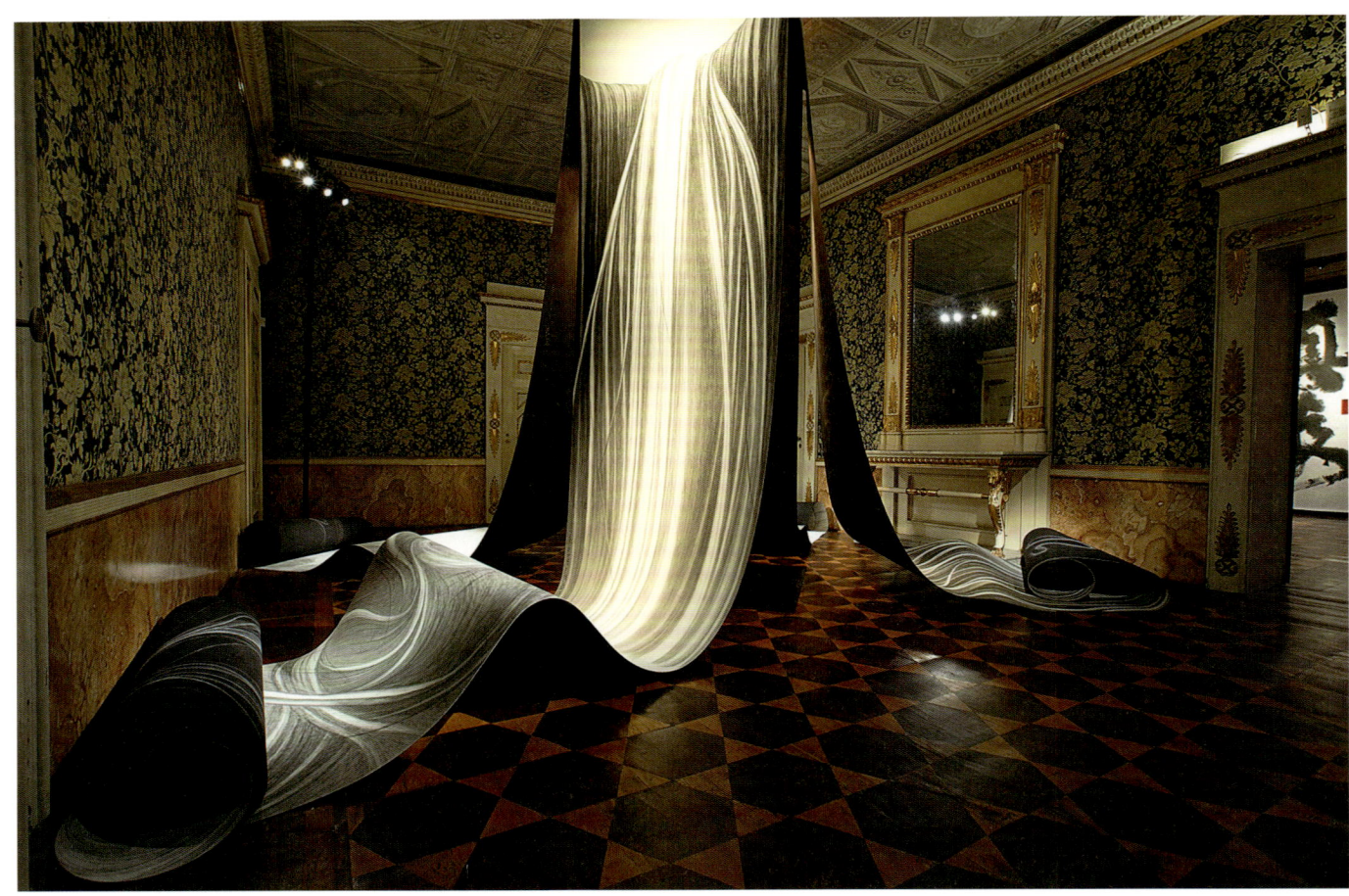

Zhang Chun Hong, "Out of the Blue", Palazzo Reale, Milan 2020

Then he starts to walk, almost jogging, along the strip of Alcantara, continuing to make black marks on the pale background. He paints as if he was writing something. They are ideograms, difficult to read, even if you know the language. But they are beautiful. Elegant and strong, equilibriums of perfect forms. Therein lies the key: filling empty spaces, and emptying spaces that are full. Nothing exists in isolation it is always a question of the relationship between presence and absence. Now the artist walks backwards, but moving very slowly, almost in slow motion. He grips the brush in both hands, his muscles taut in an effort to control the marks. The marks that he makes on the Alcantara "canvas" are light, grey, and very liquid. More drops fall. They do not have a specific meaning, but they make the work even finer. They are random details, splashes of an unexpected poetics.

In another part of the world, another calligrapher is walking barefoot on the Alcantara support, laid on the floor. Using a stiff brush he paints the shapes, he fills the empty spaces and empties the full spaces. He does so with delicacy, as if he was stroking the painting. Then he lays another sheet of Alcantara on the ink while it is still wet, and he dances on it. His feet move nimbly over the hidden letters. The dance is also part of the calligraphy: the movement writes things in the air, and on the material. One heavy step, and one light step. Writing well is an art that involves the whole body.

Wang Huangsheng, "Out of the Blue", Palazzo Reale, Milan 2020

Then there is a female master calligrapher kneeling on the platform of a mobile scaffold. The wall of her studio is covered in Alcantara. She covers huge surfaces with lines made using a small brush. A huge task, the enemy of haste. She paints waves of ink: flowing black and grey shapes on pale Alcantara, white marks on dark Alcantara. They look like long locks of hair, blowing in the wind. Underneath the painting, somewhere or other, there must be a female body, wrapped in a silk kimono. And in the background a landscape of hills, streams, and blossoming cherry trees.

The scenes flashed by on the screens at the exhibition entitled "Out of the Blue", in the rooms of Palazzo Reale in Milan. The year was 2020, while the pandemic was rife: the virus imposed a distance between people, while art brought them closer together. In the Prince's Apartment the works of six leading Chinese calligraphers were displayed. They were of differing ages, and some of them lived in Europe and the United States; their installations created an exhibition full of beauty. The videos screened alongside the works were performances of artistic creation which brought to the public's attention the intimacy of the work, too, and the hard work behind the ideas.

"Calligraphy is one of the noblest and oldest forms of art in Chinese culture," explained the curator, Dagmar Carnevale Lavezzoli. "But in the age of technology, with digital reproduction, can these centuries-old disciplines still be vehicles for the contemporary world?" The answer is yes. A definite

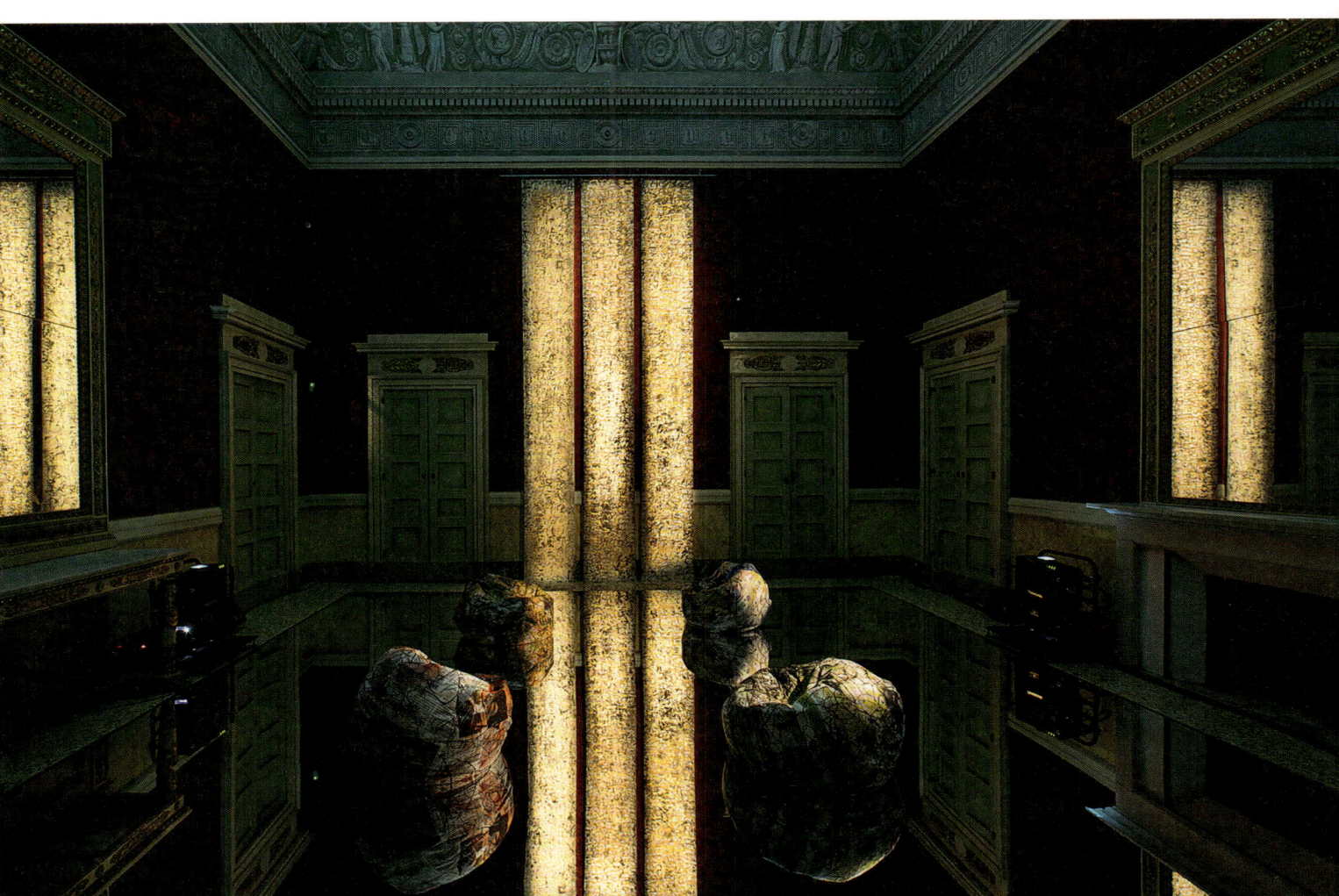

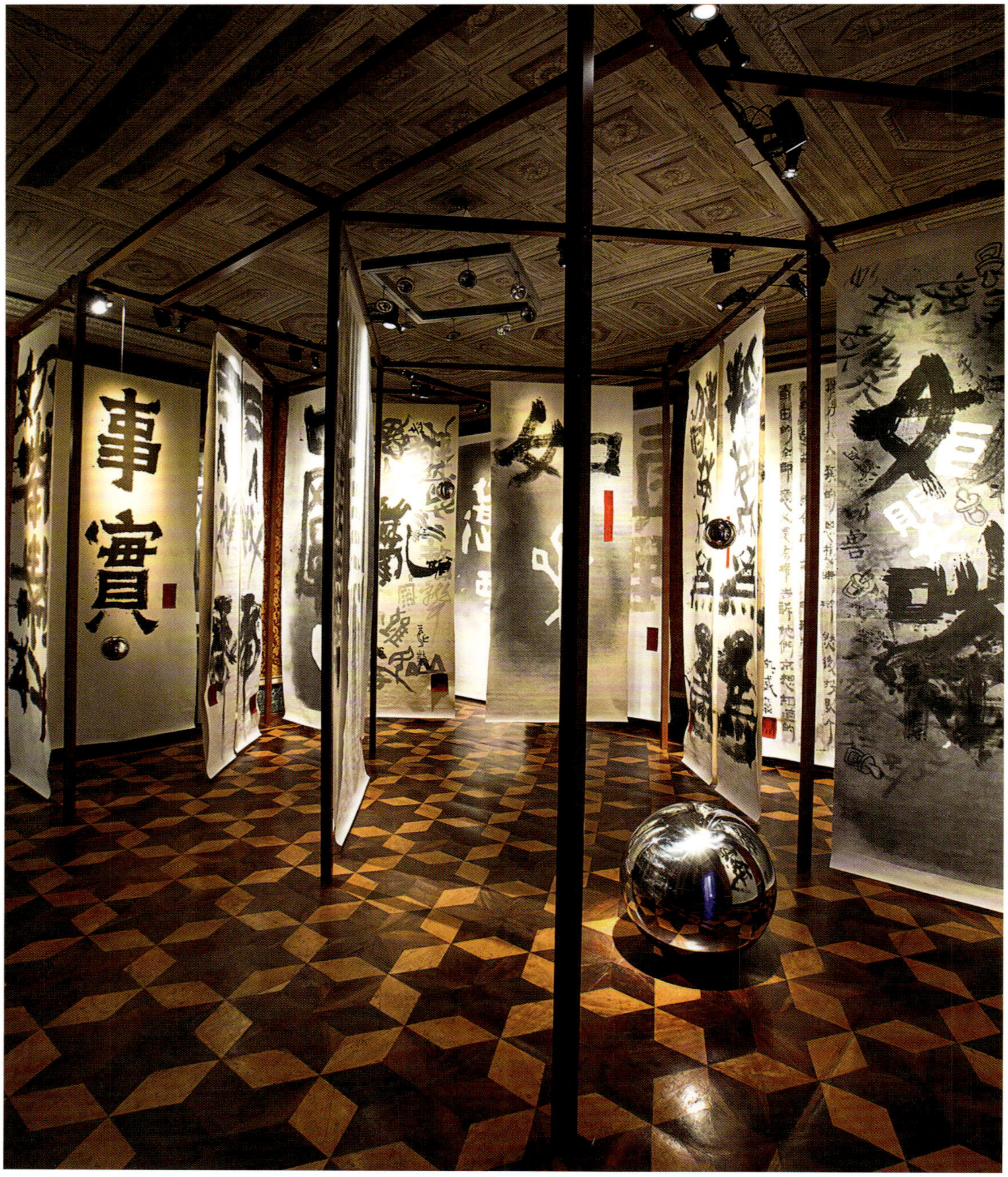

Qu Leilei, "Out of the Blue", Palazzo Reale, Milan 2020

yes. Calligraphy has gradually abandoned some of its functional aspects, and acquired a new aesthetic dimension. Ideograms have become actions, they follow the flow of internal meditations, the search for new dynamic equilibriums. "The exhibition title," the curator went on to say, "refers to this very evolution in traditional calligraphic form, which surprises us with this extraordinary ability of the artists to speak modern-day and universal languages that transcend writing."

In this process of research, Alcantara has proved to be a support capable of interacting with the works, and even inspiring them, altering the density of the ink, the fluidity of the mark that is made. A highly modern

Sun Xun, "Out of the Blue", Palazzo Reale, Milan 2020

material that is however archaic, like the traditional animal hides used by the first calligraphers, with the porousness and softness of ancient parchment. Thus, calligraphy on Alcantara becomes a bridge between the memory of the past and the race towards the future, retaining all the elegance of a delicate movement of the hand. The breath of life flows from the brush and is deposited on the Alcantara material, the material of art.

The exhibition was also a bridge between cultures, an embrace between the East and the West that was in contrast to the coldness of social distancing. One of the six master calligraphers works specifically on the spontaneity of action, which releases a primordial energy. He expresses the philosophy of acting without taking action. He uses tea, which represents the East, and coffee, a symbol of the West. On the Alcantara support, marks become liquid, the material absorbs it, and transforms it.

"It is truly surprising to see how these calligraphers have managed to pick up on the legacy of traditional Chinese culture," the exhibition's curator ended by saying, "allowing it to re-emerge in the present, enriched with new expressive potential for the future."

Ancient and delicate gestures, on a modern material.

Painted poems, abstract depictions of reality.

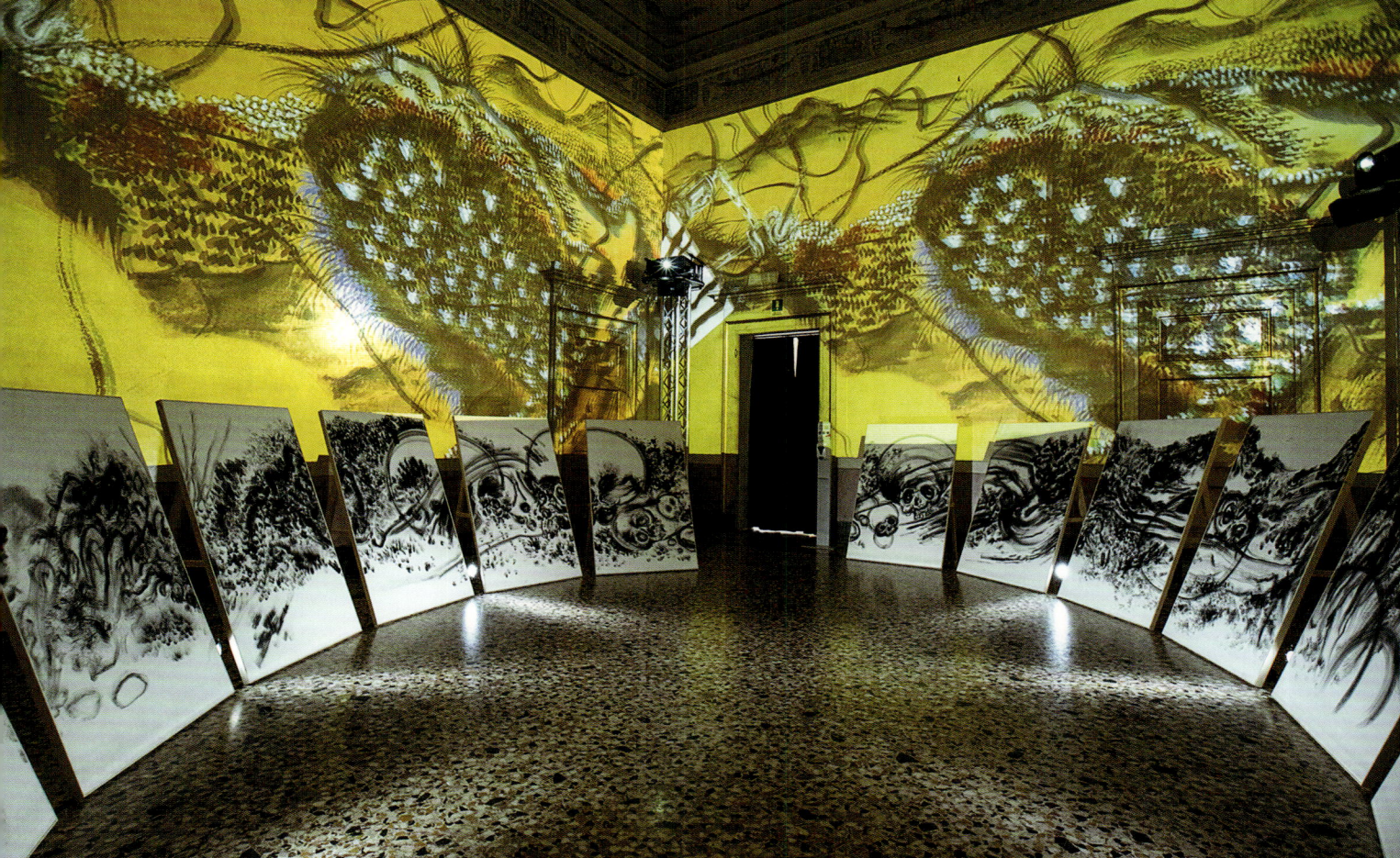

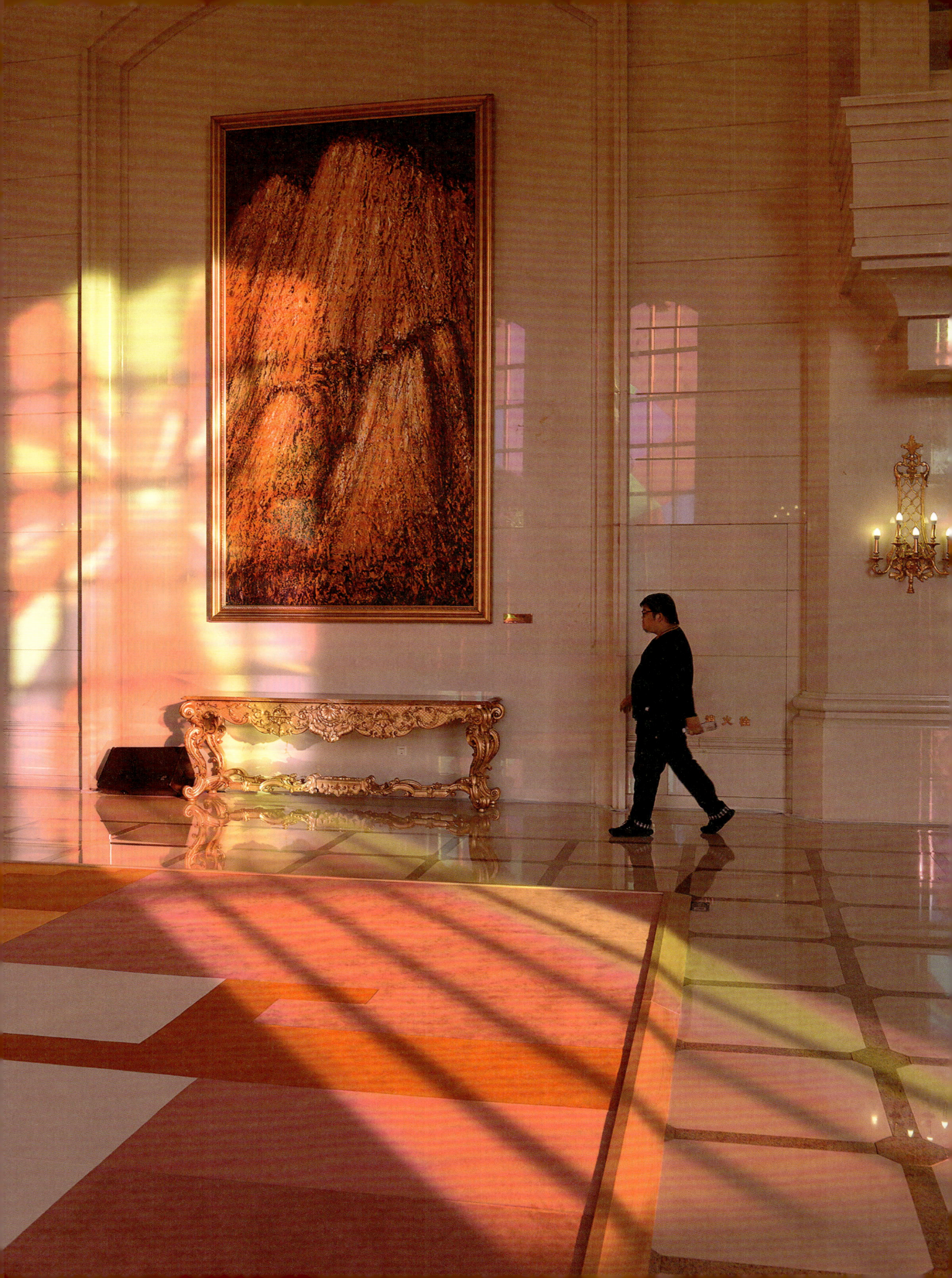

THE NEARBY EAST

In 1271 Marco Polo left Venice with his father and uncle, to travel to China. The journey lasted three and a half years. Just to give some idea, none of the world maps made between the 7th and 13th centuries showed what lay on the other side of the Ganges and the Himalayas, or beyond the Pamir and the Urals. The lands of the East were just an abstract idea, empty spaces devoid of a landscape. Map-makers used to embellish the words they wrote on maps, and make them bigger, as children do at school to make their essays seem longer. Phrases in Latin such as: *Hinc abundant leones, or Anthropophagi.* Then came *The Travels of Marco Polo*, the prose writing of Rustichello da Pisa, who transcribed the memoirs of Marco Polo, and gave an account of a vast and distant land, which was now starting to be less remote.

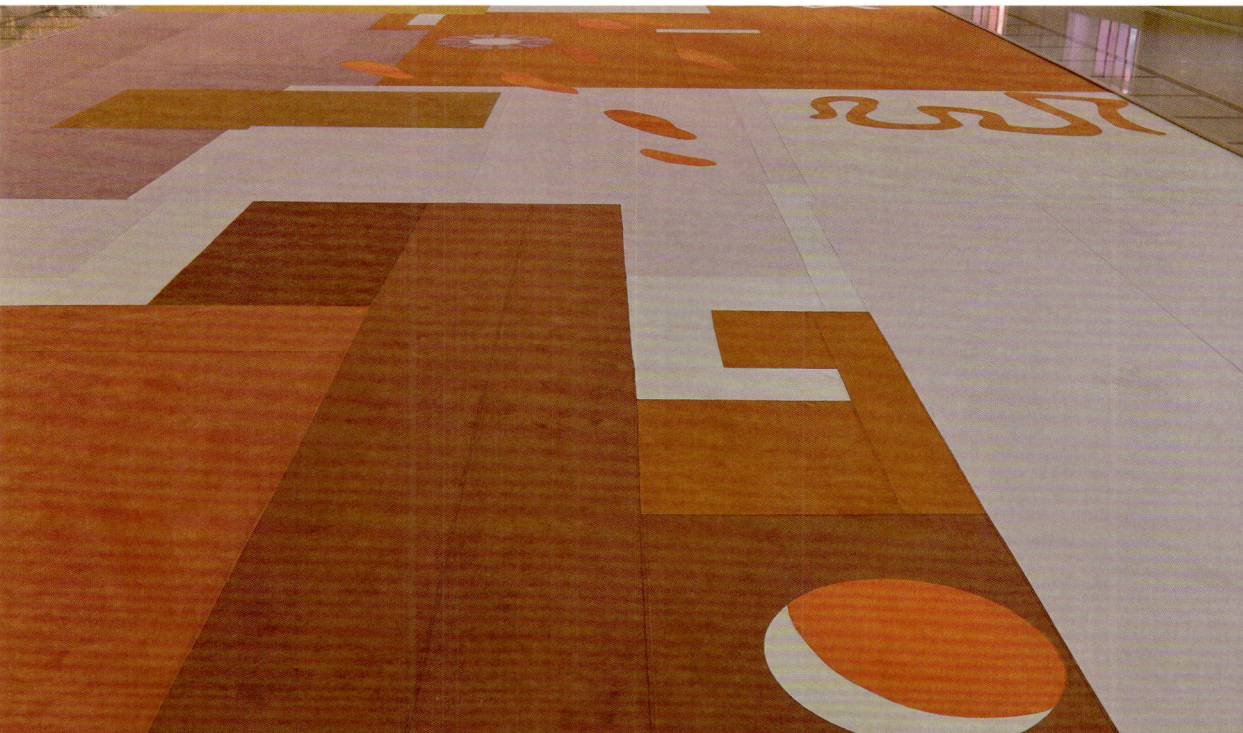

Michael Lin, *AFTER CHANDIGARH*, Aurora Museum, Shanghai 2014

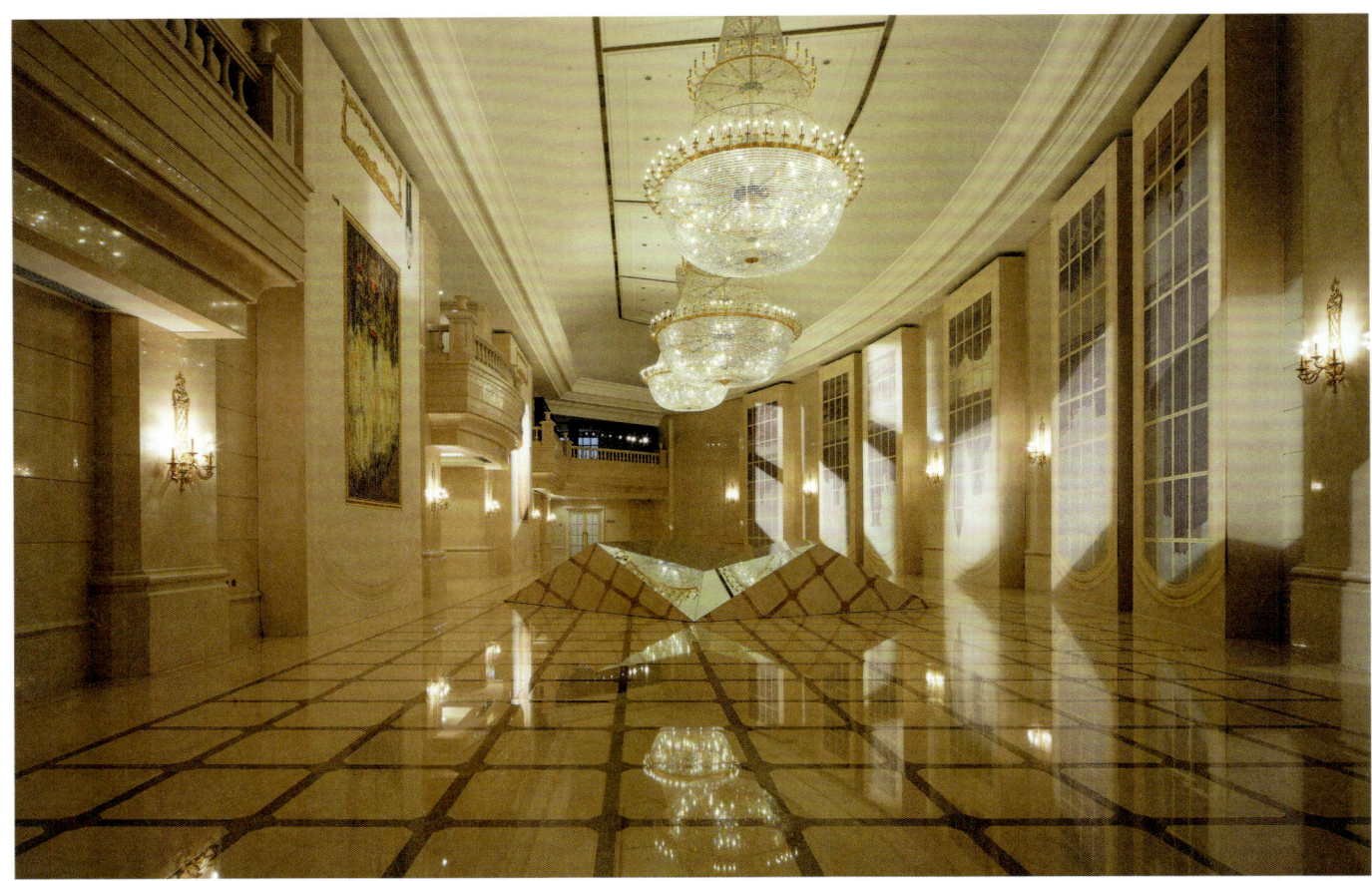

Gentuccia Bini, *Arora Mueum*, "Unordinary Space", Aurora Museum, Shanghai 2015

on the right and following pages
Yin Xiuzhen, *Digestive Cavity*, "Unordinary Space", Aurora Museum, Shanghai 2015

Marco – the man from Venice, of Latin origin – had taken the West into the Orient. Kublai Khan had asked him to travel through his lands. The eyes of the foreigner had become the gaze of the Emperor: being an alien, his eyes were open and curious, and able to connect with his mind, and thus to understand. The great Khan wanted to find out about the lands that belonged to him, but which were unknown to him. Then Marco Polo returned home, bringing the Orient to the West, opening up the Silk Routes, trade, and encounters between cultures.

Many years later, in 2014, Alcantara produced its first art exhibition in China, at the prestigious Aurora Museum in Shanghai. The Taiwanese artist Michael Lin created a site-specific installation in Alcantara with a large carpet inspired by the marble floor in the Sala del Lampadario. "The incredible versatility of the material," said the artist, "enabled me to use Alcantara like paint, to create a monumental installation that offers a new conceptualisation and configuration of space."

The show's curator was Davide Quadrio, a connoisseur of Eastern culture, who had come back to Italy to work after spending more than 20 years living and working in China.

The following year, the exhibition that Quadrio himself, and Torrigiani, had put on for Alcantara at Palazzo Reale travelled to Shanghai. The idea that works designed for such a distinctive setting, as thoroughly imbued with

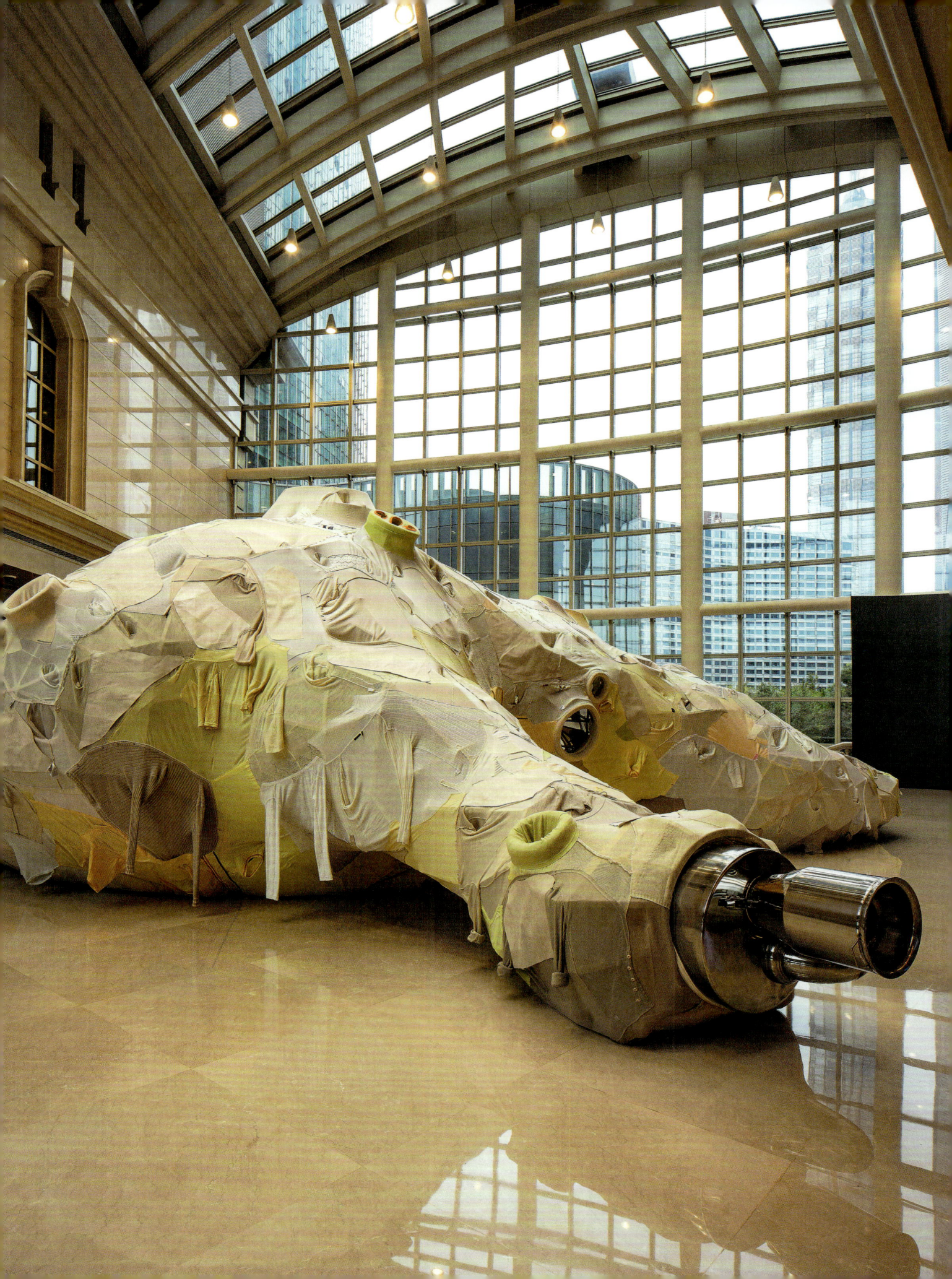

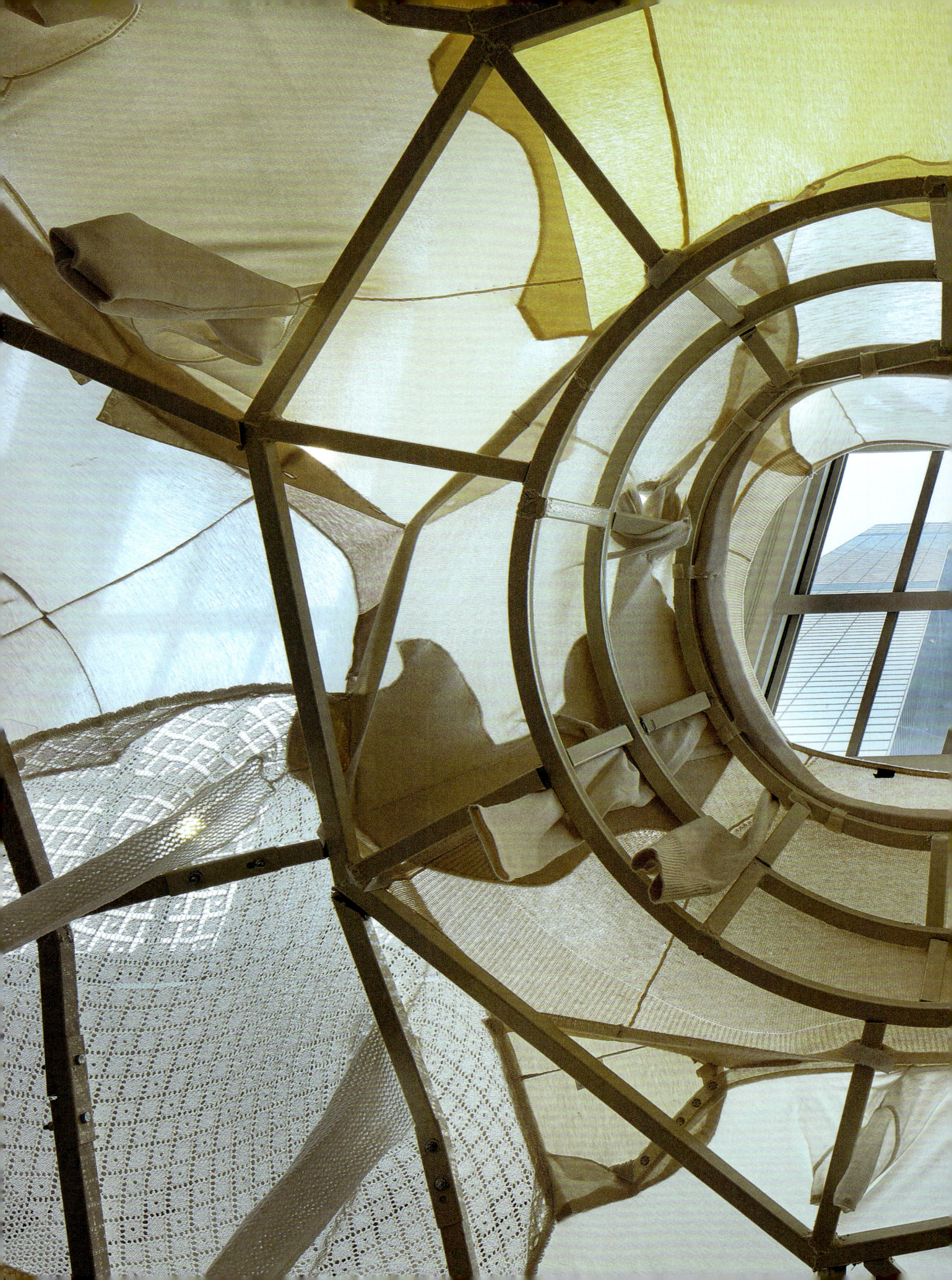

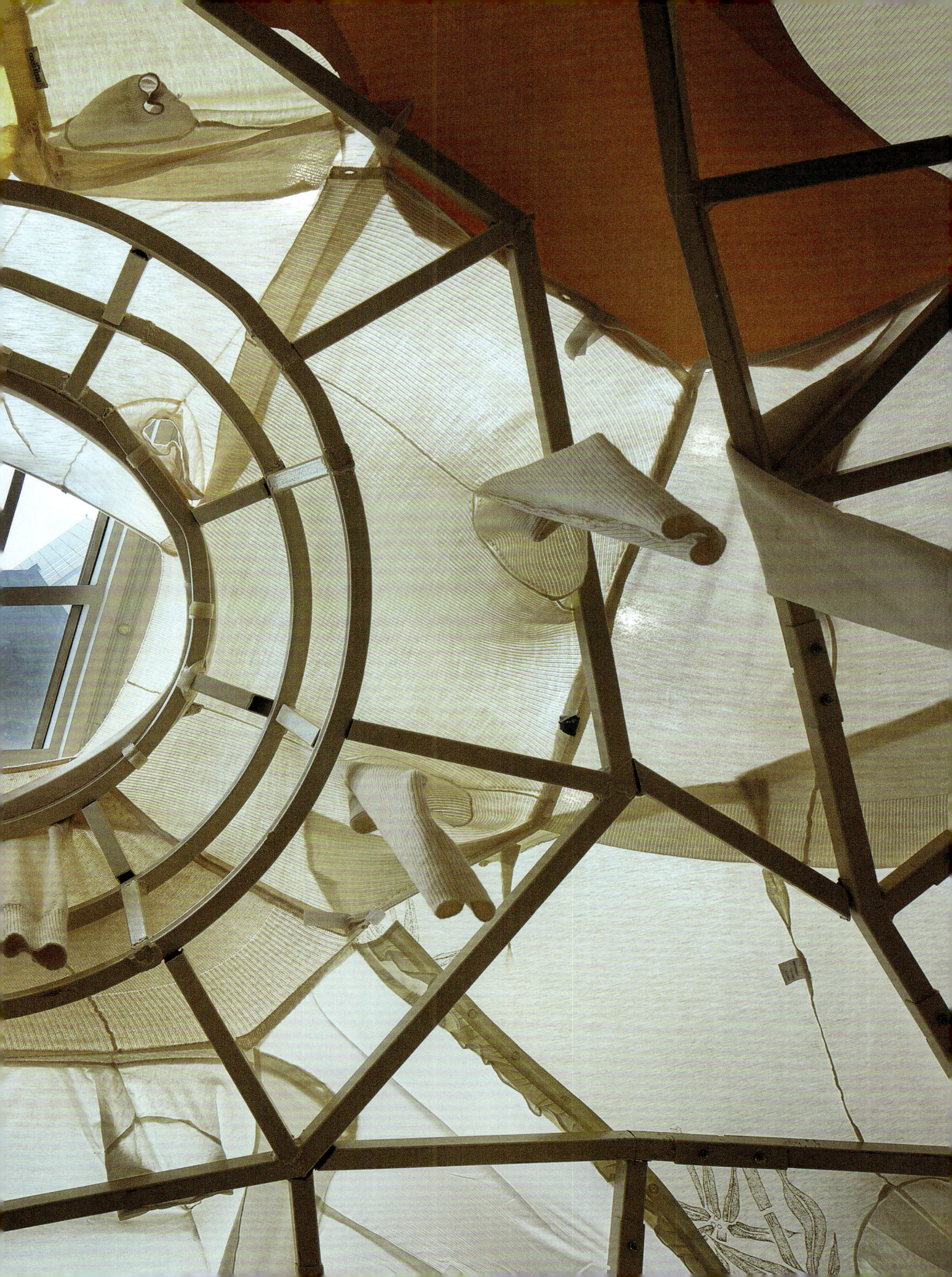

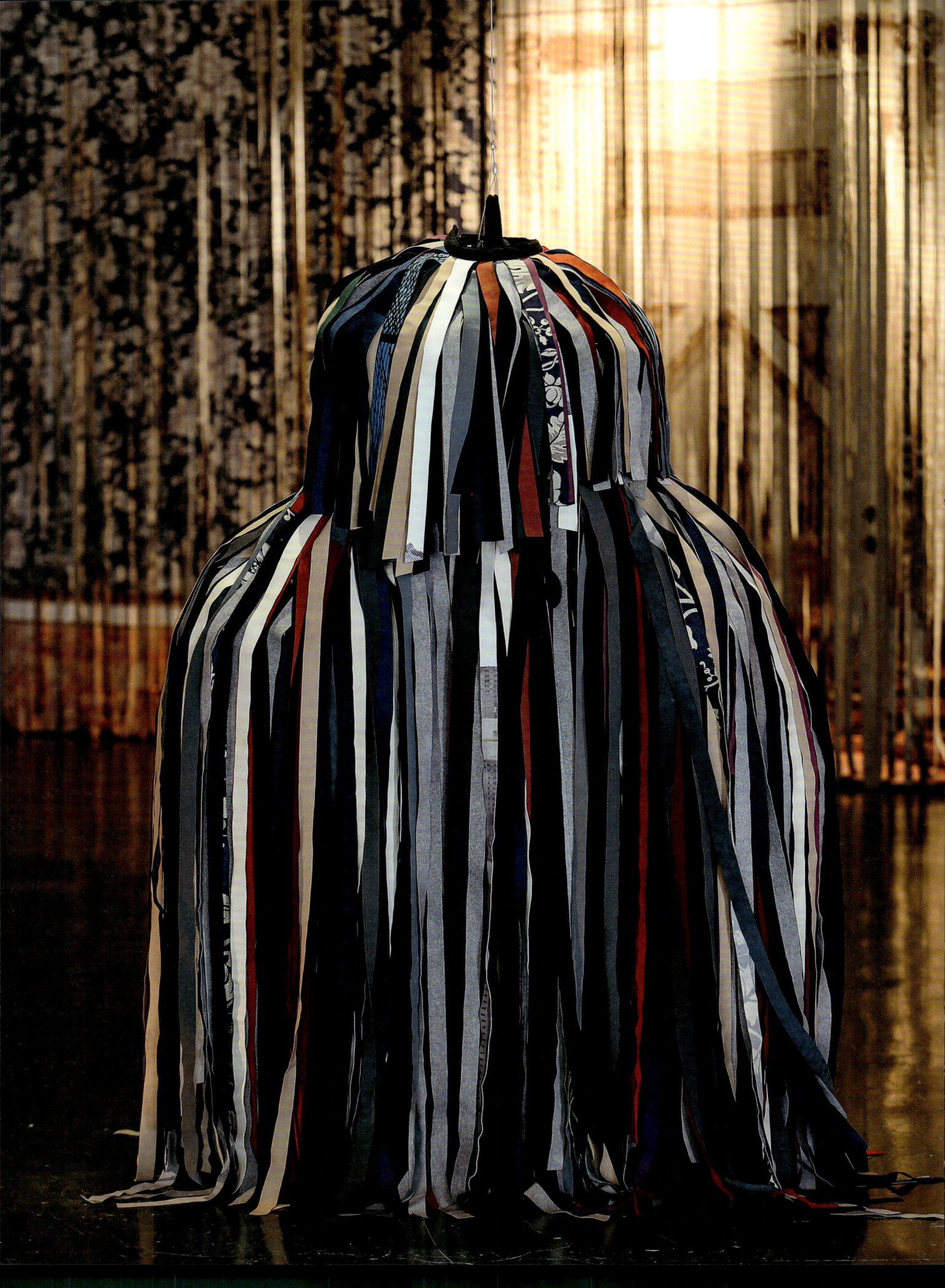

Gentuccia Bini, *Real/Royal Fringes*, "The King and I", Shanghai Gallery of Art, Shanghai 2017

Francesco Simeti, *Xanadu*, "The King and I", Shanghai Gallery of Art, Shanghai 2017

Pagine seguenti
Gentuccia Bini, *Real/Royal Fringes*, "The King and I", Shanghai Gallery of Art, Shanghai 2017

Italian identity as the Prince's Apartment in the heart of Milan, might find their way into a setting as different as the Aurora Museum, looked rather like a gamble. And indeed, it was a gamble, one that was won. The Western spirit was internalised by the works, and this later burst forth in their new location, forming unexpected connections with the new, Eastern context. The versatility of Alcantara, along with the company's international nature, and the ability of the curators and technical staff to display the works as if they were part of a film set, opened up a new channel of communication.

A new Silk Route: the protagonist being Alcantara, the material of art.

Later exhibitions at Palazzo Reale travelled to Shanghai, and were presented at the Gallery of Art and at the K11 Art Museum. Later on, the *Arch/arcology* installation that Nanda Vigo created at the MAXXI in Rome – drawing her inspiration from the visionary work of Paolo Soleri – was presented in the illustrious setting of 800 Show, the building that is a symbol of modern Chinese culture.

Finally, Chiharu Shiota. For Palazzo Reale interiors, she created the work entitled *Reflection of Space and Time*, which was dismantled and reassembled at the Mori museum in Tokyo, becoming an integral part of a major one-woman show by the Japanese artist. Constant transmissions of creativity along the routes that, from East to West, meet up and, instead of diverging again, join together. The exhibition was entitled "The Soul Trembles", and it included other works in Alcantara, such as

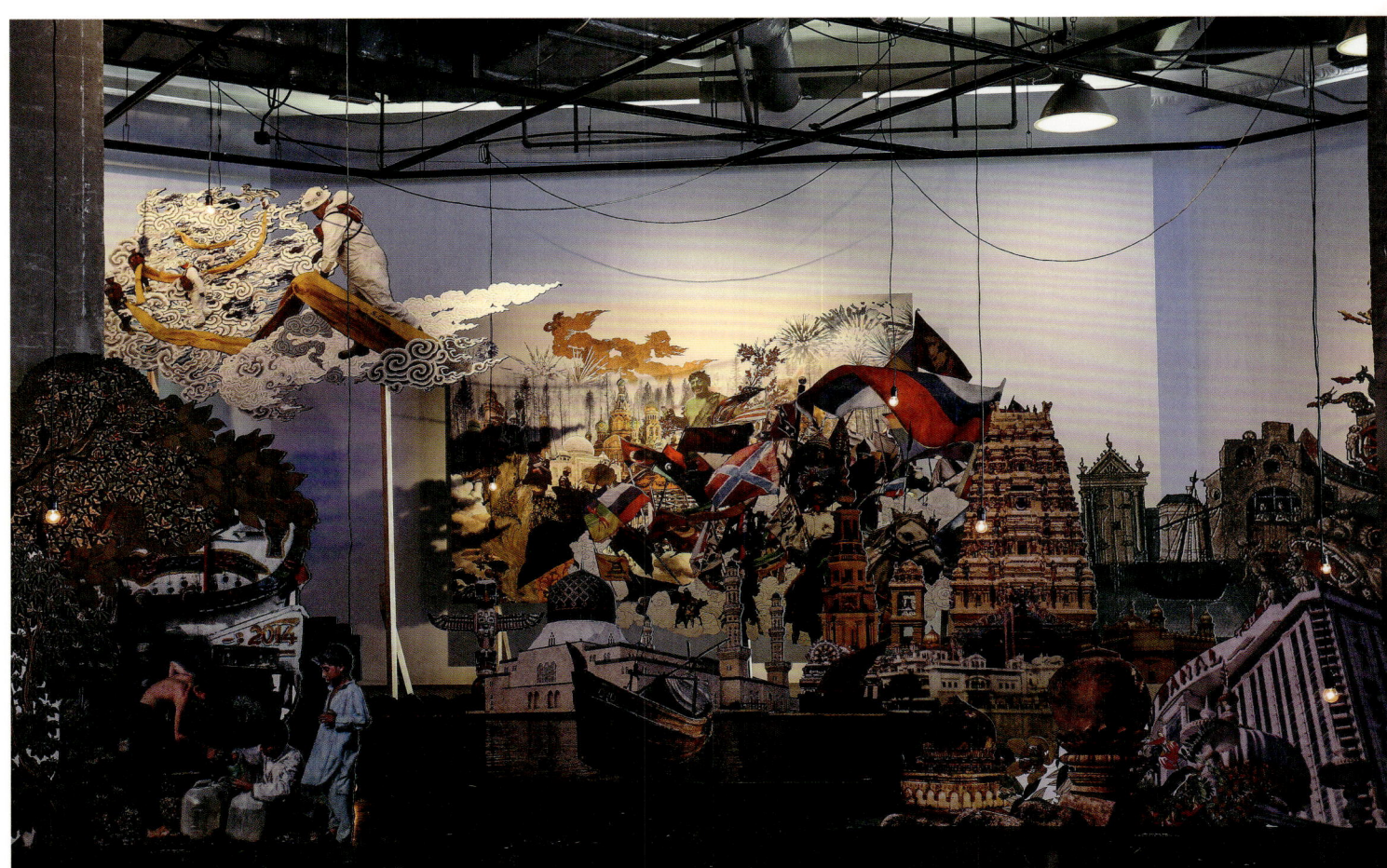

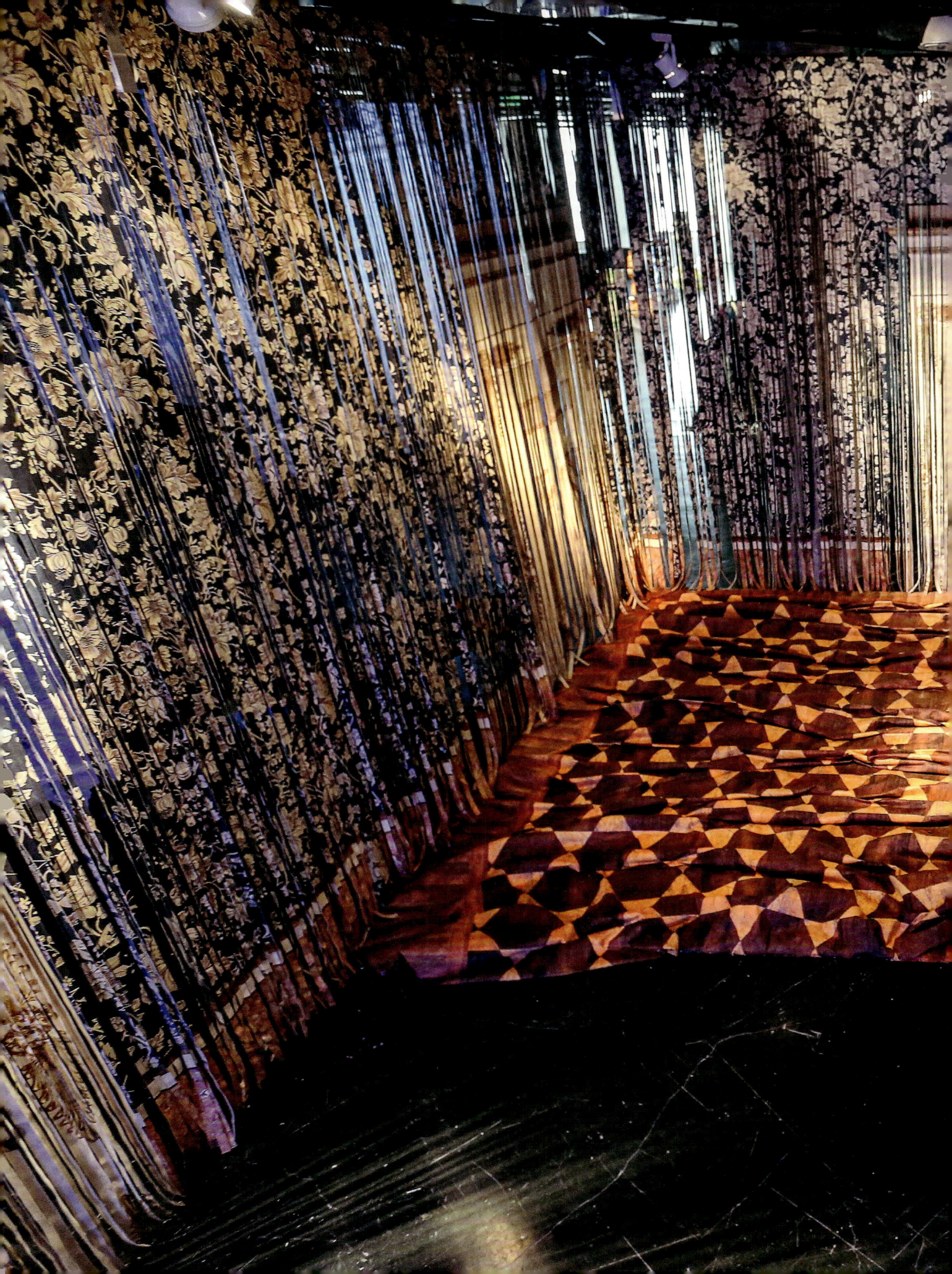

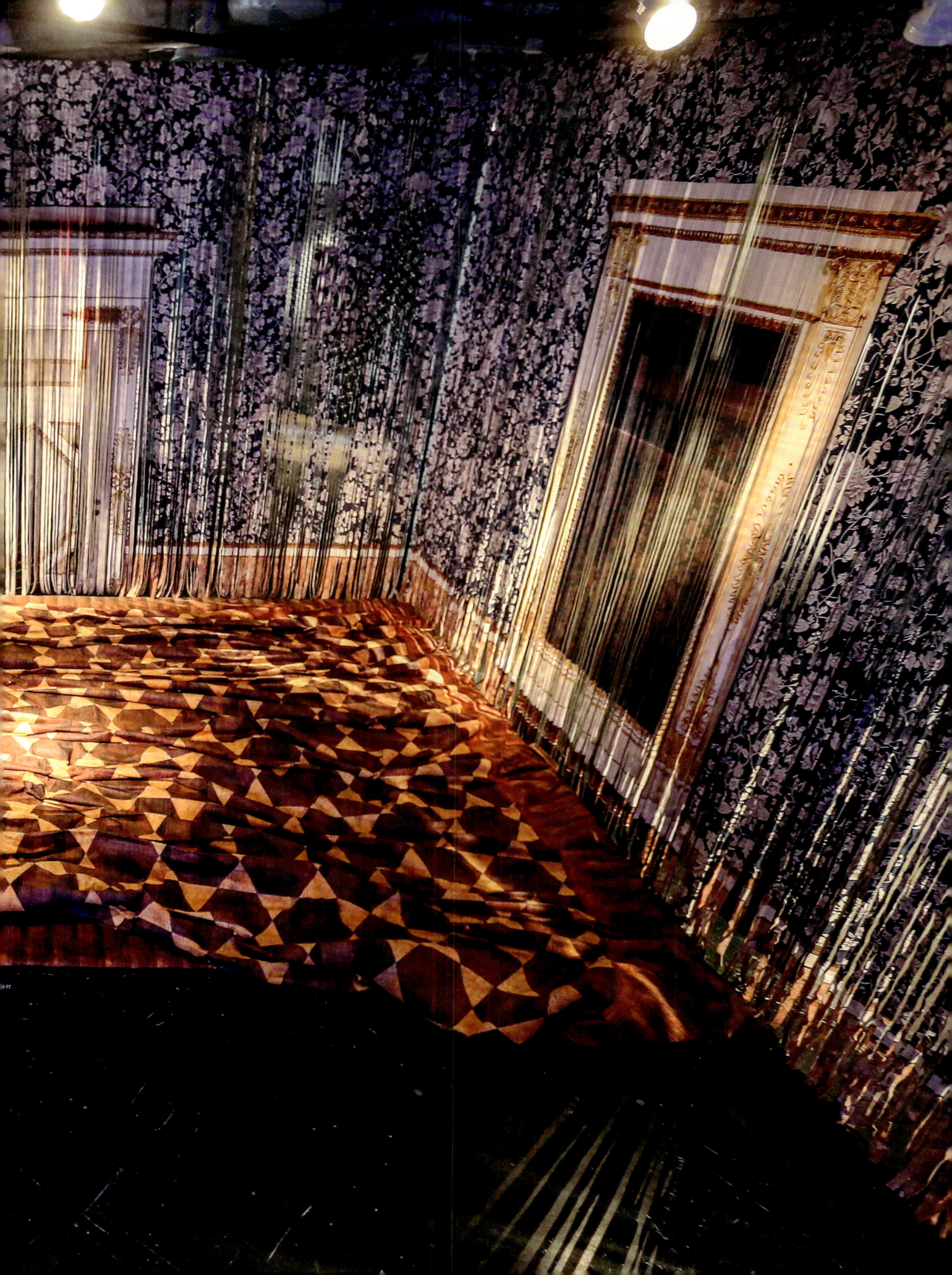

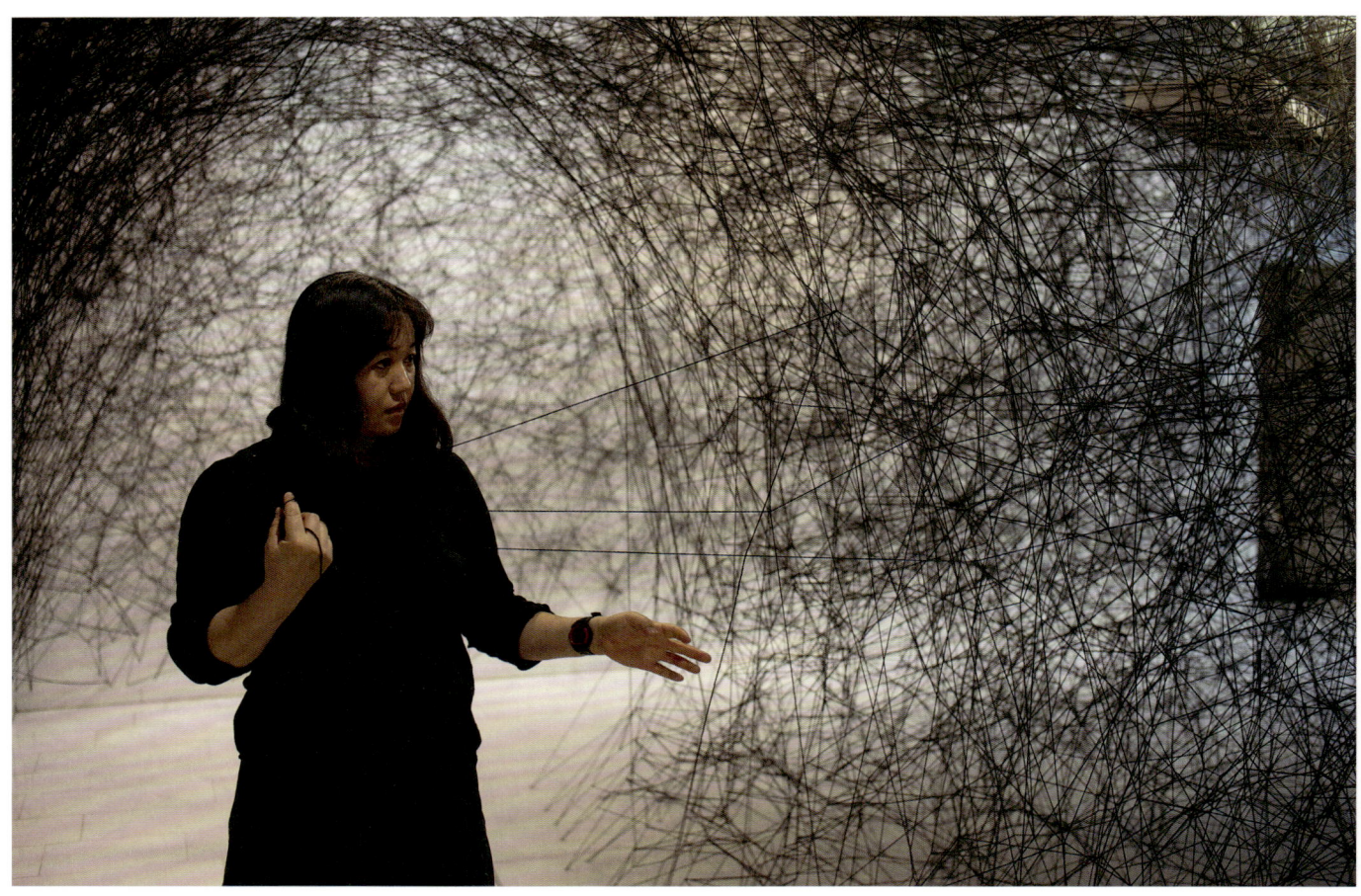

Chiharu Shiota, *In Silence*, "The Soul Trembles", Mori Art Museum, Tokyo 2019

the monumental *In Silence*. An immense web of minute Alcantara threads invaded the room, and enveloped a burnt piano. All around, the empty chairs of a mute and absent public, also trapped in the tangled threads that seemed to float in the air, taking on a dynamic, three-dimensional aspect. The work exuded life, even in the presence of death. Once again, the ability of Alcantara, as a material, to withstand tensions and twists, while absorbing light, created a poetic, magic effect of suspended reality. All Chiharu Shiota's works speak to the mind and heart. This is pointed up in a small cartouche, written by the artist herself, and placed beside the work. The text explained that, when she was 9 years old, a terrible fire broke out in a neighbours' house. The following day, outside the door, she saw a burnt-out piano, as black as night. That symbolic image became very powerfully present in the mind of the young Chiharu, who kept smelling the fire carried by the wind. The text ended as follows: "There are things that become drowned deep in our mental recesses, and things that are unable to take on either physical or verbal shape. They exist as souls, without tangible form. The more you think of these things, the more the sound of them vanishes in our mind, and their existence becomes concrete."

All those Alcantara threads, becoming intertwined and forming webs that enclose and envelop objects, are voices. Each of those threads is a

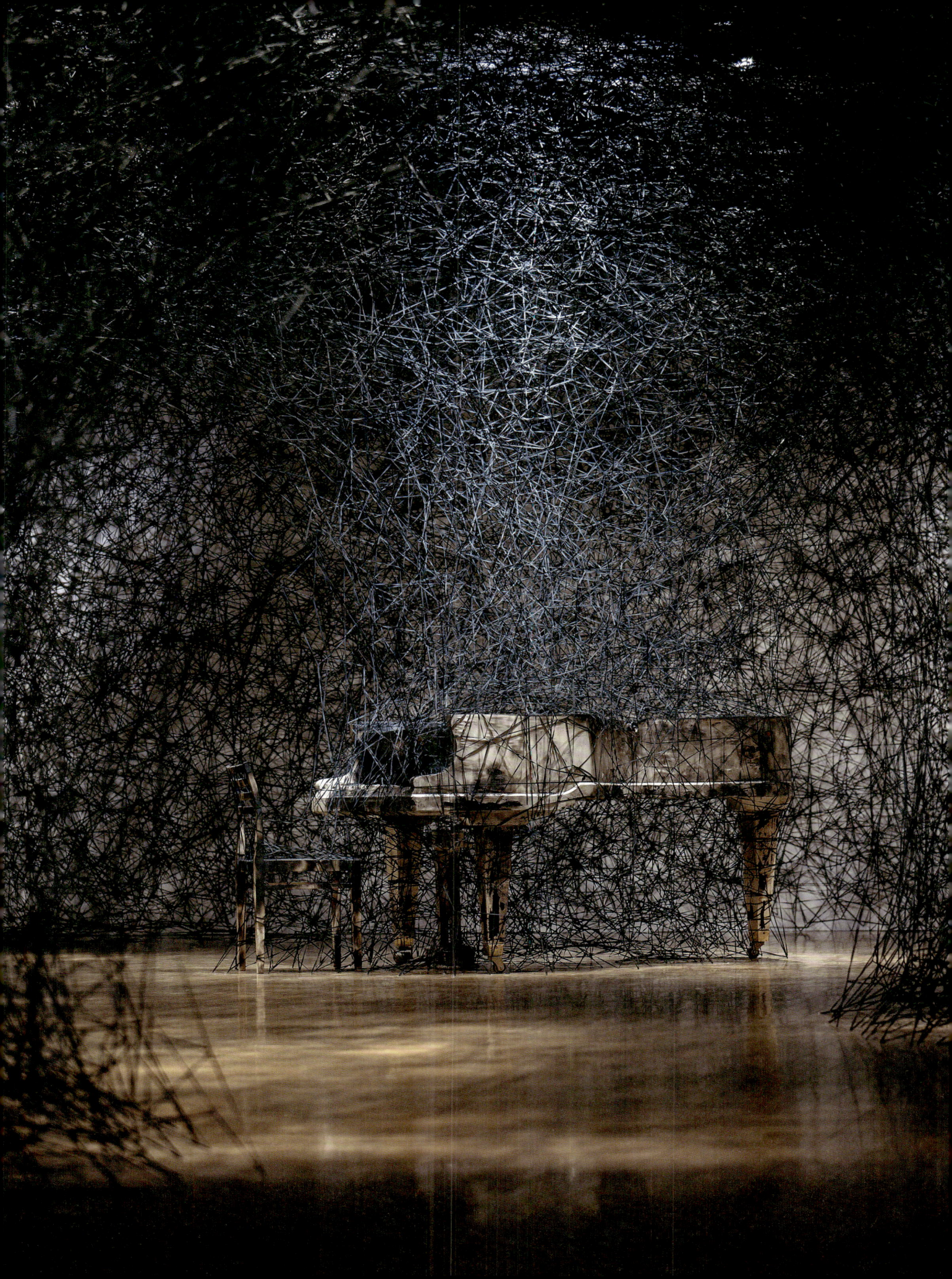

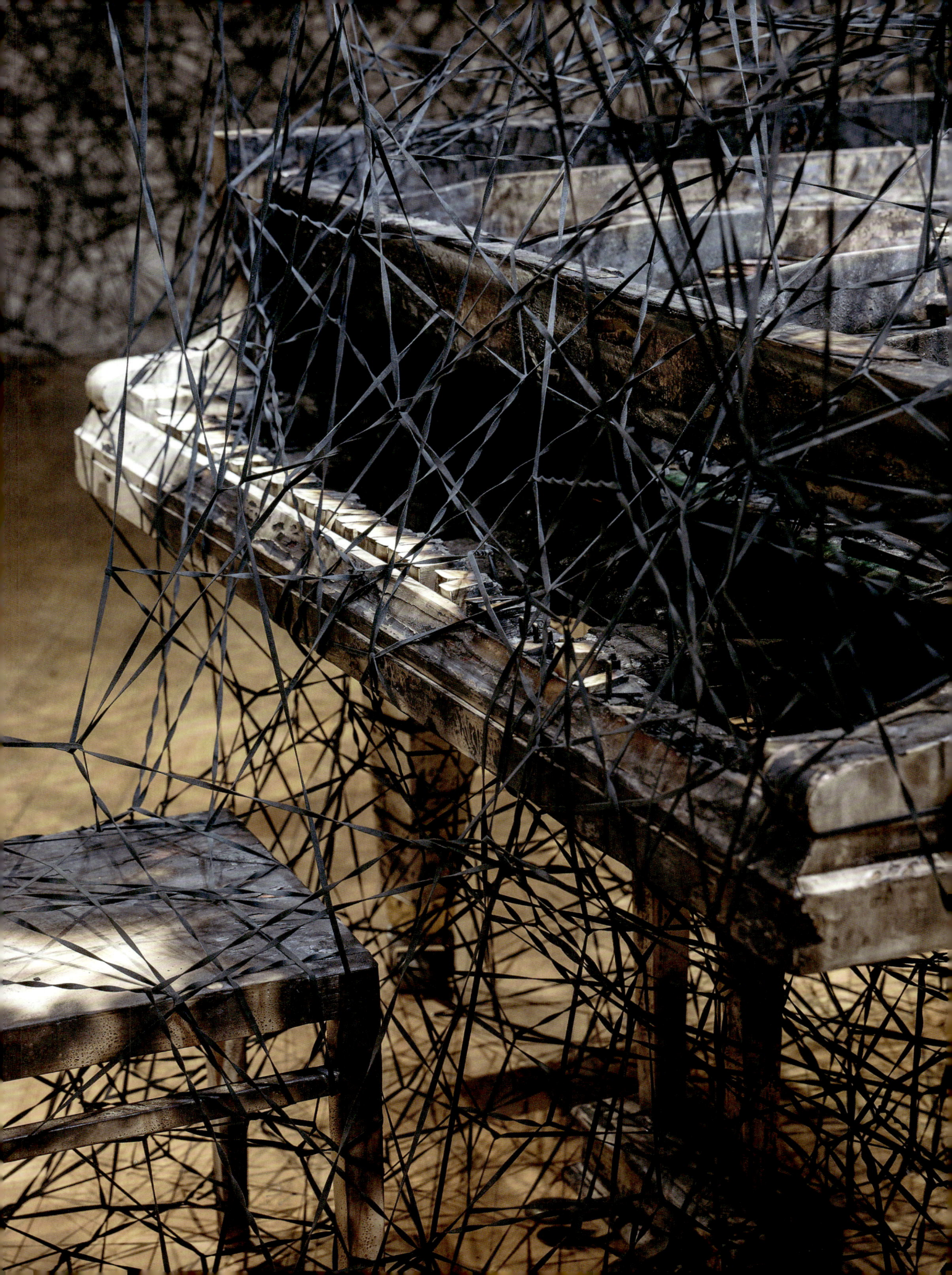

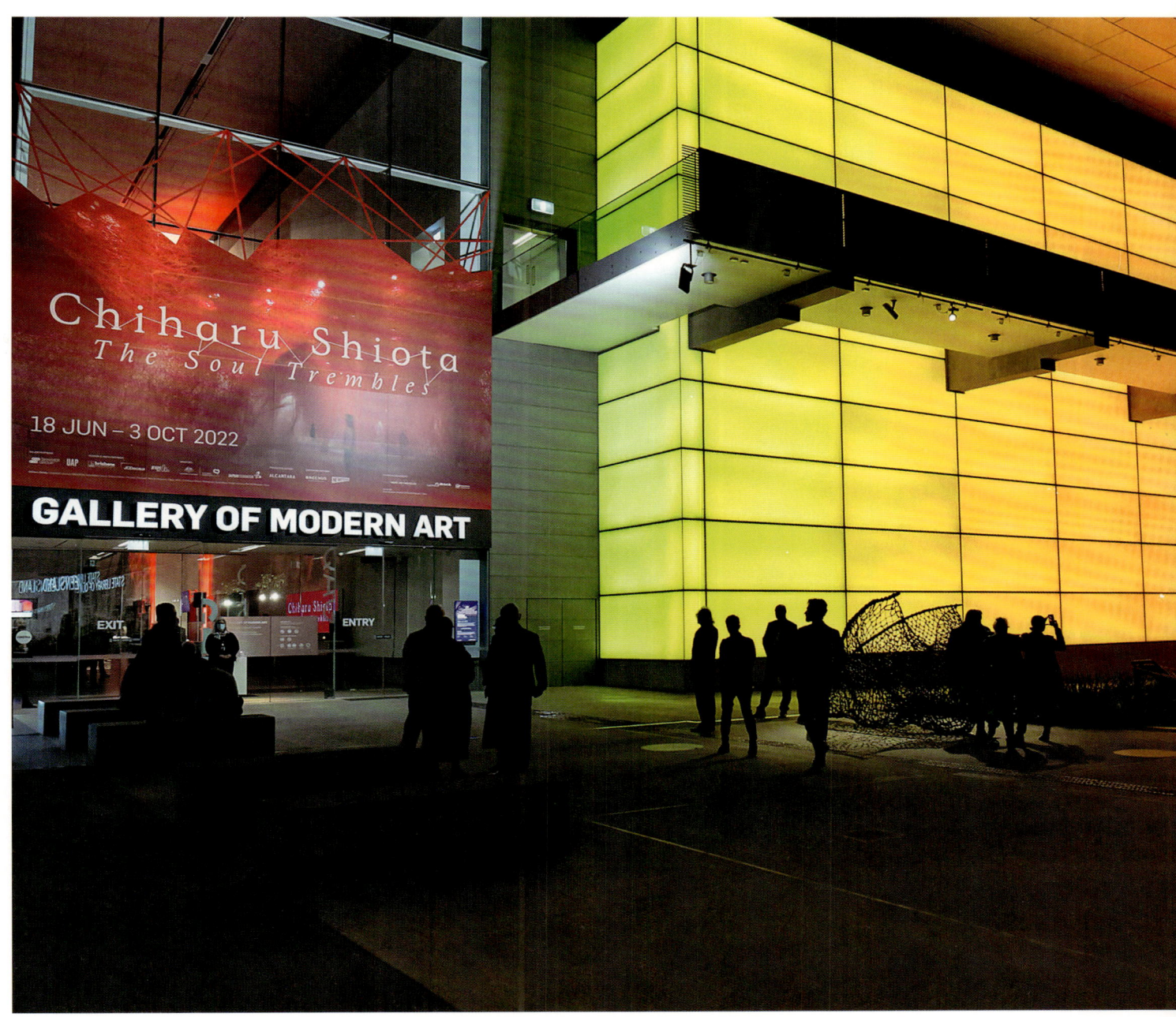

Chiharu Shiota, *In Silence* (detail), "The Soul Trembles", Mori Art Museum, Tokyo 2019

Queensland Gallery of Modern Art, Brisbane, Australia

Following pages
Chiharu Shiota, *In Silence* (detail), "The Soul Trembles", Mori Art Museum, Tokyo 2019

cry, often a desperate cry, that is in search of a mouth. Chiharu Shiota's Alcantara exhibition began to travel, exploring other parts of the East and the southern hemisphere. After the Mori, it went to South Korea's Busan Museum, and then Taipei's Fine Art Museum in 2021, then Shanghai again, and the Long Museum, and finally Brisbane, and the Queensland Art Gallery.

The journey continues.

The extraordinary journey of Alcantara: the art material.

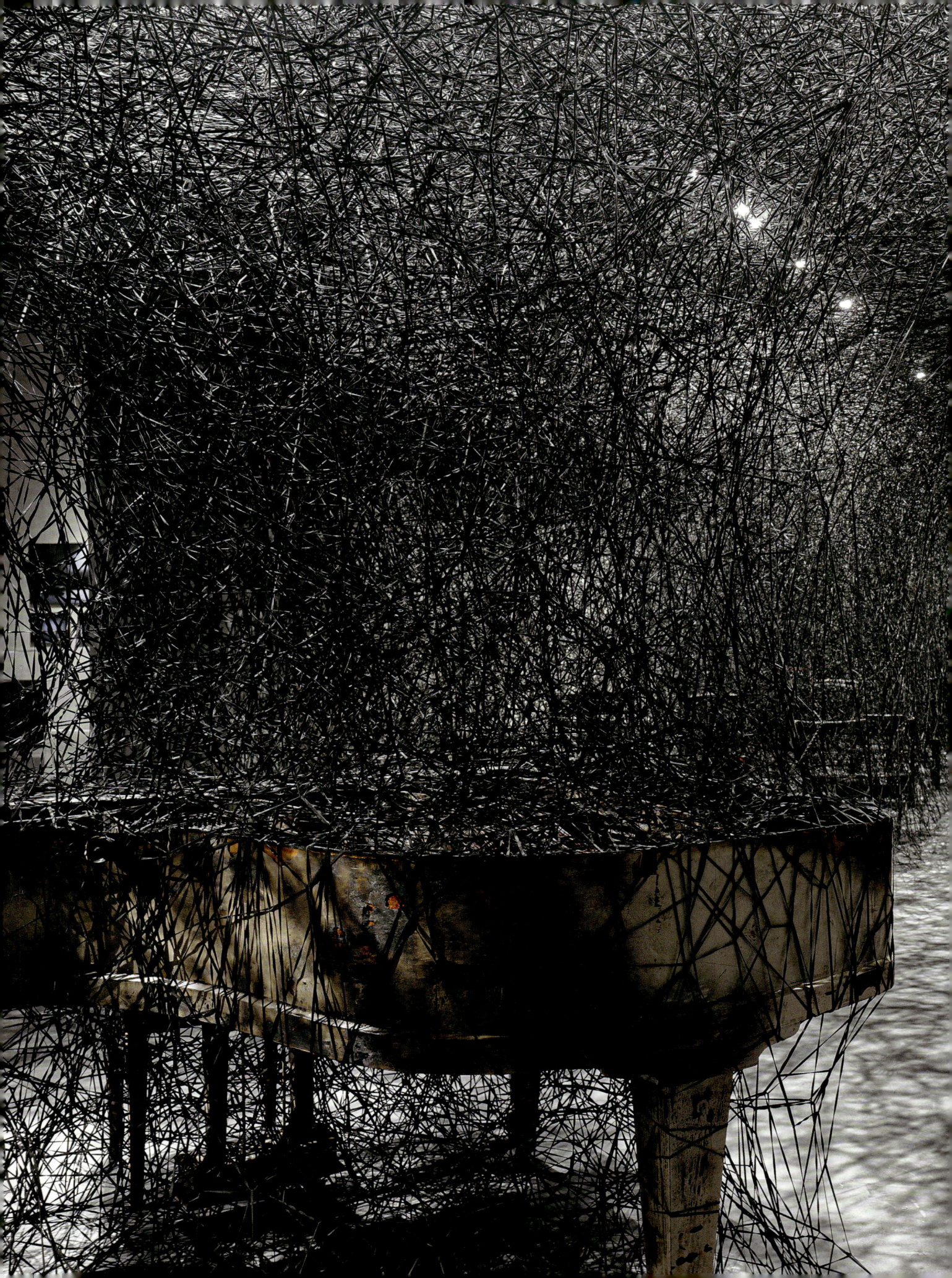

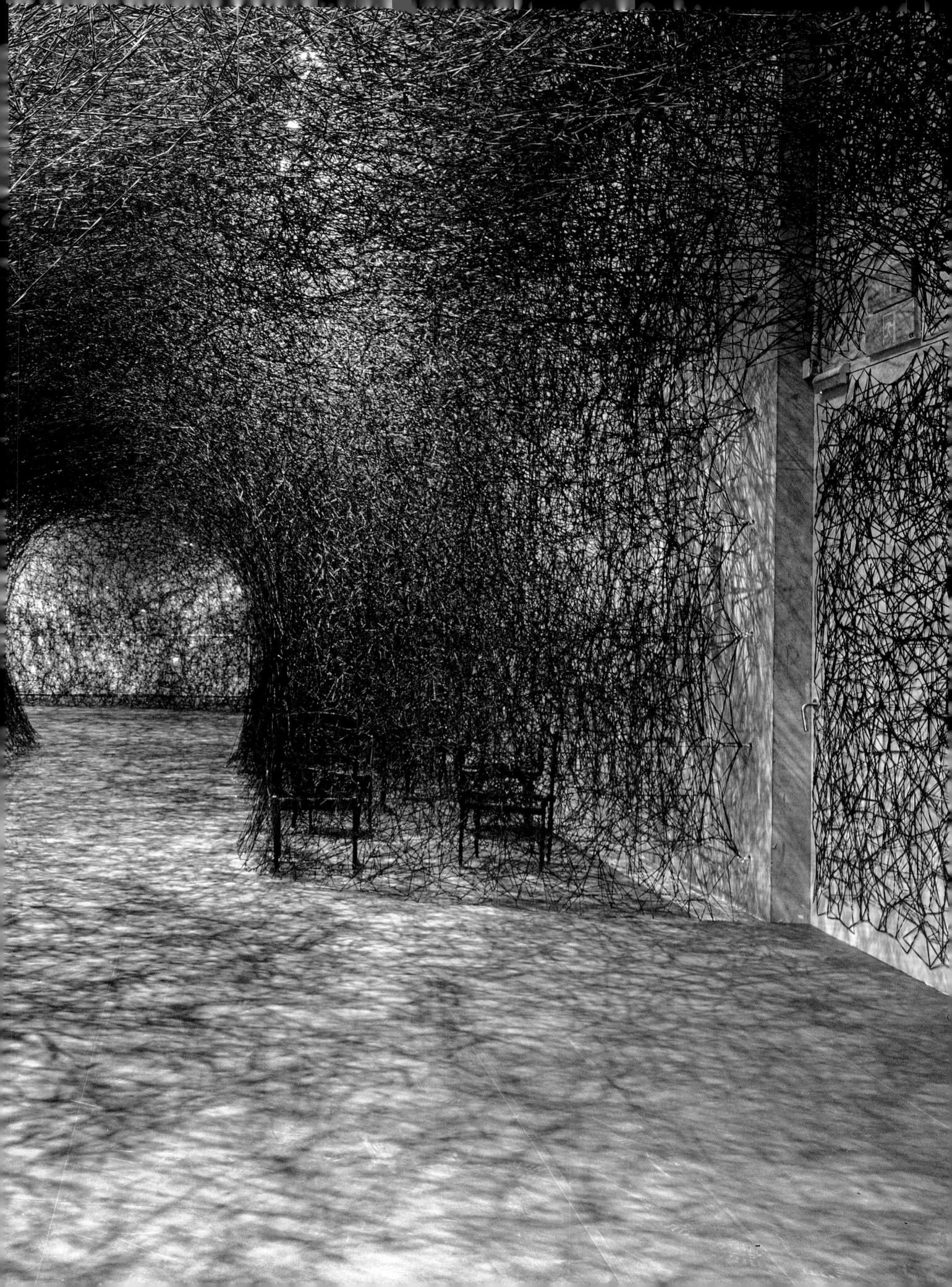